Shirley—
Thanks for all the years
of collaborating and inspiring
me in this work!
I so appreciate our
friendship and our professional
work!

Joan

Advancing Responsible Adolescent Development

Series Editor:
Roger J.R. Levesque
Department of Criminal Justice
Indiana University, Bloomington, IN, USA

More information about this series at http://www.springer.com/series/7284

Joan G. DeJaeghere • Jasmina Josić
Kate S. McCleary
Editors

Education and Youth Agency

Qualitative Case Studies in
Global Contexts

 Springer

Editors
Joan G. DeJaeghere
University of Minnesota
Minneapolis, Minnesota, USA

Jasmina Josić
Pearson
Mahwah, New Jersey, USA

Kate S. McCleary
University of Wisconsin-Madison
Madison, Wisconsin, USA

ISSN 2195-089X   ISSN 2195-0903   (electronic)
Advancing Responsible Adolescent Development
ISBN 978-3-319-33342-7   ISBN 978-3-319-33344-1   (eBook)
DOI 10.1007/978-3-319-33344-1

Library of Congress Control Number: 2016946434

Printed on acid-free paper

This Springer imprint is published by Springer Nature
The registered company is Springer International Publishing AG Switzerland

We dedicate this book to Dominik, Noah, Luka, Gabriela, and all young people who have been part of our research and work.

Acknowledgements

This volume is a testament to many collaborations among researchers in the academy, program managers in foundations, and leaders and practitioners of non-profit and non-governmental organizations in efforts to understand and improve the role of education in youth's lives and futures. We owe our appreciation to The MasterCard Foundation and CARE, USA, that funded some of this research and the many other organizations that allowed us to be participants in their schools, institutions, and communities. Each contributor worked very closely with different institutions to carry out the research. We hope that the work we have done has helped you and others to learn from the experiences of youth in new ways, and that we all have a better understanding of the contributions made by such institutions and groups in the lives of young people.

Within each organization, we got to know youth who opened their hearts and minds and shared with us their lived experiences, their realities, and their desired and imagined futures. Their thoughts and ideas are captured in each chapter, and we thank and honor them for the knowledge and wisdom they shared with us.

The ideas and chapters for this volume came about over the past decade through many conversations to conceptualize research studies and projects with graduate students and colleagues of ours in and outside the academy; many of whom have contributed chapters here, while others have furthered our thinking and understanding on the the topic of youth agency. Our profound appreciation goes to all who have engaged in these discussions in efforts to extend our knowledge and our practice. We are particularly grateful to colleagues from the University of Minnesota who have shared their curiosity with us and pushed us to think in new ways. They cannot all be named here, but we express a special thanks to Frances Vavrus, Peter Demerath, Chris Johnstone, and David Chapman, who have shared in this journey with us. Shirley Miske, Jenny Parkes, Emily Morris, and Leon Tikly have also offered valuable insights on improving our chapter and this book. Thank you for your critiques, collegial support, and friendship.

We are extremely grateful to the contributors of this volume for exploring with us diverse perspectives on the topic with such intellectual rigor. They engaged in a

peer-review process that strengthened the contributions of each chapter and allowed
for collegial dialog across institutions.

We are also thankful to the series editor, Roger J.R. Levesque, for his valuable
and timely feedback in shaping this volume, and Springer's team, especially Judy
Jones and Michelle Tam, for support and assistance in the publication process. Our
appreciation also goes to Bharath Krishnamoorthy and his team of editors for their
attention to editorial details throughout the book.

We are indebted to our families for their understanding and support and for providing us space and time to complete this volume.

Contents

About the Editors

Joan G. DeJaeghere is an Associate Professor of Comparative and International Development Education in the Department of Organizational Leadership, Policy, and Development at the University of Minnesota and an affiliate faculty of the Interdisciplinary Center for Global Change. Her scholarly work and professional practice are concerned with inequalities in education and how education can foster future livelihoods, well-being, and social justice. She has co-edited two special issues and published articles and books chapters on educating for citizenship, youth agency, gender equality, as well as international development and educational policy in journals including *Comparative Education Review, Compare, Comparative Education, International Journal of Educational Development*, and *Human Development and Capabilities Journal*. DeJaeghere's research and education and development projects have taken place in several countries including Bangladesh, Honduras, India, Pakistan, South Africa, Tanzania, Uganda, and Vietnam.

Jasmina Josić is a Manager in the Efficacy and Research team of Pearson's Global Product organization. She works with the product and research teams to develop research frameworks and implement evaluations of digital products in K-12, higher education, and English language learning sectors. Her research is concerned with examining the internationalization of higher education, dynamics of educational policies in urban spaces, youth citizenship and identity, and student engagement and achievement. Josić has conducted multiple research studies with youth and managed youth programs in urban United States settings. Josić received her Ph.D. in Educational Policy and Administration from the University of Minnesota.

Kate S. McCleary is an Associate Researcher with the LEAD Center in the Wisconsin Center for Education Research at the University of Wisconsin-Madison where she focuses on evaluation and assessment of higher education programs. McCleary has worked in international education and carried out research on gender in education, youth agency, and intercultural learning. After holding fellowships with Save the Children and CARE International, McCleary served as the director of the Global Education Office at Washington College prior to her current position at the University of Wisconsin-Madison. She holds a Ph.D. from the University of Minnesota in Educational Policy & Administration with a focus in Comparative International Development Education.

About the Contributors

Beth Dierker holds a Ph.D. in Comparative and International Development Education from the University of Minnesota. She is an independent consultant conducting research and program evaluation related to youth and community development, efforts to address educational inequities, and university-community partnerships. She is currently working with the University of Minnesota's Urban Research, Outreach, and Engagement Center. Also a parent of a child with autism, Dierker writes and speaks for a local non-profit organization that supports families and educators of children on the autism spectrum.

Marline Guerrero is a Domestic Violence and Child Welfare Specialist in Tallahassee, Florida. She has worked with various organizations serving minority communities in the United States. Guerrero received her master's degree in International and Comparative Education from Florida State University and bachelor's degree in Psychology from the University of California Santa Barbara.

Ayesha Khurshid is an Assistant Professor of International and Comparative Education at the Florida State University. Her ethnographic and qualitative research focuses on the issues of gender, modernity, and education in Muslim countries and communities. She received her Ph.D. in Education from the University of Wisconsin-Madison.

Anna Ndesamburo Kwayu holds a master's degree in Gender Studies from the University of Dar es Salaam and a B.A. in Cultural Anthropology and Tourism from Tumaini University. She has considerable experience working with non-governmental, governmental, and local organizations in her native Tanzania to represent a range of socio-economic and political concerns with a particular emphasis on gender. Ndesamburo Kwayu currently works as a policy analyst, researcher, and facilitator on gender, development, and socio-economic issues. She conducted a research project on gender and education with Joan DeJaeghere and Laura Wangsness Willemsen from the University of Minnesota.

Acacia Nikoi has her Ph.D. in Comparative and International Development Education in the Department of Organizational Leadership, Policy, and Development at the University of Minnesota. She has spent over 15 years working in higher education on issues of community development and youth and childhood well-being in East and West Africa. Her research interests center on the role of non-formal and vocational education in youth development and empowerment, and she is currently completing her dissertation on Kenyan youth conceptualizations of and experiences with empowerment.

Mohamed K. Sallam is the Director of the Pan-Afrikan Center and Instructor in the Department of History at Augsburg College—Minneapolis, USA. He holds a Ph.D. in Comparative and International Development Education from the University of Minnesota. His research focuses on examining the effects of international development discourse and national education policy formation on women in post-revolution Egypt.

Payal P. Shah is an Assistant Professor of Educational Studies in the College of Education at the University of South Carolina. Her primary research interests include girls' education, international development and education policy, and qualitative research methodology, with geographical expertise in South Asia. Shah has published in a variety of journals across the fields of research methods, gender studies, and international and comparative education. Her research has been funded by the Fulbright Program, Spencer Foundation, and the University of South Carolina. She holds a Ph.D. in Education Policy Studies from Indiana University.

Roozbeh Shirazi is an Assistant Professor in the Comparative and International Development Education Program in the College of Education and Human Development at the University of Minnesota. His scholarship examines questions of youth citizenship and national belonging in times of sociopolitical transformation; migration and globalization in education; and the role of schooling in formations of youth subjectivities. Shirazi received his Ph.D. from Teachers College, Columbia University.

Casey Stafford is a Grants Manager in the Equitable Development Thematic Area at the Ford Foundation, New York. He holds a Ph.D. in Comparative and International Development Education from the University of Minnesota. During his doctoral studies, he had the opportunity to partner with a resilient and vibrant group of Senegalese university students and learned the value of collective organizing. His research focuses on access and success in higher education.

Shawanda Stockfelt is a senior research associate and a British academy postdoctoral fellow within the Centre for Comparative and International Research (CIRE) and the Centre for Multilevel Modelling (CMM), in the Graduate School of Education at the University of Bristol. Her research focuses on key issues relating to inclusion, equity, and social justice in education. Stockfelt has a keen interest in methodologies that involve innovative qualitative, quantitative, and mixed methods approaches with an emphasis on holistic research that covers the lifespan.

Miriam S. Thangaraj is a Ph.D. candidate at the Department of Educational Policy Studies, University of Wisconsin-Madison. Her research interests encompass global policy discourses of development, education, child labor, and child rights, as they shape the daily lives of "real" children and families. In her dissertation, *Reconstructing "Childhood": Silks, Schools, SEZs*, she offers an ethnographic account of how children and families in a weavers neighborhood in Kanchipuram, India, experienced and navigated transnational projects to prohibit child labor and enforce schooling. Her account foregrounds children's voices to consider a key, if taken-for-granted, question: Do children only belong in school?

Nancy Pellowski Wiger is the Project Director for the Learn, Earn, and Save Initiative grant in the Department of Organizational Leadership, Policy, and Development at the University of Minnesota with responsibility for evaluating the overall impact of three educational initiatives on youth from marginalized backgrounds in East Africa. Her professional interests include gender and education, social capital, and youth policy. Her past scholarly work includes partnerships with CARE investigating youth empowerment and education initiatives and girls' leadership, and with UNICEF's child-friendly school standards in Ghana. She received her Ph.D. in Comparative and International Development Education from the University of Minnesota.

Laura Wangsness Willemsen is a researcher specializing in schooling, gender, and teaching with a geographic focus on East Africa. She completed her Ph.D. in Comparative and International Development Education in the Department of Organizational Leadership, Policy, and Development at the University of Minnesota, with an ethnographic study of an all-girls school in Tanzania alongside life histories of young women who attended it. With a background in anthropology and education, Wangsness Willemsen has taught widely, from English in high school classrooms in Tanzania and urban and suburban Minnesota, to seminars on qualitative research and culturally relevant teaching at the University of Minnesota.

Conceptualizing Youth Agency

Joan G. DeJaeghere, Kate S. McCleary, and Jasmina Josić

Introduction

Agency of young women and men has become a considerable focus of educational and youth research, policy and practice globally. Policymakers and educators alike use the trope of agency as a necessary part of being and becoming an independent adult and a contributing member of society. For example, McLeod (2012) argues that global institutions and goals and national policies increasingly frame agency, participation, and citizenship as imperatives that respond to and foster economic, social, and political changes. In addition, some donor and non-governmental organizations draw on discourses of agency to signify efforts toward youth participation in development projects, and, more broadly, in the future of their societies.

The urgency attributed to youth agency is in part a reflection of a growing youth population worldwide, known as the "youth bulge" (Ortiz & Cummins, 2012), and in part a refraction of changing global political, economic, social, and cultural relations in which youth are finding it increasingly difficult to politically and economically participate and contribute to their communities and countries. Much public discourse situates youth in a binary category: they are "at risk" and vulnerable, and, when their agency is not positively channeled, they cause social and political

J.G. DeJaeghere (✉)
Department of Organizational Leadership, Policy, and Development,
University of Minnesota, Minneapolis, MN, USA
e-mail: deja0003@umn.edu

K.S. McCleary
Wisconsin Center for Education Research, University of Wisconsin-Madison,
1025 W. Johnson Street, Madison, Wisconsin, USA
e-mail: kate.s.mccleary@gmail.com

J. Josić
Pearson, Mahwah, NJ, USA
e-mail: jasmina.josic@gmail.com

© Springer International Publishing Switzerland 2016
J.G. DeJaeghere et al. (eds.), *Education and Youth Agency*, Advancing
Responsible Adolescent Development, DOI 10.1007/978-3-319-33344-1_1

tensions, and possibly unrest. In contrast, some scholarship and development organizations label the large youth population the "youth dividend"—the promise for the future and the "makers" of society (Honwana & De Boeck, 2005). Regardless of whether youth are "at risk" or a "dividend" to society, agency is regarded as a necessary component to shape, and even improve, their lives in relation to a myriad of social, cultural, and political problems in societies. However, agency as it is used to describe or even change youth's lives is fraught with conceptual and practical ambiguities in diverse settings.

A common definition of agency in social science and policy discourses is the ability of young people to make decisions and take action toward their own life and well-being (Dillabough & Kennelly, 2010; McLeod, 2012). This definition assumes that youth need to be guided in developing and channeling their agency through external interventions, such as education and youth programs, to ensure that they can be productive members of a society, and so they do not become "failures" in society. From this perspective, education and youth initiatives may attend to structures that constrain agency, but they place considerable hope in the power of the educated individual to overcome obstacles she may face. Increasingly, this perspective of youth agency is tied to a neoliberal notion of self-making amidst a decline in government programs and changing social-cultural systems that support youth's futures (Honwana, 2012; Kelly, 2006). However, a large body of scholarship on youth, education, and agency also problematizes how both formal and non-formal educational efforts foster or constrain agency.

Sociological and anthropological studies of education debate how youth agency can be constrained by structures of class, gender, and racial inequalities in society, and they acknowledge that social change is not easily achieved even though education may foster aspirations and individual agency (see, for example, Bucholtz, 2002; Dillabough & Kennelly, 2010; Hart, 2012). These debates tend to position the macro-environment, such as the economy or "culture," as dominating individual agency. In contrast, scholars who focus on the micro-level, including beliefs, attitudes, and practices in daily life, argue that contradictions in the different sites or fields in which young people live, such as in schools and work, may result in uneven changes in young people's agency (Klocker, 2007; Murphy-Graham, 2010). This theorization of structures and individual beliefs and actions tends to set up agency as a binary, or, alternatively, takes it as a holism (see Maslak, 2008). As a holism, structures and agency are regarded as integrated parts and the relationships among them are not well clarified. Different from binary and holistic perspectives is a dialectic relationship in which the individual is always socially embedded in different structures and norms. A dialectic conceptualization ontologically positions youth agency in relation to others; young people do not necessarily learn and act alone, but rather with and through others (see Archer, 2000; McNay, 1999).

This introductory chapter to the volume sets out the differing conceptualizations of youth agency and the contextually specific ways that education and programs for youth foster and constrain agency. The adjective of *youth* adds particular import to the concept of agency; we take youth to be a social and physiological construct that reflects both age and critical or vital junctures in their life trajectory (Johnson-Hanks, 2005). The UN refers to youth as a specific age cohort, between 15 and 24, though some other international organizations and governments, such as the African Youth Charter, extend this age cohort to 35 years. Common social junctures that mark "youthhood" from a Western perspective have traditionally been denoted by passing through puberty, participating in education, residing with family, not being married or having their own family, and seeking to transition to work or livelihoods.[1] Bourdieu (1993), in his essay, "'Youth' is just a Word," captures the import of this category as signifying particular physiological commonalities and sets of power relations; he also challenges us to consider the differences between categories of youth. On the one hand, he notes, youth as a "classification by age (but also by sex and, of course, class …) always means imposing limits and producing an order" which is related to both social power and biological differences with adults (p. 94). On the other hand, this classification obscures differences in relation to social power among a group of youth. Since Bourdieu's writing, youth or youthhood as a social-cultural construction has been shifting, and both biological and social junctures are expanding, contracting, and becoming more diversified among a continuously growing youth population.

As the majority of the world's youth live in the global South, situating how youthhood is defined within a specific country and culture is imperative. For example, examining youth's experiences between different life junctures and social positions, such as having a child and still pursuing secondary school, warrants greater attention to the plurality of issues and challenges faced by youth. At the same time, adults in society often ascribe certain roles and responsibilities to youth that may lie within the traditional markers. Burgess (2005), in his introduction to an issue on youth in Africa draws on Brubaker and Cooper (2000) to describe this duality as "[the term youth] possesses both 'soft' and 'hard' meanings. The difference is between categories that are fluid and improvised, and those that are bounded and possess a fundamental sameness" (p. 9). There are multiple meanings to this category of youth and many differences within it. For the purpose of this book, youth as a concept has sociological importance in relation to agency in that it considers power relations within an ageist structure as well as power relations among categories of youth. Each of the chapters situates how youth or youthhood is being constructed within these different relations.

The rationale for this edited volume on youth and agency in global contexts is twofold. First, it offers a current and in-depth qualitative perspective on youth agency in different social, cultural, economic, and political environments, and in doing so, these in-depth qualitative cases contribute theoretically to the debates about agency as socially embedded and culturally and economically mediated. These qualitative case studies also offer an analysis of youth agency as constructed and reshaped over time and in specific spatial sites. The chapters in this book employ in-depth mixed methods and qualitative approaches, including ethnography and narrative analysis. The contributors to this book spent extensive time with the young people with whom they conducted the research in diverse country contexts.

---

[1] It is worth noting the distinction between adolescence and youth, where adolescence refers to the physical and psychological changes and youth is predominantly a social category. Additionally, much of the research on young girls tends to use the term adolescence, which is not necessarily applied to research with young boys.

Not only do these case studies illustrate how agency is contextually contingent (as has been argued by Bajaj, 2009; Murphy-Graham, 2012; Shirazi, 2011; and others), but they show the contradictory possibilities of youth agency with and through structures and norms. These accounts therefore are hopeful and, at times, uncertain, because as most of the scholars of these chapters proffer, agency is not always transformative or complete.

Second, this volume offers concrete examples and implications for the role of education—formal and non-formal—in fostering agency among youth. Many of the chapters suggest that particular educational practices play an important role in changing unequal social conditions and producing alternative social imaginations. While formal education particularly has taken a more individualistic turn toward the skills and competencies a young person needs to succeed in society, it also plays an important social role in preparing youth as members of their communities and countries. Additionally, non-formal education holds a prominent role in youth agency as it is often a site for critical pedagogy that potentially challenges the status quo of formal education and static political and cultural practices in communities.

The questions that are taken up in the different chapters in this volume include: How do formal and non-formal educational opportunities contribute to the construction and enactment of youth agency in specific contexts? How is agency linked with specific cultural histories, social relationships, and economic structures within country contexts and marginalized communities? In what ways do enactments of youth agency, either individually or collectively, and empowerment bring change to local and regional communities? Finally, are educational approaches to intentionally foster agency problematic and do they account for historically and culturally embedded practices in youth's daily lives? By examining these questions, we do not assume there are universal or holistic conceptualizations of agency among youth. While there may be some shared economic or social factors that affect youth, such as high unemployment in a global economy, we aim to tease out the multifarious social, cultural, and economic conditions that take on specific meanings in youth's lives at particular places and times. In doing so, these chapters contribute to conceptual and empirical examples of how agency is socially embedded. The thread woven throughout the chapters is that education is dialectically related to agency in that it is supportive and constraining depending on specific economic, social, and cultural factors affecting the education system and youth. Advancing the scholarship on youth, education, and agency, these chapters offer ways to consider agency as more socially than individually constructed, embedded in relationships with peers, family, and communities. It is through relations with others or with structures surrounding these youth that agency is imagined, shaped, enabled, or suppressed.

Theories of Agency and Education

In this section, we discuss the ongoing debates in the literature that situate agency in relation to structures, including cultural norms and systems. Social theories offer a rich, though varied, set of conceptualizations of agency, structure, and education (e.g., Archer, 2000, 2007; Bourdieu, 1990). Scholars in feminist studies, anthropology, and critical policy studies also contribute to these debates (McLeod, 2005; McNay, 2000; see also Levinson et al., 2011, for a brief summary of critical social theorists' contributions to education, agency, identities, and youth specifically). We begin with a brief discussion of Bourdieu's perspective on structure and agency, particularly in relation to education, along with those who have extended his ideas toward productive notions of agency, including Levinson et al. (2011), McNay (2000), and McLeod (2005). We then discuss Archer's (2000) scholarship as another perspective that helps us to think about the relationship between agency, culture, and social change. Finally, a capability approach offers a normative perspective of agency toward achieving individual well-being and addressing societal inequalities. This discussion is followed by a brief commentary on the concept of empowerment, in which we suggest agency serves as a dimension. After setting out these theoretical debates that position agency ontologically and epistemologically, we review studies of youth and education that draw on, critique, and extend these different perspectives.

Bourdieusian Perspectives on Agency, Structure, and Education

Bourdieu's classic work on agency and structures is often drawn on to consider how education reproduces social inequalities, or to alternatively consider if it can foster individual and social change (Bourdieu & Passeron, 1977, 1990). While the body of scholarship drawing on Bourdieu utilizes concepts of social fields, habitus, capital, and practices, agency is not often defined and has become conflated with habitus (see McNay, 2000 for a discussion of agency from Bourdieu's perspective; and Zipin, Sellar, Brennan, and Gale (2015) for conceptualizations of agency drawing on Bourdieu). For purposes of this book, then, it is useful to briefly review Bourdieu's key concepts, their meanings and the assumptions about the individual, society, and the role of education, and then to consider how other scholars have extended his work to consider agency in and through education for youth. Two key points are important for our purposes to illustrate the tension around conceptualizations of agency. First, much of Bourdieu's early work (e.g., Bourdieu & Passeron, 1977) and those who drew on him, positioned educational structures and norms as having power to influence youth's dispositions, thoughts, and actions in ways that reproduce middle-class norms. In this sense, his theorization of structure and agency, or relatedly fields and habitus, has been critiqued for being overly deterministic and primarily used to explain class differences. For instance, Farrugia (2013) notes that Bourdieu theorized subjectivity as individual practices that are produced to fit material structures—a view that is more reproductive than productive. However, Bourdieu (1990) acknowledges that there may be a lack of "fit" or dissonance between the habitus, or practices of an individual, and the conditions that structure it, producing a crisis (Farrugia, 2013). In these moments of crisis, reflexivity occurs and alternative or innovative practices may arise. A related second point is that Bourdieu's habitus is innovative, creative, and malleable (McNay, 2000). Reflexivity of one's situation and responses to it allows for a myriad of different responses that are innovative and not only reproductive. Such changes to an individual's habitus have the potential to also foster broader social change. This reproductive and productive tension is central to conceptualizations of agency in the chapters in this book.

Fields, in Bourdieu's (1990) use of it, describe the relations, rules, and norms that constitute particular social spaces, and habitus is the durable though concomitantly inventive dispositions, values, and preferences of an individual, shaped from personal and collective histories of those with whom we interact in different social spaces. Furthermore, the habitus is embodied action in day-to-day interactions in different fields. So while there is continuity in dispositions, values, and knowledge, they also change through an individual's practices as she negotiates her present reading of the field (Bourdieu, 1990). Therefore, the habitus is not static or determined solely by social structures. Individual's practices are enacted within and shared among a group and are what Bourdieu refers to as cultural and social capital as they can confer resources or power that can be convertible to other forms of capital (Bourdieu, 1986). McLeod (2005) states that this relationship of habitus with social fields is one of "ontological complicity" in which there is a complex and dynamic relationship between objective structures and the subjective self, even while Bourdieu also aims to understand the underlying and systematic relations of structures. However, some scholars continue to conceptualize structure and habitus in holistic and unitary ways, assuming that all class or gender structures have similar effects on actors; others challenge this unitary ontology and consider structure and habitus as dynamic, contradictory, and mutable, thus allowing for agency within structures of power.

Critiquing and extending Bourdieu's work, Levinson, Foley, and Holland (1996) offer a perspective of education as the cultural production of meaning and identities in contrast to a foreordained social and cultural reproduction. Reconceptualizing the relationship of structure and agency, Levinson et al. (2011) puts forth a definition of agency "as inherent creativity of the human being given expression through subjectivities that both fashion and are fashioned by the structures they encounter" (p. 116). They argue that through practice, as discussed in Bourdieu's (1990) practice theory, there is a relational conception of an individual and society in which a person both internalizes structures of power and is also an implicitly knowledgeable agent. Similar conceptualizations of agency are also taken up among some feminist scholars.

Feminist Framings of Agency and Structure

McLeod and McNay take more nuanced positions extending the theoretical linkage between habitus and fields to account for a multiplicity of change. McLeod (2005) astutely argues that Bourdieu's early work was most often used to analyze the reproductive nature of education; however, she draws on Ball, Maguire, and Macrae (2000) to argue the following:

> Some contemporary commentators have attempted to reformulate the relationship between habitus and field so that it is imagined as less tightly deterministic and rigidly presumed, emphasizing more the scope for improvization and degrees of inventiveness alongside the structural and shaping qualities of habitus. (p. 17)

McLeod also takes on the question of whether and how habitus, which is usually used to explain and examine class differentiation and hierarchies of difference, could be used to examine other social relations and distinctions. She recounts Bourdieu's (2001) *Masculine Domination* in which he applies the concept of habitus to denaturalize gender division and to "locate gender as a particular kind of habitus" (p. 18); however, she concludes that this analysis does not offer much to feminist scholarship because feminists have long theorized gender differences of labor—the focus of his research here. Despite Bourdieu's rather limited gender analysis, some feminists still find the concept of social fields useful to consider how they are differentiated by gender, as well as race and class, and to understand how the habitus is gendered. Still, some of this scholarship has tended to emphasize the domination of structure more than the inventive and productive nature of habitus. These different uses elides habitus with agency or identity and, as McLeod (2005) argues, distinctions are not always made between the practices of habitus that may be contradictory—at times reproductive and at times innovative.

The inventiveness and mutability of an individual's habitus vis-à-vis gender norms and structures are further taken up by McNay. McNay (1999, 2000) extends Bourdieu's work to complexify the relationship between structure and agency, suggesting that there is more room for instability of gender norms than most research has accounted for. McNay (2000) argues that conceptualizations of fields need to consider how they represent social differentiation. She uses the metaphor of "refraction" to explain how gendered social norms in different fields have differentiated and dispersed effects on one's thoughts, actions and embodiment of these norms. She further elaborates that "as a relational concept … [the field and habitus] provide a framework in which to conceptualize the uneven and non-systematic ways in which subordination and autonomy are realized in women's lives" (p. 70). While McNay refers to the multiple subjectivities and identities in accounts of gender, she also speaks to agency, stating that the habitus is generative, and "like the 'art of inventing' makes it possible to produce an infinite number of practices" in different social spaces (p. 55). McLeod (2005) warns, however, that the possibilities of agency should not be overstated, and that research should consider how change happens in contradictory ways, and slowly over time. Summarizing the debates between McNay and Bourdieu, McLeod (2005) argues there is a need to theorize, and we add, empirically show, "change and continuity, invention and repetition—a complex process that happens in ambivalent and uneven ways" (p. 24).

As these debates illustrate, the concept of agency is fraught with ambivalences. Other feminist scholars, such as Madhok, Phillips, and Wilson (2013), are more critical of the positive, transformative and liberation ideals equated with agency, which they say favors "the hyperindividualist liberal subject" who is autonomous, free, and independent (p. 7). At the same time, they acknowledge that many feminists call upon the ideals that agency signifies. Both the use of agency as a positive ideal and the critiques thereof suggest the contradictions and ambivalences inherent in this construct. In their edited volume, Madhok, Phillips, and Wilson situate agency in relation to coercion, arguing that agency is always exercised within constraints. Their approach to agency has two implications that are relevant for chapters in this book: first, agency is reframed based on ideals of collectivity and social relations, rather than the individual; and second, agency is embedded in social relations with deep inequalities, and such an account also allows for theorizing the social structures that frame possibilities for being agentic. A recent volume by Maxwell and Aggleton (2013) puts forward a contrasting perspective of how privilege is constitutive of agency and it asks whether agentic practices reproduce social relations or if there are possibilities for social change. These recent works point to the tension between agency as situated within privilege or coercion, thus ontologically positioning agency within dynamic social power relations.

These recent debates and developments in theorizing agency are relevant for the chapters in this book, many of which are situated in positive development discourses about youth and agency even though youth's lives are characterized by seemingly intractable material and social inequalities. Still, being educated affords some possibilities for greater privilege and power than if youth did not have these opportunities. However, education is also marked by social differences and inequalities, particularly in relation to class, race, and gender, among other social categories. We now turn to Archer's theorizations of how a social-cultural and subjective approach of agency can be used to understand differentiation among social categories.

Reflexivity, Agency, and Culture

Margaret Archer's scholarship on structure and agency is extensive and she theorizes a dual ontological approach in which structures are objective and agency is subjective (see, for example, Archer, 2000; her complete work cannot be fully discussed here). We draw on her work that conceptualizes agency in relation to cultural structures and norms. In her 2005 chapter, *Structure, culture and agency*, she argues that culture is often poorly related to structures, and theorizations of cultural properties often assume a homogenous and holistic treatment of culture. Anthropologists and sociologists, she suggests, have tended to conflate cultural systems with socio-cultural explanations. This conflation does not sufficiently differentiate what is cultural in the socio-cultural, and it further assumes coherence and closure in the system rather than possibilities for change and contradictions. Archer argues that functional theorists and Marxist theorists alike assume closure, with functionalist theorists suggest individuals are determined by a cultural system through socialization, whereas Marxists regard cultural properties as formed and transformed only by the dominant group, which universalizes cultural ideas. She acknowledges that this over-deterministic theorization has been shed; however, she asserts that the conflation of culture and agency remains in which culture is regarded as the texture of thought with little internal possibility for change. This conflation further "prevents the interplay between the parts and the people from making any contribution to reproduction or transformation" (p. 37), and precludes a two-way interaction or explanation of how change occurs in one way and not in another. She puts forward an explanatory framework in which cultural systems interact with the socio-cultural level of individuals, which in turn produces a cultural elaboration, stating that "cultural structures necessarily predate the actions that transform it and that cultural elaboration necessarily postdates those actions" (p. 43). From this perspective, agency is always present in individuals and possibilities for reproduction or transformation relate not only to material structures but also cultural systems, which have differing effects on individuals' thoughts and actions.

Further elaborating the subjectivity of agency, Archer uses the concept of reflexivity as the core of agency, and in her later work (2012) she argues that habitus is "no longer a reliable guide(s)" (p. 1). Her conceptualization of agency assumes that social order and systems are changing and that "new games" and their rules are novel, and "increasingly all have to draw upon their socially dependent but nonetheless personal powers of reflexivity in order to define their course(s) of action in relation to the novelty of their circumstances" (p. 1). Reflexivity for Archer is the internal conversations that mediate the effects of circumstances on actions, and define the courses of action taken in given situations. She is clear, however, that these internal conversations are not individualist; they are concerns formed in and of social life. Her analysis of different types of reflexivity (meta, communicative, autonomous, and fractured) among college students in the United Kingdom in the early part of this millennium is detailed and astute; however she says less about the varying material and cultural structures that affect these young people's live, assuming certain understandings of "late modernity." If, as her theory assumes, agency is always embedded in changing social, cultural, and material structures, then consideration of different cultural and structural environments as they affect reflexivity and agency need to be examined. Specific nuances of changing material and cultural environments vis-a-vis youth' agency are detailed in the chapters in this book.

Agency, Capabilities, and Well-being

Finally, another perspective on agency is offered through Amartya Sen's and Martha Nussbaum's capability approach.[2] Different from social theory that explains the relationship between agency and structures, the capability approach is informed by philosophy, ethics, economics, and development and is a normative approach that situates well-being as central to development. Sen's approach is concerned with comparatively evaluating policies and practices that can expand freedoms, foster well-being, and address inequalities (Sen, 1992, 1999, 2009). Education is suggested as a core capability—one that functions to foster well-being as well as other

---

[2] In this brief review of a capability approach and its conceptualization of agency, we primarily draw on Amartya Sen's work.

capabilities necessary for pursuing a life that individuals value. However, Walker and Unterhalter (2007) have argued that education is under-theorized in a capability approach as to how it can foster well-being and address inequalities. Other scholars have since taken up a capability approach in various ways to theorize and empirically examine educational practices that enable other capabilities, agency, and well-being (DeJaeghere & Lee, 2011; Hart, 2012; Hart, Biggeri, & Babic, 2014; Murphy-Graham, 2010; Saito, 2003; Walker, 2010; Walker & McLean, 2013). Much of this work draws on critical feminist or critical pedagogical approaches to show the possibilities for transformation and the constraints that arise for individuals as they become educated and use their education to enhance their lives.

Agency has been less theorized and examined within a capability approach, as it is assumed to be present in order for individuals to make informed choices toward their well-being. At the same time, agency is dialectically situated within social, environmental, and personal conditions that affect whether and how one can make choices (Sen, 1999). In Sen's writings on a capability approach, agency entails choices and actions linked to achieving positive well-being or addressing inequalities, even though others have argued that agency can also be used for less positive outcomes (see Walker, 2010 for an example of two women using their agency for different ends). Even if an individual has certain capabilities, such as the ability to read and write, she has to be able to convert these capabilities into well-being outcomes she has reason to value. This requires not only social and economic opportunities, but also agency. Sen further distinguishes between agency freedoms and agency achievements, and Unterhalter (2005) applies this to the context of education. Agency freedoms are having the conditions to exercise agency, including but not limited to access to information, the chance for (critical) discussion and evaluation of goals and values, and the freedom to make up one's mind without violence or shame (Unterhalter, 2005). Agency achievements are success in pursuing goals that she has reason to value, which may be the same as her well-being achievements, or it may be related to other well-being outcomes that are valued.

While there are critiques of the capability approach as being ontologically individual, others have conceptualized agency as socially and collectively embedded (e.g., Deneulin & McGregor, 2010). Deneulin and McGregor (2010) develop this view when they situate agency as "defined through our relationships with other persons … and that what we value is built from meanings which we share with others" (p. 2). They elaborate that agency to achieve well-being is for both self and others: "Rather than an individualized form of wellbeing … we argue that a broader and socially informed telos is required; this encompasses the good of oneself and others, including future generations" (p. 4). Thus, agency is not simply individual choice; it is embedded within social relations that give value to certain goals and outcomes. Further, agency is enacted not only for the individual but with and for others.

Little research, however, has examined the linkage between education and agency from a capability approach. The most recent is Caroline Hart's (2012) book on young people in the United Kingdom and their educational aspirations and agency, and Hart et al.'s (2014) book on agency and participation of young people. Lastly, DeJaeghere (2015) examines how aspirations and agency are dialectically and socially fostered through education in a rural community in Tanzania. Several chapters in this book offer insights into how agency is socially constructed and embedded in current and future aspirations, providing an alternative to the individually oriented agentic young person that other chapters critique.

Agency and Empowerment

Debates about agency require a word about its related concept, empowerment. Empowerment is equally ambiguous and varied in its uses. In the international development literature, empowerment is a positively regarded buzzword and the uses of it resemble the discourses of agency that situates youth, and particularly girls, as individually making decisions and changing one's own life amidst structural barriers. Similar to agency, feminists have both been drawn to and critique the concept of empowerment. On the one hand, it aims to explicitly bring in a conceptualization of power as changing if one is empowered. On the other hand, empowerment has also become an empty signifier, in which various actors and perspectives can give it meaning. In this way, it is often tied to neoliberal perspectives on individual power (see Sharma, 2008 for a discussion of discourses on empowerment particularly in relation to women and development). In contrast to the neoliberal uses of empowerment, Kabeer (1999) provides a useful definition of empowerment as a tripartite process, resources, agency and outcomes, in which agency is a dimension of a larger process of empowerment. Kabeer's theory of empowerment parallels a capability approach, noting that resources are important but insufficient to achieve desired or valued outcomes, and agency is a critical part of this process. Murphy-Graham's (2008, 2012) scholarship on education for empowering women also draws on a capability approach and other feminist scholars of empowerment and defines it as recognition, capability building, and action. In her work, recognition is fundamentally about recognizing one's own inherent worth and the equality of all human beings, and actions are for both personal and social betterment. This conceptualization primarily positions empowerment as subjectivities, and it does not necessarily account for objective material structures as Archer's account does. In this way, empowerment strongly parallels the constructions of agency above: as influenced by social, cultural, and historical structures/resources; as reflexive in one's thought and action; and as individual and social change. However, as conceptualizations of empowerment engage specifically with power structures, the scope is broadened to examine the dialectical relationship between individuals and their material and social worlds.

In the literature on youth and education, agency may be more frequently used than empowerment, possibly because agency does not necessarily assume marginalization of all youth, and it is related to a psychosocial process in which youth learn to become agentic over time and space. For this book, we use agency because the chapters capture how youth engage in a process of reflection and action within specific social contexts and power relations, but depending on these social, cultural, and economic contexts, the authors do not necessarily claim that these youth are empowered. In sum, agency is both a useful and a problematic concept. We recognize the limitations of this concept, including its over-usage and linkage with psychological and economic theorizations of self-efficacy, individual choice and the making of the self (see Hemmings & Kabesh, 2013 for this critique). However, all of the approaches discussed above call for situating agency as socially constructed and embedded, with more or less emphasis on the construction versus embedded. We see value in conceptualizations offered by McLeod, McNay and other critical and feminist scholars, in which agency includes inventiveness and improvisation vis-à-vis coercive and oppressive norms and structures. Such a conceptualization invokes inequalities in privilege and power, and it regards these inequalities as fluid and changing, even if in uneven ways and slowly over time. In addition, a capability approach orients agency toward specific ends, drawing attention to ethical considerations of the use of agency toward "a good life" and addressing inequalities (Walker, 2010). Finally, the role of reflexivity in relation to social-cultural structures situates cultural norms as socially constructed and also dynamic. By incorporating reflexivity into our conceptualizations of agency, we focus on how agency takes shape individually and socially. In rapidly changing societies affected by global economic, political and cultural change, we see value in continuing to examine and problematize agency among youth as they make sense of their lives in their social worlds.

Situating Agency Within Youth and Educational Studies

Youth inhabit a space and time where they are aware of and engaged with the world around them, and at the same time, they are on the fringes of change across their different life spheres (Benson & Saito, 2001). Agency as a concept allows us to understand how youth envision, negotiate and navigate their lived realities amidst social, cultural, political, and economic continuity and change, as well as during the transitions of their life from childhood to adulthood. Maira and Soep (2005) identify the term "youthscape" to describe the geographic and temporal spaces in which youth are positioned, as well as the social and political context in which they live and experience their lives (p. xv). Scholars of youth studies document how youth subcultures emerge in marginal spaces, such as urban sites (Dillabough & Kennelly, 2010) as well as over time through elongated transitions into adulthood, or what Honwana (2012) terms "waithood" in the context of many countries in Africa. These transitions of being part of and at the margins of specific life phases as well as spaces or spheres in which youth engage suggest that agency is temporally and culturally situated. In this section, we first discuss how scholarship on youth and educational studies conceptualize agency. Similar to the theoretical literature above, these scholars recognize the tension between agency as positive action and as imaginaries or possibilities of their current and future realities. This literature also suggests that agency needs to be linked with larger ethical stances or values of well-being so that it can have positive outcomes. Still other scholars take poststructural and ethnographic perspectives and argue for understanding agency as it is constructed through contradictory cultural formations, such that it responds to social forces. Following this discussion of literature specific to youth, we turn to studies that examines agency, activism and citizenship; agency and social identities; and agency and peer and family relations, all bodies of literature that have informed many of the chapters in this book.

The dynamics of youth identities as both engaged with and at the margins of change allow them to view the world from a different "vantage point" that Honwana (2012) characterizes as being "outside dominant ideologies" (p. 162). Such a vantage point allows for conceptualizing agency within these socio-cultural and temporal dynamics. In her studies in Mozambique, South Africa, Tunisia, and Senegal, Honwana suggests that youth are citizens engaged in new forms of social and civic action, which she contrasts with the assumed participation in partisan political activities (p. 135). She elaborates that these new modalities are collective protests and movements, with the possibility for broader social change. She discusses how youth's "collective action" may cause a generational change, which in turn spurs a "collective consciousness" for social and political issues (Honwana, 2012, p. 159). This action-oriented perspective of youth agency is countered by Dillabough and Kennelly (2010) in their description of youth's "urban imaginaries." They describe how youth cultures are "made and remade" through their "temporal and special understanding of how diverse young people struggle to hold together the imagined identities they constructed for themselves" (p. 204). Whereas Honwana describes a positive trajectory in which youth cultivate "collective conscious" that leads to "collective action," Dillabough and Kennelly suggest that youth at the margins are able to navigate through the broader society by constructing identities rooted in their "imaginations without hope, or without fantasy and its fictional effects" (p. 205). These collective actions and imagined identities serve as a medium of youth agency in their perceived and actual realities.

Acting upon and imagining futures or alternative realities are all forms of being agentic to create and respond to specific cultural, social, and economic dynamics in which youth are situated. Sociological, anthropological, and cultural studies of youth take different approaches to conceptualize action in relation to societal structures, such as racism, religious or gender discrimination, and class and economic structures of power. For example, Hart et al. (2014) edited volume takes up youth agency from a capability approach (Nussbaum, 2011; Sen, 1999), drawing on Sen's concept of "agency freedoms" or the "freedom to bring about achievements one values and attempt to produce" (Sen, 1992, p. 57). This concept of agency freedoms assumes that youth know—or have access to information to learn and understand— what they value. Furthermore, agency from this perspective assumes that youth have supports and conditions that allow them to pursue what they value. However, Hart et al. (2014) note that agency freedoms, while often used to achieve positive outcomes (for self and other), may be used to negatively affect self and/or others. Therefore, agency needs to be linked to larger moral and ethical stances, and as Sen (1992) has argued, for the improvement of well-being and addressing inequalities. Such an approach suggests judging whether and how educational policies and practices enhance agency and well-being. A second point raised in this book is that while an individual may be agentic and act for both individual and social benefits, the "sum of social benefits may be greater than the individual parts" (Hart et al., 2014, p. 20). This points to the need to examine the complex, subtle, and wider community benefits when youth act agentically.

While the capabilities approach of youth agency presented by Hart et al. (2014) focuses on the broader community influence on and impact of youth agency, Bucholtz's anthropological (2002) perspective seeks to link youth to their cultural context and how they negotiate and interact within that environment. She writes that researchers seeking to understand youth agency need to be attentive to "… how identities emerge in new cultural formations that creatively combine elements of global capitalism, transnationalism and local culture" (p. 525). Yet, in examining their agency, youth are seen as "responding to, not shaping, cultural forces" (pp. 532–533). This perspective of agency does not necessarily involve acting and influencing others, but rather agency is a response to and reconfiguring of oneself in relation to external influences.

While agency is always related to social, cultural, and economic context, how researchers understand the ways youth construct their agency through actions, imaginaries, and responses requires attention to how youth see themselves (and not how others see them) shaping their lives. Korteweg's (2008) feminist approach sees agency as "responding to" social forces of domination and subordination within societies. Korteweg's work, which is focused on agentic religious subjects, examines agency in relation to cultural practices. She critiques Western assumptions that certain cultural and religious practices are necessarily oppressive, challenging the assumption that Muslim women who participate in religious practices are not agentic. Korteweg suggests that if framings of agency are embedded in socio-cultural contexts, including religious practices, there is the possibility for more nuanced representations of agency particularly among women. She defines "embedded agency, which captures practices that do not have this explicit aim [of resistance to domination], yet still reflect active engagement in shaping one's life" (p. 437). She further states such a conceptualization allows us to see that "the capacity to act is not contingent on 'free will' and 'free choice' approaches to subjectivity" (p. 437). This perspective suggests that agency can be conceptualized and understood in terms of how youth shape and reshape their identities vis-à-vis cultural influences, and not only as actions taken in resistance to domination or in imagining alternative futures that are in sharp contrast to hegemonic ideals of youth. Agency, then, is not simply action to change or navigate youth's lives, it is also the subtle ways youth understand and respond to cultural forces in which they are situated and construct their identities.

Agency, Citizen Activism, and Society

One of the aims of formal and non-formal education is to foster youth to act within the larger society as citizens. However, education may serve to both facilitate and constrain agency for youth to be and act as citizens. A critical pedagogical approach, which seeks to involve youth and their perspectives in educational activities and decisions, is regarded as necessary for youth to act upon conditions in their lives (Bajaj, 2009; Bajaj & Pathmarajah, 2011; Olitsky, 2006). In her work within the Umutende school in Ndola, Zambia, Bajaj (2009) explores what she calls "transformative agency" (p. 2). "Transformative agency" was cultivated with the Umutende school students, in comparison to a group of government school students, through a focus on social justice in the curriculum and by teachers and administrators' positioning the youth as "future leaders" (p. 6). The use of a social justice discourse changed how youth thought about and saw themselves within their broader educational and community structures. Bajaj noted numerous ways in which the youth in the Umutende school expressed feelings of agency; however, she also shows that agency could be situational, stating that graduates did not always express an ability to act agentically within their broader communities (p. 13).

Shirazi's (2011) use of critical youth studies and the adoption of a postcolonial framework in his work in Jordanian schools with youth from both Jordan and Palestine allowed him to uncover ways that youth were able to enact their agency in spite of an educational environment that did not actively promote it. Rather than a perspective that views the Jordanian youth as being "marginalized" or "oppressed," the framework he employed allowed him to see and name the "agency in everyday venues and practices of schooling" (Shirazi, 2011, p. 292). For example, in an interaction between the students and Mr. Barakati, a teacher at one of the secondary schools, Shirazi documents the ways Mr. Barakati physically struck the hands of his students with a rod as a form of punishment. In turn, Shirazi shows how the students used their agency to name the hypocrisy of teaching human and children's rights when the teacher used corporal punishment in the classroom (pp. 285–286). While outwardly these acts of corporal punishment might be viewed as stifling youth agency, their naming and critiquing of the contradiction between these acts and what they were learning in class were acts of agency.

Despite constraining, and even oppressive environments in school and the larger society, youth's participation in shaping their learning experiences can enable them to be "agents of change" (Ardizzone, 2008, p. 279). Kennelly's (2011) work on youth's political engagement speaks to the effects that neoliberal policies have on youth's citizenship experiences in political and economic spheres. She argues that youth are situated within a tension between the state's construction of "good citizens," who are representations of the model students succeeding academically and engaging in the benevolent community work, and the "bad activists," who act beyond the limits of good engagement and challenge the state and economic structures, or the policies upholding them. She shows that despite constraining influences (i.e., the expectations of the citizenship curriculum to prepare youth to pass the exams or complete community service; and limited content of social injustices present in the textbooks), youth are activist in political issues that affect their lives. Kennelly highlights some of the ways youth are activists through their engagement in protests against the G-8 and G-20 meeting and how they do not conform to the expectations for and identities of becoming adults. The studies noted here also show that youth citizen agency, a term that Josić uses in her chapter, is socially constructed in relation to specific ethnic and group relations within the state.

Agency, Social Identities, and Status

Agency to resist, imagine, and act is intricately tied to social identities and statuses that are oppressed in society. These social identities are not usually singular, rather they are intersectional (gender and racial, gender and social class) and they affect youth agency in dynamic and complex ways. Gender relations have been one of the more prominent and salient social identities explored in regard to agency and youth; however, these gender relations are also often linked with ethnicity, class, or other social statuses.

Agency to negotiate gender norms and to form new gender identities can be fostered through education, though it is not necessarily the case that schooling is always agentic. Murphy-Graham's research on the curriculum of the Sistema de Aprendizaje (SAT) secondary school program showed how gender equity can be learned and fostered in the Garifuna communities in which she conducted her research in northern Honduras. Gender equity messages were incorporated within the five content areas of the curriculum and aimed to cultivate women's self-confidence and their knowledge and understanding of their own positionality as young women (Murphy-Graham, 2008, p. 31). The self-directed coursework helped the young women to set their own goals and follow-through with them. Furthermore, the curriculum promoted positive gender relations and agency. For instance, young women saw their own lived experiences through the lessons, and young men gained a better understanding of social constraints affecting women (Murphy-Graham, 2008, 2010). While Murphy-Graham's analysis provides a gender account, it does not explore the cultural embeddedness of agency at the intersection of the Garifuna racial/ethnic group status and gender status.

Agency as the capacity to change society or reshape one's response and identity also produces a new set of challenges in which existing agentic capacities are not sufficient. Greany's (2008) work on gender and education in Niger brings to light how young women who pursue schooling are set apart because they are agentic vis-à-vis norms that did not support their schooling. She problematizes that girls and young women are positioned to choose between what she terms "two distinct worlds" in their pursuit of education (p. 561). Going from a "traditional life to a more urban, modern one" changes the lived reality of girls' and young women in the type of community they feel comfortable engaging and acting in (p. 561). This study shows how gender identities and agency may take on distinct nuances in rural and urban communities, and furthermore how tradition and modernity are positioned in opposition.

Refugees are another group often seeking to reimagine their futures in new spaces, and their social status also intersects with gender, ethnic, and religious inequalities and oppression they face across different spaces in which they live and move. Gateley's (2015) study shows how refugee youth enact agency in their pursuit of higher education in the United Kingdom. Even though many refugee youth came from situations where their access to education was highly irregular or constrained due to religious beliefs or gender norms, the participants in the United

Kingdom's Refugee Integration and Employment Service (RIES) program saw higher education as a "central aspiration" (Gateley, 2015, p. 29). Agency for the refugee youth meant having the "opportunity to choose" and the "space (time) to make the choice" (p. 38). Based in Sen's capabilities approach, Gateley found that many youth were agentic in pursuing higher education opportunities despite professionals in the program discouraging them to do so and encouraging them to pursue work. While Gateley identified this population as "vulnerable" due to their marginalization in both the larger societal context and educational settings, the study showed that vulnerability does not preclude the ability to act agentically "when given both the opportunity and the space to choose" (Gateley, 2015, p. 35). This study illustrates assumptions that are often held about who can be agentic and what individuals and groups value with regard to their lives.

Agency in/Through Family and Peer Relations

Familial and peer influences are ever present when researching youth agency. Benson and Saito (2001) name the need to explore "spheres of influence" as sites in which youth engage across communities and "socializing systems." Aaltonen (2013) identifies education, peer relations, and family life as three sites where agency can be examined as they often require "action and choice." (p. 376). The presence or absence of support for youth within their family homes often sets the stage for how they can be agentic in other spheres of their lives (McCleary, 2013). In addition, peers are influential across the spectrum of choices youth make and the types of experiences in which they engage. The influence of family and peers is taken up in Tomanovic's (2012) longitudinal study of a group of Serbian youth. She tracked these young people over a decade from childhood into youthhood in order to examine the family influences and structural opportunities available to them. She uses the term "active use of opportunities" as a descriptor for how youth used agency in a setting with considerable political, economic, and social change (p. 610). For Tomanovic, youth's ability to use family resources and peer networks to actively engage opportunities available to them was demonstrative of agency. In this sense, agency is not individually held, but rather actions taken and imaginations made with others comprised a socially embedded agency.

Agency is also examined in romantic or sexual relationships among youth (Averett, Benson, & Vaillancourt, 2008; Thorpe, 2005). Having the agency to communicate about engaging in physical intimacy, responding to a request for sex or a sexual act, and making sure contraception is used are areas in which researchers discuss how youth are, or are not, being agentic. Bell (2012) found in her study on sexual agency in Uganda that young women and men extended their agency in negotiating with whom they would have sex and the material goods that would be a part of this transaction. Bell (2012) cites sexual agency as "… an individual's actions and decisions about one's body and emotions to shape and change one's sexual practice, including whether, when, where, and with whom to initiate a sexual relationship" (p. 284). In this case, youth's sexual agency had outcomes at the personal level, although the youth used their peers as barometers to consider if and how decisions around sex had positive or negative outcomes for themselves.

In sum, studies on youth illustrate different frameworks for understanding agency as constructing identities, resisting, and acting amidst cultural, social, economic, and political forces. These studies also show youth agency as being constructed individually and collectively at the macro, meso, and micro levels, including in relation to the state and economy, social groups and communities, and families and peers. The chapters in this book draw on some of these bodies of literature to explore how youth agency is taken up from different disciplinary lenses and in diverse contexts. The book is divided into three sections encompassing agency and political, social, and economic contexts, policies and discourses.

The Chapters

The first section of the book focuses on agency and youth activism as citizens at the intersection of various social positions of youth—race, ethnicity, and age. Dierker's chapter considers African American youth belonging and agency through an exploration of points of resistance and what she identifies as youth's counter-narratives of their history. She unpacks how counter-narratives about African Americans contribute to youth's agency within a broader context of racism and violence. Pulling from Chávez and Griffin's (2009) work on youth belonging and resistance, Bajaj's (2009) writing on transformational agency, and Ginwright and Cammarota's (2002) work on critical race consciousness, Dierker describes how these youth developed coalitional agency by understanding their culture and its history, and through a sense of belonging with others who participated in a youth program. In addition, she shows how this youth program supported these youth to use their coalitional agency to enable community social change.

Josić takes up how youth's practices of citizenship are shaped by community contexts and through their relations with schools and neighborhood communities. Based in research from two United States high school social studies and civic programs, Josić examines the ways institutionalized structures and practices (i.e., the social institution of education, schooling practices) condition youth's belonging to their communities, and how they are becoming and acting as a citizen. Calling on the work of Staeheli (2010) on citizenship and communities, and Lawy and Biesta's (2006) work on "citizenship-as-practice" (p. 45), Josić explores the role of school and community opportunities, resources, and practices in shaping youth's formation of their citizen agency.

The Senegalese Université Cheikh Anta Diop (UCAD) is the site of Stafford's research in which he explores how student activism is, what he terms, an "entry point" for understanding collective student agency. Stafford situates higher education in Senegal within postcolonial theory, as well as discourses of "developmentalism and global capitalism" (Gupta, 1998, p. 10). He uses "transformative agency"

(Bajaj, 2009) as a basis for examining how social expectations related to "the educated person" and the "rule of failure" are used to cultivate student activism and participation to improve their educational and university experience vis-à-vis constraining structural conditions of higher education institutions and the state.

The second section of the book examines gender, class, and religion and constructions of youth agency in various sites of patriarchal oppression. Payal Shah's 5-year ethnography of a Kasturba Gandhi Balika Vidyalaya (KGBV) residential school in Western Gujarat looks at how structures and resources within the school and community contribute to a "thickening" and "thinning" of girls' agency (Klocker, 2007). Using two case examples from her study, Shah details how Rekha's and Lata's agency has been fostered and shaped by their secondary education experiences, families, and the non-egalitarian gender system present in their communities in Western Gujarat.

McCleary's chapter explores how Honduran young women and men used their agency to "resist," "transgress," and "undo" gender norms that constricted their actions and behaviors at home and in their local communities (Montoya, Frazier, & Hurtig, 2002; Stromquist & Fischman, 2009). Her chapter also addresses how a non-formal youth program promotes reflection on and change toward greater gender equity through a local community youth sport event.

Staying within the Latin America and Caribbean (LAC) region, Shawanda Stockfelt takes up the legacy of colonialism in Jamaica, and the effect it has on Jamaican boys' participation and interest in higher education, in her chapter examining young men and masculinities in education. Using Bourdieu's work on agency, habitus, field, and cultural capital, Stockfelt looks at the intersection of government policy, young men's academic achievement, and their life experiences of education to understand the low enrollment of young men in higher education.

Sallam's chapter focuses on how the historical and contemporary urban–rural divide in Upper Egypt is exacerbated through educational programming for women's empowerment. Using a poststructural framework, Sallam critiques the role of development efforts, and particularly "second-chance" education programs, in shaping young women's agency. Bringing together Said's (1978) cultural critique on the representation of the Eastern world, particularly Arabs and Muslims, with a cultural analysis of the empowerment of women in Jordan (Adely, 2012), Sallam's research points to the historical, sociopolitical, and cultural influences of rural–urban dynamics shaping Egyptian communities and how patriarchal oppression and agency are framed differently in these communities.

Laura Wangsness Willemsen and Anna Ndesamburo Kwayu draw on two qualitative studies to examine Tanzanian secondary school students' agency and the ways peers and family are mediators in how they learn about and engage in sexual relationships. Utilizing Kabeer's (1999) concepts of agency, resources, and achievements to conceptualize empowerment, Wangsness Willemsen and Ndesamburo Kwayu show how youth's sexual agency is constructed and learned through their relationships.

Khurshid and Guerrero's chapter is a discourse analysis of the problematic ways that Western media writes about and portrays the tragedy and triumphs of Malala

Yousafzai, her family, Islamic religion, education, and Muslim culture. Problematizing the dual position of Muslim women as victims and agents, and the ways education contributes to that binary, Khurshid and Guerrero examine the discourse used by *The New York Times* and *The Wall Street Journal* to portray Malala's story as a binary between a victim of Islamic patriarchy and an agent of change for girls' education. They note how her agency is often fallaciously attributed to the West's support of her education. These authors give voice to Malala's story as counter-narrative to that of the Western media's discourse of girls' and women's positionality within Islam and the Muslim culture of the Swat Valley.

The third section of the book explores how economic and social policies intersect with and impact youth's economic agency. Thangaraj's research problematizes common understandings of children's economic agency through an ethnographic exploration of the dynamics that influence how young people in India's Kanchipuram region engage in education and labor. Providing a rich account of the dominant global discourses and conventions on child labor alongside the voices of young people and their experiences, Thangaraj offers a critique of the inflexible nature of the policy banning child labor and calls for alternative approaches to schooling and labor that are responsive to the economic agency of these youth.

Pellowski Wiger's chapter on entrepreneurship education in Tanzania examines how youth develop social capital, which serves to both foster their agency and be converted into other forms of economic capital. Drawing on critical conceptualizations of social capital (e.g., Bourdieu, 1986; Stanton-Salazar, 1997, 2011) Pellowski Wiger illustrates how youth utilize their schooling to develop peer and adult relationships that in turn assist them in pursuing enterprises and their livelihoods. Using longitudinal data of youth attending two secondary boarding schools in Tanzania that are implementing entrepreneurship training, this analysis highlights how social relations with both family and non-family peers and adults affect youth's agency and ability to further their livelihoods in constraining economic and social environments.

Nikoi's work with Kenyan youth provides insights into how a non-formal training program fosters agency and empowerment to improve their economic and social lives. Building on Murphy-Graham's (2012) framework of empowerment, Nikoi also engages with the concepts of economic empowerment and Payne's (2012) everyday agency to explain the empowerment of the young people completing the vocational programs. Nikoi's research reveals how vocational training programs, and particularly work-readiness and life skills, allow youth to make livelihood decisions in contexts of limited economic opportunities.

In sum, this book's examination of youth agency aims to problematize the intersections of the social, cultural, and economic relations that affect youth agency and their identities. Our review of the literature and the conceptualizations of agency we put forward suggest that researchers and practitioners need to understand how youth construct for themselves their actions, resistance, and imaginaries in relation to both their present situations and desired futures that are historically, socially, and culturally embedded. Bucholtz (2002) reminds us that "the lived experience of young people … [is] neither rehearsals for the adult 'real thing' nor even necessarily oriented to adults at all" (p. 532). In this sense, agency is constructed specifically among youth and their ways of seeing, resisting, and acting on the forces in their lives at different times and in different spaces.

References

Aaltonen, S. (2013). 'Trying to push things through': Forms and bounds of agency in transitions of school-age young people. *Journal of Youth Studies, 16*(3), 375–390.

Adely, F. J. (2012). *Gendered paradoxes: Educating Jordanian women in nation, faith, and progress*. Chicago, IL: University of Chicago Press.

Archer, M. S. (2000). *Being human: The problem of agency*. Cambridge, England: Cambridge University Press.

Archer, M. S. (2005). Structure culture, and agency. In M. D. Jacobs, & N. Weiss Hanrahan (Eds.), *The Blackwell companion to the sociology of culture* (pp. 17–34). Blackwell Publishing Ltd. Retrieved from http://dx.doi.org/10.1002/9780470996744.ch2.

Archer, M. S. (2007). *Making our way through the world: Human reflexivity and social mobility*. Cambridge, England: Cambridge University Press.

Archer, M. S. (2012). *The reflexive imperative in late modernity*. Cambridge, England: Cambridge University Press.

Ardizzone, L. (2008). Motivating and supporting activist youth: A view from non-formal settings. In M. Flynn & D. C. Brotherton (Eds.), *Globalizing the streets: Cross-cultural perspectives on youth, social control, and empowerment* (pp. 273–286). New York, NY: Columbia University Press.

Averett, P., Benson, M., & Vaillancourt, K. (2008). Young women's struggle for sexual agency: The role of parental messages. *Journal of Gender Studies, 17*(4), 331–344.

Bajaj, M. (2009). "I have big things planned for my future": The limits and possibilities of transformative agency in Zambian schools. *Compare: A Journal of Comparative and International Education, 39*(4), 551–568.

Bajaj, M., & Pathmarajah, M. (2011). En'gender'ing agency: The differentiated impact of educational initiatives in Zambia and India. *Feminist Formations, 23*(3), 48–67.

Ball, S., Maguire, M., & Macrae, S. (2000). *Choice, pathways and transitions post 16: New youth, new economies in the global city*. London, England: Routledge Falmer Press.

Bell, S. A. (2012). Young people and sexual agency in rural Uganda. *Culture, Health & Sexuality, 14*(3), 283–296.

Benson, P. L., & Saito, R. N. (2001). The scientific foundations of youth development. In P. L. Benson & K. J. Pittman (Eds.), *Trends in youth development: Visions, realities, and challenges* (pp. 135–154). Boston, MA: Kluwer Academic Publishers.

Bourdieu, P. (1986). The forms of capital. In J. G. Richardson (Ed.), *Handbook of theory and research for the sociology of education* (pp. 241–258). New York, NY: Greenwood.

Bourdieu, P. (1990). *The logic of practice*. Stanford, CA: Stanford University Press.

Bourdieu, P. (1993). 'Youth' is just a word. In P. Bourdieu (Ed.), *Sociology in question* (pp. 94–102). London, England: Sage Publications.

Bourdieu, P. (2001). *Masculine domination*. Stanford, CA: Stanford University Press.

Bourdieu, P., & Passeron, J. C. (1977). *Reproduction in education, society and culture* (1st ed.). London, England: Sage Publications.

Bourdieu, P., & Passeron, J. C. (1990). *Reproduction in education, society and culture* (2nd ed.). London, England: Sage Publications.

Brubaker, R., & Cooper, F. (2000). Beyond "identity". *Theory and Society, 29*, 1–47.

Bucholtz, M. (2002). Youth and cultural practice. *Annual Review of Anthropology, 31*(1), 525–552.

Burgess, T. (2005). Introduction to youth and citizenship in East Africa. *Africa Today, 51*(3), vii–xxiv.

Chávez, K. R., & Griffin, C. L. (2009). Power, feminisms, and coalitional agency: Inviting and enacting difficult dialogues. *Women's Studies in Communication, 32*(1), 1–11.

DeJaeghere, J. (2015). Girls' educational and livelihoods aspirations and agency: Imagining alternative futures through schooling in low-resourced Tanzanian communities. Paper Presented at the Human Development and Capability Conference, Washington, DC, September, 2014.

DeJaeghere, J., & Lee, S. K. (2011). What matters for marginalized girls and boys: A capabilities approach to exploring marginalization and empowerment in Bangladesh. *Research in Comparative and International Education [Special Issue on Marginalization and Empowerment], 6*(1), 27–42.

Deneulin, S., & McGregor, J. A. (2010). The capability approach and the politics of a social conception of wellbeing. *European Journal of Social Theory, 13*(4), 501–519.

Dillabough, J. A., & Kennelly, J. (2010). *Lost youth in the global city: Class culture and the urban imaginary.* New York, NY: Routledge.

Farrugia, D. (2013). Young people and structural inequality: Beyond the middle ground. *Journal of Youth Studies, 16*(5), 679–693.

Gateley, D. E. (2015). A policy of vulnerability or agency? Refugee young people's opportunities in accessing further and higher education in the UK. *Compare, 45*(1), 26–46.

Ginwright, S., & Cammarota, J. (2002). New terrain in youth development: The promise of a social justice approach. *Social Justice-San Francisco, 29*(4), 82–95.

Greany, K. (2008). Rhetoric versus reality: Exploring the rights-based approach to girls' education in rural Niger. *Compare: A Journal of Comparative and International Education, 38*(5), 555–568.

Gupta, A. (1998). *Postcolonial developments: Agriculture in the making of modern India.* Durham, NC: Duke University Press.

Hart, C. S. (2012). *Aspirations, education and social justice: Applying Sen and Bourdieu.* London, England: Bloomsbury.

Hart, C. S., Biggeri, M., & Babic, B. (Eds.). (2014). *Agency and participation in childhood and youth: International applications of the capability approach in schools and beyond.* London, England: Bloomsbury.

Hemmings, C., & Kabesh, A. (2013). The feminist subject of agency: Recognition and affect in encounters with 'the Other'. In S. Madhok, A. Philips, & K. Wilson (Eds.), *Gender, agency and coercion* (pp. 29–46). New York, NY: Palgrave Macmillan.

Honwana, A. (2012). *The time of youth: Work, social change, and politics in Africa.* Sterling, VA: Kumarian Press.

Honwana, A., & De Boeck, F. (Eds.). (2005). *Makers and breakers: Children and youth in postcolonial Africa.* Trenton, NJ: Africa World Press.

Johnson-Hanks, J. (2005). *Uncertain honor: Modern motherhood in an African crisis.* Chicago, IL: University of Chicago Press.

Kabeer, N. (1999). Resources, agency, achievements. *Reflections on the measurement of women's empowerment, 30*(3), 435–464.

Kelly, P. (2006). The entrepreneurial self and 'youth at risk': Exploring the horizons of identity in the twenty-first century. *Journal of Youth Studies, 9*(1), 17–32.

Kennelly, J. (2011). *Citizen youth: Culture, activism and agency in a neoliberal era.* New York, NY: Palgrave Macmillan.

Klocker, N. (2007). An example of 'thin' agency: Child domestic workers in Tanzania. In R. Panelli, S. Punch, & E. Robson (Eds.), *Global perspectives on rural childhood and youth: Young rural lives* (pp. 83–94). New York, NY: Routledge.

Korteweg, A. C. (2008). The Sharia debate in Ontario: Gender, Islam, and representations of Muslim women's agency. *Gender & Society, 22*(4), 434–454.

Lawy, R., & Biesta, G. (2006). Citizenship-as-practice: The educational implications of an inclusive and relational understanding of citizenship. *British Journal of Educational Studies, 54*(1), 34–50.

Levinson, B. A., Foley, D. E., & Holland, D. (Eds.). (1996). *The cultural production of the educated person: Critical ethnographies of schooling and local practice.* Albany, NY: The State University of New York Press.

Levinson, B., Gross, P. J., Heimer Dadds, J., Hanks, C., Kumasi, K., Metro-Roland, D., et al. (2011). *Beyond critique: Exploring critical social theories and education.* Boulder, CO: Paradigm.

Madhok, S., Phillips, A., & Wilson, K. (2013). Introduction. In S. Madhok, A. Philips, & K. Wilson (Eds.), *Gender, agency and coercion* (pp. 1–13). New York, NY: Palgrave Macmillan.

Maira, S., & Soep, E. (Eds.). (2005). *Youthscapes: The popular, the national, the global.* Philadelphia, PA: University of Pennsylvania Press.

Maslak, M. A. (Ed.). (2008). *The structure and agency of women's education.* Albany, NY: State University of New York Press.

Maxwell, C., & Aggleton, P. (2013). Introduction. In C. Maxwell, & P. Aggleton (Eds.), *Privilege, agency and affect* (pp. 1–14). Retrieved from http://www.palgraveconnect.com/pc/doifin der/10.1057/9781137292636.0001.

McCleary, K. (2013). *'Tomar decisiones es el futuro de uno' [To make decisions is one's future]: The gendering of youth agency within two Honduran communities.* Retrieved from the University of Minnesota Digital Conservancy, http://hdl.handle.net/11299/162502.

McLeod, J. (2005). Feminists re-reading Bourdieu old debates and new questions about gender habitus and gender change. *Theory and Research in Education, 3*(1), 11–30.

McLeod, J. (2012). Vulnerability and the neo-liberal youth citizen: A view from Australia. *Comparative Education, 48*(1), 11–26.

McNay, L. (1999). Gender, habitus and the field: Pierre Bourdieu and the limits of reflexivity. *Theory, Culture & Society, 16*(1), 95–117.

McNay, L. (2000). *Gender and agency: Reconfiguring the subject in feminist and social theory.* Cambridge, England: Polity Press.

Montoya, R., Frazier, L. J., & Hurtig, J. (Eds.). (2002). *Gender's place: Feminist anthropologies of Latin America.* New York, NY: Palgrave Macmillan.

Murphy-Graham, E. (2008). Opening the black box: Women's empowerment and innovative secondary education in Honduras. *Gender and Education, 20*(1), 31–50.

Murphy-Graham, E. (2010). And when she comes home? Education and women's empowerment in intimate relationship. *International Journal of Education Development, 30*(3), 320–331.

Murphy-Graham, E. (2012). *Opening minds, improving lives: Education and women's empowerment in Honduras.* Nashville, TN: Vanderbilt University Press.

Nussbaum, M. C. (2011). *Creating capabilities: The human development approach.* Cambridge, MA: Harvard University Press.

Olitsky, S. (2006). Structure, agency and the development of students' identities as learners. *Culture Studies of Science Education, 1*(4), 745–766.

Ortiz, I., & Cummins, M. (2012). *When the global crisis and youth bulge collide: Double the jobs trouble for youth.* Social and Economic Policy Working Paper. New York, NY: UNICEF.

Payne, R. (2012). 'Extraordinary survivors' or 'ordinary lives'? Embracing 'everyday agency' insocial interventions with child-headed households in Zambia. *Children's Geographies, 10*(4), 399–411.

Said, E. W. (1978). *Orientalism.* New York, NY: Vintage Books.

Saito, M. (2003). Amartya Sen's capability approach to education: A critical exploration. *Journal of Philosophy of Education, 37*(1), 17–33.

Sen, A. (1992). *Inequality reimagined.* Boston, MA: Harvard University Press.

Sen, A. (1999). *Development as freedom.* New York, NY: Knopf.

Sen, A. (2009). *The idea of justice.* Cambridge, MA: Belknap Press of Harvard University Press.

Sharma, A. (2008). *Logics of empowerment: Development, gender, and governance in neoliberal India.* Minneapolis, MN: University of Minnesota Press.

Shirazi, R. (2011). When projects of 'empowerment' don't liberate: Locating agency in a 'postcolonial' peace education. *Journal of Peace Education, 8*(3), 277–294.

Staeheli, L. (2010). Political geography: Where is citizenship? *Progress in Human Geography, 35*(3), 393–400.

Stanton-Salazar, R. D. (1997). A social capital framework for understanding the socialization of racial minority children and youth. *Harvard Educational Review, 67*(1), 1–40.

Stanton-Salazar, R. D. (2011). A social capital framework for the study of institutional agents and their role in the empowerment of low-status students and youth. *Youth Society, 43*(3), 1066–1109.

Stromquist, N. P., & Fischman, G. E. (2009). Introduction—From denouncing gender inequities to undoing gender in education: Practices and programmes toward change in the social relations of gender. *International Review of Education, 55*(5), 463–482.

Thorpe, M. (2005). Learning about HIV/AIDS in schools: Does a gender-equality approach make a difference? In S. Aikman & E. Unterhalter (Eds.), *Beyond access: Transforming policy and practice for gender equality in education* (pp. 199–211). Herndon, VA: Stylus Publishing.

Tomanovic, S. (2012). Agency in the social biographies of young people in Belgrade. *Journal of Youth Studies, 15*(5), 605–620.

Unterhalter, E. (2005). Global inequality, capabilities, social justice: The millennium development goal for gender equality in education. *International Journal of Educational Development, 25*(2), 111–122.

Walker, M. (2010). Critical capability pedagogies and university education. *Educational Philosophy and Theory, 42*(8), 898–917.

Walker, M., & McLean, M. (2013). *Professional education, capabilities and the public good: The role of universities in promoting human development.* London: Routledge.

Walker, M., & Unterhalter, E. (2007). The capability approach: Its potential for work in education. In M. Walker & E. Unterhalter (Eds.), *Amartya Sen's capability approach and social justice in education* (pp. 1–18). New York, NY: Palgrave Macmillan.

Zipin, L., Sellar, S., Brennan, M., & Gale, T. (2015). Educating for futures in marginalized regions: A sociological framework for rethinking and researching aspirations. *Educational Philosophy and Theory, 47*, 227–246.

Part I
Youth Agency and Community, Historical, and Political Contexts

"You Are Building on Something": Exploring Agency and Belonging Among African American Young Adults

Beth Dierker

What Made the Difference?

Having just proposed a study focused on these young adults[1] and the influences that fostered their agency for social change, I listened as the conversation circled, quickly spiraling up to the big-picture question: "What made the difference?" In a cascade of stories and laughter, the group—the most recent cohort of participants in a church-based youth-development program—and the elders[2] who led that program shared what they thought "it" entailed. "We had opportunities to go further with everything … to brainstorm and take a leap of faith," Julie recalled. "It's also about ownership of the program and freedom," Adam asserted. Michelle pointed to the importance of relationships, saying, "You can build a program around a relationship." The elders posed questions to the young adults. Amy wondered why the youth stayed when there was no money left to pay stipends and no basketball court or other fancy facilities. "You made us think and open our eyes!" Adam began to

---

[1] Throughout the chapter, the term "young adults" is used in reference to the study participants, ages 23–25. During the study, the participants considered themselves to be young adults, possibly to differentiate themselves from the children and youth; several participants worked within local youth development programs. The study took place at a time of transition into young adulthood as many participants were in college; all had full or part-time jobs, and two had children of their own.

[2] The term "elder" is found throughout the chapter and was used by the participants in reference to the Youth Space staff (Ed, Aaron, and Amy) and, occasionally in reference to respected African American local political and community leaders. Highlighting the moral dimension of eldership, Adrian, one of the participants, explained that "age doesn't necessarily make you an elder" but that an elder is one who is "instilling values in a young person" (Adrian, personal communication, March 27, 2012).

B. Dierker (✉)
Consultant, Urban Research, Outreach and Engagement Center, University of Minnesota, Minneapolis, MN, USA
e-mail: dierk020@umn.edu

© Springer International Publishing Switzerland 2016
J.G. DeJaeghere et al. (eds.), *Education and Youth Agency*, Advancing Responsible Adolescent Development, DOI 10.1007/978-3-319-33344-1_2

27

explain. Julie volleyed back with a deeply personal question for her elders at the table, "how did you know what we needed when we needed it?" (Field Notes, 2012)

I met several of the people around this table 3 years earlier in a youth-violence prevention initiative, and we had since crossed paths in the youth-development network that spanned the urban area. Over that time, I observed what I thought was a unique capacity to reflect on their actions and circumstances and to envision and enact strategies for effecting change in their neighborhood. Inspired and curious, I began shaping research questions around what I thought I saw. Now, this group was asking their own questions, revisiting powerful, shared experiences, and reflecting on the way those experiences shaped them as youth and as young adults navigating careers, college, and family life.

Having seen how structural violence and discrimination greatly affected these young men and women, but also having observed their convictions about and actions toward addressing these injustices, I situated this research in scholarship that seeks a holistic understanding of youth agency, community involvement, and activism (Bajaj, 2009; Hart & Fegley, 1995; Watts & Guessous, 2006). Hart and Fegley (1995) conducted research on youth who had been nominated by community leaders as exceptional in their commitments to helping others in their community. Their study drew a wealth of important conclusions about the youths psychological characteristics, such as self-understanding and moral judgment, and they called for research on the social context, particularly the ways community groups "provide contexts within which strong moral commitments can develop and flourish" (1995, p. 1357). From a different theoretical perspective, Watts and Guessous (2006) theorized and began to test aspects of their model of sociopolitical development—the evolving, critical understanding of the political, economic, cultural, and other systemic forces that shape society and one's status within it, and the associated process of growth in relevant knowledge, analytical skills, and emotional faculties (p. 60, citing Watts, Williams, & Jagers, 2003). Suggesting that their findings "show a link between what is good for the individual and what is good for society" and pointing out that psychological research has explored individual personal growth thoroughly, Watts and Guessous (2006) call for research on "conceptions of social (in)justice, and the social processes that lead to a collective striving for liberation" (p. 72).

This chapter's findings, drawn from a larger research study, offer a partial response to these calls for research on social processes and contexts that shape moral commitments and collective striving for social change. Taking place in city rich in diversity but marked with vast economic and educational disparities, particularly between African American and white residents, this case study explored the journeys of six young African American adults, who were recognized leaders and change-makers—especially related to youth development and advocacy—in their predominantly African American neighborhood and across the urban area. The study sought to understand the influences that the young adults articulated as contributing to their sense of agency for social change, and how they drew on those influences as they navigated young adulthood. This chapter addresses the findings related to the influences, experiences, and relationships these young adults identified as shaping their belief that they should and could effect change in, or transform, their communities. The study participants' efforts to "effect change" often focused on improving the lives of youth in the neighborhood by, for example, lending youth perspectives to neighborhood discussions and city policy related to violence, safety, health, youth programming, and community-building and by engaging in mentorship and youth development programs with younger children and youth.

The findings discussed in this chapter illuminate the relationships, narratives, and commitments that the young adults said contributed to their sense of agency for social change. They pointed primarily to ideas, experiences, and relationships that were formed in a non-formal educational setting—a church-based youth organization called the Youth Space. While they discussed the influences of family, friends, and acquaintances in school, neighborhood and professional settings, they emphasized that their relationships and experiences alongside Youth Space peers and elders helped them draw connections among individual experiences and their overall view of themselves as change-agents, as African Americans, as members of their community, and as humans. Altogether, this chapter offers illustrative examples that further develop the concept of coalitional agency put forth by Chávez and Griffin (2009), who suggested, "A coalitional agency implies that our ability to affect social change, to empower others and ourselves necessitates seeing people, history and culture as inextricably bound to one another" (p. 8).

Framing Agency: Critical Consciousness, Critical Race Consciousness, and Transformative and Coalitional Agency

Grounded in a critical constructivist approach, this study seeks to understand the meaning the young adults made from their lived experiences, while incorporating analyses of power and reflections on the influence of social, economic, and political structures in their lives (Kincheloe, 2008). Rather than Freire's notions of power as oppressive over people, which is commonly used in critical approaches to education, this study incorporates Bartlett's (2010) reconceptualization of power as "circulating, or rather, simultaneously exercised and experienced by all" (p. 170). This recasting of power aligns with the perspectives of the young adults in this study, who recognized oppressive systems and structures but have experienced and fostered power in a collaborative, more horizontal way through collective action.

Practice theory specifically provides a theoretical framework for the study. Observing a trend in anthropological scholarship toward a broader conception of actors' agency that considered how the structure constrains action but also how the system itself is created through actions, Ortner (1984) asserted that a common approach to theorizing practice still "tends to highlight social asymmetry as the most important dimension of both action and structure" (p. 147). In contrast, Ortner outlined a new understanding of practice that (1) views actions as "not just random response to stimuli, but governed by organizational and evaluative schemes" and (2) views the system as "an integral whole rather than trying to separate it out into levels" (p. 148). Ortner (1984) emphasized that actions are often part of broader human "projects," instead of simply individual, disconnected "moves," and that "action itself *has* (developmental) structure, as well as operating *in*, and in relation *to*, structure" (p. 150, emphasis in original). Of most significance for this study is Ortner's suggestion that rather than viewing rational individual interest as motivating actions, a new approach to practice theory attempts to understand

> where actors ... are coming from .... A system is analyzed with the aim of revealing the sorts of binds it creates for actors, the sorts of burdens it places upon them .... This analysis, in turn, provides much of the context for understanding actors' motives, and the kinds of [long-term] projects they construct for dealing with their situations. (p. 152)

This study adopted Ortner's approach to practice as it sought to understand how the young adults navigate their lives, drawing on relationships, ideas, and experiences that help them navigate constraints and "binds" they encountered while creating holistic and developmental understandings of themselves and their lives. During a 2-year period of planning and implementing a youth violence prevention campaign with several of the study participants, I recognized the young men's and women's keen understanding of the systems and structures that constrained their lives and damaged their communities. They demonstrated a strong conviction that they should and could change these systems and structures. The concepts of critical race consciousness and transformative and coalitional agency help to frame the meaning-making processes behind the young adults' beliefs that they should and could effect change.

Critical Consciousness and Critical Race Consciousness

Critical consciousness is part of Freire's (1970) notion of praxis, involving cycles of action and reflection. It is the capacity to recognize and understand one's circumstances in light of the power and social structures that constrain them (Freire, 1970). Ginwright and Cammarota (2002) recast praxis by describing social action and critical consciousness as an interdependent "couplet," arguing, "people can only truly 'know' that they can exercise control over their existence by directly engaging the conditions that shape their lives" (p. 87). The importance of taking direct action is clear and helps bridge the divide between belief and behavior.

Critical race consciousness is also central to this study as it offers a framing of consciousness in which "race has a deep social significance that continues to disadvantage blacks and other Americans of color" (Aleinikoff, 1991, p. 1062). Part of the "self-awareness" that contributes to critical consciousness (Ginwright & Cammarota, 2002), critical race consciousness surfaces throughout this study's findings in relation to the young adults' racial identity development and sense of agency for social change. Like critical consciousness, critical race consciousness involves analyses of power, but it importantly focuses on the role of race in the social and political structures that constrain people's lives.

Transformative and Coalitional Agency

"Agency" in this study refers to the type that is driven toward transformation or social change (Bajaj, 2009; Giroux, 1996). The study applies Monisha Bajaj's (2009) working definition of "transformative agency" which includes "belief in one's present or future ability to improve individual social mobility and transform elements of one's society" (p. 550). In her research comparing pairs of siblings with one sibling attending a public school and one a private school in Zambia that infused agency-building messages throughout its culture and curriculum, Bajaj (2009) found that although the private school students had higher senses of agency overall, their levels dropped drastically when they encountered a sparse job market and corrupt higher-education entrance processes. Bajaj (2009) concluded that transformative agency is situational, describing it as "a complex phenomenon, limited and informed by a variety of factors both temporal and ideological" (p. 552). In this chapter, the terms transformative agency or agency for social change are used interchangeably.

Coalitional agency highlights the influence of one's relationships, culture, and "belongings with others" (Carrillo Rowe, 2008; Chávez & Griffin, 2009, p. 8). Drawing on the work of Carrillo Rowe (2008) on "coalitional subjectivity," which asserts that we come to understand ourselves through our relationships with others, Chávez and Griffin (2009) proffered the term "coalitional agency." They explained, "A coalitional agency implies that our ability to affect social change, to empower others and ourselves necessitates seeing people, history and culture as inextricably bound to one another" (Chávez & Griffin, 2009, p. 8). The authors called for recognition of the way agency resides in connectedness. They assert that the "power we enact is one grounded in a profound cognizance of the interconnections and interdependences of people, privilege, and social/political/economic opportunities" (pp. 7–8). Coalitional agency is a particularly relevant concept in this chapter, and the term will be used to highlight the influence of history, culture, relationships, affiliations, and belongings with others that influenced these young adults.

Critical consciousness and critical race consciousness involve young people reflecting and acting upon their experiences, particularly the "binds" and "burdens" placed upon them by the system (Freire, 1970; Ortner, 1984, p. 152). Critical reflection involves uncovering and examining "the interconnections and interdependences of people, privilege, and social/political/economic opportunities" (Chávez & Griffin, 2009, pp. 7–8). Through this repeated process of praxis, youth form, test and reshape their beliefs about their abilities to change the world around them (Bajaj, 2009; Freire, 1970). A sense of transformative agency takes shape over time, in a variety of contexts (sometimes alongside others), and with a critical understanding of one's self and the systems and structures that shape one's lived reality (Ginwright & Cammarota, 2002). Throughout this process, it draws in coalitions with "people, history, culture [which are] inextricably bound to one another," fostering a sense of agency that is embedded in various belongings (Chávez & Griffin, 2009, pp. 7–8). According to this conceptual model, transformative agency and coalitional agency are interwoven and overlapping.

Youth Space and the Community

This study took place in a large Midwestern city in which its population is made up of European Americans (nearly half), American Indians, African Americans, as well as those from Central America, Africa and Southeast Asia. With a robust social services sector and a long history of civic engagement and activism, the city has numerous community and nonprofit organizations that focus on the needs of youth. Compared to the rest of the United States, the state boasts several strengths, including high public high school graduation rates (Stetser & Stillwell, 2014) and high levels of home ownership (Institute for Child, Youth, & Family Policy, n.d.). However, the successes expressed through the indicators of human and financial capital are not evenly distributed across the population within the state. Although the high school graduation rate for European American (usually categorized as white) students is 84%, the state is the second lowest in the nation for the rate of African Americans graduating from high school, currently 51% (Stetser & Stillwell, 2014). Homeownership follows a similar trajectory, with the state ranking among the highest in the nation at 77.1% and yet only 26.2% of African Americans own homes (Institute for Child, Youth, & Family Policy, n.d.). These inequities raise critical questions and create an overarching frame for this study about the context that affects these African American young adults and the influences that made them think they could and should effect change in their community and struggle for social justice.

The neighborhood, where the six study participants were raised and where the Youth Space was located, has a large African American population. The young adults identified strongly with their neighborhood, communicating a sense of belonging, rootedness, and pride. They referenced their family history and support networks in the community, acknowledged the generations before them who called the area home, and described their own long-term goals of improving their neighborhood and being seen as community elders. The state housing and education disparities mentioned above were evident in the young adults' individual stories of growing up in the neighborhood. They spoke of their families' financial struggles, housing insecurity, safety concerns, the presence of gangs and drugs, and frustration with neighborhood schools. More often, however, they pointed out the positives in their lives. For example, all six participants said both of their parents[3] played a significant role in their lives, an involvement that they recognized as unique compared to many peers who grew up without one or more parents being involved in their lives. In addition, most of these young people noted trusted adults in their extended families or from the neighborhood who had taken an interest in them and communicated high expectations for their futures.

The Youth Space was located at the heart of the neighborhood, in a church off one of its busiest streets. Although the pseudonym, "Community Church" was used in the study, the church's real name reflected its rootedness in Afrocentric ideology and its commitment to social action. When the church hired Ed—the elder involved in the

---

[3] In the case of one young man, a stepfather played a significant role.

study—to direct a youth development program, he designed the Youth Space as an open hangout area for teens and offered summer programming for younger children in the form of summer Freedom Schools. Created in the summer of 1964 to supplement low-quality segregated schools, to mobilize voters and to build leadership capacity among African American youth, present-day Freedom Schools, led by the Children's Defense Fund, focus on "[h]igh quality academic enrichment, [p]arent and family involvement, [s]ocial action and civic engagement, [i]ntergenerational servant leadership development, [n]utrition, health and mental health" (Children's Defense Fund, 2015). As children, five of six participants attended Freedom School programs at Community Church, often at the insistence of family members.

Upon beginning high school, a variety of opportunities for youth involvement and leadership at Community Church and the Youth Space took shape. The number of staff increased when Ed hired Aaron and Amy, who led various activities at Youth Space. For example, Aaron and Amy headed up year-round efforts to engage and support teens to lead mentorship groups for younger youth. Adrian, one of the young men, described the arrangement as "intergenerational mentorship," referring to the manner in which the elders guided and supported the youth leaders (Adrian, personal communication, 2014). Ed also selected youth to participate in leadership training, called junior servant leaders, in the summer Freedom Schools, which included undertaking political advocacy, connecting with participants and community members, and assisting the main teachers in delivering the curriculum. Adam, another young man, had dropped out of Freedom Schools in the past, but a junior servant leader role, along with Aaron's mentorship, led to his meaningful and sustained engagement. According to Ed, Aaron brought an additional level of depth to these Freedom School experiences as he mentored the youth and engaged them in critical conversations about local black history and contemporary issues in the community. The Youth Space staff were intentional about integrating the Freedom School "model of affirmation ... model of celebration ... [and] model of encouragement and direction" year-round at the Youth Space (Ed, personal communication, 2014). Ed also engaged youth as apprentices in a small videography business that documented the community's history. He drew on his extensive personal and professional network to garner video projects and foster partnerships on a variety of youth and community-related initiatives. Over several years of their engagement with Youth Space, the youth created public service announcements (PSA's) addressing neighborhood issues; shot and edited footage for numerous organizations and events; lent their voices to the formation and growth of a city-wide youth council that weighed in on policy issues and launched services on behalf of the city's youth; became part of a local branch of a national organization advocating for peace, human rights, and social justice, which later involved organizing local conferences that welcomed two Nobel laureates to the city; and contributed to the work of the city's youth violence prevention efforts, where our paths initially crossed.[4] Whenever possible, the youth were paid stipends for their work, which enabled many to stay

---

[4] These examples were selected to demonstrate the scope and variety of community involvement the youth were exposed to through opportunities at the Youth Space. Ed garnered numerous long- and short-term opportunities in response to youth's interests and needs.

involved. Several activities and partnerships that began with Youth Space connections led to sustained collaborations and additional opportunities for youth involvement and, years later, social-justice and youth-focused employment.

My engagement with Youth Space began with my support of a local university staff member who was organizing a youth-violence prevention campaign involving teams of adults and youth from local youth organizations. I came to know Ed and four of the young adults—Lance, Adrian, Julie, and Adam—when most of them were entering their senior year in high school. Through the course of our bi-weekly, large-group meetings in 2009–2010, I observed these four young adults in various leadership roles—facilitating meetings, planning and shooting PSAs, and organizing community events. In discussions framing the issues related to youth violence, they readily identified the systems, structures, and power dynamics that contribute to the problems in their neighborhood and city. They leveraged their familiarity with the issues and spoke with confidence and clarity about strategies to effect change. The large group became quite cohesive and bonds were formed around painful, personal discussions and the vision for our work together.

As the youth graduated and began college and/or their careers, the youth violence campaign came to a close and the Youth Space program ended. I continued to see Julie, Lance, Adam, and, sometimes, Adrian, at public gatherings as they pursued professional opportunities with youth-focused and/or social justice–oriented organizations as well as with the city-wide youth council. In 2011, I met with the group to gauge interest in this research project and they were receptive to my proposal, launching excitedly into the discussion that opened this chapter.

Researching Young Adults as Change-Agents Over Time

The case study involved six focal participants: three men and three women, ranging in age from 23 to 25 years old.[5] Ed, an elder and coordinator of the Youth Space, also lent his ideas and reflections, which situated and/or responded to the central ideas that the young adults shared in their interviews. Interviews and member checks were used to collect data from February 2012 to August 2014. In trying to understand what fostered their sense of agency, I asked the young adults to describe when they felt as if they had "made a difference" and what they "took away" from these experiences. I inquired about how they learned of various opportunities to effect change in their community, why they stayed involved, and about their motivations for pursuing this work.

I interviewed the six young adults and then, between 1 and 2 months later, three of them were also interviewed a second time. Each data-collection phase was followed by preliminary analysis and member checks that informed next steps. This study extended the use of member checks as a means to gather additional data, which, in turn, guided subsequent study design decisions. For example, after the

[5]The young adults in the study chose to either use a pseudonym or their own name.

first round of analysis, I had individual and paired member checks in which I shared with the young adults a statement that characterized a broader theme. I asked them to discuss which statements resonated with them or which did not fit their experience. In each case, they said the themes resonated with them. They went on to elaborate on several themes, sharing additional stories and examples. I incorporated this additional data into a deeper phase of analysis that yielded the central themes and began to write about these themes. In a second round of member checks, I shared my writing with the participants, asking them to speak to the adequacy of my unpacking of their stories and reflections. Sharing the analysis process through these member checks helped clarify or deepen emerging themes and probe further about the relevance of underdeveloped themes.

The approach described above is consistent with emergent design, demonstrating a commitment to being "sensitive to the data" and "guided by questions, educated hunches, and emerging findings" throughout data collection (Merriam, 2009, p. 150). In fact, this openness and flexibility enabled the shifting of the study design and research questions. I initially designed a study that prioritized the young adults' relationships and social networks as impacting their sense of agency for social change. With each round of interviews and analysis, it became evident that the young adults were directing me toward more intrinsic and relational factors.

This shift in study focus through the course of the research paralleled a shift in my relationships with several of these young adults and a shift in my understanding of myself as a scholar. For our first several years of knowing one another, my primary identity in the group was a professional one. In presenting the idea of doing a research project, I foregrounded my identity as a researcher, highlighting the value of this research for youth-work practice, expressing interest in the uniqueness of the group's experience, and framing myself as a listener and learner. After the young adults shared personal stories and reflections, some of them expressed interest in my story and motivations that shaped this inquiry. I shared that I had grown up in a middle-class, racially homogeneous region and had a ladder-like, individual-achievement focused lens well into my 20s. I explained that I was struck by group's drive to contribute to the world around them at such a young age. My reflections led to more conversations about identity, culture, race, and social justice in which the young adults shared about how their racial and cultural identities shaped their sense of agency. In analyzing, writing about, and sharing these themes with the young adults, I was humbled by the richness and importance of their cultural identities. Overwhelmed by the way in which my whiteness lent only guilt, privilege, and doubt about my role in social justice work, I began a cultural self-study alongside a mentor of mine to reexamine my cultural identity. In sharing this process in conversations with young adults, I received affirmation of my role in a collective struggle around "human rights," rather than just "civil rights" (Cyreta, personal communication, 2014) and the "importance of reclaiming our humanity" from the myth of race and "white supremacy ideology," which also strips white people of their cultural grounding (Ed, personal communication, 2014). These formative conversations created a deeper sense of mutual trust, fostered meaningful learning for all involved, and reinforced my commitments to participatory and engaged approaches to research. In fact, several participants attended the public presentation of the study, expressing their appreciation for the intentional approach and contributing their perspectives to this discussion.

"You Had the Feeling You Were Part of Something Else. You Are Building on Something": Agency and Belonging

In response to my questions about the ideas, experiences, and relationships that made these young adults believe they should and could effect change in their communities, they described a sense of agency rooted in a layered sense of belonging. This section is framed by Julie's words about how the Youth Space elders highlighted her social embeddedness, drawing attention to the way her choices and actions influenced others. She explained, "In [the Youth Space], they asked me to think about my role with peers who weren't in the room, with family, in the community. You had the feeling you were part of something else. You are building on something" (Julie, personal communication, 2013). Throughout the iterative data collection and analysis process, when I tried to understand how they enacted transformative agency, these young adults told me about their coalitions, their belongings—with one another and with their elders at the Youth Space, within an African American counter-narrative of courage and struggle, and to a set of shared moral commitments or values. The subsections below illuminate these layers of belonging.

Relationships in the Youth Space Community

As they shared examples, stories, and memories about how they got involved at the Youth Space, why they stuck around, and what deepened their engagement, the young adults pointed to the relationships with their elders and the group norms at the Youth Space. They experienced a level of acceptance and support from their elders related to personal, school, and family issues. The elders encouraged the youth's involvement at the Youth Space and in other organizations, often giving them rides to facilitate their involvement. For Cyreta, the trust and support of her elders gave her the confidence to take on a leadership role at the Youth Space. She recalled, "that's something I always got from Sister Amy and Brother Aaron, and, Mr. Ed, is that even though they were looked at as elders or as big brothers and big sisters to us, they were always there to serve" (Cyreta, personal communication, 2012).

The young adults also said that their elders' expectations challenged them. The questions elders asked and the way they facilitated conversations at the Youth Space reinforced the idea that the youth had a responsibility to themselves and others to critically engage and participate through their actions and their ideas. These expectations challenged them intellectually, made them see themselves and their community differently, and fostered their engagement at the Youth Space and in their neighborhood. The elders also communicated long-term expectations of the young adults to eventually "give back" by taking on mentorship roles with other youth (Adam, personal communication, 2012). The dedication their elders showed in guiding them over years and across circumstances instilled a sense of responsibility to make good decisions because "there's a lot of people betting on me" (Adam, personal communication, 2012).

All of these levels of relationships within Youth Space community illustrate the balance of challenging expectations and holistic support that participants experienced during their engagement. As described previously, the youth were exposed to numerous opportunities to contribute to projects and initiatives within and beyond the Youth Space. Many young adults said they had "stumbled into" these opportunities as Ed casually invited them to contribute before established roles, goals, or direction were in place. They were willing to try out new experiences and take risks knowing that they could go back to their peers and elders at the Youth Space to reflect upon them. Through these reflections they learned the importance of stepping out alongside peers, and were surprised with what they were able to accomplish while overcoming challenges and fears together. In essence, these young adults saw the Youth Space as the fertile soil into which the roots of their transformative and coalitional agency grew, drawing in nutrients that would feed and nourish them as they enacted their sense of agency in their neighborhood.

Learning "So Much More" Through a Counter-narrative of African American History

The part of the years-long experience that the young adults identified as fostering their commitment that they should effect change was their sense of belonging to an African American counter-narrative of courage and struggle. Learning about the courage, strength, and struggles of their ancestors—particularly through summer Freedom Schools experiences as teens, but also in discussions and activities in their subsequent, year-round Youth Space involvement—sparked a desire to contribute. Cyreta, Michelle, and Julie compared this learning to their school-based learning of African American history and stated emphatically that they learned "so much more" in the Youth Space.

Julie's in-depth reflection, summarized below, illustrates several dimensions of learning "so much more." She began by talking about "being introduced to [her] ancestors" through the narrative of slavery, which "portrayed [her] community as passive and as docile and cowardly almost" (Julie, personal communication, 2013). She pointed out that learning the slave narrative of African Americans in school alongside students of other ethnicities felt as though her ancestors' identity was "prescribed," to her, and that she felt like a powerless recipient of this characterization (Julie, personal communication, 2013). She also pointed out that, while figures like Harriet Tubman were named, school curricula didn't "talk about the courage in that" (Julie, personal communication, 2013). Instead, she drew on the counter-narrative she had embraced at the Youth Space as she elaborated on Tubman's courage, pointing out the economic blow Tubman and so many others dealt to the slave trade by escaping and resisting. Julie recalled that learning the counter-narrative "opened some, [opened] a different door. Like, it doesn't have to be that way [as the dominant narrative depicts the story]. It doesn't have to be my identity. It doesn't have to be the end of this story" (Julie, personal communication, 2013). Building momentum as she drew connections between her sense of belonging in the counter-narrative, her belonging at the Youth Space, and her sense of self, Julie went on:

> Because once you go to [the Youth Space], like, you learn so much more. Like, you learn so much more about your ancestors and your history and your community and the people around you, that, like, you can't stop there …. I've got to learn more, and I have to be able to understand more and you know, be able to contribute to this history and do things differently. So … it's always been one thing after another or, you know, coming into [the Youth Space], learning and being around other youth who kind of had similar experiences. (Julie, personal communication, 2013)

What Julie found and was attracted to in the counter-narrative was her ancestors' power, meaning their strength and courage along with the impact they had through individual and collective resistance. This story of a powerful people quickly replaced a characterization that Julie had learned in school. Seamlessly, Julie drew connections from her ancestors to her community and "the people around [her]" as examples of hope and courage, sites of power, and sources of learning that would guide her actions as a co-author of the counter-narrative. At the Youth Space, she encountered the counter-narrative alongside elders and peers where she felt safe, understood, free from judgment, and able to grapple with its complexity. The content and process of their learning honored her and other youths' struggles and strengths, helped them recognize and embrace their own power to effect change, and framed their community and their interactions with others as sites of power.

Julie also described how getting involved at the Youth Space affected the way she felt about herself. She recalled feeling "really low" and "smaller than other people" as a teenager, due, in part, to her "family and [their] situation and [their] finances" (Julie, personal communication, 2013). She identified Ed and being part of the Youth Space as helping change those feelings. She explained, "I didn't feel as important, you know, around, until you could actually have someone say to you, like, what you bring and your contribution to this is an asset and it's needed" (Julie, personal communication, 2013). Julie's in-depth reflection on learning and embracing the counter-narrative in a safe setting alongside her peers reveals her identity and tangible actions that were affirmed and framed as contributions to a broader struggle, and illustrates various layers of coalitions that informed her transformative agency.

Adam shared a similar story of finding engagement and belonging at the Youth Space. While attending middle school in a nearby suburb, Adam's teachers recommended he switch from mainstream classes to International Baccalaureate classes.

Adam struggled with the change, recalling, "in mainstream, I was with my homies and in IB, I was with all white kids ... I failed miserably. I guess I felt alienated and lost interest" (Adam, personal communication, 2014). Joining the Youth Space after middle school, Adam was exposed to readings and discussions that resonated with his experience and "put [him] on notice" about racial disparities in schools and their consequences (Adam, personal communication, 2014). He continued to explore his racial identity under Aaron's mentorship, which fostered his critical race consciousness and cultural identity—areas of personal growth that he enjoyed sharing with the youth he mentored as a young adult.

Commitments in Action: A Worldview of Connection and Embeddedness

The previous sections have illustrated that through their coalitions—their relationships at the Youth Space and in their roles as co-authors in an African American counter-narrative—the young adults came to see themselves as "part of something bigger" (Julie, personal communication, 2013). This section illuminates a third layer of belonging, one consisting of shared values, that shaped their coalitional agency. In describing the ideas that guided their decisions and in articulating the values that connected them to the counter-narrative and to one another, the young adults referenced two broad commitments they held as a group—to honor the humanity of others and to serve others and struggle for justice. I used the phrase "commitments in action" to reflect the way the commitments both guided how the young adults enacted agency in their lives through their actions and choices but also framed these actions and choices as contributions to the counter-narrative, both big (i.e., through career choices) and small (i.e., in conversations that helped others see themselves as part of a worthwhile struggle).

Honoring humanity. While this commitment was evident in many of the participants' stories, Adrian, a philosophical and spiritual young man, shared powerful examples acknowledging the inherent worth of every human being. He explained,

I'm not going to take somebody's life just because you call me the n-word. I respect your life ... and the crazy part is it's not two-way ... It's me trying to be the person I want to be. It's not about you; it's about me. (Adrian, personal communication, 2013)

Even in the face of injustice, Adrian envisioned himself choosing to honor humanity, enabling him to "be the person [he] want[ed] to be." Highlighting that "it's not two-way," Adrian affirmed how his sense of self and his commitments remained strong, regardless of how others viewed and treated him.

Adrian offered another example about learning to examine "root issues" at the Youth Space, demonstrating one way to recognize and appreciate others' humanity. Continuing with the issue of violence, Adrian pondered, "People shoot each other, but why? Are they just crazy?" (Adrian, personal communication, 2012). He continued, "... you start looking at family structures ... at their financials ... looking at vendettas, start looking at other reasons why people would go to that extreme. And you start realizing that you stop demonizing so much, start looking at them like human beings" (Adrian, personal communication, 2012). Adrian demonstrated the practice of breaking through an issue's label (e.g., violence) and delving into the complex factors that make up the issue. He recognized the tendency to "demonize" others and highlighted the importance of trying to understand people and their situations. Adrian said this way of thinking "opened [his] eyes" and changed the way he saw his community and his role in it (Adrian, personal communication, 2012). By using empathy, he was able to better understand the multiple factors that contribute to violence and honor the humanity of the people involved in it. Furthermore, honoring humanity recognized and affirmed the uncertainty of these young men's and women's journeys and their closeness with the friends, siblings, and cousins who had gotten caught up in gangs, alcohol, or drugs. For example, Lance said he had always admired his two older brothers, but when one was killed in gang violence when Lance was in high school and one was incarcerated, Lance recalled thinking, "Well, I don't want to make either one of [his brothers'] choices. So let me see what happens if I do this [get involved at the Youth Space]." (Lance, personal communication, 2012). In our conversations, Lance highlighted all he had in common with his brothers. He framed his choice to join the Youth Space as an uncertain one. For him, focusing on his own "good" decision-making and "positive" choices would not honor his brothers' humanity and the complexity of their circumstances.

Sense of responsibility to serve others and to struggle for justice. The commitment to serve others and struggle for justice is deeply tied to the counter-narrative and to the commitment to honor humanity. As Julie's story illustrated, part of finding oneself in the counter-narrative was embracing one's responsibility to contribute to the generational struggle for justice. Furthermore, human connectedness was at the core of Adrian's description of what it meant to honor others' humanity. Also, the Youth Space elders were deliberate about holding the youth responsible for their contributions and their actions in ways that "give back" and serve their community. An important part of assuming the responsibility to serve others and struggle for justice was to accept their embeddedness in and responsibility to serve in numerous relationships and spheres of their lives.

Lance related an "ah-ha moment" when Freedom School teachings of "lov[ing] your brother and protect[ing] your sister," along with the guidance of his Youth Space elders, changed the way he viewed himself and his role in his neighborhood. Whereas he would previously watch out for his own family, but ignore a fight or wrongdoing and "just keep on moving … 'cause it had nothing to do with me," Lance said, after participating in Freedom Schools and at the Youth Space, he would intervene. He explained why:

> … I look at it, like, there was somebody who told me the same thing … They stopped and said something [to me]. It was like, "OK, you actually got me to think about what I'm doing right now, like, you makin' me realize that what I'm doing may not be, like, perceived as the right thing." … It's become key, like, as far as, like, with working with like the kids and all of that, like, 'cause of Freedom School. I love the way that I work with kids 'cause of Freedom School. (Lance, personal communication, 2012)

Lance's shift from a position of minding his own business to stepping up and speaking up seemed to stem from both the Freedom School teachings and the way people in his life made him think about how others perceived his actions and the example he set. Throughout our conversations, Lance indicated that being a role model and appreciating the power and importance of that role enriched his work with youth. Lance articulated two interconnected strands of coalitional agency that influenced the way he saw himself and his actions. One was the ongoing African American counter-narrative of brothers and sisters struggling together; the second strand included his elders' impact on his thinking and he indicated the hope and pride he felt about similarly impacting the youth he encountered. In later conversations, Lance drew direct connections between his experiences as a youth and the strategies he used to connect with the youth in his after-school program. For example, when a young man told Lance he had been acting out in a class he struggled with because he disliked the teacher, Lance responded, "Man, I didn't like none of my teachers that I worked with … [but] at the end of the day, who was this class benefittin'?" (Lance, personal communication, 2012). Lance smiled remembering how the youth came to the realization that acting out was only hurting him. This example resonates with Lance's "ah-hah moment," above, and illustrates how Lance leveraged his own past struggles to connect with youth. From his experience as a young man who looked up to his brothers, and, later, his elders, Lance understood and embraced the importance of offering a positive model for youth.

The sense of responsibility to serve others and to struggle for justice was reinforced through engagement in activities developed in partnership with other youth- and social justice-oriented organizations, whose representatives also valued serving others and framed work in the community as a responsibility. Surrounded by people, including her own elders and other community leaders who were articulating this view in one particular meeting, Julie recalled how the message that she was responsible to others sunk in. Whereas she once felt like a "superhero 'cause [she was] helping" in her neighborhood, the group discussion helped her realize that "I'm no more of a hero than anyone else that's suffering from this or that's, dealing with these problems, just because I'm willing to help" (Julie, personal communication, 2012). For Julie, adopting the group's viewpoint shifted the celebration of their work and the superhero status to seeing her work as a responsibility, a given, and an expectation. Julie also felt an urgency to spread this new perspective, saying "… there needs to be more people that feel responsible, not feel … I don't even know what other word to describe that, but there should be more people that feel obligated to [help in their community and be a neighbor]" (Julie, personal communication, 2012). Julie's reflection illustrates her sense of connectedness to a broad network of community members and the mutual sense of coalitional agency defined by human connectedness, responsibility, and commitment to social justice.

Julie later talked about her first job out of high school doing youth development with a large community center. When she realized the center's goals and structures did not allow for the relationship-based, community-focused approach that she had experienced and valued, Julie left to work as a consultant, largely within the rich network described above. She explained that, while the center job offered stability, she felt she was not "following along with what [her] purpose is" and that, at the center, "[she] really didn't feel like [she] had any real responsibilities or [she] didn't really feel like [she] had any real power" (Julie, personal communication, 2012). Her enthusiasm building, Julie described "reconnecting with everybody [listing elders and organizations]" and feeling "that's where I belong, you know what I mean? That's what my purpose is to be doing things in my community constantly … [as a consultant] I'm not technically tied down and not allowed to do it the way I think it should be done" (Julie, personal communication, 2012). Throughout our conversations as Julie shared examples of her vision for "how it should be done," she drew directly on her experience as a youth at the Youth Center to articulate a relationship-based and community-focused approach.

Discussion

The findings presented in this chapter extend and deepen our understanding of agency by shedding light on the coalitions, affiliations, and belongings that informed the young adults' sense of agency for social change (Chávez & Griffin, 2009). The young adults in this study repeatedly emphasized their belongings and embeddedness—with one another and with their elders, within their neighborhood, within a courageous African American counter-narrative, and within a shared set of commitments or values—as shaping their beliefs that they should and could effect change. These layered belongings were also interconnected and reinforcing. The community that formed at the Youth Space created a safe, shared space of learning and processing where the participants made meaning of their lived experiences. The Youth Space community affirmed the participants' inherent value and their contributions, linking both to a courageous African American counter-narrative that played out daily in their neighborhood. Embracing the counter-narrative while participating in activities at the Youth Space not only reinforced the interdependent "couplet" of social action and critical consciousness (Ginwright & Cammarota, 2002, p. 87), it also provided opportunities to experience and practice the commitments in action. Through their ongoing involvement, the young adults embraced the counter-narrative and their roles as contributors to a generational struggle. The commitments in action helped the young adults see their actions as "part of something bigger" and as having the potential to effect change in big and small ways.

These interwoven findings resonate with O'Connor's (1997) study of six African American youth she called the "resilient six" youth who expressed optimism for the future *and* demonstrated high academic achievement, as distinct from other optimistic, but not highly academic achieving youth in the study. Similar to my observations of the young adults in this chapter, the resilient six articulated "a particularly acute recognition of how race and class (and, in two cases, gender) operated to constrain the life chances of people like themselves" (O'Connor, 1997, p. 605).

O'Connor (1997) supposed that this awareness could lead to discouragement but, instead, found that the youth's "familiarity with struggle"—individual or collective resistance to oppression—set them apart. The resilient six were "privy to social behavior and discursive practices which not only expressed the need for struggle but also expressed its potential to produce desirable change" (p. 605). Black adults in the youth's lives modeled these behaviors and practices. O'Connor suggested that these youth's familiarity with struggle could illustrate their "embeddedness in a cultural context which might more readily translate their penetrations into political strategies" (p. 602). She stated:

> I contend that these messages, especially those which emphasized the potential for collective action, conveyed the agency that resides (even when dormant) with marginalized communities. In short, resilient youths, unlike other optimistic respondents, appeared to have not only insight into human agency at the personal and individual level but also a basis for interpreting Black individuals and collectives as agents of change. (p. 621)

The models of agency to which youth in O'Connor's and this study were exposed framed youth's actions in political and collective terms. The young adults in this chapter learned about the courageous and impactful struggles of their African American ancestors. They were exposed to community leaders and elders who viewed themselves as responsible for contributing to an ongoing struggle for justice. In repeated cycles of action and reflection over the span of years, they drew connections between the struggles in their lives and structures of oppression in society, and they engaged in activities to address those issues. The young adults expressed a sense of "building on something," that is, a sense of connectedness, a "sense of common struggle" (Ginwright, 2007, p. 412), and coalitional agency, both across generations (as illustrated in Lance's story about speaking up because somebody stopped him and made him think) and around ideas, moral commitments, and visions for justice.

While transformative agency and coalitional agency are introduced in this chapter as two separate concepts, the young adults in this study enmesh the two. When Adrian, Julie, Adam, Michelle, Lance, and Cyreta were asked questions focused on individual beliefs that made them think they could and should make a difference in their neighborhood and city, they overwhelmingly discussed the relationships, belongings, and connectedness through a lens that views "people, history and culture as inextricably bound to one another" (Chávez & Griffin, 2009). Similarly, their own "familiarity with struggle" constituted a coalition, a sense of belonging and embeddedness within a narrative of individual and collective struggle (O'Connor, 1997).

Based on her research with students exiting school and entering the job market in Zambia, Bajaj (2009) concluded that transformative agency is situational and contingent. Perhaps, as this chapter suggests, transformative agency could be bolstered or reinforced by coalitions. This study raises other conceptual questions about the relationship of coalitions and transformative agency. Is transformative agency interwoven with various coalitions, relationships, and narratives more resilient in the face of challenges or disappointments? Does transformative agency, when supported by a sense of belonging and embeddedness, sustain agency across contexts and/or over time?

The current Black Lives Matter movement in the United States embodies many of these interwoven concepts and may offer insights to the questions posed. A social movement that began with protests when the Florida man who shot an unarmed young black man was acquitted of criminal charges, the Black Lives Matter movement has grown as several black men in cities across the country were killed in altercations with police officers who were, in many cases, also acquitted. Weaving these tragic instances together with broader trends, statistics, and stories, the movement has shone light upon systemic injustices in law enforcement and criminal justice systems across the United States. The name and the movement "Black Lives Matter" assert a counter-narrative of humanity, a story that counters the narrative of injustice and dehumanization that the movement has helped document with poignancy and through collective action. Both narratives resonate with people who have come together in Black Lives Matters chapters, gatherings, and protests across the country to call for change. As these disenfranchised individuals and their allies come together to collectively address the "binds" and "burdens" (Ortner, 1984, p. 152) placed upon them by the system, they embody a sense of transformative and coalitional agency.

Conclusion

Framed by the concepts of critical consciousness, critical race consciousness, and transformative agency and coalitional agency, this chapter illuminates the importance of the sense of belonging that shaped these young adults' identities as change-agents. The sections in the chapter discuss three coalitions or strands of belonging that the young adults said influenced their beliefs that they should and could effect change in their neighborhood and city. First, a sense of belonging with one another and with their elders at the Youth Space, a youth organization, provided a safe space in which the youth could discuss and learn from their experiences, such as their struggles in school or at home or their involvement in the neighborhood. Through these relationships, the young adults experienced full acceptance and affirmation and came to embrace their roles as contributors at the Youth Space, in the neighborhood and city, and to a broader human struggle. Second, the young adults described a sense of belonging within an African American counter-narrative of courage and struggle that affirmed their own and their ancestors' humanity and power. Third, the participants embraced two commitments in action that they learned, experienced, and practiced at the Youth Space—to honor the humanity of others and to serve others and struggle for justice. These commitments constituted a worldview of connectedness that grounded the young adults' change-agent identities and helped frame their individual actions and choices as part of a larger, collective struggle. Altogether, the young adults articulated an interwoven sense of transformative and coalitional agency—one that took shape over a long period of time and that they drew upon as they navigated young adulthood. This study further developed the notion of a coalitional agency that sees "people, history and culture as inextricably bound to one another" (Chávez & Griffin, 2009, p. 8). In social movements, activists and organizers mobilize, shape, and cultivate these coalitions as they seek democratic change through collective action. Youth workers, educators, community leaders, and policymakers who understand these interwoven forces of social transformation have valuable insights into human agency and rich opportunities to promote lasting social change.

References

Aleinikoff, T. A. (1991). A case for race-consciousness. *Columbia Law Review, 91*(5), 1060–1125.

Bajaj, M. (2009). "I have big things planned for my future": The limits and possibilities of transformative agency in Zambian schools. *Compare: A Journal of Comparative Education, 39*(4), 551–568.

Bartlett, L. (2010). Conclusion: New critical literacy studies. In *The word and the world: The cultural politics of literacy in Brazil* (pp. 167–177). G. Noblit & W. Pink (Eds.) Cresskill, NJ: Hampton Press.

Carrillo Rowe, A. (2008). *Power lines: On the subject of feminist alliances.* Chapel Hill, NC: Duke University Press.

Chávez, K. R., & Griffin, C. L. (2009). Power, feminisms, and coalitional agency: Inviting and enacting difficult dialogues. *Women's Studies in Communication, 32*(1), 1–11.

Children's Defense Fund. (2015). Five essential components of CDF Freedom Schools program Retrieved December 8, 2015, from http://www.childrensdefense.org/programs/freedom-schools/five-essential-components-of.html.

Freire, P. (1970). *Pedagogy of the oppressed.* New York, NY: The Seabury Press.

Ginwright, S. A. (2007). Black youth activism and the role of critical social capital in black community organizations. *American Behavioral Scientist, 51*(3), 403–418.

Ginwright, S., & Cammarota, J. (2002). New terrain in youth development: The promise of a social justice approach. *Social Justice, 29*(4), 82–95.

Giroux, H. A. (1996). *Fugitive cultures: Race, violence, and youth* (1st ed.). New York, NY: Routledge.

Hart, D., & Fegley, S. (1995). Prosocial behavior and caring in adolescence: Relations to self-understanding and social judgment. *Child Development, 66*(5), 1346–1359.

Institute for Child, Youth & Family Policy, Heller School of Management, Brandeis University. (n.d.). *Diversity data* [Data set]. Retrieved July 12, 2014, from http://diversitydata.sph.harvard.edu/Data/Profiles/Show.aspx?loc=912.

Kincheloe, J. L. (2008). *Critical constructivism primer.* New York, NY: Peter Lang.

Merriam, S. B. (2009). *Qualitative research: A guide to design and implementation* (3rd ed.). San Francisco, CA: Jossey-Bass.

O'Connor, C. (1997). Dispositions toward (collective) struggle and educational resilience in the inner city: A case analysis of six African-American high school students. *American Educational Research Journal, 34*(4), 593–629.

Ortner, S. B. (1984). Theory in anthropology since the sixties. *Comparative Studies in Society and History, 26*(1), 126–166.

Stetser, M. C., & Stillwell, R. (2014). *Public high school four-year on-time graduation rates and event drop-out rates: School years 2010–2011 and 2011–2012.* National Center for Education Statistics. Retrieved July 12, 2014, from http://nces.ed.gov/pubs2014/2014391.pdf.

Watts, R. J., & Guessous, O. (2006). Sociopolitical development: The missing link in research and policy on adolescents. In P. Noguera, J. Cammarota, & S. Ginwright (Eds.), *Beyond resistance! Youth activism and community change: New democratic possibilities for practice and policy for America's youth* (pp. 59–80). New York, NY: Routledge.

Community Context and Relations Conditioning United States Youth's Citizen Agency

Jasmina Josić

Citizen Agency as the Practice of Citizenship

Recent research about youth citizenship moves beyond a focus on civic knowledge and political engagement toward understanding the contexts in which youth citizenship is constructed, as well as socio-cultural processes and practices affecting youth experiences and their notions of and actions as citizens (Abu El-Haj, 2009; Biesta, Lawy, & Kelly, 2009; Bixby & Pace, 2008; DeJaeghere & McCleary, 2010; Dillabough & Kennelly, 2010; Rios-Rojas, 2011). Informed by this recent research and discussion on youth's constructions of citizenship, this chapter aims to illuminate understandings of United States youth's citizenship through the experiences in their communities. The chapter is particularly concerned with the construction of citizenship through youth's relationships with their communities, while at the same time addressing how the structural context of those communities is shaping practices of citizenship, and in turn, youth's citizen agency.

Social constructions of citizenship have shifted over time, reflecting changes in the political, economic and socio-cultural dynamics of our societies. The social construction of citizenship in the United States has been largely influenced by post-WWII political and social discourses where citizenship had been defined as "a status bestowed on all those who are full members of a community" (Marshall, 1950, in Lawy & Biesta, 2006, p. 34). This construction of citizenship provides those members with certain rights, responsibilities, and values learned through schooling which were assumed to lead to a strong level of community engagement. However, over time, these social constructions have expanded from a focus on "status" to exploring the relational nature of citizenship that reflects the more complete life experiences of individuals. This perspective on citizenship recognizes that citizenship

J. Josić (✉)
Pearson, Mahwah, NJ, USA
e-mail: jasmina.josic@gmail.com

© Springer International Publishing Switzerland 2016
J.G. DeJaeghere et al. (eds.), *Education and Youth Agency*, Advancing
Responsible Adolescent Development, DOI 10.1007/978-3-319-33344-1_3

47

is produced through the interactions of individuals within their spaces of experiences and bounded by institutionalized structures (Abu El-Haj, 2009; Rubin & Hayes, 2010). Moreover, this latter perspective acknowledges the importance of understanding citizen agency, specifically the position, responsibilities, power, and possibilities to engage and make changes in their immediate communities or a larger society (Arnot & Dillabough, 2000; DeJaeghere, 2009; Lister, 2007).

This chapter posits youth's citizen agency as a practice of citizenship encompassing one's belonging to a community through an individual's self-definition as a citizen and engagement in civic and social action in the community. Defined this way, citizen agency represents being a citizen and/or practicing citizenship through a range of actions. To understand this social construction of citizenship, the chapter delves into the relational nature of youth citizenship influenced by youth's interactions with the structures and practices within the sites of their life experiences, which also serve as the sites of their citizenship. In particular, the chapter addresses: the socio-economic structures and social networks of the communities where the participating youth live or attend school, education as an institutional structure embodied in schools, and the social practices facilitated within these structures. Moreover, the chapter questions whether citizen agency can be produced equally across the sites of citizenship and across all communities.

Conceptualizing Citizen Agency Within the Institutional Structures and Practices of Their Communities

Borrowing from critical feminist and poststructural perspectives (Anyon, 2009; Arnot, 2006; Baxter, 2002; Cook-Sather, 2007; St. Pierre, 2000), this research is shaped around the conceptual framework that views citizenship as produced through interactions of institutionalized structures and practices (i.e., social institution of the state or the institution of education and schooling practices) and an individual's struggle for self-definition and identity formation as a citizen. From this perspective, constructions of citizenship are generally shaped in an exclusionary environment where institutionalized political, economic, and social forces uphold the perplexing position of youth as "citizens in the making" (Smith, Lister, Middleton, & Cox, 2005, p. 426), but also as "good" citizens able to secure "good" jobs that sustain the economic and political system (Apple, 2006). These social practices to produce youth as particular types of citizens are also in constant interaction with the dynamics of relations between institutions and an individual. Along with this prescribed identity of citizens in the making, young people define and negotiate their self-made citizenship identities through interactions and experiences in their communities (Dillabough & Kennelly, 2010; Josić, 2016; Rios-Rojas, 2011).

Pulling from the rich debates about citizenship, Staeheli (2010) argues that "citizenship is always in formation, is never static, settled, or complete," suggesting that citizenship is constructed within different contexts and relationships that exist within and across the places of experiences (p. 398). Citizenship also signifies a status, meaning a position an individual is assigned or has earned within institutional structures and practices, which "provides moral, political, and economic resources that underlie the ability to act and to shape the conditions in which citizenship is formed" (p. 399). Thus, Staeheli notes that it is "important to consider citizenship as both a status and a set of relationships by which membership is constructed through physical and metaphorical boundaries and in the sites and practices that give it meaning" (p. 394). Although citizenship tends to connote status more than the changing constructions of its meaning, this chapter focuses on a relational nature of citizenship and on exploring its meaning through the sites and practices of citizenship. From this view, the practice of citizenship is where citizen agency is formed, further constructing or disrupting one's meaning of citizenship.

Furthermore, Lawy and Biesta (2006) argue that citizenship learning is grounded in day-to-day life experiences of young people, and as such citizenship needs to be understood through "citizenship-as-practice." In their research, they found that "young people routinely participate in a range of different practices such as the family, peers, schools and college, leisure, work and the media" (p. 45). Understanding the construction of youth as citizens incorporates aspects of all of these practices. While some of these practices are deemed as more important by adults, classifying them as engagement, other practices are not seen as representative of citizenship engagement, or youth are not seen as "legitimate participants, their voices are ignored, and they have little opportunity for shaping and changing the situations they are in" (p. 45). Despite the value placed on particular citizenship practices by adults, young people learn to be and act as citizens through a range of practices— formal ones in/through schools as well as informal ones through "participation in their communities and practices that make up their everyday life" (Biesta et al., 2009, p. 3). For instance, these authors found that the relations built with the adults and other youth through leisure activities (i.e., sports) influenced young people's constructions and experiences of citizenship and warrant further exploration. Biesta et al. (2009) argue for the importance of recognizing overall experiences and relationships developed in youth's lives, not only the formal ones delivered through citizenship education in schools.

The practice of citizenship in all spheres of youth's lives is where the possibilities of youth citizen agency lie. However, to understand agency in relation to the position of young people in their communities and their relationships, we need to move away from solely looking into school-based learning for citizenship, and include discussion about the "wider context," or in other words, various sites of citizen agency (Biesta et al., 2009, p. 8). In this study, this wider context includes material resources and social opportunities within youth's immediate communities— schools and neighborhood—as well as the structures and practices that shape their everyday lives. Therefore, both the physical context of citizenship and the relational "conditions of citizenship" (Biesta et al., 2009, p. 20) create unique identities of citizens holding certain level of belonging and engagement in their communities.

Schools represent important contexts that serve as sites of constructing youth citizenship. The school emerges as a site where young people are made into functioning citizens with a particular set of knowledge. Staeheli (2010) describes schools as the sites in which the key concepts such as equality, democracy, history, justice, belonging and citizenship are contested" (p. 395). Moreover, the school "extends beyond the physical structure to encompass cultural and political practices by which citizens-in-the-making are managed, disciplined, and enabled" (p. 396). Schools are where youth learn from the approved curriculum, organized activities, as well as everyday experiences of interacting with peers, teachers and practices. The experiences within schools align with the experiences in their neighborhood communities, with varying structures, relations, practices, and resources, producing those influential, cumulative relationships that shape youth's being and acting as citizens. These contexts also shape youth's ability to "have a say" and to influence both the neighborhood community and school contexts (Biesta et al., 2009, p. 9). The cumulative experiences and relationships of youth within these contexts influence how young people see themselves fitting and acting within their communities.

From this relational and contextual perspective, the analysis in this chapter assumes that citizen identity and agency are not constructed in isolation from the communities, spaces and sites of citizenship, as if based solely on personal responsibility and capacities; in contrast, citizenship is negotiated in relation to the many dynamics affecting those communities. In this chapter, I focus on the communities in which high school students constructed their citizen agency, namely their schools and neighborhood spaces. These communities are the spaces where youth notice commonalities between the members, and where they position themselves or their experiences as citizens. These communities are also the sites providing some boundaries of youth engagement. This chapter investigates how the citizen identity and agency of the young people is shaped by the histories of their communities, the structures, opportunities and resources provided in those communities.

Methodology

Positioned in the urban United States, this research employs an interpretive approach, with elements of critical ethnography, which encourage critical practices of understanding youth's perspectives through working with them in the spaces of their experiences (Madison, 2005). Furthermore, informed by poststructural theory and methods, this study interrogates how structures differentially affect citizenship, including youth's educational experiences (Baxter, 2002; St. Pierre, 2000). Lastly, the reflexivity embedded in this approach encourages me to reveal my position as a researcher and my engagement in translating the experiences of young people through my understanding of the study context (Cook-Sather, 2007; St. Pierre & Pillow, 2000).

Over a period of 4 months in the early part of 2009, I conducted this research in two public secondary schools in northern New Jersey and New York City. The study participants were high school juniors and seniors from Memorial High School (MHS) and Franklin Heights High School (FHHS).[1] The youth in both schools had

---

[1] The names of the schools are changed to protect the privacy of the participants.

access to advanced social studies curriculum and participated in extra-curricular activities focused on citizenship. The communities from which these students hailed differ starkly in their socio-economic status, namely in the level of wealth/poverty of the families, as well as of the overall community and educational institutions supported by the communities. Some differences between the schools included the racial/ethnic background of the students, proportion of students for whom English is not a native language, and the number of students who qualified for free lunch, a common proxy for poverty levels of students attending schools.

Located in Glendale, in northeast New Jersey, MHS's student population was mainly White (90%), with 6% of Asian and Hispanic students combined. The school did not have students considered English Language Learners (ELL),[2] and less than 1.5% qualified for free lunch.[3] FHHS was about 35 miles away from MHS, located in an area of Brooklyn, NY that had a large population of students originating from the Caribbean. About 89% of its students were African Americans, and 7% were Hispanic. Approximately 12% of students were categorized as ELLs, and over 62% of students qualified for free lunch.[4] Graduation rate in MHS was at 96%, and 51% in FHHS. The diversity in the backgrounds of the young people at these two sites allowed for multiple perspectives on how youth conceptualized and experienced citizenship.

After building relationships with the principals and two social studies teachers in each school, I started visiting classes and interacting with the students. Four teachers provided access to their classes, which I observed across the two schools. For 4 months, I conducted school and classroom observations, small group interviews, and follow-up individual interviews. These methods complemented each other and built on the data and discoveries made throughout the time I spent in the schools and with the students. Twenty-eight students from across the four classes participated in the group interviews that met over a period of 5 weeks. Seventeen of these students participated in the individual follow-up interviews. Pseudonyms are used for all the study participants to ensure anonymity.

Data analysis included an adaptation of Carspecken's (1996) stages of critical ethnography, and Kvale's (1996) suggested steps for analysis of interviews. In building the narratives around the findings, I engaged the process of "translation," which calls for attending to student voices, as well as my understanding of the "interpretation and representation … [of] students' language, lived (context-specific) experiences, and how and by whom are those represented" (Cook-Sather, 2007, p. 396). In this process it was important to acknowledge my position and interests as a researcher. Moreover, St. Pierre and Pillow's (2000) discussions on engaging in poststructural ethnographies provided assistance with questioning the relation of

---

[2] English Language Learners (ELL) is a categorization used by the states, including New Jersey and New York, for students for whom English is not a native language and are evaluated by the school for needing additional support in learning English.

[3] Data about NJ school comes from NJ School Performance Report, education.state.nj.us/pr.

[4] Data about FHHS comes from greatschools.org and schools.nyc.gov.

the institutional and social structures and processes with youth's experiences. Follow-up interviews functioned as reflexive member checks of the preliminary interpretations (Freeman, deMarrais, Preissle, Roulston, & St. Pierre, 2007). Furthermore, within the framework of interpretive qualitative design, the reported findings were supported with thick, rich descriptions of youth's experiences (Merriam, 2002).

This research on youth as citizens was influenced by my work with youth programs, starting in 2007 when I managed a summer program focused on international studies and global engagement for high school students from all parts of New Jersey. While reviewing program applications I observed a notable difference in the engagement activities of student from wealthy communities in comparison to students from more impoverished areas. From this experience, I wondered how young people (high schoolers), all of whom were actively engaging during the summer program, choose to engage, or not, as they become voting-age citizens. Could youth from different communities engage with their communities in meaningful ways? Moreover, how could youth learn to engage and act as citizens in communities lacking resources and opportunities for their members? Thus, in this study and for this analysis, my interests focused on the communities that do not have many resources and opportunities for their members.

"Community Is a Base Part of Citizenship": Belonging in Communities and Acting as Citizens

The findings of this study revealed that youth's sense of belonging and engagement varied in the spaces of their communities: their schools, and their neighborhoods within which their schools are positioned. This section first discusses youth's notions of community and the relations of a community and citizenship. It then delves into how structures and resources affect youth's sense of belonging within their communities. Finally, it highlights youth's awareness of the relations between their communities and citizenship, and how those relations shape their citizen agency.

Schools, Suburban and Urban Communities Shaping Belonging and Non-belonging

The young people in this study conceptualized citizenship around their relationship with a community.

> [Citizenship is] a community, not necessarily in a sense of just like a physical community, like our town's community or like people's community, but it's like the feeling you get when you're around the people you're comfortable [with], like you're willing to work with them for like a mutual benefit .... So, in that way, the community is, like a base part of citizenship. (Max)

Further, the youth described their communities as spaces where people lived, interacted through various processes, and impacted other individuals and spaces. The relationships they had in their communities most defined what "community" meant to them. "I guess the people who know your name, who know who you are, who you feel comfortable with … So I guess, it's knowing the area, is what makes it a community, knowing the people" (Nico). What mattered the most for these youth was the connection among community members and one's association with that community.

Young people predominantly talked about two communities: their schools and their neighborhoods. While a majority of youth identified having a strong connection with their schools, the neighborhood communities were experienced and internalized differently by the suburban and urban youth. For example, the suburban youth predominantly expressed a strong affiliation with the neighborhood community around their school, while the urban youth expressed a lack of affiliation with the neighborhoods surrounding their school or their own neighborhood community.

School as a community. Many youth in this study viewed their school as a functioning community, and sometimes the only one with which they associated. Students did not necessarily "hang out" in their neighborhoods. Nico commented, "I feel more connected to the school and feel like it's also my community." Amira echoed these sentiments when she noted, "I don't really stay in my area, but FHHS is the only community for me to think of, if that makes sense." Similarly, Amanda, who was a junior at MHS, felt that the school was a community where she belonged:

In a weird way I associate my community more with, like, the school than the town I live in just because, like, I spend a lot of time here and, like, I know [almost] everyone here …. But I know more about people here than I do, like … about some of my neighbors and stuff. So, and, like, this is the place that I understand best. If I try to associate myself with one group, I would probably say, like oh, with MHS, so it's, like, a sheltered community and whatnot. But I think it's a pretty good community.

The school was a space the youth from both schools knew and understood; a space where their personal development through learning took place and, more importantly, where they could connect and interact with others or have opportunities to engage. They considered clubs and school-driven initiatives as mini-communities where members care for each other and work toward creating something for their shared school communities.

Neighborhood communities create differing sense of belonging. Suburban and urban youth experienced their neighborhood communities differently. Suburban space of a town community was described as a "tight community" (Jennifer), where "people know each other or know a good number of other people" (Anna); they know what is happening, attend social events, or volunteer for activities. This space was also described as a "functioning community" (Kim), whose members are willing to help each other when needed.

However, many urban, and a few suburban, students did not see their neighborhoods as functioning communities; their communities were not close-knit, the members did not interact, and these youth did not feel a part of them. Moreover, a majority of urban students described various social structures as impacting this lack of integration within the community.

The urban communities were often described through community members' ethnic backgrounds, and the levels of safety and noise rather than the available support and opportunities which were commonly used for community descriptions by the suburban students. "My community has a lot of culture" (Samuel), where the culture was seen in terms of institutions (e.g., a museum, parks, or events) along with diverse ethnic groups and what they contribute. Members of varying socio-economic status were included in this definition since the urban community "has a lot of poor" people (Samuel) and "has a lot of crime" (Anthony). The poverty level of the urban community was used to emphasize the crime in the community and behaviors that were detrimental to the security of the community. Tanya reflected on her daily walk to school and passing bystanders on the street, "Where I come from, to school, I walk down this (smiles and pauses), it is dangerous! ... So, mostly, mostly it's dangerous-looking. They have that attitude. They're always fighting and all that stuff." Tanya's experience was in contrast with descriptions from suburban youth who described a "functioning community" helping students engage in that neighborhood.

The sense of safety affected how these young people related to the community and was perhaps most visible at the schools' front doors. The suburban entrance had wide glass doors observed by elderly safety personnel. Students simply went through while guests registered at the safety personnel desk and received a simple pass. However, the urban school had heavy metal doors, New York City Police Department staffed security officers, and metal detectors. Metal detectors were not placed in all NYC schools; the decision was based on the level of criminal activity within the community. FHHS was located in a neighborhood with active gangs. Additional security measures in the urban school included uniform standards for male students, and the restriction of certain color combinations of clothes, which could be associated with the gangs.

Overall, the urban communities were not perceived as having a positive impact on youth's experiences with schooling; on the contrary, several students specifically described their struggle to resist the neighborhood's negative effects. Dustin described his community, "I mean community is, my community is (pause, sad smile) ... bad. Something is always happening outside; police is always standing around the corner. It's destructive." Dustin noted that he did not want to "fall on the bad track" as a lot of youth in his neighborhood who commonly dropped out of school by their junior year; he often stayed at home after the school or went to other neighborhoods with his relatives. The lack of sense of safety, and related challenges students discussed, contributed to constructing the neighborhoods and schools as separate communities.

Regardless how they viewed their communities, these youth saw themselves as citizens of their communities through their individual relationships with that community. Growing up in the urban community that he described as poor and with high crime rate, Samuel reflected on his relationship with this community:

> As long as you are part of this, the system I mean, you're a citizen, as long as you're a part of it, just like he said, an ecosystem. Like, you might be a shark or the tadpole or the sun that keeps everything running, whatever you are, you are a citizen .... Even if the society does not accept you, you're there, and you gotta work on it. (Samuel)

Samuel's words reflected the youth's viewpoint that connection to a community started by living there. Youth felt an ascribed status of citizenship regardless of their position in the community, or whether they could practice their citizenship. However, the structure and practices of communities shaped their ability to engage in or affect their position as citizens. As a result, the urban youth talked about not belonging which was expressed through their unwillingness to be associated with a community. Living in a community did not necessarily translate into belonging to that community. Describing her neighborhood as distant from the spaces of her experiences, Amira commented, "I live there, but do I belong there? That's questionable." She indicated that she did not hang out in her neighborhood or know her neighbors. She just lived there. Similarly, discussing the level of safety and opportunities in his neighborhood, Dustin saw himself as different from others in his community. Dustin wanted to overcome the expectations about its residents and did not want to "fall on the bad track." "I see myself as a member of my community, but I don't see myself as somebody that belongs to that community," said Dustin. Aside from the ascribed nature of citizenship based on their membership in the community, these youth were more prone to discuss the conditions within their communities that shaped belonging, or not belonging, and acting as citizens.

Although youth in the study were more active than most other students at MHS and FHHS, they were aware of the opportunities in their respective communities and what was offered to peers attending other schools. The opportunities for engagement and resources supporting their involvement, for instance, extra-curricular activities, were more present in the suburban than in the urban school. The next section addresses these different opportunities and resources as they shaped their citizen identities and agency.

Community Opportunities, Resources, and Safety Shape Youth's Sense of Being a Citizen

The two sites of this study offered differing opportunities, resources, and practices to their members. Youth mentioned three particular conditions that most affected their sense of belonging and agency: access to the engagement opportunities, access to educational resources, and security practices of ensuring "safety" within schools.

"[W]here you live," or, in other words, the location of their school and neighborhood was connected to the number of the accessible resources that created opportunities for engagement and being a citizen. The amount of opportunities was singled out as the most important component of youth engagement in the community. "Some opportunities are given to people who live in, example Orange County [New York], in general, in suburban areas" (Nico). Nico saw suburban areas as having opportunities whereas urban areas were seen as having fewer opportunities. Offering an example of a friend from another high school where internships were offered through school, Nico commented, "Where you come from [is important]. I have never heard of [an internship] like that being offered in this high school." Making the connection between the neighborhood's location and its financial wealth, Nico suggested that the "opportunities go to people who have [the wealth]."

A few extra-curricular activities were available for FHHS students with the most prominent one being the program offered through the non-profit organization that supported FHHS. While Nico was very active in this after-school program, a relatively small number of students from the two observed classes in FHHS were actively engaged with the after-school program. However, as the program focused on global citizenship and engaged youth from a large number of high schools in New York City, Nico and his friends' participation in activities took place predominantly outside the school and their neighborhoods.

The opportunities were considered available in MHS. Several youth from MHS acknowledged the value of the opportunities existing in their school and community through a discussion of the challenges for nearby urban students. Anna, who was a peer mentor to an urban student, reflected on this difference through the drop-out rate in her school and that of her mentee.

> [W]ell I think that if you really look at Glendale, just as a community compared to the other communities in America, like in more urban areas … I have met a lot of people that I work with [in the urban area], and, like, he's 17. He's finished [, dropped out of school] … There are a lot of people that drop out of school, but they are like, (pause), in Glendale, I can name the four kids in my grade that dropped out of school. Like there's a lot of a difference in dropping out of school, stuff like that.

Questioning the position of the youth who "dropped out of school" in their communities, Anna and her friend Jennifer noted that the opportunities they received in MHS were meaningful and encouraged their engagement. Jennifer who lived the first portion of her life in the nearby urban area of New Jersey shared the following:

> If we hadn't moved to Glendale, like from Hackensack, I could have been one of those like sketch balls outside of the Plaza[5] parking lot, like not caring about anything. From moving I definitely received such better education, and like so many more opportunities that I wouldn't had in Hackensack … I feel like I definitely have a better perspective of the world and I am learning more than I would have in Hackensack, because it's just a different environment. Like there is a lot poverty that you're exposed to, like, and I just had a lot more opportunities here.

Therefore, opportunities available in the communities were identified as important aspects that impacted youth's relations with and engagement in their communities.

Educational resources differed quite starkly between these two sites. MHS was a fairly large school with over 1000 students offering a number of specialized programs for various types of learners, including six advanced curricula, the so-called University Programs (UP). This rather new school had modern spacious design, athletics fields, and student murals decorating almost every wall and ceiling of the hallways. FHHS, with approximately 500 students, was a part of the small-school movement in New York City and partnered with a non-profit organization to supplement curricular activities with a targeted engagement program.

---

[5] Refers to the Garden State Plaza, the largest shopping center in New Jersey.

FHHS shared a building with two other high schools and occupied the third and part of the second floors of a building from the 1930s. The interior had impressively high ceilings and large windows, with bars on the lower level floor, and was located across from a small park, museum, and residential street where students suggested that I not venture.

The differences in educational resources were perhaps the most apparent in library and technology resources. Students in the suburban school had a well-equipped library with a reading area, study area, magazine section, two computer classrooms, and access to online resources. Additionally, MHS had modern technological equipment visible throughout the school (i.e., Mac computers in their classrooms or brought in on carts). Technology in the urban school was limited and students had no easy access to the few available, refurbished PCs located only in some classrooms. In addition, during the time the study was conducted, the FHHS library was not available to students, and students had to seek library resources outside of the school. One teacher whose class was observed brought in her own magazines to class; when students finished an assignment early and waited for others, she provided them with magazines to read.

Although urban students did not center their discussion on the lack of library access, rather merely acknowledged that they do not have a library and never even questioned the state of their computers, these limited resources knowingly and unconsciously shaped their citizen agency. For example, youth in MHS used the resources in their school to engage in everyday learning and engagement activities in or around their schools, extending it beyond the course time. However, youth in FHHS had to look for additional resources outside their school and neighborhood to expand their everyday learning and engagement.

A safe and secure educational environment was not a reality for all students, as mentioned above. The material conditions of poverty and crime in the urban area affected youth's daily lives and how they saw themselves as citizens through school and community expectations. The security measures embedded in the school presumed that these youth might fail the school's expectations for becoming "good" citizens and become (or already were) involved in criminal activities. Waiting in a line and going through a metal detector in FHHS affected their relations with the community—this practice served a dual role as either positioning the youth as a part of the criminal activity or setting the school space apart from such activities. In addition to believing that the experience of going through metal detector on daily basis was preparing them for future lives where they would always be identified as representatives of minority groups, these youth felt annoyed, uncomfortable, humiliated, or aggravated by the practice and referred to the neighborhood as the reason for having it. These security practices were not perceived by some students as an ostensible measure of protection; rather the metal detector symbolized an expectation of the students as (becoming) criminals. Dustin, who lived a block away, observed:

> In my community, you are looked at as, because of who you are or [how you] look, you are looked at as somebody to be on that bad line. So, when you come to the metal detector, they treat everybody, like, ah (exhales), as if, like, we're all gonna do something and keep us on that line back purposefully and just talk to us badly.

Furthermore, talking about the morning ritual of being scanned, Anthony, Samuel, and Dustin discussed it as preparing them for failure:

Anthony: I think they kind of setting us up for that, early.
Samuel: Yeah, it feels like, like, a little training.
Anthony: Yeah!
Dustin: Like, putting us in that attitude, like, subconsciously.

These young men were referring to the statistics on the "school to prison pipeline" and they were unnervingly aware that a large number of young minority men, somewhat older than themselves, had gone to prison.

Ms. Davis, one of the teachers who participated in this study, was critical of the security practices and attempted to foster a stimulating classroom environment offering opportunities for these young people to feel safe. "Some of their lives are violent enough … and we need to provide them with the resources to learn how to have different future," responded Ms. Davis on my questions about the structure of her classes.

These institutional reactions to crime visible in the increased attention to the safety within urban schools through the use of security check points created a dynamic that shaped youth's perspectives about belonging to that community, as well as about their relations with the educational processes. While passing through a security check was an everyday routine for urban students, it was not present in the suburban educational environment. Safety concerns in an educational space were not part of the suburban students' experiences and they did not articulate it as affecting their sense of being a citizen. In their experiences, the educational environment was always safe, and in turn so was their community where they belonged and acted as citizens. However, these distinct experiences based on location beg the question of how this widely accepted security practice shaped urban students' views of education, access to education, and their ease in entering and relating to institutions of learning. In addition, these security practices in schools also affected how youth viewed their educational experiences as preparing them to be (particular kinds of) citizens in their communities.

From Belonging to Acting as a Citizen

Youth often noted that a citizen acts to benefit the community rather than just oneself; a citizen is "[s]omeone who participates to better a group as a whole" (Juliann). Their focus on active participation, as the root of citizenship, was guided by the view that the "whole idea of citizenship should not be based off what you know but rather what you can do" (Alec). These youth commented that taking actions that affect the community were expected from citizens, and include all types of activities from neighborly assistance to political engagement. Overall, they felt that belonging to a community included a sense of agency, which enabled individuals to contribute to their communities in more formal, civic actions, or informal ways such as simply being a proud member of the community. Whitney further suggested that an "ideal" citizen was a person who belongs to a community and ought to "be courageous, or maybe proud, you know, to advocate for that [community], or just represent it to the fullest."

In sharing how they engaged with their communities, these young people acknowledged that they were involved in their communities when it affected their lives and produced rewards–providing personal or material benefit such as personal growth, interaction with other members, but also improving a college application– whether through school activities, youth organizations, or religious pursuits. "I think it really just depends on your motivation and then what your goals are, and, like, whether or not you feel like you want to help other people," commented Lara who was actively involved with her church youth group and assisted in the food bank on Saturdays. However, she also noted that it is difficult for young people to understand the purpose of their engagement as various influences affected their level of engagement, such as peers, associated material or monetary benefits, or social networks of opportunities. From the perspective of these youth, the possible benefit, altruistic or material, shaped their activities.

Many of these young people participated in special curricular or co-curricular programs geared toward civic engagement. All youth enrolled in these civically focused programs identified them as defining experiences that shaped their further engagement in their communities.

> [T]he decision to join the [program], it really kind of changed my view of my decisions in the community, … changed how I view my role in the community and showed me that I can make a difference and kind of, like, shaped what I want to do with my life. (Jennifer)

Youth also identified activities in their neighborhoods through community or religious organizations as important experiences. By engaging in these activities, "you feel like you're actually doing something, because together you have a common interest and you feel a part of community" (Amira). Several youth also talked about their individual actions benefiting the community or a larger cause. For example, Kim shared that her experience as a brain-cancer survivor motivated her to assist other sick youth in her community. Instead of asking for gifts for her sweet 16 celebration, Kim raised money for the pediatric-oncology wing in the local hospital where she was treated. Like Kim, other students identified individually initiated engagement as grounded in their life experiences, including writing a letter to the president to ban smoking, purchasing and donating items for military personnel from personal savings, attending an event to question the governor about public-parks policy, or shoveling snow on the street, all of which provided certain social benefit.

However, in addition to altruistic motivations, youth noted engagements that provided personal benefit. Many of these youth remarked that life in their community was very fast, "focused on reaching goals, constantly doing something, and being successful" (Laurie). As they were reaching their high school graduation, Alec shared that the focus on "impressing colleges" with academic accomplishments and "putting together a great application," which highlighted a variety of engagements, left little time to participate in the activities that were meaningful to them.

Alec, who was active in several school clubs and was an EMT, reflected on also preparing for the SAT exam during the academic year that left less time for other engagements. Therefore, the decision to participate in a certain activity was also guided by their perception of usefulness of that engagement for their college applications.

Finally, youth from both schools recognized the relationship between their schools and communities, which provided social support and opportunities for some youth whereas other groups of youth faced more challenges and fewer opportunities in which to engage. These youth noted that the neighborhoods where they were coming from were "rather the same [either wealthy or poor] socio-economically." Growing up in their respective communities, youth were exposed only to "people of similar backgrounds" (Laurie), and they were prepared to engage within certain familiar structures and practices that existed in their communities. Alec and Samuel addressed how their engagement in communities affected them differently. Alec, a junior from MHS hoped to enter a competitive college, and shared:

> I think it's just being involved that really motivates teens like us. I mean, I'm in fencing, [the] republican club, and I used to be in skating and drama club, and I run track. And I think it's just the whole idea of being involved and willing to step up to the challenge is, like, really what motivates a lot of us.

In contrast, Samuel, a senior from FHHS, faced different challenges. With graduation approaching, he had no plans for college and was trying to figure out how to open a business. He acknowledged that his experiences and how he could engage in his community were different from some peers attending his school and some other schools. Samuel said, "I see it in terms of like lifestyles that we live, like being cool, like who has the most money, the best schools that there is, basically." Samuel sounded content with starting a business after completing high school and was not considering colleges he could attend. How these youth engaged both within their schools or neighborhood communities influenced how they imagined or positioned themselves for their futures.

Can Citizen Agency Be Produced Equally Amid Varying Conditions of Communities?

Through the narratives of these youth, this study illustrates how the school and neighborhood communities shaped their constructions of belonging and agency as citizens. Moreover, the conditional inequalities found in the communities, evident in the opportunities related to extra-curricular engagement or internships, resources available in the schools, and the safety and security practices within a community, shaped how these young people learned to become members of their communities and whether and how they could act as citizens in these spaces. In her study on youth's citizenship through urban geographies of education in the United Kingdom, Pykett (2009) summarizes that "the spatial contexts of schooling [have an] impact on pupils' conditions of citizenship. Their relationships with others, expectations of themselves and others, aspirations and behaviours at school are shaped by these geographies" (p. 34). Similar to Pykett's work, this study reveals that youth's position in and relations with their schools and neighboring communities strongly shape their notions of belonging and acting as citizens which are located within complex and unequal community spaces.

With this chapter, I highlighted how belonging is constructed in relation to schools and communities, and the importance of this belonging for the ability to act as a citizen. The findings in this chapter demonstrated that youth develop a varying sense of belonging to their schools and, to a degree, to their neighborhoods. They distinguished between being a member of and belonging to a community, which is based on the type of relationships they develop and their level of engagement. Further, belonging to and engagement in a community were shaped by the available opportunities and resources, as well as the common practices in those communities. Although they seemed to have accepted the presence or lack of opportunities (i.e., volunteering, internships), resources (i.e., school library), and practices (i.e., metal detectors and security measures) as a part of everyday reality, further research on what impact the presence or lack of opportunities and resources have on youth's belonging and acting as citizens of their communities is needed.

The research on citizenship education programs in the United States shows that they do not produce equitable outcomes in civic knowledge, skills, and attitudes, due to uneven opportunities and access to education and these programs (Avery, 2007; Kahne & Middaugh, 2008). Pace (2008) further argues that this preparation of youth as citizens in United States classrooms suggests that "citizenship education research needs to pursue unequal preparation of citizens, and how this perpetuates social and political inequality" (p. 54). This study begins to show how this unequal preparation and citizenship outcomes occur by recognizing youth's different experiences in schools and communities and how the opportunities, resources, and practices within the communities affected their belonging and action as citizen.

Conclusion

This chapter inquires about the role of community context and youth's relations with their communities on youth's being and/or practicing citizenship–their citizen agency. In addition, this chapter probes on Staeheli's (2008) question of whether community is a precursor to citizenship or "does citizenship lead to community" by illustrating how citizen agency is produced across the sites and contexts of citizenship–in particular, educational spaces–with unequal distribution of opportunities, resources, and institutional practices (p. 8). The findings in this chapter illustrate that youth citizenship is constructed within and conditioned by the contexts that frame their experiences and give meaning to their sense of belonging. Based on these findings, I argue that future research needs to better understand the role of communities (i.e., schools, neighborhoods) as sites of citizenship, and the practices of citizenship that take place within those communities. Constructing citizenship through youth's experiences and practices allows for focusing on the spaces where youth have opportunities to develop a sense of agency through belonging and meaningful activities that could lead to strengthening of their communities.

> A focus on young people's citizenship learning in everyday life settings allows for an understanding of the ways in which citizenship learning is situated in the unfolding lives of young people and helps to make clear how these lives are themselves implicated in the wider social, cultural, political and economic order. (Biesta et al., 2009, p. 8)

Therefore, it is perhaps not only the process of learning about citizenship, but more so the process of acting as citizens through which young people reflect on their experiences in their communities that contributes to developing a sense of citizen agency. In this way, youth's citizen agency represents the capacity to understand their social positions and participate in activities that influence their immediate and larger communities.

References

Abu El-Haj, T. (2009). Becoming citizens in an era of globalization and transnational migration: Re-imagining citizenship as critical practice. *Theory Into Practice, 48*(4), 274–282.

Anyon, J. (2009). Introduction: Critical social theory, educational research, and intellectual agency. In J. Anyon (Ed.), *Theoretical and educational research: Towards critical social explanations* (pp. 1–24). New York, NY: Routledge.

Apple, M. (2006). *Educating the "right" way: Markets, standards, God and inequality* (2nd ed.). New York, NY: Routledge, Taylor & Francis Group.

Arnot, M. (2006). Freedom's children: A gender perspective on the education of the learner-citizen. *International Review of Education, 52*(1), 67–87.

Arnot, M., & Dillabough, J. A. (Eds.). (2000). *Challenging democracy: International perspectives on gender, education and citizenship.* New York, NY: RouthledgeFalmer.

Avery, P. (2007). *Civic education in diverse contexts: Challenges and opportunities.* Paper Presented at the "Citizenship Education in an Age of Worldwide Migration" Conference in Muenster, Germany.

Baxter, J. (2002). A juggling act: A feminist poststructural analysis of girls' and boys' talk in the secondary classroom. *Gender and Education, 14*(1), 5–19.

Biesta, G., Lawy, R., & Kelly, N. (2009). Understanding young people's citizenship learning in everyday life: The role of contexts, relationships and dispositions. *Education, Citizenship and Social Justice, 4*(1), 5–24.

Bixby, J., & Pace, J. (2008). *Educating democratic citizens in troubled times: Qualitative studies of current efforts.* Albany, NY: State University of New York Press.

Carspecken, P. F. (1996). *Critical ethnography in educational research: A theoretical and practical guide.* New York, NY: Routledge.

Cook-Sather, A. (2007). Resisting the impositional potential of student voice work: Lessons for liberatory educational research from poststructuralist feminist critiques of critical pedagogy. *Discourse: Studies in the Cultural Politics of Education, 28*(3), 389–403.

DeJaeghere, J. (2009). Critical citizenship education for multicultural societies. *Interamerican Journal of Education for Democracy, 2*(2), 223–236.

DeJaeghere, J., & McCleary, K. (2010). The making of Mexican migrant youth civic identities: Transnational spaces and imaginaries. *Anthropology and Education Quarterly, 21*(3), 228–244.

Dillabough, J.-A., & Kennelly, J. (2010). *Lost youth in the global city: Class, culture and the urban imaginary.* New York, NY: Routledge.

Freeman, M., deMarrais, K., Preissle, J., Roulston, K., & St Pierre, E. A. (2007). Standards of evidence in qualitative research: An incitement to discourse. *Educational Researcher, 36*(1), 25–30.

Josić, J. (2016). "You are part of where you're from and a part of where you're born": Youths' citizenship and identity in America. In A. Loring & V. Ramanathan (Eds.), *Language, immigration and naturalization: Legal and linguistic issues* (pp. 145–163). Bristol, England: Multilingual Maters.

Kahne, J., & Middaugh, E. (2008). High quality civic education: What is it and who gets it? *Social Education, 72*(1), 34–39.

Kvale, S. (1996). *InterViews: An introduction to qualitative research interviewing.* Thousand Oaks, CA: Sage Publications.

Lawy, R., & Biesta, G. (2006). Citizenship-as-practice: The educational implications of an inclusive and relational understanding of citizenship. *British Journal of Educational Studies, 54*(1), 34–50.

Lister, R. (2007). Why citizenship: Where, when and how children? *Theoretical Inquiries in Law, 8*(2), 693–718.

Madison, D. S. (2005). *Critical ethnography: Method, ethics, and performance.* Thousand Oaks, CA: Sage Publications.

Merriam, S. B. (2002). Qualitative research in practice: Examples for discussion and analysis. San Francisco, CA: Jossey-Bass.

Pace, J. L. (2008). Teaching for citizenship in 12th grade government classes. In S. Bixby & J. L. Pace (Eds.), *Educating democratic citizens in troubled times: Qualitative studies of current efforts* (pp. 25–57). Albany, NY: SUNY Press.

Pykett, J. (2009). Making citizens in the classroom: An urban geography of citizenship education? *Urban Studies, 46*(4), 803–823.

Rios-Rojas, A. (2011). Beyond delinquent citizenships: Immigrant youth's (re)visioning of citizenship and belonging in a globalized world. *Harvard Educational Review, 81*(1), 64–94.

Rubin, B., & Hayes, B. (2010). "No backpacks" versus "drugs and murder": The promise and complexity of youth civic action research. *Harvard Educational Review, 80*(3), 352–379.

Smith, N., Lister, R., Middleton, S., & Cox, L. (2005). Young people as real citizens: Towards an inclusionary understanding of citizenship. *Journal of Youth Studies, 8*(4), 425–443.

St. Pierre, E. A. (2000). Poststructural feminism in education: An overview. *International Journal of Qualitative Studies in Education, 13*(5), 477–515.

St. Pierre, E. A., & Pillow, W. S. (2000). Introduction: Inquiry among the ruins. In E. A. S. Pierre & W. S. Pillow (Eds.), *Working the ruins: Feminist poststructural theory and methods in education* (pp. 1–24). New York, NY: Routledge.

Staeheli, L. (2008). Citizenship and the problem of community. *Political Geography, 27*(1), 5–21.

Staeheli, L. (2010). Political geography: Where is citizenship? *Progress in Human Geography, 35*(3), 393–400.

Confronting "The Conditions" of Sénégalese Higher Education: Reframing Representation and Activism

Casey Stafford

Introduction

Higher education in sub-Saharan Africa is often described in terms of crisis, or, in the case of Sénégal, "sheer chaos" (World Bank, 2003, p. 2). Increased enrollment rates in the region—the highest annual tertiary education growth in the world at 10 % per year (UNESCO, 2009)—have contributed to this "crisis" in that there have not been concomitant increases in faculty and facilities to meet the student demand. In Sénégal, higher education enrollment increased by 56 % from 2005 to 2010 (UNESCO, 2015). Although Sénégalese expenditures per student for higher education are comparatively high within Africa, at 193.5 % of GDP per capita, the higher education system faces considerable challenges, including overcrowded classrooms, overworked and, at times, under-qualified faculty, dilapidating facilities, lack of resources, and technological barriers (World & World Development Indicators, 2014). Each of these issues combines to form the conditions of the higher education student experience in Sénégal.

In this study, I draw upon two meanings of the conditions of higher education to introduce the structural context on campus. The first meaning is the postcolonial condition, which refers to the intersection of European colonization and contemporary relations of economic inequality and international development in the global South. As Gupta (1998) explains, this condition pertains to "a specific set of locations articulated by the historical trajectories of European colonialism, developmentalism, and global capitalism" (p. 10). The postcolonial condition, in this usage, is an analytical category that captures the position of Sénégal within inter/national political, economic, and social relations that greatly affect higher education policy-making in the country. The second meaning is one in which students at Université

C. Stafford (✉)
Ford Foundation, New York, NY, USA
e-mail: caseygstafford@gmail.com

© Springer International Publishing Switzerland 2016
J.G. DeJaeghere et al. (eds.), *Education and Youth Agency*, Advancing
Responsible Adolescent Development, DOI 10.1007/978-3-319-33344-1_4

Cheikh Anta Diop (UCAD) — Sénégal's largest university — commonly refer to "the conditions" to describe the poor material situation on campus, particularly limited food, housing, and educational equipment. Students use the term, "the conditions," in a negative way to express their discontent with the physical components of campus as well as the psychological hurdles they face, such as the stress of paying for a meal ticket when government scholarships (stipends) are not paid on time or sleeping ten students to a dorm room created for two people. Whether in reference to physical or psychological conditions, it is my view that the use of "the conditions" expresses the material reality of the current postcolonial "location" of Sénégalese society (Gupta, 1998).

On the campus of UCAD in 2011, there was a confluence of events that led to unrest, including a faculty strike, delayed scholarship payments, and the possibility of an *année invalide*, an invalid year. UCAD professors went on strike in the beginning of March 2011 in an attempt to increase the budgets of Sénégalese universities and to advocate for more recruitment of teachers, better wages, increased health benefits, and timely payment for overtime work (English professor, personal communication, 2011). The strike ended in mid-April, only days before the year was deemed invalid due to insufficient classroom time. As a result, students began coursework in April and took exams in June. Two months of schooling — down from the "official" October to June, 8-month academic calendar — left students scrambling to attend courses, write papers, and prepare for exams.

I arrived on campus March 6, 2011, amidst the turmoil at UCAD. On March 10, students clashed with Sénégalese police officers, and this confrontation resulted in the payment of scholarships. On March 15, student members of The Collective, a student organization created by the students in the Faculté de Lettres et Sciences Humaines (Faculty of Arts and Sciences; FLSH) to promote student interests in place of the defunct *amicale*,[1] marched peacefully from the campus (where students live) to the faculté (where classrooms and faculty offices are located) and requested an end to the faculty strike, which was granted a week later. Thus, by the end of my first 2 weeks on campus, there had been two student protests and both resulted in outcomes sought by students. It is within these conditions on campus that I examined agency in this study.

Against the backdrop of these conditions, studies of student agency are particularly important because failed states and decaying institutions "produce new spaces for political assertion and the creation of identities" that affect educational pathways (Durham, 2000, p. 114). Based on 4 months of research in Sénégal and the United States with Sénégalese students studying English at UCAD I will illustrate how students negotiate "the conditions" collectively and how they organized to produce new discourses and reframe the large group protest in order to establish themselves

---

[1] An *amicale* is a body of students gathering around similar interests, with an elected student governing body. The *amicale* for FLSH is important because it is the largest *amicale* on campus, and the leadership has access to resources, such as tickets to the campus restaurant, which are then distributed to students in the *amicale*. It also controls the disbursement of rooms on campus. The *amicale* is responsible for liaising between a student and the administration if a student has an issue. The faculty of FLSH disbanded its *amicale* in 2008 due to violence during *amicale* elections.

as future leaders. I contend that in the arena of Sénégalese higher education, in which classroom time is severely limited, what occurs outside of the classroom is as important for understanding agency as what occurs inside the classroom. I consider collective organizing and protest activities in which students participate to be political and educational activities. Student activism, therefore, is the entry point for understanding how agency is produced at UCAD.

"The Rule of Failure": Material and Ideological Conditions on Campus

During my time on campus, an unwritten rule of failure was pervasively felt among the student body. As one student articulated: "I will tell you an anecdote: When I first came [to UCAD], someone told me here in the university, the rule is failure. The exception is success" (Abel, personal communication, 2013). This "rule" is evident in the fact that thousands of students fail out of UCAD each year because they do not pass their year-end examinations, making failure, not success, at the university the norm.[2] The rule of failure affects other spheres of the student experience at UCAD, not only in the examination system. In classrooms, in the restaurant, and in residence halls on the campus, students fail to find adequate space for learning, eating, and sleeping due to pervasive overcrowding. Among the factors contributing to these conditions is the consistent increase in enrollment, where during the structural adjustment period in the 1980s–1990s, UCAD's enrollment grew to over 20,000 students without growth in infrastructure. Today, the student population is more than 60,000, so classrooms swell, restaurants deteriorate, and dorm rooms burst at their concrete seams.

Compounding their experience of these conditions on campus, students are also repeatedly represented in the media and by donors in negative terms such as lazy, non-studious, violent, immature, and greedy, particularly when they protest for access to scholarships or better living conditions (Marshall, 2013, 2014, 2015; N.A., 2009, 2010a, 2010b, 2010c, 2014; World Bank, 2003). Students' political and social activism is usually deemed problematic in the popular media and in development scholarship. The substance of their grievances, including poor university management, overcrowded classrooms and dormitories, and government corruption, is rarely recognized in these accounts. This problem of student representation is cogently expressed in Amutabi's (2002) overview of Kenyan higher education, and is applicable to Sénégalese context as well:

> ... crises and disturbances in Kenyan universities have received a fair amount of attention in both the popular press and academic circles, although the main emphasis has tended to be upon incidents involving physical violence. Reports invariably suggest, especially to outsiders, that Kenyan universities are occasionally disrupted by a small group of aggressive and anti-establishment students, whose criminal activities are rooted out, punished

---

[2] There are two exam periods—one in May–June and one in October. If students do not pass their exams for two cycles of July and October exams (four total exam attempts) they are no longer enrolled at the university.

severely, and then set aside so that the universities can get on with their main business of educating young Kenyans. Yet the democratic nature of the students' grievances and the autocratic nature of the institutions and structures under which they operate, are often ignored. It is rarely reported that university students in Kenya are responding to authoritarian leadership, institutional decay, and management crises at the universities and in the country as a whole. The students are always blamed; in fact, they usually are vilified by the media, parents, politicians, scholars and the public, who fail to listen to their side of the story. The public rarely acknowledges the role that university students have played in Kenya's struggle for democratization. (p. 169)

The vilification of students dislocates student action from the larger political economy, and it denigrates the calls for greater democratic and social justice at the heart of many of these movements. These reports acquit the state of any political or economic wrongdoing and frame the student as a burden to the nation rather than as its future leaders who are enacting agency to advocate for reform.

In Sénégal, the World Bank has referred to students as one of the major blockages to education reforms. For instance, the World Bank (2003) follow-up report to the Sénégalese Higher Education Improvement Project noted that "the resumption of violent student protests fueled by outside political interests led to a reversal of the many earlier ambitious reforms" (p. 2). In addition, the student movement in Sénégal has been labeled as "agitating" and "destabilizing" (Bathily, Diouf, & Mbodj, 1995, p. 369). Consistently, metaphors of violence are used to describe student activism (Konings, 2002). This negative framing conflicts with the more positive view of students as the future leaders of the nation, which is how African students were framed in the early independence period by development scholars and national governments. Reflecting on this change in representation of students, Zeilig (2009) argues that students are viewed in either positive or negative ways, as "a vanguard for democratic change *or* troublemakers manipulated by political elites" (p. 68).

Conceptualizing Student Agency: Cultural Production, Discourse and Social Justice

Informed by Bajaj (2009), Davies (1991), and Walker and Unterhalter (2007), I define agency as one's ability to recognize and act upon multiple subject positions within a given context and to choose if and how socio-cultural practices determine identity and action. The first influence on this definition is Bajaj's (2009) view of "transformative agency," which focuses on how a person conceptualizes her ability to impact society. This focus on an individual's ability to impact society is important for understanding how agency affects student's social and cultural influence in Sénégal. The second influence is the discursive constitution of agency. Davies (1991) argues that agency and freedom cannot be produced without understanding discursive relationships. Her work underscores the discursive nature of identity formation and creation by first identifying how one is being produced discursively within a cultural system. Lastly, I draw on Walker and Unterhalter's (2007) capability framing of agency, which frames people as individuals with valued goals that drive their decision-making within a context of social, cultural and environmental conditions.

My definition of agency is intended to link directly to cultural production theory, as discursive relations and culture are key elements in how students respond to the cultural system, in this case, university life. There are three important ideas in cultural production that I draw on for this study. The first is the notion of "confronting ideological and material conditions" (Levinson, Foley, & Holland, 1996, p. 14). Secondly, the conceptualization of agency is active and creative beyond the spaces in which "confrontation" occurs, including change at the household and societal level. Lastly, cultural production contends that agency is contingent on subject positions and social circumstances. Sites of education, such as universities are, from this perspective, particularly rich for exploring how social and material circumstances like "the conditions" at UCAD help to produce certain kinds of identities among students.

Cultural production theory arose as a critique of the deterministic view of schooling presented by reproduction theories and illustrated how students could be agents with the ability to transform their schools (Willis, 1981). For critical education researchers, the potential for both oppression and emancipation lies within the process of schooling. Drawing on Freire, many critical theorists see the process of becoming educated as a process of "conscientization," or becoming aware of one's political, economic, and social realities with an eye toward changing them (Bajaj, 2005). Cultural knowledge, then, is the knowledge produced through meaning-making practices in a particular context (Jasper, 2005). Through academic lectures, student organization meetings, conversations with other students, sleeping, eating, living, participating in student protest, playing sports, and the other myriad of student practices, a cultural knowledge of student life is produced that raises awareness of the social positioning of students and how to transform that position.

Critical theory enables an analysis aimed at achieving social justice or equality (Anyon, 2008) and was useful in this study because it illuminated power dynamics that often led to the suppression of student voices in various arenas (policy discussions, political discussions, on campus advocacy). Suspitsyna (2010) refers to social justice as "the silenced discourse" because of the privileging of "national economic competitiveness" discourses in the global arena (p. 67). Similarly, Samoff (2009) underscores the dominance of economic, technical terminology in higher education reports and how this suffocates discussions of social justice within higher education in sub-Saharan Africa. As Samoff elaborates:

> As they work in an aid-dependent settings, often without being fully aware of the transition, African educators and decision-makers discard education as the vehicle for national liberation, for reducing inequality, and for constructing a new society in favor of education that consists of upgraded facilities, more textbooks, better-trained teachers, and improved test scores. (p. 147)

Social justice research moves beyond a focus on production-function models typically used in higher education research and critically approaches the topic of human capabilities. A human capability approach (Sen, 1992) allows us to move beyond the dominant assumptions of the human capital model that continue to drive higher education research and policy making, and instead allows us to examine "what education enables us to be and to do" (Walker, 2006, p. 163).

In addition to cultural production of students' lives within a social justice and capability framework, drawing on Davies (1991) allowed me to keenly focus on how discourses operated in the university and how agency was enacted in light of competing discourses. There were two primary discourses circulating at the university. The first discourse is what I call, "the educated person." Students discussed the roles as well as the rights and privileges of educated people in Sénégal. Several ideas were prominent, including: the educated person is socially just; she resists injustice and racism and seeks peace in the world; and, if an educated person works hard, she is deserving of a job and the right to ask for privileges. The second discourse, "the rule of failure," mentioned earlier, shaped the context of university life and the ways in which the discourse of "the educated person" took form. The interplay between "the educated person" discourse and "the rule of failure" context in which students lived their daily lives underpin the conceptualization of agency and the discursive and cultural structures in which to examine how agency takes form. Within this framework, this chapter is guided by two research questions: (1) How do students negotiate their social-cultural and material position in society amidst negative representation and competing discourses? and (2) How do students enact agency through protest and activism?

UCAD: The Compelling Qualitative Case

In order to understand these competing discourses and how they affected students' agency, I designed a qualitative case study, drawing on ethnography and critical analysis. The first part of the design consisted of 2 months of in-country fieldwork utilizing in-person interviews, participant-observation, document analysis, and students' journals. The second part of the design consisted of 2 months of data collection from the United States; during these latter 2 months, I engaged in document analysis and depended heavily on cooperative journaling, phone interviews, and Facebook conversations with students to address findings from the first 2 months in the field.

The focus of the study was the student body in the English Department, the largest departments at UCAD, which is housed within FLSH,[3] the largest of the UCAD faculties. FLSH students, and English students in particular, deal with many of the worst of UCAD's physical conditions and are very involved in student activism. As students in the largest department, they deal with overcrowding inside and outside of the classroom; additionally, these students face very limited job prospects upon graduation due to large graduating classes and already saturated markets.

I gathered data on students'[4] home region, religion, gender, and ethnicity, as well as contact information and used maximum diversity sampling to identify

---

[3] Faculty of Arts and Sciences.

[4] I established three criteria for involvement in this project: (1) Student was currently enrolled in the UCAD English Department at the time of research fieldwork; (2) Student had studied at UCAD for at least 3 years; (3) Student had participated in student protest at least once.

participants that represented regional, ethnic, religious, and gender diversity within the English department. Five male and five female students, ages 21–28, were chosen. I conducted multiple interviews[5] with each of the students for a total of 41 student interviews. Additionally, I conducted interviews with three English faculty members to better understand how they perceive agency and if they attempted to cultivate student agency in their classrooms. One of the faculty members had been previously involved in student activism at UCAD, described in Zeilig and Ansell's (2008) reserach and Zeilig's (2009) research, and was very helpful in providing insight into the history of activism at UCAD. I also conducted a survey in collaboration with a professor that was administered to Masters level students. The survey was completely voluntary and I received 180 completed responses.

To answer the research questions, this chapter analyzes these data to illustrate how agency was shaped and demonstrated when students at UCAD found themselves between the proverbial rock of deteriorating material and ideological conditions on campus and the hard place of misrepresentation when they attempt to advocate for themselves in a volatile political environment.

Confronting the Politics of Education via "The Educated Person" Discourse and *In Loco Cura* Critique

Students at UCAD confronted the politics that engulf higher education in "chaos" and crisis (World Bank, 2003) through collective action. First, students organized themselves in order to meet their own needs in the midst of administrative neglect and outside political influence on campus. The "educated person" discourse facilitates students' notions of responsibility to care for one another and for their country, a concept captured in the phrase *in loco cura*. Second, as a collective endeavor, students confronted negative representations and reframed activism by intentionally advocating for their needs in nonviolent and socially just ways.

"The Educated Person" Discourse

"The educated person" discourse derives from notions that the university-educated individual has the responsibility and moral fortitude to engage in future leadership and service to the nation. This orientation to their community impacted student actions on campus. Students identified as intellectuals with an obligation to serve their communities and ultimately the nation and they began such service by helping

---

[5] Interviews were conducted in English because students were fluent and proficient and desired to practice their English with a native speaker. Interview citations throughout this chapter do not reference student names so that students remain anonymous, as requested.

fellow students whose needs were not being met by the university staff. The discourse was acted upon by students as they envisioned a leadership driven by social justice and they upheld the responsibilities they believed to be representative of an educated individual. One student described these responsibilities as filling the gaps left by others who are unable or unwilling to serve the community:

> What is an intellectual? It is someone who fills a gap. Filling a gap fills a very important role in life. Before leaving this world, you have to leave some very important things. If I leave this world into the other world without doing anything, for me, I think there are other people who paved this way. You understand. I could not speak English [if not for those people before me]. Who taught me this English? My professors and speaking with other students. So, [filling in a gap] is very important. (N'deye, personal communication, 2011)

Students frequently linked being an educated person to responsibilities beyond those at the university when they spoke of leading their communities and, ultimately, the nation. The educated person, in this sense, had certain expectations placed on her shoulders that were framed in terms of moral obligations. This moral underpinning was used to contrast the responsible, educated person with the person who is powerful or successful in terms of wealth accumulation but morally bankrupt. One student summarized this moral dimension of the educated person as follows:

> What I see as good things, for example, be serious, responsible, don't spend your time lying, respect others. If a person is older than you, you have to respect him. If a person is younger than you, you have to give him respect also, in order to gain his respect and then try to help him, because sometimes they need your help because you're elder than him. You have more experiences than him. Sometimes, it's your duty to help him to grow, or to become more intelligent or to gain more experiences. (Moustapha, personal communication, 2011)

Giving back intellectual and material talents to the community was one of the major components of the "educated person" discourse, which drives the discursive critique of *in loco cura*.

In Loco Cura: *Student Organizing for Community Provision*

Before the 1960s, United States on-campus higher education policy was driven by the theory of *in loco parentis*, meaning "in the place of a parent." From this perspective, the university took the responsibility for student conduct, discipline, and moral and life guidance. A related term (that I coined to apply to student life at UCAD), *in loco cura*, means "in the place of administration" or "care," and both terms applied to the university setting at UCAD but with students, not paid staff, playing this role of caring parent. Students organized to fill the gap left from cuts to administrative staff due to structural adjustment and downsizing of higher education budgets, or the lack of hiring adequate numbers of staff when enrollment expanded. They also filled the gap created by university officials who did not work their posted hours or when they neglected student requests. The lack of administration and care was one of the primary manifestations of the material conditions at UCAD. Students confronted this problem by creating their own formal and informal systems to advocate for student needs, such as providing informal orientations to new students and distributing rooms in the *pavillon* (student dormitories), in collaboration with COUD, the campus administrative staff. In sum, *in loco cura*, was used as a discursive critique and an active response to the lack of student support at UCAD.

One way students modeled *in loco cura* was by filling in for the limited number of faculty members who are burdened with too many classes. In the English department, for example, there were 39 faculty members for almost 7500 students, too many students for the faculty to provide proper advisement, teaching, and administration. Additionally, frequent faculty strikes limited classroom learning opportunities for students. Students filled in these gaps by organizing study groups, planning academic events through the English Club, and by utilizing resources outside of the university, such as those available at the West African Research Association (WARC)—a research center located blocks from campus. Each of the students in this study was also formally or informally tutoring younger students, standing in for professors and earning a small amount of money. Primarily, students utilized consistent study groups to learn the material needed to pass the examinations, as one student explains:

> If we do not see the teacher or the courses are not sufficient, we can go to [Internet] sources for research and then after that we form groups of students, and most of the time these are formed during the examination period. And, we discuss about a given subject. You are supposed to bring your knowledge from the classes and the Internet. It is a rendezvous of giving and taking. [...] We've been doing it since our first year. With friends you can discuss something you can't with the teacher. Because of the great numbers of [students in] the amphis, we do not have the possibility to ask questions so it is in these gatherings that you ask your friends what you'd like to understand. So, it worked in the 1st, 2nd, and 3rd year, and now we're in the 4th year. (Tapha, personal communication, 2011)

Because classroom time is limited, proactive scholarship and supplemental learning opportunities are required to overcome the "rule of failure." For example, The English Club hosted events for English students, such as grammar competitions and study sessions that allow first- and second-year students the opportunities to learn from older students in the English Department. While such supplementary learning is not unusual in higher education, the students participating in this study did not have the regular instruction (inside or outside of the classroom) or homework assignments, and therefore, they believed they must meet together *in order to* overcome this gap and pass the courses.

The problems of insufficient instructors and instructional time were compounded by the lack of accountability by the administrative staff. COUD, the administrative body at UCAD—not including faculty—was comprised primarily of political appointees, who contributed to the politicization of the campus. Additionally, as the ruling party appoints many of the administration, students lamented that their needs were often cast aside in pursuit of a political agenda. In this environment, students were frequently treated poorly in their interactions with administrative staff. The comments of one participant, after a particularly emotionally disruptive experience with administration, reflected on nepotism and corruption in Sénégalese society:

> For example, if you need something in the administration here at UCAD, you pay with your time and we have no time to waste. Instead of coming at 8:00 AM, they do not respect the hour and the hour is very precious. ... [administrators] don't respect what they should do in

their office because they have no experience, or no higher education. I think this is the main reason [for this behavior]. (Abel, personal communication, 2011)

This student identified several key tenets of the *in loco cura* phenome at UCAD, including administrators not taking seriously the work that they had been assigned and displaying a lack of care for UCAD students. Students lost a lot of time by waiting in lines at the restaurant, waiting for scholarships to be disbursed, waiting for classes to begin, and, as seen here, waiting for administrative staff to fulfill student requests. The shortage of administration, and their inadequate preparation as higher education administrators contributed to very little student support, which created the environment of *in loco cura* and essentially contributed to the "rule of failure."

Collective Student Leadership and Activism

In addition to the *in loco cura* actions taken by students, one of the major ways they enact agency to confront these conditions is through activism. The educated person discourse, with its moral leadership and social justice underpinnings, underlied the promotion of a "new" nonviolent collectivism for UCAD students. This activisim is exhibited through *Le Collectif* (The Collective), which was established in 2010 in an effort to re-establish the FLSH *amicale*. There is no official membership for The Collective, but their involvement was apparent during the March 15, 2011 rally when 600–750 students protested. As representatives standing in for the disbanded *amicale*, The Collective's group leaders committed themselves to an ideology of advocacy based on nonviolent leaders such as Martin Luther King and Mahatma Gandhi. They utilized these ideologies in interviews about nonviolence as well as in large group settings to rally student support. Recalling the reason for the March 15th Collective-led march, a student stated:

> [The Collective] stood up so as to go and speak our minds, as we represented students. So as not to stay there with mouths and eyes shut during this situation and I think it has been a good advancement to the [faculty] strike because they stopped it and asked students to resume classes. (Oumar, personal communication, 2011)

Students used the language of human rights and social justice to frame their activism ideology—they viewed the protest as an opportunity to care for students' rights to education and a valid academic year, modeling *in loco cura*. The success of this nonviolent approach contrasted with years of violent protest on campus. According to one professor:

> So, [the students] are right, they have the right to organize themselves to defend the interests of the students, but then it should be on a brand new basis which is that no one should promote violence in this space because this is a space in which we should all be defending our ideas using the brain and not using the strength of brutality or force. It should be the strength or the force of the brain and nothing else. So if we all agree on that, I think we could all live in this university, in this space, with peace, live in peace, live in harmony, for the three components: the students, the teaching staff, and the administration, which is something that is very important for all of us. (English professor, personal communication, 2011)

This assertion of their rights as citizens and students vis-à-vis the politics of education was most apparent in the realm of activism. Students, for instance, had advocated for the right to protest and demonstrate off campus. However, this was not possible due to police restrictions; once a demonstration, even if peaceful, moved off campus, the police had the right to arrest students. The following conversation with a student illustrates this perspective of students' rights and the need to advocate for increased freedoms from the government:

> For example, we are in a democratic country and we don't have the right to march, to celebrate. Because if you march outside of the campus ... we can do it inside the campus because the police don't have the right to get into the campus, but if you do it outside the campus, the policeman will beat you or catch you and take you to the police. These kinds of things are rights, it's our rights that the authorities are denying. They don't want to give us the right to express ourselves, the right to march, the right to do things that we have the right to do. (Tapha, personal communication, 2011)

This student intentionally framed this conversation as a discussion of rights, appealing to Sénégal's democracy as a reason for students demanding access to resources and defending their rights in order to open up new freedoms for Sénégalese citizens. Students saw this demand for their rights as a responsibility of the educated person, and aligned this demand with both the historical traditions of intellectual leadership in Sénégal, as well as with the discourse of universal human rights.

Re-presenting the Large Group Protest: Nonviolence and Diplomacy

Drawing on this human rights discourse, students were reframing advocacy-through-politics on the university campus. Students commonly confronted the narrow representation of their motives and found pathways to succeed within the higher education system despite the "rule of failure." In this final section, I focus on activism to show how students reframed the large group protest, which had often been used to misrepresent student collective action. As a participant in the March 15th protest organized by The Collective, I witnessed how their activism was reframed as nonviolent large-group advocacy.

As the protest began at 11:00 a.m., students were gathering and organizing themselves, to march around campus. They finally ended up at the Rector's office to file their request for the end to the faculty strike. My field notes begin with the gathering of students at Pavillon A:

> In front of Pavillon A, on campus, the march is about to begin. The students will proceed from the campus to the faculté and onto the Rector's office. A student on a microphone appeals to identity asking "Qui sommes-nous?" (Who are we?) while imploring students not to divide on this issue. Another student gets on the microphone and says, "Come out of your rooms and participate and discuss this situation!" I ask a student, "Why are you participating in this march?" and he says, "Because otherwise, I am here wasting my time learning". He is referring to the année invalide that could occur if faculty members don't end the strike. There are at least 500 students and the march has not yet begun. (Field notes, 2011)

From the beginning of the rally, students appealed to their identity as students. The protest was based on an intellectual framing that students must unite and they "should" advocate for their own needs. They positioned their concerns within a discourse of the educated person in contrast to one of violence, such as the throwing of rocks and shouting of profanities in the protests that had occurred only 4 days earlier. Additionally, a community orientation was emphasized, encouraging students to stick together in an effort to fight back against the approaching *année invalide*. There was one clear goal throughout the protest: Fight the *année invalide* and continue education for the year. In contrast to the 1988 and 1994 protests in light of potential *invalide* years, The Collective protest was based in peaceful ideology and a rights discourse.

> *The march has now begun and students are chanting, "Nous voulons etudier!" (We want to study!) As we march down the road between Pavillon A and C, police officers are blockading the exit located by the women's dorms. Journalists are interviewing students as we walk. Most of the participants are male students, maybe 2–3% are women. What an interesting sight! Students demanding to study when many of them do not pay to study. The difference between the march and the strikes just four days ago is so stark: this is so calm and peaceful. There is no police presence on this side of campus. As usual, they only gather at the entrance to the campus near Avenue Cheikh Anta Diop.* (Field notes, 2011)

The protest began with students chanting, "We want to study!" From the beginning, before they started walking towards the Rector's office students made their intentions clear. The outcome of this rally was to end the strike and begin classes for the year.

Not only did students protest for primarily academic reasons, but the media also took notice. Student leaders of The Collective were able to speak to reporters and researchers and challenge their representations of students as violent and selfish.

> *The leader of the Collective holds up a peace sign and the crowd explodes with cheering and clapping. He approaches the microphone, taking his time to speak, eloquently articulating the reason for the strike using French, Wolof, and English. He references UCAD as the premier institution of West African intellectualism. He [identifies/notes] student representation as violent and aggressive and says "not today", then begins a chant "Nous sommes etudiants!" "Nous sommes etudiants!" "Nous sommes etudiants!" (We are students!) Students wave their student cards in the air as they chant. He makes multiple references to students as the future of Africa and calls out despotism, nepotism, and corruption on campus and in Sénégal.* (Field Notes, March 15, 2011)

Again, the leadership of The Collective was very aware of their representation in the media and addressed it directly in the speech made by the leader. In addition, the leader spoke in three different languages to reach the multiple audiences present at the protest, illustrating their engagement with a larger global discourse about students' rights and positioning them as the "educated persons." The leader also framed his argument within a Sénégalese historical context, recalling the history of UCAD in a proud way, and then calling upon their collective student identity. He ignited students' passion as future leaders and critiqued non-moral leadership in the nation:

> *He now turns his attention to the professors and asks them to end the strike. He chronicles the history of UCAD proudly recalling that UCAD began as the only faculty of medicine in*

West Africa. Other references include Rosa Parks, Nelson Mandela, and MLK for their nonviolent approaches to social justice. His oratory skills are excellent. I feel myself becoming more excited as he speaks. His voice intonation is similar to Barack Obama's, but even more resolved to his point. He shouts (in English), "We need education, They [the world] need Africa!" He then addresses students again, "Don't ask what your country can do for you, but what you can do for your country!" He then presents a letter to the Rector and asks him to pass the message on to President Wade. (Field notes, 2011)

Throughout his speech, the leader of The Collective emphasized the nonviolent approach to conflict resolution and recounted the long history of UCAD as a leading West African institution. He also made an international reference, placing Sénégalese students in the greater global political economy, and he directed his request to President Wade to appeal for a continued school year.

Making Sense of the UCAD Case: Re-presenting Student Activism

The 2015 protest provides an example of student activism in the form of political and educational participation at UCAD through which students are attempting to re-present themselves in relationship to the nation. The use of the educated person discourse worked to place the protest in the larger picture of the Sénégalese political economy, and to advocate for leadership within the community and the nation. The motivation for community organizing was social justice concerns, rights of students, and reasonable governance in order to ensure that students continued to have access to education and a valid school year. Confronting the representation of students as uninterested in their studies and disobedient of the rules, students in this study believed being educated comes with certain responsibilities. Namely, they were committed to contributing to national development, building their communities, pursuing social justice, ending violence, and upholding moral leadership in the process. Students wanted to fulfill duties to their communities and the nation. They felt that they could be current and future leaders, and more importantly, they acted on these ideas to change their representation as students and to promote broader social justice in a potentially transformative way. In 2012, following the success of the nonviolent protest, the FLSH *amicale* returned and students in FLSH now have a representative group with access to resources, such as meal tickets and dormitory disbursement. This successful activism, in turn, affected students' beliefs in their ability to contribute to national development and their conceptualizations of the nation and their future within it.

This re-presentation of their activism had three important effects. First, by taking a nonviolent approach to activism, students challenged the notion that it takes violence to "grab the attention" of the government on campus or in the suburbs of Dakar. Second, the March 15th protest did not take up material concerns, such food or scholarships; instead it revolved around academic issues, thereby limiting the influence of political parties who work through student organizations that distribute dorm rooms and meal tickets. Third, the localization of the rally was very important. The protest stayed on campus and dealt with an on-campus issue in campus terms, rather than engaging the police or national authorities. Zeilig and Ansell (2008, 2009) have shown how Sénégalese students use their proximity to national politics to engage national leaders. In this case, there was an academic focus that allowed students to deal with their issues without disrupting the rest of the city. By remaining "local" in their activism, students were able to achieve their goal, impressing faculty and administration in the process because they did not cause destruction to the campus. This march demonstrated a different kind of student activism—nonviolent, local, and focused on learning—and it had the potential for long-term impact on the broader political sphere during a period of youth-led political activism across the continent.

Implications of UCAD's Student Activism for Agency Research and Theory

Agency in educational research has tended to focus on two types of resistance: oppositional and transformative (Bajaj, 2005). Additionally, in Africa, scholars have used agency as a category for examining African youth and their relationship with schooling (Comaroff & Comaroff, 2005; Diouf, 2003; Sharp, 2002). Oppositional resistance usually focuses on action taken against a dominant force or structure, as in the cultural production notion of confrontation. Transformative behavior, instead, includes the concept of "possibility" beyond resisting a dominant force, such as a student starting a trash cleanup day on campus (Bajaj, 2005). As Bajaj (2005) points out, agency in educational literature does not always have a positive connotation because it is used primarily as an analytical category to explore resistance to domination regardless of the outcomes of this resistance, rather than focusing on the form of the resistance undertaken and the impact it has on self and others. Conceptualizing possibilities within resistance allows us to theoretically move beyond oppositional resistance and consider agency as neither pre-determined nor prescriptive.

Within the low-resourced and politically intense environment of UCAD, students enacted agency in productive ways that shaped the student experience. Confronting their representation and using activism showed their ability to recognize and act upon the conditions and discourses that shape their lives as educated people. This moves beyond the student belief in transformation (Bajaj, 2005) to acting on this belief. The examples in this chapter highlight the importance of discourses as they "acted" upon and shape the conditions of students' daily lives. By confronting and reframing these discourses and utilizing a nonviolent approach to protest, student actions have the potential to serve as a model for citizens who seek change within the country.

Students were not only made into objects and subjects through their activism, they were also active participants in creating their own discourses and reshaping those available to them. Students represented themselves in particular ways based on the discursive, material, and political condition in which they lived even though these representations were often subsumed within dominant media representations of students as negative societal actors. As Torfing (2005) summarizes:

> Identity is always constructed within a particular discourse. However, the formative order of discourse is not a stable self-reproducing structure, but a precarious system that is constantly subjected to political attempts to undermine and restructure the discursive order. (p. 154)

In this way, discourses, rather than *concealing* power in social relations, actually *contribute* to the exercise of power in social relations (Nash, 2010). They construct the range of ways most people see the world and themselves in it: it 'governs' the conduct of people and groups even though it does not completely determine it. In brief, discourses operate "on [people's] own bodies, on their own souls, on their own thoughts, on their own conduct" (Foucault, 1980, as cited in Rabinow, 1984, p. 11). The negative discourses and representation of students had a material effect on students and their confrontation constructed a new way of moving forward as a student community, impacting identity and community organizing. The re-presentation and enactment of the "educated person" discourse took place through participation in these re-presentative events, such as the nonviolent protest; they shaped and reshaped their conceptualization of agency and their identities through these productive and socially transformative events. Drawing on Davies (1991), understanding how students change, resist, and appropriate discursive constitutions allowed me to see how individuals positioned themselves in social situations and therefore allowed me to better understand transformation and change within UCAD's "precarious system." In other words, by focusing on student discourses, scholars can better understand how students conceptualize and participate as "educated persons" and link this discursive constitution to their actions in order to understand their motivation for activism.

Utilizing the capabilities framing of agency (Walker & Unterhalter, 2007), I was able to understand how access to resources— representation in the *amicale*, a valid school year and classroom time, and the right to protest—enabled students to "function in and through education" (Walker, 2006). A capabilities framing of agency focuses on the freedom to choose and to act on one's beliefs and goals. This focus allows scholars not only to concentrate on the outcome of agency enactment (activism, in this case), but enables us to understand freedom (the ability to act on one's belief and goals) and unfreedom (the constraints on choice). For the students in this case study, standing up for what they perceived to be "right," reflecting and acting on their values, and organizing were motivated by their goal to become the future leaders of the nation. By understanding the resources available to them and how to access them, students were able to achieve their short-term goal of a valid academic year and, eventually, the re-establishment of the *amicale* and representation at the university.

Conclusion

This chapter explores the ways Sénégalese students enacted agency to confront "the rule of failure," a set of issues including difficult living conditions, high-stakes exams, limited faculty interaction, and financial struggles, in order to succeed at the university level. An analysis of the means through which students enacted agency, including the large group protest and student organizing, provided insight into the active and discursive production of student identity and representation as well as how students negotiate their future role as leaders of the country. Three primary theories informed this analysis: transformative agency to examine how student action was driven by belief, discursive constitutions of agency to understand how students confronted discourses, and the capabilities framing of agency to illuminate how access to resources affects agency. The findings reveal how students reframed the traditional means of accessing educational and financial resources—the student protest—in a nonviolent way in order to change the discourses that negatively affect their educational experience and create new venues to promote their interests on campus. The chapter provides insights into how agency operates outside of the classroom, the role of discourse in agency studies, and how youth agency operates in resource-limited educational environments.

References

Anyon, J. (2008). Critical social theory, educational research, and intellectual agency. In J. Anyon, M. J. Dumas, D. Linville, K. Nolan, M. Perez, E. Tuck, and J. Weiss (Eds.) Theory and Educational Research: Toward Critical Social Explanation. New York, NY: Routledge.

Amutabi, M. N. (2002). Crisis and student protest in universities in Kenya: Examining the role of students in national leadership and the democratization process. *African Studies Review, 45*(2), 157–177.

Bajaj. (2005). *Conceptualizing agency amidst crisis: A case study of youth responses to human values education in Zambia.* Unpublished Doctoral Dissertation Thesis, Columbia University.

Bajaj. (2009). 'I have big things planned for my future': The limits and possibilities of transformative agency in Zambian schools. *Compare, 39*(4), 551–568.

Bathily, A., Diouf, M., & Mbodj, M. (1995). The Sénégalese student movement from its inception to 1989. In M. Mamdani & E. Wamba-Dia-Wamba (Eds.), *African studies in social movements and democracy* (pp. 369–408). Dakar, Senegal: CODESRIA.

Comaroff, J., & Comaroff, J. (2005). Reflections on youth. In A. Honwana & D. de Boeck (Eds.), *Makers and breakers: Children and youth in postcolonial Africa* (pp. 19–30). Oxford, England: James Currey.

Davies, B. (1991). The concept of agency: A feminist poststructuralist analysis. *Social Analysis: The International Journal of Social and Cultural Practice, 30*, 42–53.

Diouf, M. (2003). Engaging postcolonial cultures: African youth and public space. *African Studies Review, 46*(2), 1–12.

Durham, D. (2000). Youth and social imagination in Africa: Introduction to parts 1 and 2. *Anthropological Quarterly, 73*(3), 113–120.

Gupta, A. (1998). *Postcolonial developments: Agriculture in the making of modern India.* Durham, NC: Duke University Press.

Jasper, J. (2005). Culture, knowledge, and politics. In T. Janoski, R. Alford, A. Hicks, & M. A. Schwarts (Eds.), *The handbook of political sociology: States, civil societies, and globalization* (pp. 115–134). New York, NY: Cambridge University Press.

Konings, P. (2002). University students' revolt, ethnic militia, and violence during political liberalization in Cameroon. *African Studies Review, 45*(2), 179–204.

Levinson, B., Foley, D. E., & Holland, D. C. (Eds.). (1996). *The cultural production of the educated person: Critical ethnographies of schooling and local practice.* Albany, NY: State University of New York Press.

Marshall, J. (2013, March 30). Protesting students self-immolate, threaten suicide. *University World News.* Retrieved May 24, 2015, from http://www.universityworldnews.com/article.php?story=20130328121528213.

Marshall, J. (2014, August 22). Crisis at top university after student dies in clash. *University World News.* Retrieved May 24, 2015, from http://www.universityworldnews.com/article.php?story=20140821142205904.

Marshall, J. (2015, August 14). Students disrupt President's launch of major HE revamp. *University World News.* Retrieved May 24, 2015, from http://www.universityworldnews.com/article.php?story=20150812152906508.

N.A. (2009, September 27). SÉNÉGAL: Stormy run-up to UCAD's new academic year. *University World News.* Retrieved March 10, 2011, from http://www.universityworldnews.com/article.php?story=200909250239287.

N.A. (2010, July 18). SÉNÉGAL: Students on the rampage again. *University World News.* Retrieved March 10, 2011, from http://www.universityworldnews.com/article.php?story=20100716193747836.

N.A. (2010, January 31). SÉNÉGAL: Student riots cause widespread damage. *University World News.* Retrieved March 10, 2011, from http://www.universityworldnews.com/article.php?story=20100128200635924.

N.A. (2010, January 17). SÉNÉGAL: Students demonstrate for grant payments. *University World News.* Retrieved March 10, 2011, from http://www.universityworldnews.com/article.php?story=20100114190020865.

N.A. (2014, June 20). University crisis was "necessary" and "predictable". *University World News.* Retrieved May 24, 2015, from http://www.universityworldnews.com/article.php?story=20140618101102519.

Nash, K. (2010). *Contemporary political sociology: Globalization, politics, and power.* Oxford, England: Wiley-Blackwell.

Rabinow, P. (1984). Introduction. In R. Rabinow (Ed.), *The Foucault reader* (pp. 3–29). New York, NY: Pantheon.

Samoff, J. (2009). Foreign aid to education: Managing global transfers and exchanges. In L. Chisholm & G. Steiner-Khamsi (Eds.), *South-south cooperation in education and development* (pp. 123–156). New York, NY: Teachers College Press.

Sen, A. K. (1992). *Inequality re-examined.* Oxford, England: Clarendon.

Sharp, L. (2002). *The sacrificed generation: Youth, history and the colonized mind in Madagascar.* Berkeley, CA: University of California Press.

Suspitsyna, T. (2010). Purposes of higher education and visions of the nation in the writings of the Department of Education. In E. J. Allan, S. Van Deventer Iverson, & R. Ropers-Huilman (Eds.), *Reconstructing policy in higher education: Feminist poststructural perspectives* (pp. 63–79). New York, NY: Routledge.

Torfing, J. (2005). The linguistic turn: Foucault, Laclau, Mouffe, and Zizek. In T. Janoski, R. Alford, A. Hicks, & M. A. Schwarts (Eds.), *The handbook of political sociology: States, civil societies, and globalization* (pp. 153–171). New York, NY: Cambridge University Press.

UNESCO Institute for Statistics. (2009). *Global education digest 2009: Comparing education statistics across the world.* Montreal, QC, Canada: UNESCO. Retrieved March 10, 2011, from http://www.uis.unesco.org/template/pdf/ged/2009/GED_2009_EN.pdf.

UNESCO Institute for Statistics. (2015). Enrolment in tertiary education, all programmes, both sexes (Number). [Data file]. Retrieved December 10, 2015, from http://data.uis.unesco.org/Index.aspx?queryid=131.

Walker, M. (2006). Towards a capability-based theory of social justice for education policy-making. *Journal of Education Policy, 21*(2), 163–185.

Walker, M., & Unterhalter, E. (Eds.). (2007). *Amartya Sen's capability approach and social justice in education*. New York, NY: Palgrave Macmillan.

Willis, P. (1981). *Learning to labor: How working-class kids get working-class jobs*. New York, NY: Columbia University Press.

World Bank. (2003). Implementation completion report on a credit in the amount of US$26.5 million to the Republic of Sénégal for a higher education project. Retrieved March 2, 2009, from http://www-wds.worldbank.org/external/default/WDSContentServer/WDSP/IB/2004/01/06/0 00160016_20040106165923/Rendered/PDF/271700SN.pdf.

World Bank, World Development Indicators. (2014). Government expenditure per student, tertiary (% of GDP per capita). [Data file]. Retrieved December 10, 2015, from http://data.worldbank.org/indicator/SE.XPD.TERT.PC.ZS?page=1.

Zeilig, L. (2009). Student resistance and the democratic transition: Student politics in Sénégal, 1999–2005. *Social Dynamics, 35*(1), 68–93.

Zeilig, L., & Ansell, N. (2008). Spaces and scales of African student activism: Sénégalese and Zimbabwean university students at the intersection of campus, nation, and globe. *Antipode, 40*(1), 32–54.

Part II
Youth Agency and the Intersectionality of Gender, Religion, and Class

Agency as Negotiation: Social Norms, Girls' Schooling and Marriage in Gujarat, India

Payal P. Shah

Introduction

Within development discourses, there has been movement towards promoting empowerment within schools as a means of addressing persisting inequality and gender based discrimination. Adolescent schooling—the transition period where in many countries girls become women and drop out of school—is seen as an important means to empower girls so that they can move beyond basic education and achieve greater social mobility, increase their quality of life, and escape the confines of poverty and marginalization. However, still left out of these discourses is a clear understanding of the schooling–empowerment link: *how* educational processes at the adolescent level can promote empowerment and address gender inequality (Chismaya, DeJaeghere, Kendall, & Khanm, 2012; Monkman, 2011; Murphy-Graham, 2010; Ross, Shah, & Wang, 2011; Shah, 2015; Stromquist, 2002).

Integral to empowerment is the concept of agency—the capacity of an individual to make choices and act. This capacity is conditioned by various factors including educational contexts and pedagogies, students' backgrounds, and the larger socio-cultural and economic contexts in which they live (Bajaj & Pathmarajah, 2011; DeJaeghere & Lee, 2011; Murphy-Graham, 2008). While considerable scholarly work examines how education fosters or constrains agency, there are few rich qualitative case studies that illustrate the complexities and contingencies of the education–agency relationship for adolescent aged girls, especially when they transition from education to other futures, including marriage.

In this chapter, I examine a component of the empowerment process by focusing on the experiences of educated girls as they exercise their agency when embarking on significant next steps in life. Specifically, I look at how two *educated* girls

P.P. Shah (✉)
College of Education, University of South Carolina, Columbia, SC, USA
e-mail: pshah@mailbox.sc.edu

© Springer International Publishing Switzerland 2016
J.G. DeJaeghere et al. (eds.), *Education and Youth Agency*, Advancing
Responsible Adolescent Development, DOI 10.1007/978-3-319-33344-1_5

navigate the strategic life choices (Kabeer, 1999) of continuing their education and getting married, to gain insight into the multiplicity of factors that influence their aspirations and decision making authority and ability. To do so, I draw from Kabeer (2001) and Boudet, Petesch, Turk, and Thumala (2012) where a focus on the intersection between social norms and agency is useful to better understand constraints on and opportunities for empowerment and gender equality. This chapter draws from longitudinal ethnographic data, following girls who were educated as adolescents at a *Kasturba Gandhi Balika Vidyalaya* (KGBV) public residential school in Western Gujarat. This chapter illuminates the extent to which education can act as a "thickener" of girls' agency, and provide insight into what it means for girls to understand and negotiate the systems, structures, and expectations that surround them while making decisions to improve their own lives (Klocker, 2007).

Conceptualizations of Youth–Agency Dynamics in Education

There has been significant scholarship dedicated towards exploring the issues of agency and empowerment to better understand how individual action can influence the very social structures that shape them (Murphy-Graham & Leal, 2015; Ross et al., 2011; Shah, 2015). In particular, in this chapter I focus on how girls are or are not able to influence their life choices within a non-egalitarian gender system that constrains their agency. I begin by discussing the link between empowerment and agency, social norms and agency, and then discuss the link between agency and schooling.

Empowerment and Agency

Empowerment and agency are interlinked concepts used widely in the development and education discourses. Empowerment is recognized as a process that expands the assets and capabilities of marginalized people to participate in, negotiate with, and influence the social and cultural practices/institutions in their lives (Narayan, 2005; Rowlands, 1997). The expansion of agency is considered one of the primary components of the empowerment process—the ability to participate, enact ones voice, and take action (Alsop, Bertelsen, & Holland, 2006; Narayan, 2005). An increase in agency is thought to enable "women to move from enduring complete compliance to constraining and unequal gender norms, to questioning those norms in face of potential opportunities, to changing their aspirations, as well as their ability to seek and achieve desired outcomes" (Boudet et al., 2012, p. 11). Integral to agency is also the concept of choice. Benhabib, Butler, Cornell, and Fraser (1995) and Fraser (1997) discuss agency as comprising the subjective capacity for choice and the capacity for self-determination, where individuals get to play an active role in the formation of their identity. Here, individuals are considered active agents who do not passively internalize external constraints.

However, agency exists in relation to a larger structural context of resources, institutions, and socio-cultural processes including traditions, moral codes, and gender norms (Alsop et al., 2006; Boudet et al., 2012; Narayan, 2005). Research on empowerment and agency tends to focus on the opportunity structures themselves, such as education, land ownership, and rights (Alkire, 2002; Kabeer, 1999, 2001). However, access to these structures does not necessarily translate into individuals being able to enact agency. Alsop (2005) suggests engaging in research that looks at agency from a broader perspective including: whether an opportunity for choice exists; whether the individual chooses to use the opportunity; and whether the choice brings about the desired outcomes. I argue that research must go beyond descriptions of context and outcomes, to focusing on how girls navigate the complex intersections between opportunity and structures, especially when we focus on marginalized adolescent girls and education.

In order to provide insight into the complexities that Gujarati adolescent girls face in exercising their agency and its link with education, I draw from Kabeer (1999, 2001, 2005) and Boudet et al. (2012) where a focus on the intersection between social norms and agency is useful to better understand constraints on and opportunities for empowerment. Additionally, I draw from Klocker (2007) and her distinction between thin and thick agency to help clarify the nature of agency that these girls may be able to exercise and to identify the various intersecting factors that shape their agency. Understanding the extent to which girls are able to act in agentic ways vis-à-vis these norms can help us better understand processes of girls' empowerment.

Social Norms and Agency

Social norms refer to informal, implicit rules that are often internalized and they prescribe particular roles, thus involving powerful external and internal commitments. Roles are ascribed and reinforced by the adherence to and collective agreement on social norms, and are powerful tools permeating individual daily life, action, and choice (Bicchieri, 2006; Boudet et al., 2012). Gender roles tend to cut across other facets of society including caste, socio-economic status, and geographic location, although their adherence and the extent to which roles are performed vary. Understanding prevailing gender norms, as well as the factors that affect adherence to such norms is necessary to gain insight into how individuals are able to enact agency.

Here, I use two cases to examine how norms and agency dynamically interact to influence how individuals make strategic life choices. By focusing my analysis on how social norms intersect with agency in individual decision-making, I show how agency is not only contextual, but also relational. Given the positioning of the two girls within a socio-cultural structure that is highly constrained, I analyze how their agency occurs amidst social norms, and the ways in which their decision-making happens in relation to family. Further, I seek to use the experiences of these to girls to illuminate how relationships with parents, siblings, and in-laws impact girls' decision-making processes which in turn influence the practice of social norms. Many of these social norms are governed by a rigid patrilineal kinship system that orders the Gujarati social world (DasGupta, 2009). Within this system, marriage represents one of the most significant and important socio-cultural and economic institutions for families and communities. As marriage decisions directly intersect with girls' further schooling opportunities, I focus on the two girls' decision-making processes as they make choices related to marriage and continuing to go to school.

Dimensions of Agency: Thin and Thick

To provide a more nuanced understanding of the opportunities for and constraints on exercising agency, I draw from Klocker's (2007) conceptualization of thin and thick agency. The distinction between thick and thin agency is useful as it seeks to take into account the various socio-cultural structures and institutions that impact the nature of girls' agency, without denying them agency. Thin agency refers to participation and action carried out under "highly restrictive contexts, characterized by few viable alternatives" (Klocker, 2007, p. 85). This is in contrast to thick agency where individuals are able to act within a context of multiple options. In this case, I focus on the girls' contexts in relation to choices around marriage and schooling. I analyze to what extent schooling experiences, agency, and social norms influence each other in dynamic ways. Therefore, I see the concepts of thin and thick agency not as a dichotomy, but rather as a continuum where factors such as structures or relationships can simultaneously mediate thin and thicken agency. Here the assumption is that all people are "actors with varying and dynamic capacities for voluntary and willed action" (Klocker, 2007, p. 85). This framework allows us to see how choice is conditioned by a variety of intersecting factors, including formal and informal institutions, social norms and expectations, and resources. Characteristics such as age, place in family, and socio-economic standing (i.e., caste, rurality, and poverty) also affect Gujarati girls' agency. In addition, I assess whether, and if so how, schooling might thicken individual agency as well as influence social norms.

Institution of Education/Schooling and Agency

Kabeer's (1999, 2001) conceptualization of empowerment comprises three interrelated components: resources, which form the conditions under which choices are made; agency, which is at the heart of the process through which choices are made; and achievements, which are the outcomes of choices. Resources, such as education, are seen as preconditions to exercising agency. Education, and in particular schooling, plays a significant role in the ordering and structuring of society. Through cultural transmission, socialization, and social selection, schools directly affect individuals' opportunities and the development of their capabilities.

Schools also contribute to processes of socialization, and cultural and social reproduction. The knowledge and pedagogy enacted in schools is not separate from the knowledge generated within families, and the two work in concert to create and transmit a cultural heritage that permeates the broader society (Bourdieu, 1973). To understand how schooling may contribute to empowerment, this chapter seeks to understand the ways experiences in school influence agentic capacity. Specifically, I examine how schooling might thin or thicken one's agency, and consider the various structures, contexts, and relationships that affect the nature of their action (Balagopolan, 2010, 2012; Kumar & Gupta, 2008; Murphy-Graham, 2008; Stacki & Monkman, 2003).

Research Context: "Educated" Adolescent Girls in Rural Gujarat, India

Examining empowerment and agency in the state of Gujarat presents a complex yet intriguing picture. Gujarat, and modern Gujarati society, is full of contradictions and paradoxes. It has a long history of diversity through migration, its entrepreneurial spirit has resulted in a unique culture and the emergence of alternative livelihood opportunities, and its high levels of industrialization and development position it as the most prosperous state in the nation. However, this spirit of enterprise is accompanied by a tradition-bound and socio-culturally conservative environment. Additionally, there has been historical opposition to the education of women and raising the status of women in Gujarati society. Instead, parochial practices of women's isolation (purdah) and subservience continue today. As a result, Gujarat provides an interesting place to examine how social norms and roles intersect with education to influence girls' agency.

Adolescent Girls in Saurashtra, Gujarat

The girls at the center of this study are considered marginalized due to their rural and low caste status. They come from castes whose primary occupations include tenant farming and migrant pastoral farming. It is generally regarded that their living conditions exacerbate their marginalization, equating migration and living in makeshift huts on farms with severe poverty (Shah, 2016). While caste is a marginalizing characteristic, many girls come from families who own substantial assets mostly in the form of land or livestock. Despite their relative "wealth," their daily living conditions are difficult. Examples of the difficult living conditions include the complete absence of access to hygiene and sanitation facilities, limited access to water for bathing, and safe, clean water for drinking. As a rural region, many communities in Saurashtra find themselves cut off from larger society and living outside the confines of the modern political state, which impacts the attitudes and beliefs of the members of these communities. Saurashtra's unique history as a princely, feudally administered state throughout British colonialism contributes greatly to its conservative outlook and maintenance of traditional practices. This conservatism manifests itself in attitudes that emphasize the subservience of females.

Given the context, the opportunity structures to which these girls have access are influenced by various interlinked socio-cultural factors. The two most prominent factors that condition their agency include decisions around marriage and strong ascribed gendered practices that include practices of *laaj* [veiling], subservience towards males and elders, responsibility for household duties, and caring for brothers and husbands (Kumar, 2010; Shah, 2016). Additionally, practices of patrilocal exogamy impact the extent to which families are willing to invest in the education of their daughters. These socio-cultural factors combine to produce a unique context within which Gujarati girls exist and act.

The KGBV Program

The participants in this study are "educated" adolescent aged girls who completed upper primary school (grades 5–7) at the *Kasturba Gandhi Balika Vidyalaya* (KGBV) *Gharwal* school from 2007–2010. The KGBV school program was initiated in 2004 as a part of the National Program for the Education of Girls at the Elementary Level (NPEGEL), and was a joint effort between the Ministry of Education and the non-governmental organization (NGO) CARE India. To alleviate many of the barriers girls face going to school—including the lack of nearby schooling facilities, distance and safety issues while traveling to schools, and domestic and livelihood-related burdens that interfere with them attending school—the KGBV schools are designed as single sex, residential institutions.

In addition to the physical aspects of the school, the KGBV program recognizes that experiences at traditional government schools tend to be disempowering for girls due to the curriculum and pedagogies traditionally used. The social learning curriculum and pedagogy developed by CARE India, and adapted by the KGBV schools in Gujarat, targets the widespread belief that education is unimportant and irrelevant for Indian girls. Based upon the goal of mitigating discrimination uniquely faced by girls in school, the KGBV life skills curricula emphasizes building self confidence, positive images, and a wider world view so that girls can become determinants of their own lives (CARE, 1998, 2008). This orientation positions the KGBV schools with the potential to provide its students a more empowering educational experience. Here, I assess how these experiences might influence the nature of the girls' agency when it comes to decisions about schooling and marriage.

Strategic Life Choices: Marriage and Education in Gujarat

Marriage represents one of the most significant socio-cultural and economic institutions for families and communities in Gujarat, as in the rest of India. Of the 52 girls enrolled at the KGBV *Gharwal* school, 28 of them were already engaged, and the majority of the remaining girls were likely to become engaged shortly after completing the seventh grade (around the ages of 14–16). Thus, marriage preparations consumed much of the parents' lives as they first prepared for their own weddings, and then spent years arranging their daughters' marriages.

The cultural practice of patrilocal exogamy greatly affects the amount of time and money a family is willing to invest in a girl. In particular, families are less willing to invest in girls' education beyond the lower primary level as they turn their attention towards securing marriages for their daughters daughters (Ross et al., 2011). The communities represented at the KGBV *Gharwal* school practiced dowry, where the girls' family is obliged to give gifts at the time of the wedding; there are significant costs associated with a daughter's marriage. Families' turned their resources and efforts towards securing their daughter's marriage at the "right" time, which directly conflicted with the efforts required to keep an adolescent aged girl in school. Given this socio-cultural climate, the girls at the KGBV *Gharwal* school existed in a reality far more constrained, rule-bound, and physically demanding than many girls around the globe. Extreme practices of patriarchy manifested themselves in daily action, form the opportunity structures to which girls have access, and greatly influence the nature of agency these girls can exert.

Methods and Participants

In this chapter, I use data from a larger 5-year longitudinal study of 11 girls who studied at the KGBV *Gharwal* school in one district within the Saurashtra region of Gujarat. From 2008–2010, I lived at the school with the girls and teachers conducing ethnographic and participatory research.[1] I built relationships with both teachers and students so that I was considered their *didi*, meaning older sister in Gujarati in terms of both respect and family intimacy, and not an outsider or just a researcher. This relationship enabled me to build meaningful relationships with the girls and their families during my time with them and in subsequent visits. After these girls completed their primary education at the KGBV school, I followed 11 of the original 15 girls from 2010–2014, over three fieldwork trips. My fieldwork sought to elicit their experiences and reflections of their schooling as they prepared for the next stages of their lives; I also incorporated perspectives of others close to the girls, including parents, other family members, teachers and community members. I used semi-structured interviews, observations, and general discussion with the girls and broader community. In this chapter, I use the experiences of Rekha and Lata as information-rich cases because they provide detailed descriptions and insights "that

---

[1] See Shah (2015) for more information on research methodology and researcher positionality conducted during 2008–2010.

manifest the phenomenon of interest intensely" (Patton, 2002, p. 234) on how educated rural girls exercise agency. These participants provide distinct yet overlapping illustrations of thin agency, illuminating the multiplicity of factors that affect their ability to act. While Rekha and Lata's experiences may not be typical or representative of all rural Gujarati girls, their stories do provide important, revelatory insights into the complexities that shape many rural Gujarati girls' capacities to act. By focusing on two cases, I am able to provide more detail to illuminate the relationship between education, agency, and social norms about marriage.

Rekha, a charismatic and intelligent 16-year-old girl who many other girls followed, belonged to a caste within the larger *Kodi Patel* caste. The *Patels* are a large caste that occupationally tends to be either small-scale, land-owning farmers or tenant farmers. Rekha had one older sister and one older brother. Rekha's father passed away when she was young, making her the daughter of a widow who was left in deep poverty after her husband's passing, due to inheritance and landownership practices that limited her access to land and other resources of the family. Rekha's mother worked as a day laborer on a farm and her brother was a truck driver. Economic pressures forced Rekha's sister to agree to an arranged marriage where she was physically abused, and after months of marriage, committed suicide. Suicide carries significant stigma across these communities, and her sister's action brought shame to her entire family.

Rekha was strikingly articulate and reflective, and was one of the first girls to engage with me in discussions regarding patriarchy and tradition. She enjoyed reading the newspaper and debating issues that she read. She also had a sullenness to her, most likely due to family circumstances, and she felt deeply the severe pressures of her mother. Her continuation at the KGBV school was facilitated by the local administrator of the school who believed in her potential, and saw education as the key to which Rekha and her mother would be able to live a better life.

Lata was a 17-year-old girl with three sisters and two brothers who also belonged to the scheduled caste of *Kodi Patels*, but a sub-caste higher than Rekha's. Her family did not own any land, and neither of her parents had any formal education. Her father was a laborer, in which he worked on someone else's farm during the day, and drove a *chhakda*, a local three-wheeled taxi, in the mornings and evenings/nights. Her mother took care of the family home and was also a day laborer on a farm. From my time at the KGBV school, Lata's situation was unusual as she continued to live at the KGBV school after completing it, while continuing her education at the nearby girls' secondary school. An exception was made for Lata to remain in the dormitory by the local administrator of the KGBV *Gharwal* school as she and her sister were among the first girls to enroll at the school in 2005. Like with Rekha, the school administrator believed that Lata had a lot of potential and wanted to support her continuing education. Her mother believed that the boys from her village were vulgar and did not feel safe sending Lata on the *chhakda* with the boys to the local village for school. It is customary in her caste that girls finish their schooling after the seventh grade. Her mother and father feared that if she were to commute to *Gharwal* with the boys, her reputation in the village would have been ruined.

Girls' Agency and Negotiating Socio-cultural Norms

Educational Aspirations and Social Norms

Both Rekha and Lata completed upper primary school at the KGBV *Gharwal* school (seventh grade), positioning them as "educated" young adults. Their unique educational experiences, their articulations and reflections on their education, and their participation in strategic life choices illuminate the relationship between education and agency. The descriptions below illustrate the primary arenas that the girls navigated after completing the seventh grade including decisions related to marriage and continuing their education within the larger context of family economic circumstances.

Patrilocal exogamy practices in the Gujarat region leads to son preference and discrimination against daughters (DasGupta, 2009; Ross et al., 2011). These practices require girls to take on household responsibilities and informal labor. However after graduating from the KGBV school, Rekha and Lata both expressed desires to continue with their schooling. They had aspirations of a better and different life after being educated. Rekha explained:

> If we have studied, then we may be of great benefit to our in-law's house. We also might be required to work less, and maybe work from home. If we are illiterate, then mother-in-law and father-in-law will ask us to look after the farm and would not allow us to do a job. If we are literate then perhaps we will even not have to do much household work.

Living at the KGBV school, Lata had already begun secondary school. She explained how she managed to continue studying:

> I have pushed my mother and father to let me study. I am very interested in studying. I do not like labor and farm work, I love to study. Whenever there is a vacation, I work as a laborer and earn money to recover the expenses of my education – I earn all the money to pay for my books – and that way I am able to keep studying. From childhood I have been asking questions – why boys can study and girls cannot? Why do the women have to do all the housework? They know that this is my nature, and they are slowly trying to understand what I say. At the KGBV school I learned how to speak with them, and I gained strength to fight for what I want. For now, they are respecting and listening to me.

Each of these girls' comments illustrates a belief in education as an investment in future well-being, and a desire to value this investment over traditional gender norms and roles.

At the time of their graduations, Lata's and Rekha's families also had aspirations for their daughters. In Lata's case, her father wanted to be supportive of her schooling, as they did her brothers, but he said, "It is now the time for Lata to get married. It is not common in our community for a girl to go to school when she should be married." Within Lata's family, marriage took precedent to schooling. For Rekha, her mother's status as a widow and her family's caste status led her to think that she would not continue with school. Rekha shared, "[My mother] says that the only way to secure my future is to ensure that I marry. At this age we are not supposed to go to school."

Leaving the safe space of the KGBV school meant that the girls re-entered a formal, patriarchal, and hierarchical socio-cultural environment. Embedded in this context are powerful norms that order Gujarati life to which the girls must adhere. Many of the communities (Hindu and Muslim) in Saurashtra practice *purdah*, where women and girls are expected to remain silent and exhibit conservative and subservient behaviors (Ebrahim, 2000; Papanek, 1973; Perez, 2006; Shah, 2015). It is the girls' age and position in the family and their associated norms that greatly affect how they can exercise their agency and what path they take after completing seventh grade. During my follow-up visits I learned that after graduating from the KGBV school, Rekha did not continue onto secondary school, despite her love of learning and positive educational experiences. She was the only girl from her KGBV cohort who secured employment after completing the seventh grade. Rekha became a local doctor's assistant where she wrote prescription letters, directions for care, and helped work with patients. She described her work as "interesting and I can use what I learned at the KGBV school about how to speak with people, and reading and writing, and I am learning so much." Rekha explained that there was too much pressure to go out and earn money. In addition to supporting the household, she stated that her mother was very worried about securing her marriage, and needed more money for her dowry. Rekha felt as though she only had one option which was to give up on schooling and seek employment.

During my third visit with Rekha, she had left her job and at 16 she was in another village living with her husband, in-laws, and a 4-month-old baby girl. Her husband, who had completed eighth grade, was a bus conductor on a "luxury bus," private, long-distance coach, and was frequently gone on overnight trips. In her new home, Rekha practiced *purdah* and *laaj*. When her father-in-law was in the house, she had to retreat to the kitchen. She was not able to speak directly to her father-in-law, and had to cover her head and look down when in his presence, a noted change from her family's home.

Lata's experience was different than she had envisioned. After completing the seventh standard at the KGBV school she lived at the KGBV school and attended the local girls secondary school for 2 years. At the time of my third visit, she was in her first year of college. She attended the local college in the nearby city while living at home. Lata's mother also revealed that she was engaged but that the marriage date was not set yet. Lata and her mother shared that her future husband would let her continue studying. While he had only completed tenth grade and his mother and father were illiterate, he and his family supported Lata furthering her education as they saw it benefitting their own home. Lata's mother explained the benefits of her furthering her education: instead of engaging in difficult labor on a farm, she could do a house-based job, such as tailoring, or work in a more comfortable environment like a school or office. From Lata's mother's perspective, her in-laws supported this because she would be able to earn money and contribute to the family's finances. Lata was proud that she was the only person in her "vicinity," her extended family and sub-caste, to have studied this far, and she stated, "It gives me inspiration that I want to study further. I want to become a teacher."

Rekha's and Lata's experiences after completing upper primary school provide differing accounts of how social and cultural norms condition their life trajectories.

These gender-based norms are combined with intergenerational power and adult–child relationships. Both Lata and Rekha negotiated these norms differently illustrating that while the norms were powerful, they were constantly changing and dynamic. Rekha's agency was especially impacted by the social norms of the family she married into. While she worked in a doctor's office, an agentic act for a girl from her community, her agency was later mediated by the family she married into. Rekha and Lata's experiences show the ways that social norms, specifically gender norms, change, although unevenly, within families and communities which in turn can add to the thickening of agency in some situations, while the thinning in others. In the following sections I use Rekha and Lata's experiences to illustrate how decision-making authority might be negotiated amidst these powerful and enduring norms.

Negotiating Schooling Decisions

Lata and Rekha's experiences reveal how decision making is a relational process. Both vignettes illustrate differently what negotiation and participation can look like in terms of influencing the nature of the decision-making process, not only the outcome. For Rekha, her difficult family circumstances were catalysts for the decision to drop out of school and work. Her mother spent long days working as a tenant farmer. Rekha stated, "There was nobody left at home to do work. Mother was having a hard time doing it all. So I had to drop out. It does not look good that I leave my mother to study." Rekha's remark alluded to the strong sense of intergenerational responsibility prevalent in Gujarati society, and the importance of family obligations. Rekha's situation illustrates how the decision to go to school was not a cut or dry decision; it is not only about a family recognizing the value of education as an investment. When I asked Rekha if her mother supported her in her studies, she replied, "Of course, *Didi*, she wanted me to continue. But there was no way I could. It was not the path for me, even though I was very fond of studying." Here, their economic circumstances, the social stigma of being the daughter of a widow and sister of a suicide victim, and strong gender related socio-cultural norms conditioned the opportunities available for Rekha. Their, and many others across Gujarat and India, circumstances did not allow them to invest in education for their future well-being. In a sense, despite recognizing education as an investment, short-term needs trump potential long-term gains.

Lata's story, unlike Rekha's, was more unique than the norm in this region, but provided additional insights into how Gujarati girls might understand and actively negotiated the expectations around them while making decisions about their future. Throughout our discussions Lata explained how she continuously worked to convince her parents to let her continue in school. Lata's mom shared:

> Yes, earlier it was not ok to educate girls, and these days even it is not safe to put girls outside for education. But our this [Lata] girl was very smart so made her educate outside of the village, she will give answer to anybody in front of her, that is why we made her study in Chorvira, KGBV, and now she goes to Surendranagar. She can answer to anybody but most other girls can't do that.

Due to Lata's persistence and willingness to speak up to her family, Lata was able to participate in decision-making related to continuing school. Through these actions, Lata challenged traditional gender norms where girls do not study past seventh grade. Further, Lata explained that her insistence to keep studying had effects on her family. She says that "my father's thinking, it has drastically changed… he is now willing to educate me, earlier he was not interested in me studying further." Lata's mother added:

> Their father is completely illiterate, both of us are completely illiterate but we made our children educate so that their lives can become good. They can get some good job so they don't have to do the labor that we have done. And in earlier times, people used to think that they will go to their in-laws' home so what is the need for providing education to them.

In one sense, Lata's experience illustrates how girls themselves can play a role in helping push back against traditional norms and roles and change the expectations or attitudes of family members around them—family members who hold significant decision-making authority for these girls.

However, Lata's experiences also revealed how parents' decision-making authority is likewise conditioned by socio-cultural factors such as age and gender. Her parents were subjected to wider social norms that hinder the extent to which girls can influence their parents in relation to decision-making. Lata explained that her efforts were primarily directed towards convincing her father, as he made most of the decisions in the house. She was also chastised by her father for addressing him in a public space. She learned that any type of negotiation had to take place within the private sphere of her home. She explained the nuance of these situations when she said:

> Yes, I can speak with my father, but since he is elder to me… but my father was doing wrong by getting me married after 10th so I told him that this is wrong and so he got me engaged only after 12th. One should not allow wrong things to happen. but then there are elders to them also so…otherwise I always say that papa this ritual is wrong, papa we should not do this thing, but many times he cannot listen.
>
> In our neighborhood when everybody is chatting and my father speaks and I try to speak, he tells me that you don't speak in between, you stay quiet. We girls are not allowed to talk much in home or especially outside in front of others.

These examples show that while she had a unique relationship with her parents and was able to exercise some agency in life related matters, there were limits, affected by community social norms to which she and her parents had to adhere. This insight parallels the circumstances surrounding Rekha's social position and limited opportunities.

Lata's experiences also highlighted a third significant insight regarding socio-cultural norms, context, and girls' agency. Lata's continued schooling came at significant costs to other family members. Her extended family broke local social norms by allowing her to stay with them while she attended school, which is typically only done for boys. Further, the responsibilities that Lata would have had to assume as the eldest female child fell to her two sisters who dropped out of school to do the household duties. In the absence of any income from Lata, and the costs associated with her attending school, her sisters additionally had to work in the fields:

> It was not so much that they didn't want to continue studying. I was studying and if they all were studying then my mother-father would not have been able to cope up. So they gave up their studies and started working at home and as laborers so I can study.

Her mother also clarified how these choices affected the family:

> Yes, we said no, at that time these children were very young so when I go for doing labor work, I required somebody to take care of them. But when Lata continued with school I got her [other daughter] dropped out of the school instead of her.

The example of what happened within Lata's family addresses how the gains for one in the family can come at the expense of others. In Rekha's experience, she had to drop out as she did not have any other sisters or extended family to support her. Contributing to the household income was a necessity. Rekha's and Lata's experiences illuminate the relational nature of agency and decision-making. Their experiences show that while negotiation within a family could result in a slow shifting of socio-cultural norms, overall, agency that is thinned due to a socio-culturally restrictive environment is less able to challenge the larger gender system.

The Role of Education in Agency and Marriage Decisions

In addition to parental authority over educational decisions, parents in rural Gujarat also decided when and with whom a girl will marry. There are a multitude of intersecting factors regarding social mobility through marriage such as family resources, family history, position within sub-caste/community, occupation, and educational levels. Both Rekha and Lata came from communities where engagements were decided at a very early age, and families followed strict rules regarding marriage within caste. Many times the idea of "marrying up" counter-intuitively acts as a disincentive for educating females, as it tends to increase dowry costs. Further, educating a female does not necessarily mean that the girl is viewed as a more desirable marriage partner. Thus, in order to save for marriage related costs, and to ensure that the widest array of suitors is available, education costs are often forgone (Ross et al., 2011).

Below, Lata described how her education helped her participate in marriage related decision-making:

> My mother-father and everybody wanted to get me engaged after 10th and I would not have been able to study 11-12th because after engagement I would have got married but then I told my father that I am not yet 18 and let me complete my 11th-12th and then you do my engagement. My grandfather is not there and everybody else told my father that do her engagement but still I told him that let me study so he agreed and he let me complete my 11th-12th and then only he did my engagement. So in that way if I say anything to my father he agrees. In the meantime many boys came to see me but I rejected them because I didn't want to get married at that time so only after completing my 12th when my aunty showed me a boy I said ok for engagement.

Given Lata's persistence and insistence, she was able to at the very least influence her father's decisions regarding when and whom she should marry. She attributed the non-cognitive skills strengthened during her time at the KGBV school, and the confidence she gained from those experiences, as giving her the strength to assert her desires to her father. "It is what I learned from Priyankadidi and Manishadidi [teachers at the KGBV school] that supported me in discussing about my marriage." Despite the various influences—her parents, the role of future in-laws, and her status, etc.—affecting decisions to continue schooling, she regards her schooling as not only important to continue but as influencing how she positions herself in her future in relation to her in-laws' family.

As detailed previously, Rekha's difficult circumstances led to her dropping out of school to get a job, and 1 year later quitting her job and getting married. Looking back at her KGBV experiences, Rekha stated, "It is a shame I am not studying now as I was in the KGBV school. It would have been good had I continued my studies. Instead, it is like I have been married off so young." When asked to talk about her current situation she explained that she did not want to drop out of school, but had to bring in an income and contribute to her family. She felt very lucky that she was able to get a job at a health center, which paid well, where she was able to use her education, and was a much better alternative to working in the fields. However, when she was married 1 year after starting her job, her in-laws did not allow her to continue working.

Rekha shared that there were two primary reasons she could not keep working, "In our community married girls do not roam about out of the house. Working after marriage is generally not permitted. After marriage I had to focus on household work and having children." Rekha's example illustrates how her strategic life decision-making authority primarily rested in the hands of her parents, and then her in-laws. For Rekha, education was not seen as an important investment in her future. Moreover, her autonomy and ability to work was not considered more important then adhering to traditional gender norms and roles. While Rekha did improve her economic and social standing by marrying into a family with more resources than her natal family, it came with her having to make significant compromises. Rekha's last comment that it was her duty to now focus on having children is significant as it reveals the nature of her agency in relation to child bearing. When I asked her what she thought about being a mother, she looked over at her mother in law, and then looked down, and said, "I am so young. But it is what *we* [emphasis added] have to do." From Rekha and Lata's experiences, we see that girls' agency can be thickened and thinned by a multitude of factors including economic resources, family obligations, hierarchical adult–child relationships, and gender norms and roles.

Discussion

The selected life experiences of Rekha and Lata illuminate what agency, as action or influence that is carried out within highly restrictive contexts, can look like for rural Gujarati girls. Their stories underscore that it is not sufficient to learn about an individual's ability to make choices by only looking at their life choices and outcomes. It is necessary to deeply consider the context and conditions under which they exercise their agency. Further, we need to go beyond descriptions of context to consider contexts as dynamic, or in other words, to examine how contexts themselves change as a result of agentic action. For example, on the one hand for Rekha, her context thinned her agency as it restricted her options and opportunities. Lata, on the other hand was able to influence and change her context and the norms embedded in it through her negotiations with her family, in a way thickening her agentic capacity. Thus, Rekha and Lata both provide us a sense of the multiplicity of factors that affect young Gujarati girls' agency as well as how their agency can cause shifts in contexts. These mutually reciprocal factors include but are not limited to socio-cultural norms, roles, economic conditions, and family relationships.

As educated adolescents, Rekha and Lata's experiences provide insight into whether schooling, as an institution, can act as a thickener of individual agency. As was explored in the findings, for education to garner support and increase opportunity, it has to be valued as an investment in future well-being (DeJaeghere, 2016). Such an investment often conflicts with gender norms and roles, making their intersection an illuminating site to examine negotiation. We see that both Rekha and Lata, and to a certain extent, both of their families, value education. However, this value is placed alongside other competing factors such as economic circumstances and strong community expectations/pressures. For a girl to continue her education, we see that larger family sacrifice is necessary.

Rekha's experience illuminates the idea that further schooling, and in particular secondary schooling, becomes a luxury for many families given their circumstances, regardless of their belief in the value of education. However, investment in Rekha's primary schooling experiences did provide tangible benefits for her. After dropping out of school, instead of working as a day laborer in the farms, as was the norm for girls from these communities, Rekha was able to secure employment in a health care center. She was able to use the academic skills she learned in school along with important non-cognitive skills in this position. Having the skills developed in school such as knowing how to read, write, and appropriately "talk" with others was central in improving the quality of Rekha's life.

Therefore, while Rekha and Lata's educational experiences did provide them additional opportunities to exercise agency and contribute to their future well-being, it was interlinked with other factors. Lata was able to work with her parents to find future in-laws that would support her continuing to study and potentially get a job, and Rekha was able to marry into a family with more financial resources than her own. Therefore, we can consider schooling a "thickener" of agency in that both girls had an increase in opportunities, and to differing extents, the capacity for action. However, overall choices for both girls were still limited and they exerted agency in a way that still conformed to more traditional gender norms. While both Rekha and Lata were positioned to be more effective in gender-assigned tasks and roles, they were not yet been able to sufficiently challenge the gender system, particularly related to their roles within marriage.

Rekha and Lata's stories provide an alternative to the traditional perspective that the desire to "marry-up" counter-intuitively acts as a disincentive for educating females. Their experiences illustrate that in Gujarat things are changing and, an educated girl is seen as desirable, and girls can be more educated than their husbands, if their husbands earn more. In Rekha's case, her in-laws said that Rekha's education was valued as they considered her more capable of running the household and supporting her illiterate in-laws—even if she would never be able to work herself. For Lata, the idea that she would be able to contribute to the household monetarily was a significant factor in arranging her marriage. Here, Gujarat's economic mobility represents movement away from traditional rural livelihoods by engaging in non-agricultural work and moving closer to the city. Given the state's unique mercantile ethos where social mobility is linked with increasing one's economic position, the instrumental value of education for girls now seems to be gaining value, shifting gender norms along the way.

Conclusion

In relation to gaining insights into the empowerment process and social change, these cases highlight the value of examining individual agency as a more dynamic process that occurs in relation to the family. Lata's story, in particular, illuminates how in negotiating the decision to continue with her schooling, her parents' and in-laws changed some of their views, demonstrating that at micro-levels some norms can change. However, their stories also show that not all norms change, despite movement along the thin–thick agency continuum. In particular, both girls were not able to escape gender related duties and obligations specifically within the household and in marriage. Therefore, while changes in individual agency are important components of the empowerment process, changes in agency alone are not clear predictors of processes of normative social change. The wider structures of opportunities and constraints, including relationships with these structures, also have to be taken into account. Nonetheless, this study shows that to empower girls and challenge the gender system, small-scale changes within the family are necessary preconditions for potential wider change at the community level.

References

Alkire, S. (2002). Dimensions of human development. *World Development, 30*(2), 181–205.
Alsop, R. (Ed.). (2005). *Power, rights, and poverty: Concepts and connections.* Washington, DC: World Bank.
Alsop, R., Bertelsen, M., & Holland, J. (Eds.). (2006). *Empowerment in practice: From analysis to implementation.* Washington, DC: World Bank.
Bajaj, M., & Pathmarajah, M. (2011). Engendering agency: The differentiated impact of educational initiatives in Zambia and India. *Feminist Formations, 23*(3), 48–67.

Balagopolan, S. (2010). Rationalizing seclusion: A preliminary analysis of a residential schooling scheme for poor girls in India. *Feminist Theory, 11*(3), 295–308.

Balagopolan, S. (2012). Does 'gender' exhaust feminist engagement with elementary education? *Contemporary Education Dialogue, 9*(2), 319–325.

Benhabib, S., Butler, J., Cornell, D., & Fraser, N. (Eds.). (1995). *Feminist contentions: A philosophical exchange.* New York, NY: Routledge.

Bicchieri, C. (2006). *The grammar of society: The nature and dynamics of social norms.* New York, NY: Cambridge University Press.

Boudet, A. M., Petesch, P., Turk, C., & Thumala, A. (2012). *On norms and agency: Conversations about gender equality with women and men in 20 countries.* Washington, DC: The World Bank.

Bourdieu, P. (1973). Cultural reproduction and social reproduction. In R. Brown (Ed.), *Knowledge, education and cultural change: Papers in the sociology of education* (pp. 71–112). London, England: Tavistock.

CARE. (1998). *Social learning in elementary education: Promoting gender equity and diversity: A reference manual.* New Delhi, India: CARE India.

CARE India. (2008). *Social learning for upper primary schools: A reference manual for teachers.* New Delhi, India: CARE India.

Chismaya, G., DeJaeghere, J., Kendall, N., & Khanm, M. (2013). Gender and education for all: Progress and problems in achieving gender equity. *International Journal of Educational Development, 32,* 743–755.

DasGupta, M. (2009). *Family systems, political systems, and Asia's "missing girls": The construction of son preference and its unraveling.* Washington, DC: The World Bank. doi:10.1596/1813-9450-5148.

DeJaeghere, J. (2016). Girls' educational aspirations and agency: The critical role of imagining alternative futures through schooling in low-resourced Tanzanian communities. *Critical Studies in Education.*

DeJaeghere, J., & Lee, S. K. (2011). What matters for marginalized girls and boys in Bangladesh: A capabilities approach for understanding educational well-being and empowerment. *Research in Comparative and International Education, 6*(1), 27–42.

Ebrahim, A. (2000). Agricultural cooperatives in Gujarat, India: Agents of equity or differentiation? *Development in Practice, 10*(2), 178–188.

Fraser, N. (1997). *Justice interrupts: Critical reflections on the "postsocialist" condition.* New York and London, England: Routledge.

Kabeer, N. (1999). Resources, agency, achievement: Reflections on the measurement of women's empowerment. *Development and Change, 30,* 435–464.

Kabeer, N. (2001). Reflections on the measurement of women's empowerment. In A. Sisask (Ed.), *Discussing women's empowerment: Theory and practice.* Stockholm, Sweden: International Development Cooperation Agency.

Kabeer, N. (2005). Gender equality and women's empowerment: A critical analysis of the third millennium development goal. *Gender and Development, 13*(1), 13–24.

Klocker, N. (2007). An example of 'thin' agency: Child domestic workers in Tanzania. In R. Panelli, S. Punch, & E. Robson (Eds.), *Global perspectives on rural childhood and youth: Young rural lives* (pp. 83–94). New York, NY: Routledge.

Kumar, K. (2010). Culture, state, and girls: An educational perspective. *Economic and Political Weekly, 45*(16), 75–84.

Kumar, K., & Gupta, L. (2008). What is missing in girls' empowerment? *Economic and Political Weekly, 42*(26/27), 19–24.

Monkman, K. (2011). Introduction. Framing gender, Education and empowerment. *Research in Comparative and International Education, 6*(1), 1–13.

Murphy-Graham, E. (2008). Opening the black box: Women's empowerment and innovative secondary education in Honduras. *Gender and Education, 20*(1), 31–50.

Murphy-Graham, E. (2010). And when she comes home? Education and women's empowerment in intimate relationships. *International Journal of Educational Development, 30,* 320–331.

Murphy-Graham, E., & Leal, G. (2015). Child marriage, agency, and schooling in rural Honduras. *Comparative Education Review, 59*(1), 24–49.

Narayan, D. (Ed.). (2005). *Measuring empowerment: Cross-disciplinary perspectives*. Washington, DC: The World Bank.

Papanek, H. (1973). Purdah: Separate worlds and symbolic shelter. *Comparative Studies in Society and History, 15*, 289–325.

Patton, M. (2002). *Qualitative research & evaluation methods* (3rd ed.). Thousand Oaks, CA: Sage Publications.

Perez, R. (2006). The limits of feminism: Women and untouchability in rural Gujarat. In L. Fruzetti & S. Tenhunen (Eds.), *Culture, power and agency: Gender in Indian ethnography*. Kolkata, India: Bhatkal & Sen.

Ross, H., Shah, P. P., & Wang, L. (2011). Situating empowerment for millennial schoolgirls in Gujarat, India and Shaanxi, China. *Feminist Formations, 23*(3), 23–47.

Rowlands, J. (1997). *Questioning empowerment: Working with women in Honduras*. Oxford, England: Oxfam.

Shah, P. P. (2016). Adolescent girls' education, empowerment, and marginalization in Gujarat, India: Inclusion, exclusion, or assimilation? In S. Stacki & S. Baily (Eds.), *Educational challenges, opportunities, and implications for young adolescent girls around the globe* (pp. 77–95). New York, NY: Routledge.

Shah, P. P. (2015). Spaces to speak: Photovoice and the reimagination of girls' education in India. *Comparative Education Review, 59*(1), 50–74.

Stacki, S., & Monkman, K. (2003). Change through empowerment processes: Women's stories from South Asia and Latin America. *Compare, 33*(2), 173–189.

Stromquist, N. (2002). Education as a means for empowering women. In J. Parpart, S. Rai, & K. Staudt (Eds.), *Rethinking empowerment: Gender and development in a global/local world* (pp. 22–38). London, England: Routledge.

Enactments of Youth Agency to Resist, Transgress, and Undo Traditional Gender Norms in Honduras

Kate S. McCleary

Introduction

The plurality of how young people identify and negotiate their agency is shaped by internal and external factors to themselves. From the socio-cultural characteristics that construct the ways youth identify, to norms and behaviors youth observe within their homes, on the streets, in churches or community centers, there is a constant negotiation with the social norms and cultural traditions of their local and national communities in regard to who they are and what they feel they are able to do (Honwana & De Boeck, 2005; Maira & Soep, 2005). Gender norms and identities play a large role in these negotiations of agency. The nexus of gender and agency is a topic taken up by many education, gender, and development scholars interested in investigating the ways a significant socio-cultural construction, gender, influences the agency youth are able to express and enact. Bajaj and Pathmarajah's (2011) work on gender in educational settings in India and Zambia found agency "as differentially experienced, influenced, and acted upon by boys and girls" in relation to their educational access and opportunities based on gender (p. 63). Conceptually situated in Deutsch's (2007) framing of "undoing gender," Bajaj and Pathmarajah's "differentiated agency" speaks to the ways that girls and boys were able to "act upon new understandings of gender and gender relations" (p. 50). However, the question of whether, and how, girls and boys "differentiated agency" challenged, shifted or changed the traditional gender norms to alter those relations remains less explored.

K.S. McCleary (✉)
Wisconsin Center for Education Research, University of Wisconsin-Madison,
1025 W. Johnson Street, Madison, Wisconsin, USA
e-mail: kate.s.mccleary@gmail.com

© Springer International Publishing Switzerland 2016
J.G. DeJaeghere et al. (eds.), *Education and Youth Agency*, Advancing
Responsible Adolescent Development, DOI 10.1007/978-3-319-33344-1_6

103

Gender plays a role in how a young person's agency is enacted vis-à-vis the relationships s/he has with family, peers, and their community. Investigating the "micro-transformations" within gender relations, Arnot, Jeffery, Casely-Hayford, and Noronha (2012) identify the transitions in youth's lives where their knowledge and understanding of gender relations and agency shifts (p. 184). These shifts serve as critical junctures in order to understand how youth's gender identities "shape the possibilities of agency" and the ways they react and enact their agency as young women and men relative to the gender norms of their community (Husso & Hirvoenen, 2012, p. 41). Arnot et al. term this a "normative biography" that each young person brings in their role and relation to local gender norms that includes a story of acceptance, challenge, or shift to how they seek to engage with the norms around them.

The intent of this chapter is to examine the ways in which young women and young men from two peri-urban communities outside Tegulcigalpa employed their agency to "resist" (push back), "transgress" (push past), and undo (*desalambrar*) traditional gender norms to make change for themselves and others (Deutsch, 2007; Montoya, Frazier, & Hurtig, 2002; Stromquist & Fischman, 2009). To start, a discussion of themes pertaining to gender relations and youth challenges in Honduras is presented. The theoretical framing of agency as it relates to gender follows. From there, a brief overview of the qualitative methodology employed to conduct the study is explained. Vignettes from my fieldwork explored through the words and experiences of the youth illustrate the ways youth's agency impacted local gender norms and relations in home (private) and community (public) spaces. Lastly, a short discussion on the ways changes to gender norms take hold and the role that community groups play in those alterations closes the chapter.

Resisting and Transgressing Gender Norms Through Gender Relations

Research on gender relations has evolved over the past 25 years from a sole focus on overarching social structures, such as laws and policies framing women's rights, to addressing themes of power and privilege with and through relationships that speak to gender equality (Francis, 2006; Holter & Borchgrevink, 1995; Molyneux; 2001; Stromquist, 1992). Early scholarship on gender relations focused on power and structural dimensions of the relationship between men and women, including "interpersonal power" and how that played out in a larger societal context (Molyneux, 2001). The often binary focus on "male dominance" and "female subordination" in gender relations (McNay, 2000, p. 11) has given way to an examination of how unequal gender relations and the continuation of conventional gender constructs, which I refer to in this chapter as "gender norms," privileges one gender's contribution over another; such as men's work being more valuable or women's participation in community governance less necessary (Deutsch, 2007). Moving beyond this binary, the scholarship shifted to how we "do gender" (West & Zimmerman, 1987), and also "undo gender" (Deutsch, 2007), bringing attention to the interactional and relational aspects between women and men. Porter (2012) writes, "Institutionalizing new ideas of gender relations is a slow process, which needs to be addressed at multiple levels, including the rules and assumptions of behavior at the micro-level of people's lives and work" (pp. 301–302). Porter's thoughts also resonate with Butler (2004) when she frames relationships between men and women as "situated within the context of lives as they are lived" (p. 8). These scholars call attention to the need to examine how gender norms are lived on a quotidian basis, and therefore, how they can also be resisted and transgressed in specific relationships at specific times.

Murphy-Graham's (2009, 2012) study serves as an example of fostering positive gender relations between women and men through education within a local community context, specifically within Garifuna communities of northern Honduras. Murphy-Graham (2009, 2012) found that the mainstreaming of gender equality content in a curriculum for an alternative education program, *Sistema de Aprendizaje* (SAT), raised awareness of gender-based inequalities faced by women in their communities. She asserts, "Education can promote more equitable gender relations; it can mine gems of inestimable value inherent in both males and females" (2012, p. 149). An increase in awareness and consciousness of gender equality can, according to Murphy-Graham (2009), be fostered through the exploration of gender relations in everyday life. Her work prompts and further explores the question of how education fosters agency through awareness and alters the gender norms that affect young women and men's daily lives.

Agency Vis-à-vis Acts of Resistance, Transgression, and Undoing of Gender Norms

Bourdieu's (1977, 1990) theorization of habitus and field offer ways to understand agency in our daily practices. Bourdieu states that we carry out our daily practices within different fields in our society. For the young people who took part in this study, the fields they traversed regularly included their schools, jobs, home life, and community spaces such as churches and soccer fields. Within these fields, how we act and what we do is negotiated by what Bourdieu terms the habitus. Habitus is the practices we think and act on which are influenced by both social structures and cultural practices. The field serves as the site of negotiation and practice of habitus, which in turn impacts our own perceptions and attitudes of our lived realities (Swartz, 1997). In Swartz's writing on Bourdieu, he explains:

> Bourdieu's idea that action is generated by the *interaction* of the opportunities and constraints of situations with actor dispositions – the repository of past experiences, tradition, and habit – seems to constitute a considerable advance over these alternative views.
>
> While habitus calls attention to the dynamics of self-selection in competitive social processes, the internationalization of objective chances into expectations and the adaptation of aspiration to actual opportunities are often more complex and contradictory processes than the concept suggests. (p. 291)

The interaction between habitus and field in the ways that they are both constrictive and permeable raises the question as to the role that agency plays. Agency can alter and be altered by habitus depending on the field and social structures that are known from "past experiences and traditions" (Swartz, 1997, p. 291). So within the field, what are the ways that agency is enacted that alters habitus? And in what ways is one's agency differentiated in that negotiation?

Stromquist and Fischman (2009) attend to these questions in their introduction to a special issue of the *International Review of Education* that calls for a greater investigation of gender in educational practices and programs. Their article serves as a call to understand gender in education in new ways that (1) address the intersectionality of gender and other socio-cultural factors, (2) takes into account not only the ways that gender is expressed through the binary of masculinity and femininity, but also through how gender is "produced and reproduced;" (3) seek to understand the role agency has in making change through "resistance (refusing to act in conventional ways) and for transgression (acting in new ways and toward new realities)" (p. 468), and (4) investigates how Deutsch's (2007) work on "undoing gender" speaks to the "oppressive structures" that maintain gender gaps and inequalities in education (p. 471). The latter two points made by Stromquist and Fischman (2009) on agency as acts of resistance, transgression, and the undoing of gender roles serves as a framework of analysis in this chapter. Resistance and transgression to traditional gender norms speaks to the plurality of agency as looking to moments of both action and inaction in making change. It is not only about what individuals are doing, but also what they are choosing not to do that is significant.

As a way to better situate these ideas in the context of Latin America, I sought to combine Stromquist and Fischman's (2009) use of "undoing gender" (Deutsch, 2007) with the notion of "*desalambrar*" [to undo fences] used by feminist anthropologists Montoya et al. (2002). Montoya et al. (2002) re-envisioned the concept *desalambrar* from the land-rights movements of the 1960s and 1970s in Latin America that speaks to the untethering of gender roles and norms in contemporary Latin America. The term gained popularity during the liberation theology movement when Uruguayan singer Daniel Viglietti wrote it as an anthem for landowners to *desalambrar* [tear down the fences] that shut out local communities to spaces owned by foreigners and the elite of the country. In Montoya, Frazier, and Hurtig's use of *desalambrar*, the concept "allows us to see the emancipator potential of ordinary people's gendered practices" but also remain "keenly aware of the hegemonic force of gender ideologies in legitimizing and naturalizing structures of power" (p. 4). Within this concept is a sentiment of people working together to make change. This mirrors Stromquist and Fischman's (2009) emphasis on working together against gender injustice and towards "purposeful change" (2009, p. 469). The use of *desalambrar* in this chapter speaks to the call to "undo gender" (Deutsch, 2007) with and through acts of resistance or transgression. In the Honduran context where this study was carried out, *desalambrar* means to undo those barriers that divide girls from boys, young women from young men, and to challenge and change the gendering of community spaces within which young women and young men interact and inhabit. It is about challenging the perceived roles of both genders, and shifting gender norms in ways that advocate for gender equality.

Gender Norms and Relations Confronting Honduran Youth

Youth living in urban areas of Honduras occupy a vulnerable space where youth recruitment into gangs and gang violence (El Heraldo, 2015; Programa Nacional de Prevención, Rehabilitación, y Exclusión Social, 2010; Wolseth & Babb, 2008), the highest homicide rate per capita in the world with 90.4 murders per 100,000 habitants (United Nations Office on Drugs and Crime, 2013), the highest adolescent birth rate in Central America (Guttmacher Institute, 2006), and the sixth highest rate of gender-based violence in the world are all part of their daily lives (University of California-Hastings, 2011). While there is considerable vulnerability for young people, there is also a narrative of empowerment in national policies and discourse. *La juventud* [youth], defined by the Law for the Integral Development of Youth in Honduras (Republic of Honduras, 2006), are individuals between the ages of 12 and 30. This law is an acknowledgement by the Honduran government of the pivotal role that youth play in the development of the country.

Following the implementation of the law, the *Instituto Nacional de La Juventud* [National Youth Institute] put a 15 year plan in place that seeks to increase youth citizenship, lessen legal and socio-cultural discrimination that prevents youth from exercising their rights, create a democracy inclusive of youth voices, and lessen social inequities for women, indigenous groups and those of African descent (e.g., Garifuna communities) (Instituto Nacional de La Juventud, 2007). The *Instituto Nacional de La Juventud's* attention to issues addressing specific social inequalities for women raises the question of how and where gender inequalities exist in the Honduran context. Educational attainment is often a site to examine gender inequalities; however, the educational data shows attendance rates that are equal for primary education, and in favor of young women at the secondary level (World Bank, 2012). If not in educational access, what is fueling continued gender inequalities in Honduras?

Gender-based violence for young women and the effects of gang involvement for young men are two structural concerns that continue to fuel gender inequities at a broader social level in Honduras. Domestic violence remains one of the worst threats to young women's well-being. The *Centro de Derechos de Mujeres* [The Center for Women's Rights] reports that within the first 6 month, January through June, of 2015 there were 438 assaults against women in Honduras. Out of the 438 assaults, 189 resulted in the homicide of the victims (Centro de Derechos de Mujeres, 2015). Honduras has passed two laws, the *Ley de Igualdad de Oportunidades para la Mujer* [2000 Law of Equal Opportunity for Women] and the *Ley Contra la Violencia Domestica* [1997 Law Against Domestic Violence], seeking to offer protections to women (Republic of Honduras, 1997, 2000). Yet finding ways to alter the cultural view of gender-based violence, and the view of women from within the "gender regime" (Connell, 2002), not only takes enforcing existing legislation and new judicial practices in response to the violence but a deeper understanding of the gender relations within families and peer groups.

The "aggressive or machismo masculinity" (Preito-Carrón, Thomson, & Macdonald, 2007) discussed by researchers as a threat to women is also a threat to young men as they negotiate their own identity and respond to the pressures they feel to behave and act in certain ways (see Barker, 2006; Gutmann, 1996; Wolseth, 2008a). Within the Honduran context, gang affiliation is leading to an infiltration of violence into young men's lives. Pine (2008) identifies neoliberal economic policies in Honduras, the lack of employment opportunities, and ongoing issues of structural violence as contributing factors to the rise in young men's involvement in gangs. Estimating gang membership in Honduras is problematic but of those involved with gangs it is estimated that 80 % are young men (Programa Nacional de Prevención, Rehabilitación y Reinserción Social de Honduras, 2010), and 35 % of gangs members in the country are thought to be younger than 18 years of age (El Heraldo, 2015). While young men are not often portrayed as victims within a cultural tradition where men hold more social power and privilege, there is a vulnerability for young men who choose not to be involved with, or want to opt out of, gang life and select what young people identify as "the good path" (McCleary, 2013; Wolseth, 2008a). Peer pressure within the larger cities such as San Pedro Sula and Tegucigalpa make avoiding gang affiliation problematic, and leaving a gang for a reason other than finding religion is unlikely for most young men as it could mean death (Pine, 2008; Wolseth, 2008b). The norm around gang participation in urban areas, in addition to the protector/breadwinner role that many young men esteem to, makes any alteration to gender relations complicated (Steans, 2006). The ways in which young women and young men in this study sought to alter these roles and relationships through their agency is explored in the *Findings* section.

Methodology

In what ways are constructions and enactments of agency different or similar between young women and young men? That is one of the original questions that I posed going into the study, and the starting point for examining the ways agency was resisted, transgressed, and undone, or *desalambrado*, by the young women and men who were involved in the study. The findings documented in this chapter are from a 6-month qualitative case study I conducted in cooperation with the Honduran CARE Education Unit in the El Valle and El Pino communities (pseudonyms are used to protect anonymity) outside of Tegucigalpa, Honduras[1]. The research study allowed me to carry out two semi-formal interviews with each of the young women

---

[1] The study was conducted in collaboration with the former Education Unit of CARE Honduras and CARE USA. From 2008–2010 I served as a graduate student researcher with the Minnesota International Development Education Consortium (MIDEC) on the Patsy Collins Trust Fund Initiative project. Dr. Joan DeJaeghere (PI) and Dr. Chris Johnstone (co-PI) led the project, and Nancy Pellowski Wiger, fellow contributor to this manuscript, was a close collaborator on the MIDEC work in Honduras. Having worked remotely with the Education Unit from 2008–2010, I partnered with them on this research and served as a fellow in their office from February until August 2010. The Education Unit had a large portfolio of projects across the country. The four-person Education Unit staff provided an impressive amount of support, training, and program development and implementation across the many communities with which they collaborated (see Moll & Renault (2014) for additional information on the project).

and men, to spend approximately 360 hours within the communities and conducting participant observations, and to spend 42 hours in the CARE Honduras office, the NGO implementing the youth non-formal education program, working with participants (CARE, Republic of Honduras, n.d., 2008 and 2010). In addition to this 6-month period, I returned to Honduras in March of 2011 for 1 week to meet with participants and conduct a participant member check (Johnson & Christensen, 2010) and I remain in touch with many of my participants and the former employees of the CARE Honduras Education Unit.

The findings in this chapter chronicle the experiences of a small subset of the 19 focal participants from my original study. The experiences of and interviews from my time with Arianna and Juan, both from the El Pino community, and Milton, David, Jordi, Jessica, Lisa, and other members of the CARE Youth Program, in the El Valle community, were selected to provide a depth of understanding as to the acts of gendered agency in how youth resisted, transgressed, and undid conventional gender norms held for them. Details on the lives of these key informants are woven into the "Findings" section as their life details inform the interplay between their agency and gender.

As I focus on a subset of participants, it is important to note that the larger population of youth I worked with included five young women and four young men from the El Valle community, and five young women and five young men from the El Pino community. This group of 19 participated in at least two semi-structured interviews, and I spent time conducting participant observations in the different venues (e.g., church, schools, soccer games, youth groups) in which they were active. Purposeful sampling was used in the recruitment of participants (Cresswell, 2007). The focal participants in El Valle were selected first and foremost based on their participation in the CARE Youth Group. After that, the participants were selected based on their (1) willingness to participate and be interviewed, (2) their friend/family affiliation in order to have a range of thoughts and opinions from within the group, and (3) their age. The El Pino youth were selected based on their involvement in at least one non-formal education program within their community, and their interest in improving their communities. For the purposes of this chapter and analysis, vignettes from only a few participants were selected to provide a depth of understanding as to the acts of gendered agency in how the youth resisted, transgressed, and undid conventional gender norms held for them.

Ethical considerations and my own positionality in this research as a White, United States woman in my thirties, working in an area identified by CARE Honduras as marginalized, were informed by a feminist epistemological approach. Olesen (2005) reminds us of a few central questions when undertaking research in contexts where power differences exist. Oleson advocates asking: "Whose knowledge? Where and how obtained, and by whom; from whom and for what purposes?" (2005, p. 238). The questions were beacons in the ways I conducted my work and interactions with the youth. In addition, Watts (2006) notion of reciprocity was also central to how I sought to engage with these young people.

Another consideration was the translation of my work from English into Spanish, and Spanish into English. Having studied the Spanish language for 10 years and having lived for 2 years in Spanish speaking countries, I was self-reliant in writing the interview questions and protocols. However, I used "decentering," a translation technique that allows for "an ongoing process of revisions in both languages as often as needed until a similar but culturally relevant instrument is validated" (Sperber, Devellis, & Boehlecke, 1994, p. 502), in the editing of my work. This included meeting with the CARE Education Unit personnel to ensure shared understanding of the questions I posed, and that the consent forms used with the youth and families would be understood within the local communities. Upon initial analysis in the fall of 2010, I returned to Honduras in March of 2011 to meet with the participants and the CARE Education Unit to further ensure clarity of ideas, and that my interpretation of findings held resonance with the group and within the Honduran context. I translated the quotes throughout this text, and they were reviewed by a Spanish-speaking colleague. For purposes of space in this chapter, I include only the English translations from the interviews with the youth.

Findings

The analysis focuses on three vignettes from the study that feature youth's acts of resistance, transgression, and *desalambrando* [undoing fences]. Each section introduces a pivotal conversation or event that demonstrates the gendering of youth's agency as they resisted, transgressed, and "undid" the conventional gender norms that bound them. The ethnographically informed nature of my research relies on a narrative story that tells how Arianna, Milton, and the Sport and Culture Committee of the CARE Youth Program demonstrated their agency in addressing conventional gender norms that constricted the ways they themselves, or members of their community, could act and engage within their homes and community spaces. A discussion of the vignettes, and implications for community organizations, will follow the sharing of these key findings.

Resistance

I met Arianna through her brother Juan, a university student studying Sociology at the time, who had helped with the demographic mapping of youth in El Pino in 2009. He was one of the first young men from El Pino who agreed to talk with me for this study. Arianna, who was 2 years younger than her brother, and 19 at the time when we met, was also enrolled in university as a Journalism and Communications major. Both Arianna and Juan were thoughtful and articulate young people who had a pulse on the contemporary challenges they and their generation faced; they also had strong opinions about Honduran politics and the reasons their country was struggling. In trying to set up a time to talk, Arianna had been challenging to meet. During my time in Honduras, she visited an aunt who lived outside of the Tegucigalpa region perdiodically. Arianna and Juan's mother, an education consultant, typically left Arianna to care for the house and her two younger siblings. However, due to Arianna's visits to her aunt, Juan had taken on the household responsibilities when she was away. The tension around household responsibilities had not been outwardly present in my talks with Arianna and Juan individually, but when I met with them together, the resentment and *choque* [clash] over their roles and responsibilities within their household became evident. Arianna was clearly resisting gender norms held within her home space by choosing to spend time at her aunt's home rather than remain as the caretaker.

As we talked, I posed a question I had asked others in my study: "Are there different spaces for men and women inside of your community?" While all 19 young women and men had agreed that there were different spaces for them in the two communities, the male-female sibling relationship between Juan and Arianna elicited a response in which they challenged each other. Arianna immediately responded that there were more spaces for men. She shared that a woman is almost always at home while men hang out with friends or play soccer or basketball. Juan quickly jumped in and said, "Sure, but there is the exception to the rule. For example, sometimes there are girls, daughters even, that travel and that are lost for months." Juan laughed as he said this, looking at his sister for a response as she had just spent the last month visiting her aunt. Arianna had left her home for an extended stay and household chores had been re-appropriated to Juan. Juan shared that he thought everything in the house was going to fall apart when she first left because she had always been in charge of everything. Now, he explained, he had given his other two siblings chores at home so everyone did their part.

"But why was she in charge of the household and not you?" I posed to Juan. His reply was that she knew how to cook and organize everything in the house; Arianna added she knew how to clean the house too. "But why?" I queried. Arianna replied that when she was asked to do things by her Mother she did them nicely; whereas some "other people," referring to her brother, would complain about doing them. I pushed further. "But your mom, who did she teach to do things in the home?" "Me," replied Arianna. "Well yeah, her," said Juan. "But why only her?" Arianna and Juan's thoughtfulness, intelligence, and disagreement over the responsibilities within the home space spurred me to pursue this and the following conversation unfolded.

Juan:	Ah, because this is the mentality people have - the women in the home.
Arianna:	It's machismo.
Juan:	No, because it's also feminism – because everything should be equal, yes or no?
Kate:	Explain this to me. Explain how this is feminism to me.
Juan:	If she [Mom] had taught me to cook from when I was very young I would do it, but ...
Arianna:	[she cut Juan off] No, but it's never too late to learn something. Every day we learn new things.
Juan:	And what happened when you left? I learned to do all of it.
Kate:	And now do you still do it [housework]?
Ariana:	No, no he doesn't
Juan:	Of course not.

Arianna: Right there, see?
Kate: If you are talking about equality shouldn't you both help at home?
Juan: No ... Well yes of course. But right now everyone in the house is doing their own
            thing. For example, in the house right now, everyone makes their own food, every-
            one does what needs done ....
Arianna: I am in charge of the food, sweeping the house, caring for my younger brother and
            sister, to make sure everything is good at home, and once in a while helping out my
            Mom as well (Arianna and Juan, personal communication, 2010).

There are multiple layers to what Arianna and Juan shared in their dispute over women's (and men's, or the absence of their) roles within the home. Juan, the burgeoning sociologist and eldest son/brother within the household, misappropriated feminism to explain why women were culturally assigned housework within the Honduran context. Juan conceded that in order to have equality within the home, the woman should not be the only one responsible for household chores. His disclaimer to this issue was that he distributed the chores evenly among the siblings, which did not leave the burden to any one individual. But Arianna contended that in returning home, she had reassumed that sole responsibility. It remained a contested issue for her and her role as the eldest daughter and sister within the family. Arianna was quick to identify women's work within the family space as "machismo," an explanation that the majority of other focal participants offered when discussing women's work within the home.

Arianna's resistance to this gendered role was a source of stress. During a meeting in April, 3 months prior to a conversation with Juan, Arianna mentioned the stress that caring for her siblings and the household caused her, and the loss of educational opportunities that helping out at home caused other young women in her community. Her self-described daily schedule involved a long commute to and from the university where she studied, preparing a midday meal for herself and her siblings, an afternoon language class, and then an evening of cooking and cleaning up at home. "It's a lot of stress," is how she characterized her daily routine. While Juan sought ways to delegate chores to his younger siblings in her absence, Arianna felt the weight of those responsibilities when she returned home.

Her frustration with her brother and her household responsibilities extended to how she viewed the situations of other *muchachas* [young women] in her community. Arianna said, "Girls almost always are in the kitchen. Moms put them to work" (Arianna, personal communication, 2010). Her solution to this, and something she sought to teach Juan, was that girls and boys should not have "egoísmo" [egoism] in helping each other. She stated that young women and young men alike need to take responsibility and compromise in what they are doing at home and in their community (Arianna, personal communication, 2010). Arianna's resistance to the gender norms assigned to her by others was to retreat to her aunt's home to avoid it, and was demonstrative of how agency was deployed in a subtle way through acts of resistance. Other youth participants involved in this project sought to not only resist (push back), but transgress (push past) the gender binaries within their communities. Milton is one of those individuals who transgressed gender roles held for young men in his community.

Transgression

Milton was 20 at the time of our conversations together. Married to Ines, who gave birth to a healthy baby boy in May 2010, Milton was working with his father, not his biological father but the man who raised him and who he called "Papa," at an automotive store during the 2 years that we were in ongoing communication. He was lauded by CARE staff, his parents, his brother, and his wife as *un buen hombre* [a good man/a good guy]. Growing up the eldest of three boys, Milton's mother, a seamstress, called on him to help around the home and care for his brothers when she was out or with clients. "My Mom taught me to do everything in the house because I was the oldest and I had to take care of the two younger ones (brothers). I also did housework" (Milton, Personal Communication, 2010). Milton went on to say, "My mom said to me, 'Always walk helping and when you can, you should.' Because I know that someone will help me when I need it." (Milton, personal communication, 2010). The strong family relationship within Milton's childhood home, and perhaps the absence of sisters in the household, shaped the responsibilities he was both assigned by his mother and that he took on.

The close-knit relationship that Milton had with his Mom, who was a single parent for part of Milton's childhood as his biological father left when his middle brother Tomas was born, spurred him to care for his Mom, siblings, and family home in a way that fell outside the scope of traditional gender roles in Honduras. Milton shared how he wanted to lighten his Mom's workload; he explained, "I had friends that saw me washing dishes in my house [and] sweeping, and they said to me, 'Hey stop that. That's women's work. [And I would reply] So? I have to do it. There isn't a woman here" (Milton, personal communication, 2010). Milton was agentic in the way he stood up to and confronted the taunts of his peers as he conducted what they identified as "women's work." He transgressed the passive role of men within home spaces and supported his mother in the care for their home and his siblings.

His role as a caretaker extended beyond his parents' home to the family he started with his wife Ines. Milton explained,

> Women come over to the house to visit my wife and they say to me, 'How good that you help. Oh, how I wish my husband would help me.' And it is true, it's not every man that helps at home. So I hear this a lot that they [the women's husbands] only go home to bed or watch television. (Milton, personal communication, 2010)

Ines, who was present for one of our discussions, confirmed that Milton's involvement at home surpassed that of other young men in her community. She was quick to add that while he helped at home, he still spent some free time on the soccer field. She shared how meaningful it was to have a husband who cared for and was there for his family beyond the traditional role as breadwinner and protector.

In addition to his Mother, Milton shared that others, including the staff of the CARE Education Unit's youth program and Milton's Papa, validated his actions as a caring and engaged young man in ways that encouraged his behaviors (Milton, personal communication, 2010). In many ways, he and his family promoted what Gutmann (1996) terms "contradictory consciousness." "Contradictory consciousness" is the way that men, and women, may not adhere to the "monochromatic image' of the gender stereotypes held within their society. Contradictory consciousness pushes people past "dominant understandings, identities, and practices in relation to" how gender is negotiated and acted on (Gutmann, 1996, p. 14). The ways in which Milton used his agency to transgress the traditional role that many in his community had for him as a young man was fostered by adults who supported him constructing another narrative of what it means to be a Honduran young man. Milton said that the staff of the CARE Education Unit helped all the youth see themselves in different ways as to what they could do and what they could bring to their work with the community (Milton, personal communication, 2010).

Desalambrar *[To undo fences]*

This final section explores the notion of *desalambrar* [to undo fences] (Montoya et al., 2002) in relation to ways the Sport and Culture Committee of the CARE Youth Group used their collective agency to create access for girls and young women to participate in a soccer match in the El Valle community. Public fieldnotes and personal reflections from meetings of the CARE Youth Group leading up to and the day of the community soccer tournament held on May 8, 2010 were used in documenting the ways there was an undoing of the barriers that girls confronted in playing soccer in El Valle.

In mid-March of 2010, the Sport and Culture Committee shared with the CARE Education Unit (CEU) that they wanted to sponsor a soccer tournament in El Valle. While the group originally wanted to invite boys from community churches and schools to participate, Doña Pilar, the head of the CARE Education Unit, shared with the committee that if they wanted to host the soccer tournament with CARE's support the event had to be inclusive of young men and young women players. On April 22, 2010, Javier, a staff member with the CEU, and I met with Jordi and David, two focal participants, and Daniel, a member of the youth group, who were all part of the Sport and Culture Committee of the CARE Youth Group to plan the tournament. Javier helped them with writing invitations to the school principals and ministers of the churches, putting together an agenda, and to-do list; while I helped them make flyers and talked to them about why they initially did not want to invite girls.

The young men did not think that girls had any real interest in soccer. David explained that for boys soccer is really important, but for girls they do not really care. At the time, David did not see any connection between girls not being permitted to play soccer, and having *access* to a soccer field, and their perceived interest in the game. David's perception did not also hold true to what he knew of the girls' interests. A few of the young women from the CARE Youth Group were avid soccer players. Lisa and Jessica both played in an all girls/women's league in Tegucigalpa. During an interview with Lisa and Jessica on June 14, 2010, Lisa explained that the soccer field in El Valle was for *los chavos* [the guys]. She shared, "It's not everyone who likes *the idea* of girls playing soccer, and for this reason there are more community spaces for guys to be out in than girls" (Lisa, personal communication, 2010). Over the course of planning the tournament; and in conversations with Doña Pilar, Javier, their peers in the Youth Group and myself; the young men's changed perspectives of who *should* be on the soccer field and who *wanted* to be on the soccer field started the undoing of the traditional gender trope within the community that soccer was for boys.

Getting others in El Valle to endorse girls' involvement in the tournament was the next "fence" that the youth and CEU staff confronted. Below is a section from my Public Fieldnotes that provides insight into the response the youth got from the school principals:

> About a week prior to the event David called me to tell me that the school principals in two El Valle schools were not going to send teams of girls. The one school director told David that they did not have a soccer team for girls, girls do not know how to play, and she did not know how parents would respond. The other director told David that there was no girls' team and she wasn't going to organize one. The reaction of the school directors was not surprising to David. He said he had tried to explain to me that girls do not play here like boys do. He asked if we should cancel the event. I said no and told him we could talk to Javier to see what could be done about the situation.
>
> Javier spoke to the school principals. The one principal told him that she wants girls to participate; she just didn't know how to get them organized in such a short amount of time. It was determined that the Parent Association (P.A.) could help get the group organized, and the vice president of the P.A. decided to help organize a group of girls. (Public Fieldnotes, May 8, 2010)

The Sport and Education Committee reached out to other members of the Youth Group to help promote having girls participate in the soccer tournament. Mariela, Angela, and their friends were encouraged to talk with the minister at one of the largest evangelical churches in the community. Laura, Hilda and Janet were asked to talk with the school director near their homes northeast of the El Valle community. In the end, with outreach from the Youth Program, the CARE staff, and the one Parent Association, the schools and churches sent equal teams of girls and boys to participate in the soccer tournament. The Youth Group, with the help of adult advocates, was agentic in beginning to undo both the physical and mental fences to having girls play in a community tournament. All the girls who participated that day shared that it was the first time they had been permitted to play on the field, which was privately owned but used weekly by teams of boys and men (Public Fieldnotes, May 8, 2010). While teams of girls played in the tournament, other occurrences throughout the day indicated that there was more work to do in continuing to dismantle the barriers to girls' access and participation. The lack of parental support for the girls in relation to the boys at the event, access to soccer uniforms, and places to practice between community events were all things that had to be continuously worked on. But the symbolism in having two trophies, one for the girls team and one for the boys team, set a strong precedent that day as to the needed inclusion of girls and young women in future soccer events.

Discussion

Arianna, Milton, and the Youth Group's enactments of agency by resisting, transgressing and undoing conventional gender norms within their Honduran communities altered gender relations in everyday practices. These examples illustrate two points that need to be problematized in how the youth's agency towards challenging and shifting gender norms was perceived and received. First, the response of family, friends, and the broader community to a young man's attempt to alter gender norms was more positively received than when a young woman advocated for changing the same gender norms. Other scholars, such as Bajaj and Pathmarajah (2011), noted this finding in their research with youth. They write, "… structural inequalities tend to privilege boys in many countries … and enable them to experience more transformative agency and efficacy when asserting new understandings of gender and gender relations in households, workplaces, and other settings" (p. 50). Milton, in his willingness to take on household responsibilities, and David, Jordi, and Daniel, in their openness to having gender parity in the soccer tournament, were all lauded for the ways they were open to and willing to go against the traditional gender norms. However, Arianna's resistance to her role as caretaker and Lisa and Jessica's interest in playing soccer were perceived negatively by those around them. Juan described Arianna as "deserting her family" (Arianna and Juan, personal communication, 2010), and Jessica's father would not talk to her when she went out to play soccer as he strongly disapproved of her participation (Jessica, personal communication, 2010).

Second, young women's advocacy for more equitable gender relations challenged the locus of power in those relationships. Their stances, which were often taken in private home spaces, need to be recognized and supported. Helping young women link their experiences to broader national efforts and policies (e.g., The Law for Integral Development of Youth or The Law of Equal Opportunity for Women) that promote gender equality can situate their individual efforts within a larger, national calling. Future research on how organizations and community groups in Honduras find ways to validate the stand young women take in confronting gender norms that subordinate them in private and public spaces is needed. A key barrier to this call is the invisibility of young women within their home space as there is more visibility to public acts than private ones.

Another point of note is that the Youth Group would not have been able to mobilize the El Valle community to host a soccer tournament inclusive of girls and boys teams on its own. While the young people were agentic in advocating for the event, their age influenced how community leaders perceived and responded to them. The CARE Education Unit played an instrumental role in promoting changes in gender relations in El Valle and the other communities in which they worked. The role they played as a local non-governmental organization (NGO) implementing an international gender program positioned them to take "… local discourses to make claims for justice" that elevated the issue of gender equality in new and culturally relevant ways (DeJaeghere & Pellowski Wiger, 2013, p. 557). For example, the CARE Education Team employed children's rights and human rights dialog to elevate issues and concerns pertaining to girls and young women in the community (Public Fieldnotes, March 2, 2010). Asking a question such as: "Don't you want your sons and daughters to be successful?" attracted community participants to engage in discussions that in the end focused more on girls' and young women's educational and community experiences. Lastly, the CARE Education Unit's and Youth Group's broad-based efforts in addressing traditional gender norms in El Valle is an example of how acting agentically as a group through collective action can promote a change in attitudes towards gender relations (Monkman, Miles, & Easton, 2008).

Conclusion

This chapter explores the ways that acts of resistance, transgression, and *desalambrar* [the undoing of fences] demonstrate how agency is being used to challenge and shift gender norms and the gender relations within families, friends, and communities. It is not a question of whether gender norms can be changed, but how they are changing, and how to raise the consciousness of change agents to see, support, and advocate for ongoing change. Young women and young men's ability and willingness to address gender norms that were restrictive to themselves or peers is influential in recognizing how gender relations are negotiated within the home and community spaces of El Valle and El Pino, Honduras. The narratives from within home and community spaces, or as Butler states, the "context of lives as they are lived" (2004, p. 8), draws attention to the "micro-transformations" (Arnot et al., 2012) that occurred as young women and men employed their agency for change. The experiences of Arianna, Milton, and the Sport and Culture Committee of the Youth Group do not represent large shifts in social structures, but they do represent a shift. Many of the issues around gender and agency in Honduras need to be addressed at multiple levels. Young women and young men benefit from having adults and community change agents mentor them and draw attention to the gendered social inequalities that exist within their homes and communities. The CARE Education Unit's work with the Sport and Culture Committee on understanding why girls should be included in a community-wide soccer tournament is a tangible example of how they enacted a shift in traditional gender norms. The receptivity of the young people in El Valle and El Pino to take in another point of view speaks to the fluidity of their life stage. Partnering with these young people in challenging and shifting traditional gender norms and practices that subordinated one gender to another was, and is, an opportunity for broad base change in gender relations.

References

Arnot, M., Jeffery, R., Casely-Hayford, L., & Noronha, C. (2012). Schooling and domestic transitions: shifting gender relations and female agency in rural Ghana and India. *Comparative Education, 48*(2), 181–194.

Bajaj, M. & Pathmarajah, M. (2011). Engendering agency: The differentiated impact of educational initiatives in Zambia and India. *Feminist Formations 23*(3), 48–67.

Bannion, I., & Correia, M. C. (Eds.). (2006). *The other half of gender: Men's issues in development.* Washington, DC: The International Bank for Reconstruction and Development/The World Bank.

Barker, G. (2006). Men's participation as fathers in Latin America and the Caribbean: Critical literature review and policy options. In I. Bannon & M. Correia (Eds.), *The other half of gender: Men's issues in development* (pp. 43–72). Washington, DC: The International Bank for Reconstruction and Development/The World Bank.

Bourdieu, P. (1977). *Outline of a theory of practice.* London, England: Cambridge University Press.

Bourdieu, P. (1990). *The logic of practice.* Stanford, CA: Stanford University Press.

Butler, J. (2004). *Undoing gender.* New York, NY: Routledge.

CARE, Republic of Honduras. (n.d.). Plan operativo anual de jóvenes. Tegucigalpa, Honduras.

CARE, Republic of Honduras. (2008). *Informe estudio situacional.* Tegucigalpa, Honudras: CARE Honduras.

CARE, Republic of Honduras. (2010). Education Unit data collection of El Valle and El Pino (the location names are pseudonyms), Honduras. Report compiled by CARE Education Unit. Tegucigalpa, Honduras.

Centro de Derechos de Mujeres (CDM). (2015). Mapa de las violencias contra las mujeres—Honduras 2015. Retrieved November 28, 2015, from http://www.derechosdelamujer.org/observatorio.html.

Connell, R.W. (2002). *Gender.* Cambridge, England: Polity Press.

Cresswell, J. W. (2007). *Qualitative inquiry & research design: Choosing among five approaches* (2nd ed.). Thousand Oaks, CA: Sage.

DeJaeghere, J., & Pellowski Wiger, N. (2013). Gender discourses in an NGO education project: Openings for transformation toward gender equality in Bangladesh. *International Journal of Educational Development, 33*, 557–565.

Deutsch, F. (2007). Undoing gender. *Gender and Society, 21*(1), 106–127.

El Heraldo. (2015, February 2). Proponen que se estudia la edad punible en Honduras: Al menos el 35% de los 187 mil miembros de pandillas en Honduras son menores de 18 años, según el Proyecto Victoria. Retrieved November 24, 2015, from http://www.elheraldo.hn/pais/792247-214/proponen-que-se-estudie-la-edad-punible-en-honduras.

Francis, B. (2006). The nature of gender. In C. Skelton, B. Francis, & L. Smulyan (Eds.), *The SAGE handbook of gender and education.* London, England: Sage.

Guttmacher Institute. (2006). Early childbearing in Honduras: A continuing challenge. In brief 2006 series, no. 4. Retrieved November 19, 2015, from http://www.guttmacher.org/.

Gutmann, M. C. (1996). *The meanings of macho: Being a man in Mexico City* (10th anniversary edition). Berkeley, CA: University of California Press.

Holter, O. & Borchgrevink, T. (1995). *Labour of love: Beyond the self-evidence of everyday life.* London, England: Ashgate/Avebury.

Honwana, A., & De Boeck, F. (Eds.). (2005). *Makers & breakers: Children & youth in postcolonial Africa*. Trenton, NJ: Africa World Press, Inc.

Husso, M. & Hirvonen, H. (2012). Gendered agency and emotions in the field of care work. *Gender, Work, and Organization, 19*(1), 29–51.

Instituto Nacional de la Juventud. (2007). *Política nacional de juventud 2007-2021: Por una ciudadanía plena*. Tegucigalpa, Honduras: Presidencia de la República de Honduras.

Johnson, B., & Christensen, L. (2010). *Educational research: Quantitative, qualitative, and mixed approaches* (4th ed.). Thousand Oaks, CA: Sage Publications, Inc.

Maira, S., & Soep, E. (Eds.). (2005). *Youthscapes: The popular, the national, the global*. Philadelphia, PA: University of Pennsylvania Press.

Maslak, M. A. (Ed.). (2008). *The structure and agency of women's education*. Albany, NY: State University of New York Press.

McCleary, K. (2013). *'Tomar decisions es el future de uno' [To make decision is one's future]: The gendering of youth agency within two Honduran communities*. Doctoral dissertation. Retrieved from ProQuest, UMI Dissertations Publishing (3607817).

McNay, L. (2000). *Gendering and agency: Reconfiguring the subject in feminist and social theory*. Cambridge, England: Polity Press.

Moll, A., & Renault, L. (2014). Rebirth, empowerment and youth leading social change: Nonformal education in Honduras. *Gender & Development, 22*(1), 31–47.

Molyneux, M. (2001). *Women's movements in international perspectives: Latin America and beyond*. London, England: Palgrave Macmillan.

Monkman, K., Miles, R., & Easton, P. (2008). The dance of agency and structure in an empowerment educational program in Mali and the Sudan. In M. A. Maslak (Ed.), *The structure and agency of women's education* (pp. 107–125). Albany, NY: State University of New York Press.

Montoya, R., Frazier, L. J., & Hurtig, J. (Eds.). (2002). *Gender's place: Feminist anthropologies of Latin America*. New York, NY: Palgrave Macmillan.

Murphy-Graham. (2009). Constructing a new vision: Undoing gender through secondary education in Honduras. *International Review of Education, 55*, 503–521.

Murphy-Graham, E. (2012). *Opening minds, improving lives: Education and women's empowerment in Honduras*. Nashville, TN: Vanderbilt University Press.

Olesen, V. (2005). Early millennial feminist qualitative research: Challenges and contours. In N. F. Denzin & Y. S. Lincoln (Eds.), *Handbook of qualitative research* (3rd ed., pp. 235–278). Thousand Oaks, CA: Sage.

Pine, A. (2008). W*orking hard, drinking hard: On violence and survival in Honduras*. Berkeley, CA: University of California Press.

Porter, F. (2012). Negotiating gender equality in development organizations: The role of agency in the institutionalization of new norms and practices. *Progress in Development Studies, 12*(4), 301–314.

Preito-Carrón, M., Thomson, M., & Macdonald, M. (2007). No more killings! Women respond to femicides in Central America. *Gender & Development, 15*(1), 25–40.

Programa Nacional de Prevención, Rehabilitación y Reinserción Social de Honduras. (2010). Situación de mara y pandillas en Honduras. Retrieved November 23, 2015, from http://www.unicef.org/honduras/14352_23534.htm.

Republic of Honduras. (1997). Ley contra la violencia domestica: Decreto no. 132–97. Tegucigalpa, Honduras: Corte Suprema de Justicia.

Republic of Honduras. (2000). Ley de igualdad de oportunidades para la mujer: Decreto no. 34-2000. Tegucigalpa, Honduras: El Congreso Nacional.

Republic of Honduras. (2006). La Gaceta: Ley marco para el desarrollo integral de juventud en Honduras. [Law on the integral development of Honduran youths]. Retrieved June 28, 2009, from http://www.inj.gob.hn/.

Sperber, A.D., Devellis, R.F., & Boehlecke, B. (1994). Cross-cultural translation: Methodology and validation. *Journal of Cross-Cultural Psychology, 25*, 501–524.

Steans, J. (2006). *Gender and international relations* (second edition). Cambridge, England: Polity Press.

Stromquist, N. P. (Ed.). (1992). *Women and education in Latin America: Knowledge, power and change*. Boulder, CO: Lynne Rienner Publishers.

Stromquist, N. P., & Fischman, G. E. (2009). Introduction—From denouncing gender inequities to undoing gender in education: Practices and programmes toward change in the social relations of gender. *International Review of Education, 55*, 463–482.

Swartz, D. (1997). *Culture & power: The sociology of Pierre Bourdieu*. Chicago, IL: The University of Chicago Press.

United Nations Office on Drugs and Crime (UNODC). (2013). *Global study on homicide*. Vienna, Austria: UNODC.

University of California-Hastings. (2011). Central America: Femicides and gender-based violence. Center for Gender and Refugee Studies. Retrieved November 20, 2015, from http://cgrs. uchastings.edu/our-work/central-america-femicides-and-gender-based-violence.

Watts, J. (2006). 'The outsider within': Dilemmas of qualitative feminist research within a culture of resistance. *Qualitative Research, 6*(3), 385–402.

West, C., & Zimmerman, D. H. (1987). Doing gender. *Gender and Society, 1*(2), 125–151.

Wolseth, J. (2008a). Everyday violence and the persistence of grief: Wandering and loss among Honduran youths. *Journal of Latin American and Caribbean Anthropology, 13*(2), 311–335.

Wolseth, J. (2008b). Safety and sanctuary: Pentecostalism and youth gang violence in Honduras. *Latin American Perspectives, 35*(4), 96–111.

Wolseth, J., & Babb, F. E. (2008). Youth and cultural politics in Latin America. *Latin American Perspectives, 161*(35), 3–14.

World Bank. (2012). Education statistics: Education equality (Honduras). Retrieved November 21, 2015, from http://databank.worldbank.org/data/reports.aspx?source=Education-Statistics:-Education-equality&preview=off#.

Exploring Boys' Agency Towards Higher Education: The Case of Urban Jamaica

Shawanda Stockfelt

Introduction

Boys are under-represented in higher education institutions across the English speaking Caribbean (Caribbean Community on Youth Development, 2010; Jha & Kelleher, 2006; Ministry of Education Youth and Culture, 2004). This is particularly the case in Jamaica where girls outnumber boys at a ratio of two to one. According to the Jamaican government, boys' failure to progress through the school system begins from year 9 where many drop out and join dangerous gangs in the inner cities (Government of Jamaica (GOJ), 2009a, 2009b). This creates a massive burden on the Jamaican society as a whole where, as early as 1996, nearly eight out of every ten arrests made by the police were presumably committed by males under the age of 30 (Chevannes, 2002). More recently in 2005, the Jamaica Constabulary Force reported Jamaica's murder rate a high 56 per 100,000 residents (United Nation's Office on Drugs and Crime, 2007). The National Security Policy of Jamaica (GOJ, 2013a) states explicitly that crime, violence and corruption, presumably by young men, are now the foremost threats to the overall economic welfare of the country. According to the policy, within the last decade, Jamaica has fallen 51 places in the world ranking, one of the most rapid declines in the world (GOJ, 2013a, pp. 6–7). This level of loss is normally equivalent to a profound catastrophic disaster; however, in the case of Jamaica economic development is retarded by crime and the fear of crime. The result is an investment in programs and strategies to encourage boys to complete secondary school and possibly progress into post-secondary education. One of the core objectives of the national security policy is to keep boys off the street and encourage them to view education as a means of social mobility. However, what are the root causes of their under-representation, and what are their aspirations

S. Stockfelt (✉)
Graduate School of Education, University of Bristol, Bristol, UK
e-mail: shawanda.stockfelt@bristol.ac.uk

© Springer International Publishing Switzerland 2016   121
J.G. DeJaeghere et al. (eds.), *Education and Youth Agency*, Advancing
Responsible Adolescent Development, DOI 10.1007/978-3-319-33344-1_7

towards higher education? Overall, what is the role of their personal agency within the dynamic structure between home, school, community, culture, and policies?

Educational aspiration is operationalized in this chapter as a desire and an intention towards higher education (Stockfelt, 2015). The term is conceptualized in relation to the literature and the narratives of the participants within the Jamaican research context. I explored these questions in relation to an ethnographic case-study conducted across two schools in urban, Jamaica. Theoretically, Bourdieu's theory of practice and the narratives of the boys themselves were used to discuss boys' educational aspirations and the role of agency in achieving them. The chapter begins with an outline of the background literature used to position and clarify the root of the problem. Bourdieu's theory of practice is then introduced briefly as the theoretical framework but placed within context of the Jamaican situation. The ethnographic approach is described and justified followed by a discussion of the findings rooted in the conceptual and theoretical framework.

Boys' Under-representation in Higher Education

Boys' under-representation is not unique to the Jamaican context but a reflection of a gendered social deviance that seems to be rapidly expanding across various countries globally (Education for All, 2009). Within the Caribbean, the literature attributes this to a variety of historical, cultural, economic and sociological factors. Overall, there seems to be a consensus that boys' under-representation is directly a result of their underachievement at the end of secondary schooling. Underachievement, defined in terms of boys' limited success in the Caribbean Secondary Examination Certificate, is based on Caribbean-wide standardized examinations taken at the end of secondary school across almost all subject areas, in which boys tend to have fewer passes at levels A–C across most subject areas. The Ministry of Education's 2013 results showed that only 37 % of those with five or more subjects at passes A–C were boys (Government of Jamaica, 2013b). This is the standard for matriculating into higher education, with only 3878 males achieving that standard to 7373 females in 2013 (Government of Jamaica, 2013b). Despite this disparity, boys in Jamaica are definitely not marginalized as they assume many leadership posts across social systems. According to Chevannes (2002), regardless of this educational discrepancy, males are usually in roles of power in the homes, schools, churches, and political institutions. For Chevannes, males' underachievement and subsequent under-representation is a case of under-participation, defined as lower enrollment, lower attendance rates and higher dropouts at mid to upper level of secondary schooling (2002). Such assertions in the literature put the focus more on personal agency in relation to other factors, such as the disadvantages experienced from lower socioe-conomic backgrounds. Chevannes (2002, 2005) thesis of male under-participation being a precursor for their under-representation has been supported by research in the literature (Caribbean Community Commission on Youth Development, 2010; Education for All, 2009; Evans, 2000; Ministry of Education

Youth and Culture, 2004; Parry, 1996; United Nation's Office on Drugs and Crime, 2007). The Global Monitoring report (Education for All, 2009) and the Caribbean Community (CARICOM) Commission on Youth Development report (Caribbean Community Commission on Youth Development, 2010), recognize this as a major problem that results in their eventual discontinuation in the school system.

Historically, some research highlights boys' under-representation as being linked to a gendered view of formal education that has its roots in slavery. According to Beckles (1996), males in Jamaica have undergone a form of hegemony during slavery where their masculinities were negated to an "otherness" not akin to power or glory (Beckles, 1996; Parry, 1996). Slavery existed for over 200 years in Jamaica. During that period, White slave masters had a right to abuse Black men in whatever capacity they chose fit. This was usually undertaken in a brutal manner in a bid to dominate and reduce any possibility of rebellion. According to Beckles (1996), the narratives in the literature of White slave owners showed how effeminate characteristics were transferred to the Black men through a variety of means. These included denying them their roles as fathers and husbands by taking/owning their wives and children. According to Johnson (1996), such practices helped to establish a distinct gender divide in attitudes, with Black men rejecting any behavior seen as "feminine" amongst themselves. Unfortunately, within a modern context, this sometimes has included excelling at formal or traditional schooling. Some sociologists perceive this gender-based view of formal schooling as stemming from cultural practices beginning from primary socialization. Miller (1991, 1992) pioneered the notion of male marginalization through a dominant colonial power impacting the Jamaican subculture. However, this notion has to be visited carefully as it has the potential of vilifying Black girls and further emasculating Black boys by removing their personal agency.

Other sociologists takes a different approach in explaining boys' apparent lack of progress into higher education; that is, boys' are under-participating in schools which leads to their underachievement at the end of secondary schooling and henceforth under-representation. According to the literature, (Bailey, 2003; Chevannes, 2002; Evans, 2000; Figueroa, 2000; Parry, 1996) the Jamaican culture prepares girls for the ethos of schooling that at the same time disadvantages boys. This is a socially constructed "feminized" version where girls co-exist as passive learners and boys are unable to fit in. According to Figueroa (2000), Jamaican males are actually more privileged and are socialized to be dominant, strong and tough. They are expected to be self-sufficient and the provider in their families. For many, schooling is not viewed as means to fulfill this obligation as it is not necessary to increase their earning power. On the other hand, this constructed image sees "femaleness" as sensitive, submissive, and needing protection. This view also sees female upward mobility as tied to their educational achievements and provides a sense of security. Chevannes (2005) theorized this aspect of the culture as stemming from the historical dimension that has infiltrated the home, school, and society.

According to Brown and Chevannes (1998) this gendered aspect of the culture results in parents encouraging more formalized education for girls but practical career-oriented ones for boys. By the time children begin schooling, boys value formal education much less. Brown and Chevannes (1998) view these cultural ideas as continuing within the schools, with boys receiving harsher punishments because of their attitudes to school, resulting in them fulfilling the expectation of being indiscipline and tough. This attitude is adopted by peer culture as well, with positive attitudes to formal schooling viewed sometimes as feminine. Such behavior may include the practice of Jamaican English versus the Jamaican Creole, spending time at home doing homework, conforming to school rules and getting high grades in traditional non-vocational subjects (Bailey, 2003; Brown & Chevannes, 1998; Chevannes, 2002; Evans, 2000; Figueroa, 2000; Miller, 1991). The result is a form of "feminization" of high academic performance that seems to reflect a marginalization that is self-inflicted.

In the literature, the historical and cultural dimensions of boys' under-participation in Jamaica have one thing in common, a consensus tied to a search and a need for economic independence. This might seem contrary since HE is seen as an important factor in development, especially for many low-mid-income countries like Jamaica. However, HE does not necessarily translate to economic independence for many in low-income countries, with a high level of unemployment amongst graduates. In addition, youths (ages 14–25) make up 30 % of the unemployed population. According to the Government of Jamaica (2009a), of the youth population, 26.2 % of the males are illiterate in comparison to only 7.9 % of the females. Of those who dropped out of secondary school, 25 % has below grade 9 level of education (p. 5). The Jamaican government theorized that for many boys from low-income backgrounds in the inner city, crime is seen as a way out of poverty. The United Nations Office on Drugs and Crime (2007), through multivariate regression analysis, identified a significant correlation between higher crime rate and lower education levels amongst large numbers of young men in Jamaica, Barbados, Trinidad and Tobago; highlighting the connection between gender, low-level of education and crime. Overall, boys are not transitioning into higher education, which is a problem for the Jamaican government as the future of the country depends heavily on its youth population.

The Role of Policy

At the level of policy, the Jamaican government views this under-representation as impacting the development of the country as a whole. Many studies have established a strong connection between education and development, based on the idea that investing in education will lead to economic growth as measured by the Gross Domestic Product (Cutler, Deaton, & Lleras-Muney, 2006; Hanushek & Wößmann, 2007; Jamison, Jamison, & Hanushek, 2007; Namsuk & Serra-Garcia, 2010; Preston, 2007). In this manner, education is seen as a human capital that will boost development. The Government of Jamaica white paper "Education: The way upward" that was tabled in parliament in 2001 stated, "The building of human and social capital represents our best hope for economic growth and social peace, the major requirements for an improved and sustainable quality of life." It also stated in an earlier format that: "This Green Paper 2000 represents a commitment of the Government of Jamaica to engage our people in the strongest possible partnership for development through education and training" (Ministry of Education, Youth and Culture, 2001). This policy aims to be achieved through an investment in education and skills that matches the current global trend and boosts Jamaica's competitiveness on the global market.

The important role that education plays in relation to economic growth is still evident approximately 10 years later, as presented in the new National Development Plan "Vision 2030 Jamaica," emphasizing a move away from "a lower form of capital" based on Jamaica's natural endowment from the soil and nature, to "higher forms of capital" including "human" and "knowledge." Amongst its many objectives, Vision 2030 aspires towards "world-class education and training" with a minimum requirement that pupils should successfully complete secondary schooling with a proficiency in English Language, mathematics, Information technology, a science, foreign language and a vocational subject (Government of Jamaica, 2009b). This also includes enhancing tertiary level education to establish an "innovative" and "knowledge-based" society. This policy focus on human capital in Jamaica is very much tied into the human capital theory propagated by aid/loan institutions like the World Bank and the International Monetary Fund through their establishment of finance driven reforms. These reforms included shifting public spending from higher to lower levels of education and opening the way for the private sector to fund secondary and higher education (Mundy, 2005). This means that parents in Jamaica share the cost of funding education with the government at the secondary level of schooling and to a much greater level at the tertiary. Even with Jamaica's recent middle-income status, this is still problematic as the larger portion of the population is working class. Shifting public spending away from secondary and tertiary levels of education increases social and economic inequalities based on levels of capitals that families have at their disposal to finance education.

Bourdieu Structure and Agency

A key theory utilized in this chapter is that of the French sociologist/anthropologist Pierre Bourdieu. Central to his theory is the notion of agency and structure and the connection between them. According to Bourdieu (1992), agency is the capability to engage in social action while structure consists of both material and symbolic contents co-created by us as agents. This chapter builds on this view of agency to present an extended re-conceptualized version; dynamic and malleable within the structures of the local and international policy context. Bourdieu (1992) views structure as existing when social practice becomes institutionalized into viable systems of power through which and within which agency becomes regulated. However, both agency and structure is united through practice. Practice is action or behavior on the part of agents that occurs consciously or unconsciously, based on habits or experiences, which Bourdieu (1977) defines as "doxa." This concept is used to explain a taken for granted belief, one that is seen as true by a society or a culture. Bourdieu perceives practice as being informed by agency; while at the same time this is limited by the objective structures in place within that culture.

In Jamaica, boys' educational experience is somewhat regulated on one hand by a centralized educational system influenced by top-down international policies from aid/loan organizations (e.g., the International Monetary Fund) and countries (e.g., the United Kingdom, the United States). Top-down is italicized to emphasize a clear-cut system of demand and control with respect to these agencies (Hill, 2014). On the other hand, the Jamaican diaspora exists as a strong form of bottom-up influence from localized agencies; that is, more in tune with family and/or agent-based aspirations. This may at times contradict the local/international educational policy expectations impacting on boys' personal agency. Understanding practice from such a framework includes a deeper exploration of Bourdieu's three key concepts: field, habitus, and capital. According to Bourdieu (1977), habitus are dispositions created within highly prescriptive social structures, i.e., beliefs that become "habituated" through primary and secondary socialization. Bourdieu defines habitus as "the durable installed generative principle of regulated improvisations [which produces] practices" (Webb, 2008, p. 36). These dispositions guide behavior and practice of agents.

Capitals are sources of advantage that is the basis for class differences (Bourdieu, 1986). They are three forms: social, cultural and economic. Social capital are those that create benefits from group memberships; cultural include non-financial assets like education; and economic are those stemming directly from wealth. Bourdieu surmised that both social and cultural capital is transferable to economic capital. Re-conceptualized within the Jamaican and research context, economic capital refers to the boys' socio-economic backgrounds[1] (Stockfelt, 2015, 2016); social capital as type of school (traditional grammar versus newly upgraded—see subsections "Schools"); and cultural capital as beliefs or dispositions towards and about higher education. Social capital was interpreted in this manner due to the level of credence it holds within these boys' educational space. Being included as a member of a traditional high performing school (School A) brand pupils as being smart, with a potential for success; while the latter school (School B) possessed no such value or prestige. Bourdieu views cultural capital in three ways: embodied, objectified and institutionalized. Cultural capital in its embodied form had the most relevance in the study as it focuses on dispositional traits influenced by beliefs.

Field exists as the space within which habitus develops. For Bourdieu, the concept of a field is quite layered and based on the different existing social forces (social structures and capitals) exerting their influence on the agents, internalized to create the habitus, and externalized by the habitus through agency and practice;

---

[1] Measured based on a summary of the following: occupation of parents (usually mothers as the sample reflected the Jamaican context of majority single-mother household), size of family, and number of individuals in one household and the location of their community (see Stockfelt, 2016, for a deeper discussion of SES in this context).

henceforth, exerting its influence within this field. Bourdieu (1990) defines field as structured spaces of positions with its own regulations and tiers of dominance, where agents compete for limited resources. Within the context of this paper, field is operationalized with respect to the educational space where these boys co-exist. I hesitate to label this as "school" as within the Jamaican culture and subculture, formalized education exists in a shared space between the home, school, community, and educational policies. Homework, extra-lessons, and after-school clubs were very much a part of the participants' learning spaces. Bourdieu's thesis perceives agents as being demarcated by their position in relation to their access to resources that confer power and status (capital) (Bourdieu & Wacquant, 1992). Their resultant experience based on their level of capital within their field help to define the intrinsic traits (habitus) of the agents themselves. However, within the local context, the Jamaican diaspora exists as an outlier that provides an alternate source of influence and possibilities that help shapes the educational experiences, practice, and agencies of these boys (see summary of findings below).

Ethnographic Approach

Exploring the notion of agency with respect to such a dynamic concept as aspirations requires a bottom-up, detailed qualitative methodology. An ethnographic "approach" was selected due to its bottom-up methodology that engages the researcher and the participants in a meaningful relationship (Samnani & Singh, 2013). Approach is placed in quotation since I moved away from the anthropological roots of ethnography and engaged with the participants in a reflective participatory manner. This is highlighted as the researcher shared much in common culturally with the participants. As a Jamaican, former teacher, and having been educated at numerous levels within Jamaica, I was able to relate to the young men with whom I worked. In addition, a systematic holistic approach was adopted to engage with pupils, teachers, parents and community members in an effort to gain an experiential understanding of the context and subculture in which these boys' educational aspirations were shaped.

The research was conducted between September 2008 and August 2009 across two secondary schools in urban, Jamaica: a traditional high achieving one (School A) and a newly upgraded low achieving school (School B) with high male drop-outs at/near year 9. The main method used was participant observations accompanied by semi/unstructured/narrative focus and one-to-one interviews. Sixty-four participants were included in the study. This is an approximate figure, as with the nature of participant observation, knowledge gained is sometimes through secondary observation and experience with others not directly participating in the study. The participants included mainly pupils with some parents, community members and teachers. The sampling method involved a mixture of snowball, random and purposive sampling. The pupils were selected randomly across year groups 7–11, the parents and teachers were selected purposively based on the involvement of their offspring/pupils, and community members were selected mainly through snowball sampling. Most of these group interviews were supported by random discussions at different time periods across both schools and throughout the research to ascertain a deeper level of understanding. The data were analyzed thematically using Nvivo for managing the dataset.

Jamaica has different types of secondary schools. Two main types were the focus of the study: traditional grammar and newly upgraded. These were selected as they represented two main contrasts within the Jamaican school system. Traditional grammar schools are those that have always been secondary schools and usually host pupils with the highest passes from the grade six achievement test. This is a standardized test taken at the end of primary schooling that determines which "type" of secondary school pupils are sent to. Pupils with the lowest scores are usually sent to newly upgraded or junior secondary (secondary schools that stops at year 9). In this manner, the education system creates a clear demarcation from the outset based on standardized grades. These grade six achievement test results are indirectly interpreted as measures of ability as pupils are grouped accordingly in a process known as streaming (Evans, 2000). An added consequence of this is a clear demarcation between the pupils based on social-class—or in a Bourdieuian context, economic capital. Pupils from lower socio-economic backgrounds tended to perform much worse at the secondary level, which creates further segregation as schools also practice internal streaming where pupils are grouped annually based on an end of year examination. The result is higher dropout rates for boys from lower socio-economic backgrounds at newly upgraded schools. School A represents a high status traditional school, while School B represented a lower status school with lower attainment at the Caribbean Secondary Education exams and higher drop-out rates for boys. This contrast was purposive to provide a comparative element in an attempt to understand the nature of boys' educational aspirations and the role of their agencies within their educational field.

Influence of Schools, Community and Family on Boys' Educational Aspirations

School, community and the family were identified as social structures that had the strongest impact on boys' personal agencies with respect to having educational aspirations. Boys regaled the positive impact of their maternal families, the negative impact of their communities and the surprising almost non-existent impact of their schools—except for the level of social capital it provided—as the reason for, or not, having educational aspirations. The positive role of maternal family had the strongest representation in the narratives, highlighted in its role in motivating educational aspirations and shaping positive dispositional beliefs about the role of higher education. These boys with maternal family support expressed strong desires/intentions to complete secondary school and move into higher education to establish careers, professions, or skills. This also includes further practical education, which for many without the economic means of financing university, was a way of staying in formal education and establishing viable careers for themselves. The inclusion of family members in the Jamaican diaspora in the United Kingdom, the United States, and Canada was quite common and represented an extension of their maternal family. For those boys with educational aspirations educational aspirations, their maternal family (locally and overseas) facilitated their agency by providing economic support and motivation, thereby allowing them to realize this.

The narratives surrounding the community included a tragic mix of fear of death and violence impacting their academic performance; as well as exemplary role models that motivated their educational aspirations. The role of the community as a deterrent to educational aspirations came mainly from boys in the inner city from lower socio-economic backgrounds. Their stories included intense fear of: being killed in gang-related activities when communities were at war; and being forced to drop out of school and join gangs to "protect" their communities or avenge the death of loved-ones and community members. In addition, many of these boys were unable to relate to success stories of higher education from within their communities — with the exception of community members that had migrated. An extended aspect of this theme involved an altruistic view of education for the greater good, linked to citizenship values that these boys "owned." Citizenship values emerged as a narrative of education being important for themselves as agents, their families, wider communities and the nation as a whole. As one young man commented:

> Miss, our (Jamaican) motto says out of many we are one people... Jamaica nah (not) go betta (better) unless we fix it... Right now, mi (my) mother deh a foreign a wash people dirty clothes fi (for) years fi (to) make sure me can get a good education...

Such ideas were common amongst participants across different backgrounds/ schools and highlighted two subthemes in relation to citizenship values. These values seemed to exist in isolation with respect to many boys from School B (lower attaining school) and those from lower socio-economic backgrounds. That is, they echoed these sentiments in relation to it being an ideal, an existence within a world where they all had the same level of capitals and henceforth opportunities. However, in practice they exhibited limited tolerance of education as seen in their lower participation in their school's day-to-day activities, and evidenced in their lack of educational aspirations. Additionally, these values reflected those embedded within the educational policies (see below), however, boys' "ownership" of them is related to the diaspora instead of the actual policies. "Foreign" is the Jamaican vernacular expression for the diasporic space that is usually the United Kingdom, Canada, and the United States. The above quote highlights the boy's respect and appreciation of his mother's hard labor (as a domestic worker) in the diaspora to boost economic capital and create a competitive opportunity for him through education.

The narrative about the role of the school in educational aspirations was astonishingly limited. When mentioned, boys tended to relate some positive and negative experiences with teachers that confirmed their already existing view of education as being important or pointless. At face value, this gave the impression that the role of school was minimal. However, what became apparent during follow-up interviews was the importance of the type of school these boys attended. This was already informed from the literature on streaming, however, as discussed below, boys exhibited different values toward education based on the schools they were affiliated with.

The Boys' Stories

The results of the study showed no comparative difference across both schools in the nature of these boys' educational aspirations. Their educational aspirations were goal-oriented and based on an instrumental view of higher education as a means to help them realize their life aspirations. In this manner, it was based on a desire and an intention towards higher education but the onus was more on an intention as most see higher education in terms of its transferability to economic and/or social capital. In doing so, boys tended to place the onus of their educational aspirations on them-selves, in this manner showing ownership of their agencies within the institutions of homes, schools, and communities. As one boy stated:

> Miss, we come here fi (to) drink milk, wi (we) nuh (do not) come here fi count cow; so mi (me) haffi (have to) work hard fi get weh (where) mi a go. Education a my milk, a nobody decision but my own whether mi go college or not... Some a dem (these) bwoy (boys) yah (here) a just a waste time... Fi dem choice!

Such sentiments were echoed by a majority across both schools. However, many from school B, the lower status school, tended to ascribe to the following:

> Yeah, a my decision (intention), but at the end of the day, what's the point? My teacher have up her degree and she live inna (in) my community (poor inner-city community)... Mi nah go bruk nobody house mek (so) police come shoot mi, but might as well go hustle (join the small informal business sector)... Education nuh (do not) mek (make) no (any) money unless yuh name Mr. So-and-So (implies a male that is wealthy) or yuh deh a foreign. (Jamaican diaspora of the United States of America, United Kingdom, and Canada)

Implicit within this argument and the narratives was the idea that having limited economic capital interacts with the transferability of higher education to wealth; therefore they felt as if they were exercising their personal agency by choosing not to have educational aspirations. The problem with such a viewpoint is that agency in such a context is not freely acted, but it is hindered by their perception of and/or actual position within that field and their belief about how this impacts them. Indirectly, their beliefs about the value of higher education is based on their view of social class, as both an economic and a social capital, as many viewed it as an exclu-sive group that replicates the social-structure that they have experienced within the confines of the inner-city. To elaborate, another boy explained:

> Miss, mi neva see nobody from my community get rich from college yet! Well, unless dem run (athletics) or play ball (football)... Sometimes yuh just tie yourself in debt and then yuh can't get a job... Unless embassy free yuh up. (implying migrating to the Jamaican diaspora)

In this manner, they related to their primary and secondary experience and obser-vation of and with higher education within their community to make—what they perceived as—an informed decision about their intention towards higher education. Such arguments connect with Bourdieu's critique of the space of school, that it repro-duces social inequalities (Bourdieu & Passeron, 1977). According to Bourdieu and Passeron (1977), education operates as a source of social control in its reproduction of social structures by the dominant class who utilizes their power to ensure schools operated in this manner. Pupils begin schooling on unequal footing based on their level of cultural capital. Schools do nothing to offset this, but instead reward those with higher capitals, henceforth increasing and maintaining inequalities. Working class pupils are theorized as passively accepting their "failure" based on class disadvantages, or establishing counter-school cultures as a form of resistance. Whatever their "choice" the outcome still results in reinforcing their subordinate positions.

The problem with this critique of the space of school within the Jamaican context was the fact that some boys across both schools, who were from lower socio-economic backgrounds, also had educational aspirations. The main reason provided in the narratives was what I referred to as *deferred higher educational aspirations* (Stockfelt, 2016). This is a term that was coined in relation to the result of the study that showed some boys across both schools reporting educational aspirations if the opportunity to migrate to the Jamaican diaspora presented itself. Boys who demonstrated and narrated this phenomena justified this based on their experience of witnessing family/community members becoming economically and socially successful through education only after migrating to these higher income countries and receiving an education. Here, boys did not demonstrate a passive acceptance of the rules of their field, neither failing nor rebelling, but aspiring towards a route not written into the script of their school but very common within their home/community environments. That is, Jamaica has a large diaspora in the United Kingdom, the United States, and Canada. The diaspora exists as an alternate form of income that provides economic capital to families and the country on a whole through remittance (McLean, 2008). According to McLean (2008), the diaspora accounted for 15.3 % of Jamaica's Gross Domestic Product in 2007. This figure was higher than Bauxite and tourism, which are two of Jamaica's main sources of income. The impact of the diaspora goes beyond the economic to encourage the development of cultural capital in its embodied state. This was identified within the narrative based on the constant encouragement and support provided by relatives in the diaspora to ensure the educational success of their younger family members in Jamaica. According to most boys, the diaspora echoes the message of "education for the greater good," "education to boost Jamaica's global competitiveness," "education to reduce crime/violence," and "education for personal/financial growth/gain." Participants at School A identified and echoed this in their narratives. This also occurred at School B, but viewed by many participants as "true" only if one migrated to the diaspora itself, or if one hailed from a higher social-class.

In many ways, the message from the diaspora supports the perspectives in the local educational policies. However, it seems to do so from a bottom-up practical view of education as a way to counteract the socio-economic inequalities within the society that were reproduced within the educational field of these boys.

Policy Perspective

Educational aspirations are multi-dimensional and develop throughout the socialization process within these boys' educational field, limited by the governing political and economic situation; that is, policies relating to cost sharing of secondary/tertiary education and the country's economic downturn, which decreases opportunities for employment. As reflected in the discussion so far, education was only viewed as a capital for these boys insofar as their perception of its transferability to economic and social capital. This revealed a discrepancy between a top-down policy implementation towards education for development, and the targeted "at-risk" boys' limited view and experience of it. That is, boys aspired towards schooling and higher education if they perceived it as a route to realize their wider life aspirations. "Life aspiration" is used here in reference to their overall and most distinctive goals and desires for the future—both intrinsic and extrinsic life goals. Intrinsic life goals are those stemming from the self and motivated from within, for example, goals like becoming the best they can be and pro-social ones like helping their family, community or their country (citizenship values) (Ryan, Huta, & Deci, 2008; Williams, Hedberg, Cox, & Deci, 2000). Extrinsic life goals were those based on outside motivation, like life aspirations towards wealth, fame and power (Kasser & Ryan, 1996). As explained by a boy from the inner-city at School A:

> All this war, killing and violence, not putting anything any better... I want to become a soldier, help people, help the community, stop the crime and all that stuff that has been going on in this country... That's why I need the subjects (getting the 5 A-C's synonymous with high attainment), you need this to go university and to get in the army... I need to educate myself so I can teach the little youths them... That was our parents responsibility, nuff (lots) a them failed, so it's up to us... Jamaica is up to us.

Such beliefs exhibit educational aspirations built on pro-social goals and feelings of responsibilities towards their immediate and local communities. Here boys voiced an intention towards higher education despite being disadvantaged by limited economic and social capitals. At School A, such ideas were usually accompanied by highly embodied cultural capital exhibited in their avid belief in the exchangeability of higher education for social and economic advancement. However, as mentioned earlier (see summary of findings), some boys—with limited economic and social capital—echoed this view but were more motivated by extrinsic life goals. At School B, these boys tended to have lower levels of embodied cultural capitals, that is, did not see higher education as being instrumental in attaining economic and social advancement. These boys represented the "at risk" category that is the target of many government policies to increase development and reduce crime rates.

Boys' educational aspirations become more complex when evaluating from the global perspective. The role of the diaspora existed as an anomaly that boosted the idea and the feasibility of boys having educational aspirations based on its narrative of education for socio-economic advancement. However, within the local context, this conflicted with the increased burden of the cost of higher education and taxation experienced by the private sector, i.e., a belief in the role of higher education unsupported by the reduced ability to support this. Such burden is a reflection of the overarching global trends and "tied" policies in relation to education and human development (Sullivan & Shreffin, 2003). For example, Jamaica receives loans from the International Monetary Fund based on a conditionality of acceptance of its neoliberal policies including those connected to education (International Monetary Fund, 2011; Johnston & Montecino, 2011). Jamaica also receives similar influence from the human capital agenda through aid/loan from the World Bank (World Bank, 2009). These reforms are sometimes seen as a deterrent to development as it limits the government expenditure on education, increase taxes and freeze wages; measures that may have a demoralizing impact on an already weak economy and structures (Johnston & Montecino, 2011). The result is a limited economy that in turn limits the experiences, possibilities and personal agency of the targeted population—youths.

As reported in the Jamaica Gleaner (Clarke, 2011), Mark Weisbrot, the director for the Centre for Economic and Policy Research, a think tank stated that, "Jamaica is a clear case where the International Monetary Fund and other international actors have put the economy in a straitjacket" (Clarke, 2011). This was further elaborated in the actual report by Centre for Economic and Policy Research concluding that:

> Jamaica's agreement with the IMF has included pro-cyclical macroeconomic policies during the current downturn. This unfavorable policy mix risks perpetuating an unsustainable cycle where public spending cuts lead to low growth, exacerbating the public debt burden and eventually leading to further cuts and even lower growth. (p. 19)

The International Monetary Fund agreement with Jamaica, places a high burden of taxation on a struggling private sector (parents) that is also "encouraged" by the World Bank to help finance higher education. The Government of Jamaica has abolished tuition fees at the secondary level of schooling to increase the quantity of the student population and meet their target for improved participation (Government of Jamaica, 2009b). However, while doing so, it reduced the subsidiary to HE and to payment of external examinations at the secondary level (Jamaica Observer, 2010). In addition, secondary schools still charge a fee equivalent to tuition, usually disguised as "maintenance" since the government has not provided proper replacement for the loss of this income. Overall, this situation creates a clear discrepancy between the view of education as an instrument for development and the reality of students/ families that are expected to finance this. Overall, the discrepancy between these two opposing principles, created by the overarching local (and global) political and economic situation impacted these boys educational field and placed a strain on the quality of education offered, as schools, staff, students and their families sometimes existed under economically and socially strenuous circumstances.

A male student's educational experience is related to the level of economic capital he has at his disposal. Evaluated within the context of this study, it is unsurprising that boys' educational aspirations are based on their instrumental view of its transferability to economic capital. If boys are unable to connect education to their wider aspirations, it is unlikely that they will aspire accordingly. The narratives showed a tendency of boys from lower socio-economic background and lower performing school (School B) has having educational aspirations that were contingent on the broader socio-economic environment. These pupils reported weaker beliefs in the value of education within the Jamaican context where many had no intention to move on to higher education and in extreme cases expressed the desire to drop out of secondary school altogether. This goes to the root of Jamaica's problem with boys' poorer participation in school and representation at the tertiary level. The government's abolishment of tuition fees at the secondary level of schooling was a step forward in terms of supporting their view of education as a means to enhance development, both on the part of pupils and for the country on a whole. It can be said — based on the result of this study — that these boys shared a similar and also different view of education to that of the government. The similarity existed in their instrumental view of education, i.e., its potential for intrinsic and extrinsic growth. However, they differed based on their extrinsic reality and beliefs about the value of education. Their extrinsic reality included not only their limited economic capital and sharing the cost of education, but their level of social capital is dependent on the "value" of their school within their educational field. Such capital is based on the view that these group memberships inferred limited academic ability and less potential for success through education. This view is not farfetched since, according to Evans (2000) and Bailey (2003), traditional grammar schools far outshine newly upgraded high schools on the major standardized high school examinations — the Caribbean Examination Council exams (now Caribbean Secondary Education exams). Bailey (2003) further elaborated that attaining five passes — including mathematics, English language and Information Technology — is connected to future attainment. Such perspectives are called upon in the government strategies supporting education as a human capital critical for development (Government of Jamaica, 2009a, 2009b).

The educational field that is comprised of structures of the family, school, community and the government (through educational policies) provides the context through which socialization occurs and dispositional beliefs about/towards higher education are shaped. These experiences are shared in a form of "class habitus" where boys' personal agency is mutually limited by their level of capitals in a false sense of autonomy; i.e., the view that practice is based on their personal agency. Personal agency is one of the ingredients behind them having educational aspirations or not, however, this is limited not only by their level of capital but also by the regulating structures with their educational field. The family and diaspora are structures that help to provide a route for boys to exercise their agency. However, the complex dynamic between the various structures within their educational field seems to result in a dynamic personal agency dependent on their perception of the possibilities, such as that evidenced in their *deferred higher educational aspirations*.

Discussion

Boys' agency is limited by the social structures within their educational field. This in turn affects practice, mediated by educational aspirations. Based on the nature of these boys' educational aspirations — goal-oriented, practical and connected to their life-aspirations — it seems necessary for them to see the link between schooling, education and practice in order for them to "have it." For example, in relation to the current global trend, the Jamaican government needs to focus more on skill-based education to enhance practical knowledge and increase employability. Therefore, at the school-level, it is critical to flag the importance of a skill-based further education along with higher education; to make clear the connection between education/

schooling and possible future outcome; and to expose boys to other possibilities or success stories of higher education outside of what they have experienced within their communities.

The significant influence of the family and community highlights the need to focus more on home-school-community cooperation. This could range from an active Parents Teachers Association to programs where relevant parents/community members could share their stories of success/failures, hopes/regrets with boys. Such real life stories may help to connect the content learnt in school, their level of partici- pation and the decisions they make about the future with that of their "real world." In this manner, making the connection between education and possible outcome as well as incorporating the family and the community. Such a venture could be more beneficial if the family/community of the diaspora were also involved in the process. This is quite relevant as most participants in the study identified a direct contact and positive influence of some family member(s) (and community) from the diaspora on their educational experiences and aspirations. Therefore, the diaspora could be incorporated more at the level of schools. This effort would match the government's objectives and reduce the possibilities of boys dropping out of the school system, joining gangs, and increasing the country's economic and social burden.

Finally, at the policy level, educational policies might be more effective if they match the needs of the target population. In this manner, understanding the educa- tional aspirations of these boys and finding ways to reduce the negative impact of limited capitals. For example, removing the practice of streaming pupils both at the beginning and during secondary schooling. Studies have consistently highlighted the positive impact of mixed-ability classes and the negative impact of streaming (Boaler, 2008; Higgins, Kokotsaki, & Coe, 2012). In addition, more needs to be done about providing materials like access to computers, after-school homework clubs etc., to make it feasible for boys disadvantaged by limited economical capital to thrive. The Government of Jamaica has attempted to improve instructional mate- rial—like access to computers—as stated in their policy (Government of Jamaica, 2009b). The impact of this is yet to be seen.

Conclusion

The chapter utilizes the literature to provide a detailed analysis of reasons for boys' under-representation in higher educational institutions in Jamaica. It offers an added explanation about the nature of boys' educational aspirations based on the findings of a study conducted across two very different schools in urban Jamaica. The find- ings are discussed in relation to Bourdieu's concept of structure and agency and the role these play in guiding practice. Boys' educational aspirations were shown to be goal-oriented, and based on a practical view of higher education in its transferability to economic and social capital. That is, boys tended to have educational aspirations insofar as their view of it as being instrumental for social and economic advance- ment. Generally, fewer boys from the lower status/achieving school (School B) and lower socio-economic backgrounds perceived higher education as important in the success of their life aspirations and tended not to have educational aspirations. The exceptions were those with deferred educational aspirations, encouraged by the Jamaican diaspora in the United Kingdom, the United States, and Canada. Overall, boys' agency to have and achieve educational aspirations or not is limited by social structures in relation to their level of capital within their educational field. However, the family and the Jamaican diaspora provide alternate possibilities that can counteract the disadvantages experienced from limited capitals and in turn can impact boys' personal agency.

References

Bailey, B. (2003). *Gender sensitive educational policy and practice: The case of Jamaica.* Kingston, Jamaica: UNESCO.
Beckles, H. (1996). *Proceedings from the West Indies Centre for Gender and Development Symposium: Black masculinity in Caribbean slavery.* Trinidad and Tobago: St. Augustine.
Boaler, J. (2008). Promoting 'relational equity' and high mathematics achievement through an innovative mixed-ability approach. *British Educational Research Journal, 34,* 167–194.
Bourdieu, P. (1977). *Outline of a theory of practice.* Cambridge, England: Cambridge University Press.
Bourdieu, P. (1986). The forms of capital. In J. G. Richardson (Ed.), *Handbook of theory and research for the sociology of education.* Westport, CT: Greenwood Press.
Bourdieu, P. (1990). *Sociology in question.* Cambridge, England: Polity Press.
Bourdieu, P. (1992). *Logics of practice* (R. Nice, Trans.). Cambridge, England: Polity Press.
Bourdieu, P., & Passeron, J. (1977). *Reproduction in education, society and culture.* London, England: Sage.
Bourdieu, P., & Wacquant, L. (1992). *An invitation to reflexive sociology.* Chicago, IL: University of Chicago Press.
Brown, J., & Chevannes, B. (1998). *Why men stay so?* Mona, Jamaica: University of the West Indies.
Caribbean Community Commission on Youth Development. (2010). *Eye on the future: Investing in youth now for tomorrow's community.* Georgetown, Guyana: Caribbean Community Commission on Youth Development.
Chevannes, B. (2002). What you wow is what you reap: Violence and the construction of the male identity in Jamaica. *Comparative Education, 2*(1), 51–61.
Chevannes, B. (2005). *Boys left out, from 'Gender achievements and prospects in education: The gap report'.* New York, NY: The United Nations Children's Fund (UNICEF). Retrieved December 15, 2015, from http://www.ungei.org/gap/interviewsChevannes.html.
Clarke, L. (2011, May 6). *Think tank says IMF agreement bad for Jamaica.* Retrieved December 11, 2015, from http://jamaica-gleaner.com/gleaner/20110506/business/business7.html.
Cutler, D., Deaton, A., & Lleras-Muney, A. (2006). The determinants of mortality. *Journal of Economic Perspectives, 20*(3), 97–120.
Education for All. (2009). *Overcoming inequality—Why governance matters. Education for All: Global monitoring report.* Retrieved July 15, 2015, from http://unesdoc.unesco.org/images/0017/001776/177683e.pdf.
Evans, H. (2000). *Gender differences in education in Jamaica.* Kingston, Jamaica: Planning Institute of Jamaica and UNESCO.
Figueroa, M. (2000). Making sense of male experience: The case of academic underachievement in the English-speaking Caribbean. *IDS Bulletin, 31*(2), 68–74.

Government of Jamaica. (2009a). *National report of Jamaica on the Millenium Development Goals.* Kingston, Jamaica: Planning Institute of Jamaica and Ministry of Foriegn Affairs and Foriegn Trade, Government of Jamaica.

Government of Jamaica. (2009b). *Vision 2030 Jamaica: National development plan.* Kingston, Jamaica: Government of Jamaica Planning Institute.

Government of Jamaica. (2013a). *A new approach: National security policy for Jamaica.* Kingston, Jamaica: The Government of Jamaica.

Government of Jamaica. (2013b). *Caribbean secondary education certificate (CSEC) examination 2013: Analysis of the public schools' performance.* Kingston, Jamaica: GOJ: Ministry of Education. Retrieved July 15, 2015, from http://www.moe.gov.jm/sites/default/files/2013%20 CSEC%20Report_0.pdf.

Hanushek, E. A., & Wößmann, L. (2007). *Education quality and economic growth.* Washington, DC: The World Bank.

Higgins, S., Kokotsaki, D., & Coe, R. (2012). The teaching and learning toolkit. *Education Endowment Foundation and Sutton Trust.* Retrieved December 15, 2015, from https://educationendowmentfoundation.org.uk/uploads/pdf/Technical_Appendices_(July_2012).pdf.

Hill, M. (2014). *Policy process: A reader* (2nd ed.). New York, NY: Routledge.

International Monetary Fund. (2011). *Jamaica: Third review under the stand-by arrangement staff report; informational annex; staff supplement; and the press release on the executive board discussion (No. Country Report No. 11/49).* Washington, DC: International Monetary Fund.

Jamaica Observer. (2010, January 27). Opposition concerns about impact of IMF on education. *The Jamaica Observer Online.* Retrieved December 11, 2015, from http://go-jamaica.com/ news/read_article.php?id=16363.

Jamison, E., Jamison, D., & Hanushek, E. (2007). The effects of education quality on income growth and mortality decline. *Economics of Education Review, 6*(26), 771–788.

Jha, J., & Kelleher, F. (2006). *Boys' underachievement in education: An exploration in selected commonwealth countries.* Vancouver, BC, Canada: Commonwealth Secretariat and Commonwealth of Learning.

Johnson, U. (1996). *Proceedings from the West Indies Centre for Gender and Development Symposium: The reconstruction of masculinity: Breaking the link between maleness and violence.* Trinidad and Tobago: St. Augustine.

Johnston, J., & Montecino, J. (2011). *Jamaica: Macroeconomic policy, debt and the IMF.* Washington, DC: Center for Economic and Policy Research.

Kasser, T., & Ryan, R. (1996). Further examining the American dream: Differential correlates of intrinsic and extrinsic goals. *Personality and Social Psychology Bulletin, 3*(22), 280–287.

McLean, E. A. (2008). *An investigation of recent trends in the remittance industry: Evidence from Jamaica.* Kingston, Jamaica: Bank of Jamaica.

Miller, E. (1991). *Marginalisation of the Black Jamaican male.* Kingston, Jamaica: Jamaica Publishing House Ltd.

Miller, E. (1992). *Men at risk.* Kingston, Jamaica: University of the West Indies Press.

Ministry of Education, Youth and Culture. (2001). *White paper: The way upward.* Kingston, Jamaica: Ministry of Education Youth and Culture. Retrieved January 20, 2009, from http:// www.moeyc.gov.jm/policies/whitepaper.shtml.

Ministry of Education, Youth and Culture. (2004). *The development of education: National report of Jamaica.* Retrieved January 20, 2009, from www.ibe.unesco.org/National_Reports/ ICE_2004/jamaica.pdf.

Mundy, K. (2005). Globalization and educational change: New policy worlds. In A. Bascia, A. Datnoa, K. Leithwood, & D. Livingstone (Eds.), *International handbook of education policy* (pp. 1–17). Dordrecht, The Netherlands: Springer.

Namsuk, K., & Serra-Garcia, M. (2010). *The effects of the economic crisis on the well-being of households in Latin America and the Caribbean.* New York, NY: United Nations Development Programme.

Parry, O. (1996). In one ear and out the other: Unmasking masculinities in the Caribbean class-room. *Sociological Research Online*. Retrieved December 11, 2015, from http://www.socre-sonline.org.uk/1/2/2.html.

Preston, S. (2007). The changing relation between mortality and level of economic development. *International Journal of Epidemiology, 3*(36), 484–490.

Ryan, R. M., Huta, V., & Deci, E. (2008). Living well: A self-determination theory perspective on eudaimonia. *Journal of Happiness Studies, 1*(9), 139–170.

Samnani, A. K., & Singh, P. (2013). Exploring the fit perspective: An ethnographic approach. *Human Resource Management, 52*(1), 123–144.

Stockfelt, S. (2015). Capital, agency, family and the diaspora: An exploration of boys' aspirations towards higher education in urban Jamaica. *Compare: A Journal of Comparative and International Education, 45*(1), 5–25. doi:10.1080/03057925.2013.812426.

Stockfelt, S. (2016). Economic, social and embodied cultural capital as shapers and predictors of boys' educational aspirations. *The Journal of Educational Research*. doi:10.80/00220671.2014.968911.

Sullivan, A., & Shreffin, S. (2003). *Economics: Principles in action*. Upper Saddle River, NJ: Pearson Prentice Hall.

United Nation's Office on Drugs and Crime. (2007). *Crime, violence, and development: Trends, costs, and policy options in the Caribbean*. United Nation Office on Drugs and Crime and the Latin America and Caribbean Region of the World Bank.

Webb, J. S. (2008). *Understanding Bourdieu*. London, England: Sage.

Williams, G. C., Hedberg, V., Cox, E., & Deci, E. (2000). Extrinsic life goals and health-risk behaviours in adolescents. *Journal of Applied Social Psychology, 8*(30), 1756–1771.

World Bank. (2009). *Jamaica-World Bank group country partnership strategy: 2010–2013 (consultation report)*. Kingston, Jamaica: World Bank International Finance Corporation.

The Last Great Hope for Transforming the Lives of Girls: The Rhetorics of Girls' Education in Upper Egypt

Mohamed K. Sallam

Introduction

Since the early 1990s young women and girls have been the focus of much of the development work undertaken in Egypt. While development remains multi-faceted, education is widely understood to play a key role in promoting gender equality and economic empowerment. These educational interventions, targeting girls and young women, aim to empower them through skills, mainly literacy and numeracy, regarded as a necessary first step to overcome social and cultural barriers associated with transitions to adulthood (namely early marriage practices and cost-prohibitive marriage customs) and realize their development potential.

Educational interventions in Egypt associated with two major international development strategies (1990 Child-friendly Schools Movement and 2000 Girls' Education Initiative) were implemented against already complex socio-cultural and political landscapes (UNICEF, 2007). Many of the communities targeted by these strategies were located in rural areas, as it was understood that girls and young women living in these contexts had little to no access to quality education. Since much of the coordination of these programs took place in urban centers, international development programs targeting rural residents were enmeshed in broader socio-cultural and historical debates concerning the rural–urban divide in Egypt.

The purpose of this chapter is to complicate the core–periphery binary that for decades has been used to describe the social, political, and spatial order that exists between Egyptians living in the urban centers of Cairo (and to a lesser extent Alexandria) and the residents of outlying regions, particularly in Upper Egypt.

M.K. Sallam (✉)
Pan-Afrikan Center, Augsburg College, Minneapolis, MN, USA
e-mail: sall0063@umn.edu

© Springer International Publishing Switzerland 2016   139
J.G. DeJaeghere et al. (eds.), *Education and Youth Agency*, Advancing
Responsible Adolescent Development, DOI 10.1007/978-3-319-33344-1_8

This divide is significant as it is suggestive of how participants articulate relationships of power that operate upon spatial and temporal constructions of modernity, in which Cairo is Egyptian modernity and much of Upper Egypt is pre-modern. Through examining the *Ishraq* (Sunrise) program, this chapter illustrates how a second-chance girls' education intervention can exacerbate the divide that exists between Cairo and rural Upper Egypt by enhancing the role of teachers and program staff at the expense of students. Inspired in part by the 2000 Girls Education Initiative, Population Council (large United States-based international NGO) developed Ishraq with the understanding it could serve as the last hope for reaching the out-of-school population of adolescent girls in rural Upper Egypt through literacy and life skills training (Population Council, 2007).

The Ishraq program frames formal education as an integral social dimension for adolescent girls to realize their development potential, and to enhance their ability to have more voice in matters affecting their lives. Through highlighting the critiques of Abu-Lughod, Adely, and Hasso (2009) and Adely (2012), this critical poststructural analysis reveals how Ishraq draws on the neoliberal rhetorics of agency and empowerment deployed across the international development landscape as the basis for intervening in the lives of girls and young women in rural Upper Egypt. These critical feminist scholars argue the Middle East and North Africa (MENA) is uniquely and decisively cast as having a retrograde culture, making enhancing the status of women and girls possible only through large-scale external reforms. These critiques not only complicate what it means for development programs to promote empowerment and agency for women, they push practitioners and scholars to consider the broader historical context, socio-cultural realities, and structural conditions that affect the lives young women and the communities where they live.

In discussing the legacy of educational intervention in Egypt since the colonial period (1882–1922), this analysis draws on Mitchell's (1988, 2002) works concerning the mechanisms of social control used by the British colonial administration as they relate to the practice of schooling. This contextual framing is particularly important as Ishraq was implemented against the backdrop of larger national level reform strategies. Through a critical examination of Ayrout's (1938, 2005) work on rural development and Egyptian peasant life during the interwar period, this analysis illustrates how the State and non-State actors historically favored interventions that focus on eradicating behaviors deemed "backwards" or "pre-modern" in rural areas. In addition to this historical analysis, this chapter draws on ethnographic fieldwork conducted over a 6-month period between 2011 and 2014 to reveal the uneven experiences of Ishraq staff and students are largely sustained through the schooling practices employed by teachers. Through examining program documents and conducting interviews with program staff and their locally based Egyptian NGO partners, this chapter demonstrates how Ishraq is contributing to an emergent binary in Upper Egypt that places girls' education at the center of the divide that exists between residents of rural communities and those living in urban areas.

Conceptualizing Girls' Education and Agency in the MENA

To examine the rhetoric of *agency* and *empowerment* applied to the MENA region, the conceptual framework for this research draws on Said's (1978) work *Orientalism*. This seminal piece of postmodern social theory interrogates the ways in which the *Orient*, or the MENA, has been intentionally and un-intentionally fashioned, through a process of knowledge production, into a region with an unchanging and retrograde cultural legacy. Said (1978) argues the representations of Arabs and/or Muslims are produced to cement the region as subservient to the West, rendering the lands and people of the MENA as legitimate targets for intervention. This work is particularly useful for examining how the expert knowledge typically represents youth in the MENA, particularly young women, as lacking essential cultural qualities that make it possible to develop and/or enact agency. In the context of this analysis, Ishraq can be understood as promoting some of these same colonial era (and more recently neoliberal) notions of empowerment that conflate individualism with enhanced forms of agency.

Several leading critical-feminist scholars have applied Said's (1978) critiques to international development policy and practice. In her work on the women's mosque movement in Egypt in the 1990s, cultural anthropologist and feminist theorist Saba Mahmood (2005) challenges the notion that enacting agency is synonymous with resisting hegemonic patriarchal social structures. This is described as *oppositional agency*, and until recently has been promoted externally as the only legitimate form of agency for women in the MENA to strive towards. She argues these narrow considerations emerging from Western notions of personhood, individualism, oppression, and freedom have come to define the extent to which development programs, interventions, and social movements taking place in Egypt are deemed successful and/or transformational. Despite this critique, Ishraq program documents implicitly frame individualism (a product of enhanced forms of agency) for girls as the solution for addressing the gender-based discrimination that prevails in rural Upper Egypt and is preserved by male relatives (Population Council, 2013). More recently, in their work Abu-Lughod et al. (2009) argue that empowerment and the promotion of agency in the MENA remains the end game for most development theorists and practitioners, where education for women and girls is understood to serve as the primary vehicle for creating and sustaining change. Specifically, drawing on her years working in Jordan, Adely (2012) contends that young women understand how others (particularly in the West) perceive them, and are aware of the narratives that describe education as the gateway to empowerment. Adely (2012) goes on to suggest that the homogenization of women in the MENA and the treatment of their cultural "condition" coupled with prevailing notions of agency and successful womanhood, "makes it difficult for us to recognize alternative goals and behaviors as important and powerful" (p. 13).

Drawing on the works of these scholars is essential for beginning the work of disentangling broader social, political, historical, and structural dimensions of power that have come to shape the experiences of adolescent girls, teachers, and staff associated with the Ishraq program. In this case what is more important than examining the extent to which the program empowers girls through literacy and life-skills training, is that programs like Ishraq can also perpetuate and enhance certain social, political, and spatial hierarchies in Egypt.

Contextualizing the Research

Upper Egypt and the "Modern" Egyptian Development State

Upper Egypt has occupied a very unique place in Egyptian history since before the colonial period. This region is home to nearly one-third of the Egyptian population, and extends along the Nile River more than 500 miles southward from below Cairo to Aswan. This region is geographically, linguistically, and culturally distinct from the Nile Delta in the north, Red Sea coast to the east, and the Western Desert area. Upper Egypt is frequently presented in popular media as largely poor and destitute, whose residents use strong family ties and tribal networks to defy the authority of local officials to the detriment of the State (Hopkins & Saad, 2004). Additionally, ethnic and religious differences among residents and a culture of social conserva-tism are often blamed for social and political disputes. For decades these types of descriptors have created an overly simplified and inaccurate narrative of a socially, culturally, and religiously diverse region of the country (Hopkins & Saad, 2004).

These problematic depictions are taken up in the ways Ishraq program staff explain how Upper Egyptian parents intentionally and maliciously falsify their chil-dren's birth records to postpone their sons serving in the military or to avoid accusa-tions of violating early-marriage laws[1] (Fouad, 2015). The State has tended to see this behavior as associated with the region, while many parents simply feel they are act-ing in the best interest of their families. Parents who are found guilty of defrauding the State not only run the risk of being jailed, their children are often not able to enroll in school or access government hospitals, clinics, and/or other public services.

The development profile of Upper Egypt during the last three decades has rein-forced problematic characterizations of residents (particularly those living in rural areas) that have come to dominate the social and political landscape in Egypt. Since the 1980s, the State and private companies have targeted rural contexts as sites for significant industrial investment and development. However, aside from a small number of superficial attempts to include Upper Egyptian farmers and business owners, the national government has largely left these residents out of national development discussions. These conditions account in part for the disparities in educational access that exist between Upper Egypt and the rest of the country

---

[1] Law No. 126 of 2008 amended the provisions of the Child Act (No. 12/1996), defining a child as any persons younger than 18 years of age, and by extension under the age of consent for marriage (Al-Jarida Al-Rasmiya, 2008).

(Hopkins & Saad, 2004). The 2003 *Egypt Human Development Report* (UNDP/INP) indicates, despite the efforts of the 1990s to enhance educational access for girls in Upper Egypt, the literacy rate for women in rural Upper Egypt remained around 20 %. The national urban rate (both men and women) for that same year was 78.5 %. The same report also indicates the national literacy rate in 2003 to be 65.6 %, while the rate of those living in Upper Egypt (rural and urban) was 56.4 %.

In the past, the tension described above has created mutual resentment between the State and Upper Egyptian communities. More recently, the international development community used the demographic profile of Upper Egypt to compel Egyptian policy makers to support the implementation of the aforementioned educational reforms of the 1990s and 2000s, which brought the region greater attention. More recent reports suggest the disparities in school enrollment and completion between urban and rural residents have been greatly reduced (UNICEF, 2007). Despite these positive developments, the implementation of educational interventions in Upper Egypt has come at the price of reinforcing already narrow characterizations of the region.

Ishraq

Following the Millennium Declaration of 2000, Egyptian policy makers partnered with UNICEF to develop the GEIE, a large-scale reform aimed at providing educational access to girls and women at various levels. While this effort proved successful in increasing net enrollment from around 80 % at the primary level to over 90 % in less than a decade, it was not necessarily designed to meet the needs of the out-of-school population (UNICEF, 2007). In the decade that followed the implementation of this initiative the overwhelming majority of children who previously enrolled in primary school and did not return were girls and young women, particularly those living in remote rural areas in Upper Egypt. In 2001, the Population Council's Cairo office unveiled a program targeting adolescent out-of-school girls from the poorest governorates in Egypt (nearly all of which are located in Upper Egypt) to address the areas not met by the national level reform (Population Council, 2013).

The Ishraq program was designed to provide Egypt's most marginalized girls aged 12–15 with opportunities for a second chance by preparing participants to successfully complete school re-entry exams. The goal of Ishraq was to transform the lives of participating adolescent girls through literacy and life-skills training. Specifically, "The program [was] intended to raise self-confidence and empower girls and young women to make informed choices by increasing knowledge and building the skills required to apply that knowledge to real-life situations" (Population Council, 2007, p. 13). Additionally, Ishraq's curriculum included special attention to reproductive health, civic engagement, and access to organized sports. These curricular dimensions were designed so that students who complete the program would not only pass the school re-entry exam, but also go on to complete secondary and in some cases post-secondary school (Population Council, 2007).

Ishraq program objectives also suggested that girls' entry into government schools and completion of the life-skills curriculum represented a last hope for them to experience personal transformation and for broader social reform in rural Upper Egypt, thus implying that as girls become more agentic they will also positively affect their communities. At the completion of the pilot phase (2004), Ishraq expanded from four villages with 50 participants per village to more than 30 villages with over 5000 participants. Ishraq was in operation until the summer of 2013 and was implemented in three phases: program pilot (2001–2003), expansion (2004–2007), and scale-up (2008–2013). In order to grow and sustain the intervention over such a long period of time, Population Council sought out partnerships and funding opportunities from numerous private and governmental (international and domestic) organizations and agencies. Additionally, Population Council employed a program director in each of the urban centers in Upper Egypt where the program was operating to oversee the activities at the local level. At the local level, Ishraq program staff were responsible for forging strategic relationships with local government officials and community members to ensure the program would be appropriately supported throughout the different levels of implementation. The regional program director was also charged with managing partnerships with local organizations, particularly the locally based NGOs that were contracted to implement the program at the village level. These organizations were made responsible for hiring teachers from Ishraq communities, mobilizing community support (through community meetings and home visits), and providing the logistical support for all monitoring and evaluation activities (Population Council, 2013). Ishraq teachers were civil servants who previously worked as either licensed (through the Ministry of Education) public schoolteachers or with the *Department of Adult Education* (DAE)[2] as licensed adult-literacy instructors.

Methodology

The methodological considerations this analysis employs are informed by critical and poststructural theoretical frameworks. Over the last two decades, educational researchers have utilized these approaches to explain human phenomenon as socially constructed and historically and contextually contingent on power differentials (Howarth & Griggs, 2012). This approach is adept for examining far-reaching implications of national development strategies and their socio-cultural effects not typically captured by mainstream development metrics (Adams et al., 2001). Additionally, these frameworks attempt to apply interpretive logics to socio-cultural worlds from program design that takes place at the transnational level to implementation at the most local levels (Levinson & Sutton, 2001). Practically speaking,

---

[2] The DAE serves as the primary governmental partner for all public or private programs working in the areas of literacy and/or basic education (Population Council, 2013).

poststructural approaches include a broader range of questions concerning power, more so than conventional outcomes based analysis of program effectiveness that utilizes linear and inferential reasoning.

In examining the complex relationship between Population Council and its Ishraq partners, this chapter presents data from a combination of textual analysis and open-ended interviewing techniques. This study also utilizes intertextual analysis (Fairclough, 1992) to examine the dialogic qualities of texts, particularly in the relationship between historical literatures on development in rural Upper Egypt and the 2007 and 2013 Ishraq program reports. Intertextuality refers specifically to the ways texts communicate by building on previous knowledge and as a result contribute to and reinforce existing discourse/s. Fairclough (1992) suggests the two types of intertextuality, manifest and constitutive (the focus of this analysis centers on the latter), are different strategies employed by authors unconsciously to bolster a given argument. Constitutive intertextuality involves *indirect* references to prior knowledge and not necessarily specific texts. Identifying the ways in which constitutive intertextuality operates in these reports is essential for examining the role power plays in legitimating particular understandings concerning colonial-era and contemporary notions of empowerment and agency in rural Upper Egypt. Examining constitutive intertextuality is an essential component for uncovering the hidden meanings found in texts, and represents their relationship to social practices and to the social world at large (Fairclough, 1992).

To examine the experiences of former Ishraq participants and teachers, this study employed open-ended interviews and informal conversations. The purpose of open-ended interviewing techniques was to provide participants with the opportunity to lead conversations about the thematic areas of the study. This informal approach to the interviews and conversations was more appropriate given the social and cultural context, and congruent with the ethnographic design and interpretive assumptions that inform this study (Fetterman, 2010).

During three visits to Egypt between 2011 and 2014, I conducted interviews with a total of 25 women; 18 former Ishraq participants ages 18–24 and seven teachers all between the ages of 35 and 50. All of the women were from the same villages in Beni Suef, Upper Egypt where Ishraq operated during the programs "Expansion Phase" between 2004 and 2007. Additional observations and informal conversations took place during field visits with many other community members around the Youth Centers[3] where the girls studied, and were almost all of the interviews took place. I conducted the interviews in Arabic, and translated their meanings into English from an audio recording. During the summer of 2014 I also worked intermittently with Mona (a pseudonym), a Cairo-based educational researcher who volunteered to participate in two field visits to Beni Suef that took place over a 2-week period. In addition to facilitating some of the focus group interviews with Ishraq

---

[3] Youth centers are public facilities that operate under the direction of the Ministry of Youth and Sport, and are located in nearly every community (rural and urban) across Egypt (Population Council, 2013).

teachers, she was present during a small number of interviews conducted with former Ishraq participants and program staff. The logistical arrangements for planning visits to Ishraq villages were facilitated by a program director from a locally based NGO (one of many) responsible for overseeing the implementation of Ishraq across Upper Egypt. The director was among the women interviewed for this study and her experiences are discussed later in the chapter.

Findings

Education as Nizam, *Rural Life as* Fouda

Through discussions and interviews with former Ishraq participants, teachers, and program staff, classroom dynamics emerged as one of the most important themes for examining how notions of empowerment and agency were taken up in the daily lives of those associated with the program. Ishraq teachers across the various centers shared during the interviews that establishing and maintaining order (*nizam*) in the classroom was the most significant challenge in their implementation of the Ishraq curriculum. More importantly, teachers discussed establishing order through employing mainly non-physical disciplinary practices as necessary for combating the chaos (*fouda*) they believed presides over the lives of adolescent girls in rural Upper Egypt. For many teachers, participants who learned to enjoin *nizam* ("order") where described as "in control," which in turn was framed as a prerequisite for participants to become agentic youth. This "order" included codified frameworks and structures operating as mechanisms of control and surveillance in modern social contexts. In the context of this analysis these are best described as the pedagogical techniques and schooling practices employed by Ishraq teachers. The order–chaos binary served as a discursive formation, where the social and cultural values of rural Upper Egyptians were understood as incompatible to enacting agency, and therefore required modification in order to operate more effectively within the bounds of modern systems of power.

In a focus group interview with three Ishraq teachers, Sana,[4] a woman in her late 20s who had been an adult literacy teacher with a government sponsored program in a neighboring village shared:

> The girls would regularly come to class with messy hair and tattered gowns and scarves. They often spoke in a rough tone with each other and when addressing the other teachers. Early in the course the girls did not know the rules, so we needed to be very gentle with them, but also very firm so that there would not be chaos in the class. If we found girls fighting (physically) with each other we would handle them until they would stop. We never hit them, but we would isolate the girls who caused the most trouble until they were ready to

---

[4] The names of all study participants are pseudonyms.

follow the rules. Since we did not hit the girls who were misbehaving we would tell them that we would not let them return to the class if they did not stop. Many of these girls never had the opportunity to attend school before. So, it is important that they know they have to sit quietly in their chairs and respect their classmates, so that when they leave Ishraq and go on to middle school they are the most respectable and professional.

When asked what they believed were the causes for poor classroom dynamics, there was a general consensus among these three women that the disharmony was largely an outgrowth of the chaotic family situations girls experienced at home. Two other teachers explained that parents and older family members often employed ineffective disciplinary practices when dealing with their adolescent girls, such as yelling and hitting. After asking each of the three women to clarify how they understood the relationship between the girls' home life and participation with Ishraq, Fatima, an Ishraq teacher in her late 30s provided the following perspective:

The parents we deal with often discipline their children in random ways. A lot of times it doesn't make much sense. Some days a girl may say that she was reprimanded at home for doing something that her father or mother just doesn't want her to do at that moment. Parents may yell at their daughter at these times and when their daughter does the same thing the next week nothing happens, and it's okay. This is why we often have trouble with the girls when they are in class. They are used to adults in their families being upset with them in random ways. At the same time a father may be very happy with their daughter and her progress in the program one day, and the next time will not express the same kind of pride for what their daughter has accomplished. Sometimes this is because parents don't fully understand what their girls are accomplishing. One time my student was talking to me about something her parents said to her after she passed her literacy exam. They asked her, "What are you going to do now?" When she told them that passing the exam meant that she could continue to go to school they would say, "Why don't you just get a job with your literacy certificate so that you can save money until the right suitor comes along?" Many parents just don't understand.

At the surface, what is described in these conversations represents the different and presumably effective approaches to classroom management employed by Ishraq teachers to create safe and productive learning environments for their students. It also represents a sort of "clinical gaze" upon the rural subject by the teachers. The order–chaos duality was reflected in how the Ishraq teachers understood the educational intervention as a catalyst for producing personal and social transformation based in colonial-era understandings of life in rural Egypt, particularly in the south.

In her work examining the intersections of education and child rearing in the nineteenth and early twentieth century Egypt, Shakry (1998) writes, "Crucial to the discourses of *tarbiya* [upbringing or education] was the indigenous concept of *adab*, entailing a complex of valued dispositions (intellectual, moral, and social), appropriate norms of behavior, comportment, and bodily habitus (p. 127)." Shakry (1998) goes on to suggests that in the Egyptian case it was not the influence of the European colonial project alone that created the conditions for the emergence of the modernizing discourses of noble mothering and domesticity. The rise of nationalist modernizing projects including integrating women in education systems with the hopes of fashioning an ideal modern Egyptian family where mothers are understood as responsible for the moral and physical upbringing of their children, as well as master caretakers of the home. Nonetheless, these colonial and anti-colonial (liberal-secularist and Islamist) discourses on mothering and motherhood where largely in agreement on what was understood as the backwardness of poor and rural Egyptians, chaotic home lives. These discourses (albeit in contention at times) produced normative conceptions of child rearing and domesticity in which order and cleanliness of the home and of home life represented the model for transforming Egypt's poor and rural social classes.

The order–chaos duality is also examined in Mitchell's (1988) work on colonial discourses in nineteenth century Egypt, wherein the author argues the practice of schooling during this period aimed to disrupt the pre-colonial master–pupil relationship that centered on the idea of largely unsupervised individual apprenticeship. Like many pre-colonial institutional mechanisms, this pedagogical approach failed to satisfy fundamental conditions of modern schooling, namely the establishment of order through discipline and the use of surveillance as a form of control. As cited in Mitchell (1988), the Inspector-General of Schools (appointed in 1873) explained a teacher's influence over a student as:

> …a magnetic fluid which transmits itself in a manner that is slow, hidden, and permanent… without external manifestation. At the moment when you attempt to surprise it, it may be absent, because it does not like to be under surveillance. Remove yourself and it will return, reactivated once more; the current will be reestablished. (p. 79)

Mitchell (1988) goes on to report that colonial accounts regarding the state of education, and particularly religious schooling, provided the necessary evidence for making the case for large-scale education reform in Egypt. Also, included in these accounts are descriptions of scholars at the most famed Egyptian Islamic institution Al-Azhar. These educators, mentors, and scholars of Islamic theology and jurisprudence are portrayed almost exclusively by colonial writers as incapable of stimulating the intellectual curiosity of their pupils due to their apprenticeship-based academic training. Similarly, their students were portrayed as lacking direction and discipline, while their learning environments (open spaces in mosques) were characterized as haphazard, noisy, and endlessly distracting.

Scholars like Said (1978) and more recently Massad (2001, 2007) draw attention to how colonial-era thinkers systematically distorted social and political life of the peoples and places associated with the Middle East and North Africa in their writings. These critical scholars characterize colonial-era accounts and writings as destructive expressions of colonial power. Like Ishraq teachers, British colonial reformers and their Egyptian collaborators understood *fouda* ("chaos") as manifesting the reality that requires relentless attention. The educational experiences of the Ishraq have largely been shaped by these nearly 150 year old reforms.

The observations shared by Ishraq teachers are the representation of how the social and cultural values held by rural Upper Egyptians are understood by the program staff as essentially incongruent with modern life. The "chaos" that enveloped these young women was characterized as a seemingly insurmountable barrier to establishing order in one's life. The teachers' views also exemplified how these disciplinary discourses could be internalized in framing the establishment of order in the classroom as a necessary precondition for addressing the chaos that prevailed in young women's home lives. Rather, on the subject of classroom management, these teachers appeared convinced that order in the classroom necessarily precedes personal growth and development. Ishraq teachers almost always discussed classroom management as a struggle between establishing order and repelling chaos. The importance of order as a necessary condition for effective classroom management speaks to the central role the order–chaos binary played in the work of Ishraq program staff at the local levels.

After examining Ishraq program documents and through asking related questions to program officers, it was difficult to conclude whether the dynamics of order–chaos describe above were solely a result of program implementation on the part of local staff. In the context of this study, Ishraq teachers' insistence on disrupting certain types of classroom behavior and outward appearances deemed disorderly points to deeper structural conditions of privileging of colonial-era understandings of order in schooling contexts. In this regard, it became clear that those responsible for designing and implementing of the Ishraq program simply reproduced the views of early colonial reformers and their postcolonial replacements in their treatment of life in rural Upper Egypt as a foil to modernity. The Ishraq Final Report (Population Council, 2007) further illustrates this point:

> Adolescence represents the last opportunity to prepare girls for the challenges of adulthood. Failure to reach girls now may well doom them to lives of isolation, poverty, and powerlessness. It also may be their last chance for organized learning and play. In rural Upper Egypt, participation in the Ishraq program provides disadvantaged girls the opportunity for structured learning, mentoring, and participation in community life. (p. 39)

These program reports suggest a clear link between adolescent girls experiencing organized and structured learning and play and the extent to which they are able to effectively navigate the challenges associated with transitioning to adulthood. It also creates a perspective that without Ishraq, the young women in rural Upper Egypt are likely to suffer from generational poverty and social exclusion. Additionally, it is understood that without appropriate intervention, the lives of girls in rural Upper Egypt lack the discipline required to overcome social and cultural barriers.

Similarly, the experiences of the young women included in this study demonstrate how teachers' notions of "order" can be internalized as well as how "chaos" is problematized by girls themselves. The following example complicates the rigid notions teachers held about the lives of women in rural Upper Egypt, while addressing how former participants were affected by the order–chaos binary. During a conversation with Shaymaa, a 24-year-old Ishraq graduate, she suggested there is a great deal of instrumental value in education. She argued that women with higher levels of educational attainment are able to more effectively negotiate the terms of their marriages. Later in the conversation she stated that women who are educated are generally happier and that their lives are more disciplined than those who live in rural areas and have lower educational attainment. When asked to elaborate on what she meant by the idea that education necessarily leads to happiness, she shared the following:

Shaymaa: When I was in the Ishraq program I learned it is important to wear nice clothes and speak in a pleasant tone. I also learned it is important for me to help my mother and sisters keep the house clean. In my class, when we used to talk to the teachers in a bad tone they would tell us that it is important to talk to people in a pleasant way, not like the way we were used to talking. It made me happy when my teachers told me I was doing a good job.

MS: Can you talk more about how this relates to the relationship you had with your teachers?

Shaymaa: I used to look up to my teachers, they are like us. They come from the same communities as we do, and I know their families. They are also older than us and have been to school. This means they know what we need to learn so that we can do well when we go to (middle) school. When I think about what I wanted to do after finishing Ishraq and school, I thought about teaching. I want to help other girls like my teachers helped me.

After having refused numerous proposals Shaymaa eventually married at around 19 years of age. Shaymaa and her husband also have a 2-year-old son named Karim who accompanied his mother to the Youth Centers occasionally where we conducted these interviews. Her husband, who is about her age, was initially very supportive of her decision to return to school after she stopped attending following the completion of the Ishraq program. However, shortly after the start of her marriage her husband asked her to stay home. While she claimed that returning to school was at the time not her main priority, her studies were periodically the subject of some of the discussions she had with her husband. Before Karim was born these conversations took place more frequently, as they considered the possibility that with additional schooling Shaymaa could contribute significantly to the poor wage her husband earns as a day laborer. However, after Karim was born it was no longer possible for Shaymaa to return to school, as she suggested, "Who is going to watch my boy? I have no time or the support that I need to finish school or find a job." What is significant in Shaymaa's experience is that independent of the complex set of circumstances described above, Shaymaa agreed that before she attended the Ishraq program, the biggest barrier to her personal development was a chaotic home life. She was adamant that the most important lesson she learned from her participation was the value of being neat and orderly at school and at home. In addition, Shaymaa believed that being an educated woman has as much to do with the way someone behaves as it does with the skills they can acquire by completing their schooling. This example demonstrates how particular notions of order and discipline are internalized by young women like Shaymaa and quickly become the lens by which their world is brought into focus.

This section focused on examining how order–chaos dynamic guided the classroom practices of the Ishraq program. The following section examines the ways in which Ishraq appears to widen the already significant social and cultural distance that exists between urban and rural communities in Upper Egypt, where largely educated, urban men and women were responsible for the implementation and management of core program functions and simultaneously served as the conduit between "local" communities and Cairo-based professional staff.

Just Outside the City Limits and Yet a World Away

During one particular visit to the office of an Ishraq implementing NGO, Nourihan (the program director) and Mona engaged in an extensive discussion about "appropriate" ages for women to marry. This conversation began after Mona asked Nourihan rather forwardly to share her age. This discussion between two highly educated women illustrated one of the many ways social relations in rural Upper Egypt are framed by urban Egyptians (from Cairo and from within Upper Egypt) in narrow and problematic terms. Shortly after arriving to the meeting, Mona remarked to Nourihan, "you know, you sounded much older over the phone. I did not realize you are so young." Nourihan responded, "oh, I am not young. I am 32 and I have three kids. I got married when I was 27." This conversation appeared to become slightly uncomfortable for Nourihan as Mona argued, "27, that sounds later than I would imagine someone to get married here in Upper Egypt." Nourihan laughed awkwardly and addressed Mona rather firmly stating, "Women in urban Beni Suef delay marriage until after they complete high school and university." She added, "… local marriage conventions also make it difficult for women to marry when they are young," something she believed is a cause for the rising marriage age in rural areas. Nourihan referred to the convention known in Egypt as the *gihaz*, a type of dowry that includes the sets of home furnishings typically provided by the betrothed and/or her family. For most women and their families the *gihaz* can be tremendously expensive; in some cases families report spending more than half of their savings. When families cannot afford to support their daughters, the bride-to-be is responsible for raising the money necessary for securing the items included in the *gihaz*. Nourihan suggested that in rural areas many young women respond to these challenging circumstances by leaving school early to work, while in urban areas women can wait until their families can afford the expenses. This exchange illustrates the extent to which participants perceive the rural–urban divide, and more importantly how this divide operates to affect relations between and among communities in Upper Egypt.

In her pivotal work documenting informal political networks in Cairo's popular districts, Diane Singerman (1995) argues that the *gihaz* is more than a cultural practice, a sentiment shared by Nourihan but also others included in this research. In the context of this conversation, the *gihaz* is one of many ways where Nourihan described her experiences as an educated urban resident of Beni Suef in opposition to her less-educated rural counterparts. This discussion regarding the practice of the *gihaz* perplexed Mona greatly; she shared that while she was aware there are differences between Upper Egypt, the Nile Delta, and Cairo in how the practice of the *gihaz* is understood, she had a hard time believing that a family could spend half of their wealth buying home furnishings that may never be used. Mona exclaimed, "no, no, no! You must be kidding. I can understand if the bride to be is expected to buy a set of dishes or cups, but that is the end of it." Nourihan explained that in Beni Suef and in Upper Egypt in general, it is common for women to buy ten sets of plates or six sets of tea glasses, or even 12 sets of bath towels. She went on to state that when she was preparing for marriage her situation was more reasonable, "I was only asked to provide four sets of everything; in rural areas women are usually asked to provide more sets of everything." Nourihan saw her experience of *gihaz* as different from more rural practices.

To further illustrate this divide between rural and urban within Beni Seuf, Nourihan called Oum Mohamed, the office caretaker. Oum Mohamed was responsible for nearly everything in the office from greeting guests to cleaning, and even making copies. It was not un-common for Oum Mohamed to prepare and serve meals and tea for staff and/or guests of ODYE during the day. Given her profession, and that she was a parent in her mid to late-40s, which was considered an older age, people called her by the name Oum Mohamed instead of her given name. It is common throughout many parts of Egypt for women of a certain demographic—middle-aged mothers from urban working class or rural farming communities—to be referred to as a mother of (*Oum*) and the name of their eldest son, or daughter if the mother has no sons. Immediately after joining the conversation Oum Mohamed was asked by Nourihan to share her experience as a mother who recently made arrangements for her daughter's wedding. Oum Mohamed responded by stating:

> You know, I am no longer married. I have to take care of my children alone and we could not afford to keep my daughter in school any longer. She had to earn enough money to cover her *gihaz* and that was not going to be possible while we still pay for school fees. So, before high-school I pulled her out of school to give her enough time to earn the money she will need to prepare for marriage. In our village the bride-to-be is required to produce around 12 sets of each item; towels, bed sheets, plates, cups, silverware. You know what I mean. Also, it does not matter if a bride is poor; every girl is expected to come up with this amount of home furnishings. That is just the way it is.

Although Nourihan used Oum Mohamed's experiences to make a larger point about the difference between rural and urban Upper Egyptians, she was also visibly bothered by what she was hearing. She told us angrily that Oum Mohamed's daughter was one of the brightest young women she had ever known, and that it was a shame that her sons could complete their schooling, while her daughter had to leave to raise money for what she described as a silly practice. While it was clear Oum Mohamed's decision was motivated by the cultural practices as well as the social pressure to meet the expectations associated with a proper *gihaz*, this was not acknowledged by Nourihan as a legitimate reason to remove her daughter out of school. This encounter like many others included in this chapter, speak to the ways in which the divide between rural and urban Upper Egyptians operates socially and structurally. Nourihan thanked Oum Mohamed for joining us and after Oum Mohamed exited the room, she turned to Mona and said, "Can you imagine? Oum Mohamed lives in a village right outside of town, but it seems more like she lives a world away." To which Mona responded, "I had no idea the situation here was so troubling." This exchange suggests the rapid urbanization of Upper Egypt, growing out of former town-centers like Beni Suef, have become the sites where rural–urban development contests are most intense. The discourses employed by Nourihan and Mona in this exchange that frame rural life as an impediment to progress are products of the intellectual legacy of the colonial period and the mission of programs like Ishraq that seek to "empower" a modern Egyptian woman.

Colonial-era thinkers and writers have historically cast Egypt's development dilemma as hinging on effectively disrupting and transforming rural life. This dynamic is best illustrated through examining the writings of Syrian-Egyptian sociologist and educator Henry Ayrout. In his polemic work concerning the life and condition of the Egyptian peasantry, Ayrout (1938, 2005) described rural Egyptians as, "… impervious and enduring as the granite of their temples, and once the form is fixed, they are as slow to change as were the forms of that art" (p. 20). Ayrout, informed largely by the work of colonial-era French sociologist Gustave Le Bon (1841–1931), blamed the core differences between advanced and not-advanced segments of Egyptian society on the naiveté and cultural backwardness of the Egyptian peasant. As a result, the solution to Egypt's poverty problem and habits (like the *gihaz*) rests on the shoulders of few; namely it is the responsibility of the social and political elite "to liberate the *fellah's* (peasant) spirit from its stifling envelope of mud" (Ayrout, 1938, 2005, p. 23). However, Ayrout viewed the policies of the colonial and postcolonial governments, where the elite in Cairo imagined themselves in opposition to the rest of the country, as ineffective and morally bankrupt. He also suggested that rural populations lack the ability to even be aware of the dreadful conditions they suffer. As a result, Ayrout believed that building a strong rural middle class represents the key for creating conditions favorable enough to produce gradual change to the social and political order of rural Egypt, especially in the south (Mitchell, 2002). This idea did not take root in the ways Ayrout had intended in the 1930s and 1940s, or for that matter during the socialist period of the 1950s and 1960s.

Revealed in this analysis of the discussion between Nourihan, Mona, and Oum Mohamed are the ways in which the ideas of making structural changes through development of a modern middle class in rural areas have become internalized by urbanites living in former rural town-centers like Beni Suef. Nourihan, and other program staff participating in the study, described their rural counterparts similarly as they were described by their counterparts in Cairo. There appears to be a reluctant acknowledgement that "everybody's" forefathers and mothers where once peasants. This in turn fashions the contemporary "peasant/farmer" into a living embodiment of a pre-modern past. In the spirit of Ayrout, it becomes the responsibility of individuals like Nourihan to ensure their rural counterparts embrace modernity in all shapes and forms despite recognizing that this is only a remote possibility. Nourihan only partially understood the experience of Oum Mohamed as the two share cultural practices like the *gihaz*. The differences between how the two women and members of their respective "groups" enacted the *gihaz* illustrates how the cultural practices of some rural people suggest that they stand opposed to modernity in principle and practice by assuming an unbearable burden in the name of "tradition."

Conclusion

The preceding discussion of the research findings illustrates how Ishraq enhances the role of program staff and teachers as they wield considerable power and authority over their students. This was observed mainly in the analysis of schooling practices employed by Ishraq teachers. Further, the ways in which these pedagogical techniques, particularly of embracing order and admonishing chaotic behavior, affected the experiences of former students was apparent in the ways former Ishraq participants explained how their own rural backgrounds were positively affected by the program.

This chapter also forwards the argument that social relations in Upper Egypt are increasingly shaped by an emergent rural–urban dualism as an extension of the historical divide that has existed between Cairo and Upper Egypt. The goal of Ishraq was to promote empowerment and enhance youth agency in the hopes of slowly changing the way girls and young women in Upper Egypt were treated. However, through examining Ishraq program documents against the backdrop of historical narratives of rural development in Upper Egypt, this study reveals that disrupting certain social and cultural practices are deemed as essential component for promoting broad social reforms.

The dominant literature on agency and empowerment for girls in the MENA has tended to center on culturally oriented theorizing for explaining why empowerment has not been realized in ways it has elsewhere. This examination of Ishraq reveals how the program furthers the divide between rural and urban contexts in Upper Egypt under the pretext of promoting empowerment and enhancing agency for adolescent girls. The narratives and experiences of practitioners in Cairo and Beni Suef are critically important for drawing attention to the socio-cultural complexity that exists across the landscape of development in Egypt. Problematizing these prohibitively narrow culture-bound arguments begins the work of uncovering the dimensions of power that affect contemporary development work on youth agency and empowerment in Egypt, and more broadly across the MENA region.

References

Abu-Lughod, L., Adely, F. J., & Hasso, F. S. (2009). Overview: Engaging the Arab Human Development Report 2005 on women. *International Journal of Middle East Studies, 41*(1), 59–60.

Adams, D. K., Ginsburg, M. B., Clayton, T., Mantilla, M. E., Sylvester, J., & Wang, Y. (2001). Linking research to educational policy and practice: What kind of relationship in how (de) centralized a context? In B. A. U. Levinson & M. Sutton (Eds.), *Policy as practice: Towards a comparative sociocultural analysis of educational policy* (pp. 59–76). Westport, CT: Alex.

Adely, F. J. (2012). *Gendered paradoxes: Educating Jordanian women in nation, faith, and progress*. Chicago, IL: University of Chicago Press.

Al-Jarida Al-Rasmiya. (2008). The Egyptian Penal Code (No. 58/1937); and the Code on Civil Affairs (No. 143/1994).24, 2–27.

Ayrout, H. H. (2005). *The Egyptian peasant* (J. A. Williams, Trans.). Cairo, Egypt: The American University in Cairo Press (Original work published in 1938).

Fairclough, N. (1992). *Discourse and social change.* Cambridge, England: Polity.

Fetterman, D. M. (2010). *Ethnography: Step by step* (3rd ed.). Thousand Oaks, CA: Sage.

Fouad, A. (2015, August 26). Here comes the … child bride? Despite legal restrictions, underage marriage persists in rural Egypt. Al-Monitor. Retrieved November 2, 2015, from http://www.al-monitor.com/pulse/tr/contents/articles/originals/2015/08/egypt-underage-marriage-wedding-law-officiant-bribery.html.

Hopkins, N., & Saad, R. (2004). The region of Upper Egypt: Identity and change. In N. Hopkins & R. Saad (Eds.), *Upper Egypt: Identity and change* (pp. 1–24). Cairo, Egypt: American University in Cairo Press.

Howarth, D., & Griggs, S. (2012). Poststructuralist policy analysis: Discourse, hegemony, and critical explanation. In F. Fischer & H. Gottweis (Eds.), *The argumentative turn revisited: Public policy as communicative practice* (pp. 305–342). Durham, NC: Duke University Press.

Levinson, B. A. U., & Sutton, M. (2001). Introduction: Policy as/in practice; a sociocultural approach to the study of educational policy. In B. A. U. Levinson & M. Sutton (Eds.), *Policy as practice: Towards a comparative sociocultural analysis of educational policy* (pp. 1–22). Westport, CT: Alex.

Mahmood, S. (2005). *Politics of Piety: The Islamic revival and the feminist subject.* Princeton, NJ: Princeton University Press.

Massad, J. A. (2001). *Colonial effects: The making of national identity in Jordan.* New York, NY: Columbia University Press.

Massad, J. A. (2007). *Desiring Arabs.* Chicago, IL: University of Chicago Press.

Mitchell, T. (1988). *Colonising Egypt.* Berkeley, CA: University of California Press.

Mitchell, T. (2002). *Rule of experts: Egypt, techno-politics, modernity.* Berkeley, CA: University of California Press.

Population Council. (2007). *Providing new opportunities to adolescent girls in socially conservative settings: The Ishraq program in rural Upper Egypt.* New York, NY: Brady, M.

Population Council. (2013). *The Ishraq program for out-of-school girls: From pilot to scale-up.* Cairo: Selim, M., Abdel-Tawab, N., Elsayed, K., El Badawy, A., & El Kalaawy, H.

Said, E. W. (1978). *Orientalism.* New York, NY: Vintage Books.

Shakry, O. (1998). Schooled mothers and structured play: Child-rearing in the turn-of-the-century Egypt. In L. Abu-Lughod (Ed.), *Remaking women: Feminism and modernity in the Middle East* (pp. 126–161). Princeton, NJ: Princeton University Press.

Singerman, D. (1995). *Avenues of participation:* Family, politics, and networks in urban quarters of Cairo. Princeton, NJ: Princeton University Press.

UNICEF. (2007). *The girls' education initiative in Egypt.* New York, NY: R.G. Sultana.

United Nations Development Program/Institute of National Planning (UNDP/INP). (2003). *Egypt Human Development Report 2003.* Cairo, Egypt: UNDP/INP.

Malala Yousafzai as an Empowered Victim: Media Narratives of Girls' Education, Islam, and Modernity

Ayesha Khurshid and Marline Guerrero

Introduction

> For us girls that [school's] doorway was like a magical entrance to our own special world. As we skipped through, we cast off our headscarves like winds puffing away clouds to make way for the sun then ran helter-skelter up the steps. (Yousafzai & Lamb, 2013, p. 4)

This was the everyday for Malala Yousafzai[1] [Malala from here onwards] as she arrived to school. The joy of learning, interacting with her friends and competing for the highest grades in her class made her happy (Yousafzai & Lamb, 2013). Her "magical" place became a target, as the Pakistani Taliban took control of the Swat Valley. Her father encouraged her to join the activists who raised their voice against the oppressive Taliban regime. She wrote a BBC blog about everyday life in her hometown as Taliban shut down girls' schools and restricted women's mobility and visibility outside of home. The Pakistani state regained control of the Swat region in 2009 as a result of an extensive military operation. In the following years, Malala received national recognition in Pakistan for her activism to support girls' education. Her work turned her into a symbol of resistance against oppressive ideologies and forces. On October 9, 2012 a young man stopped Malala's school bus and demanded to know who Malala was. He fired three shots, one hit Malala and went through her left eye and out her left shoulder and the other two bullets hit the girls sitting next to her (Yousafzai & Lamb, 2013). The Taliban accepted responsibility for this attack.

---

[1] Malala Yousafzai is a girls' education activist and the youngest-ever Nobel Prize laureate. Her work has inspired a large number of global and local policy initiatives and projects all over the world to support education for girls.

A. Khurshid (✉)
College of Education, Florida State University, Tallahassee, FL, USA
e-mail: akhurshid@fsu.edu

M. Guerrero
Domestic Violence and Child Welfare, Tallahassee, FL, USA
e-mail: mg12@my.fsu.edu

© Springer International Publishing Switzerland 2016   157
J.G. DeJaeghere et al. (eds.), *Education and Youth Agency*, Advancing
Responsible Adolescent Development, DOI 10.1007/978-3-319-33344-1_9

Malala's story became international news as the world gathered to condemn the attack and applaud the bravery of a young girl. Her activism became the source of inspiration, as the local and global organizations including the United Nations named different global campaigns after her. For instance, the UN Special Envoy for Global Education, Mr. Gordon Brown, launched a campaign to promote education for children in Pakistan a month after Malala's attack. He also introduced a petition for universal access to primary school for girls called, "I am Malala." Malala wrote a book, *I am Malala* (2013) and received financial support to start a non-profit, The Malala Fund, to advocate for girls' education. In 2014, she became the youngest-ever Nobel Prize laureate for her advocacy on girls' education.

In this global narrative, Malala has become an icon of girls' education, youth agency, and gender empowerment. She is presented as a reflection of how education can instill agency in youth, especially in girls, and be the movement for progress even in the most oppressive conditions (Khoja-Moolji, 2015). In this chapter, we argue how this global narrative around her activism mobilizes her image, not merely as an *agent*, but also as a *victim*. Our work is grounded in critical feminist and development scholarship that shows how the "victimhood" of Muslim women has been the site for different colonial, development, political, and even military interventions in Muslim societies (Abu-Lughod, 1998; Hirschkind & Mahmood, 2002; Kandiyoti, 2005; Mahmood, 2005; Scott, 2007). This critical scholarship highlights how the concepts of agency and empowerment that guide these interventions are shaped by a Western understanding of Third World and Muslim women as *victims* of their own culture (Abu-Lughod, 2009; Mahmood, 2005; Scott, 2007). The dominant and Western discourse conceptualizes empowerment as an expression of individual women's choice and free will against the oppressive frameworks of family, community, and religion and education is conceptualized as being central to enabling Muslim women to become agents of change (Abu-Lughod, 2009; Adely, 2009; Najmabadi, 1998). We argue that in the case of Malala these mainstream narratives about Muslim women overlap with the discourses about "girl affect" (Moeller, 2014) and "girl power" (Gonick, 2006) that position girls as agents who can resolve the structural and social problems that impact their lives.

In this chapter, we examine how the United States media tells Malala's story as a victim/agent primarily through mobilizing the binaries of the *oppressive* Islam versus the *modern* West. We argue that for many, a surface reading of Malala's story may portray her as a symbol of the oppression that women face in a Muslim society. However, Malala herself has problematized the stereotypical images of Islam and of Muslim women in her autobiography, *I Am Malala* (Yousafzai & Lamb, 2013). She talks about Islam, her family, and her culture as the inspiration for her activism and the sources of her strength, rather than oppression. Our discourse analysis of United States news articles investigates how the features of her story become invisible in the media discourse that presents her as the icon of girls' education, youth agency, and gender empowerment. This media discourse mobilizes her as a symbol of not only the cultural and religious oppression of the Muslim women, but also of the potential of Western modernization to empower Muslim girls through education. The analysis of this media discourse in this chapter provides insights on how the stereotypes about Islam, Muslim societies, and Muslim women continue to persist despite being challenged by the very subjects whose images and stories are used to reinforce these stereotypes. It highlights the need to critically engage with the discourses of these stereotypes as they claim to empower Muslim women through education.

Malala Yousafzai's Story

In October 2012, Malala was shot during the bus ride home by the Taliban. Malala's father, Ziauddin Yousafzai, was an educator and ran the school that Malala attended in the Swat District of Pakistan, her hometown. In 2007, Taliban seized control of this scenic valley and banned girls' education for a community that had a long tradition of educating both girls and boys. However, Ziauddin refused to close the school despite Taliban threats. Following her father steps, Malala raised her voice against this brutal regime that had not only denied girls the right to attend schools but had also announced the death penalty for barbers, music shop owners, and thieves. In a blog for BBC Urdu, she used a pseudonym to talk about the community's daily life in her beloved Swat Valley under the Taliban (Yousafzai & Lamb, 2013). Pakistan military drove the Taliban out of Swat after an operation in 2009. As Swat became a safe and peaceful city again, Malala and her father decided to reveal her identity as the author of the popular BBC blog. Malala received recognition in Pakistan and internationally for her brave and articulate depiction of the value of education for girls. Her activism, however, also made her the target of extremist groups such as the Taliban who had retreated from Malala's hometown but continued their violent activities against the Pakistani state and people. After Malala was attacked in 2012, she became even a greater global symbol for girls' education for development organizations as well as for wider public (Khoja-Moolji, 2015).

The Victimhood and Agency of Muslim Women

> ...when Lord Cromer in British-ruled Egypt, French ladies in Algeria and Laura Bush, all with military troops behind them, claim to be saving or liberating Muslim women. (Abu-Lughod, 2002, p. 3)

Abu-Lughod (2002) in her article, *Do Muslim women really need saving?*, argues that the post-9/11 media discourse in the United States presented Muslim women as subjects who could somehow help the Western audience understand the tragic attacks of 9/11. This media discourse mobilized their "victimhood" subjectivity to examine the cultural values that had allegedly also promoted religious extremism. The plight of Muslim women became the lens to explain not only religious extremism, but also Islam itself. For example, the impoverished conditions of a large number of Afghan women living under Taliban regime in Afghanistan became a reflection of Islam rather than an extremist religious group. These media discourses construct reality by choosing certain social and cultural images rather than being "transparent windows or simple reflections of the world" (Share & Kellner, 2005). However, such media presentations are the major source of education for the majority of the society (Macedo, 2007). In the aftermath of 9/11, Western media used the images of *burqa*-clad women and terrorists to examine the "so-called Muslim world" (Watt, 2012). This discourse reduced the complexity and diversity of Muslim societies to a homogenized entity that reflected the patriarchal nature of Islam (Abu-Lughod, 2002).

These media images have shaped the mainstream Western imagination of Muslim women and their roles in their families and societies (Awan, Sheikh, Mithoowani, Ahmed, & Simard, 2010; Falah, 2005; Jhally, Earp, Shaheen, & Media Education Foundation, 2006; Jiwani, 2005). In this paradigm, Muslim women are presented as silent, anonymous, and victims of their traditional culture, families, and communities (Jiwani, 2005; Kassam, 2008; Watt, 2008, 2011). Sensoy and Marshall (2010) argue that since 9/11 there has also been a proliferation of books about the plight of Muslim women that are mass-marketed in North America. *Princess: A true story behind the veil in Saudi Arabia*, supposedly the true story of a female member of the Saudi royal family, is just one example from a large body of popular literature about the victimhood of women in patriarchal Muslim societies.

This discourse of Muslim women as "real or authentic victim subject" (Kapur, 2002; Mohanty, 1988) is embedded in the projections of Islam as an antithesis of the *modern* West (Asad, 2003; Kandiyoti, 2005; Mahmood, 2005; Najmabadi, 1998; Scott, 2007). This narrative of modernity also drove the Western colonial projects that claimed to empower Muslim women in *backward* Muslim societies (Ahmed, 1992; Lazreg, 1994). In post 9/11 era, the focus on Muslim women as the focal point for modernity and the vessel for stopping religious extremism and modernizing Muslim countries has been further intensified (Watt, 2012).

Coupled with these discourses about Muslim women, contemporary international development discourse presents girls' education as the primary strategy for gender empowerment and modernity of Muslim societies (Herz & Sperling, 2004; Schultz, 2002; Tembon & Fort, 2008). This discourse does not clearly define how education may lead to gender empowerment within the cultural contexts at hand (Chismaya, DeJaeghere, Kendall, & Khan, 2012; Guin'ee, 2014; Stromquist, 2006). However, this discourse of girls' education approaches families and communities as manifestations of the Islamic practices that continue to oppress women (Abu-Lughod, 2009; Adely, 2014). In this context, education is meant to provide Muslim women access to individual rights, and choice to transform their culture and family (Ahmed, 1992; Hesford & Kozol, 2005; Kandiyoti, 2007; Khurshid, 2012, 2015). Following this logic, an empowered Muslim woman is viewed as an agent—an agent who is willing to not only distance herself from, but also actively challenge her culture, community, and family (Hirschkind & Mahmood, 2002; Jamal, 2009; Kandiyoti, 2007; Mahmood, 2005; Najmabadi, 1998). In this discourse, education is equated with the *modern* West whereas women's oppression is associated with the *traditional* institutions of family and community that embody Islam. In contrast to this logic of girls' education some feminist scholars have highlighted how women mobilize local discourses of modernity to define the meaning and importance of education for themselves and their communities (Adely, 2009; Khurshid, 2015; Stambach, 2000).

Ironically, Malala's story can be employed not only to problematize but also to substantiate these binaries of Islam–West and victim–agent. She, and many other women and men in her community, survived the violent regime of the Taliban. Her story is also a validation of the role education plays as a powerful motivator for change. It also shows how women's rights activist, such as Malala, pose a potent threat to the extremist groups. These features can be employed to confirm Pakistani Muslim society as a reflection of the Islamic patriarchal values.

However, Malala's own autobiography problematizes this dominant narrative that presents Islam and all Muslim societies as representative of patriarchal structures (Yousafzai & Lamb, 2013). She asserts her identity as a Muslim woman, and does not blame Islam or her community for being attacked. In fact, she talks about Islam, her Pashtun culture, and family as an inspiration for her. Her narrative does not present Islam or Pakistan as an antithesis of modernization or of the West. Instead, she terms Islam as a modern religion that has been misinterpreted and misused by the extremist groups like the Taliban. She challenges such distortions of Islam by stating in her book:

> I couldn't understand what the Taliban were trying to do. 'They are abusing our religion,' I said. How will you accept Islam if I put a gun to your head and say Islam is the true religion? If they want every person in the world to be a Muslim, why don't they show themselves to be good Muslims first? (Yousafzai & Lamb, 2013)

Malala's story reveals a rich and multilayered subjectivity of Muslim girls and women who have been the subject of different modernity projects. Muslim women from diverse contexts engage with different local and global discourses and institutions to create and recreate their gendered identities in complex ways (Huisman & Hondagneu-Sotelo, 2005; Hutson, 2001; Killian, 2003; Khurshid, 2012, 2015; Marshall, 2005; Predelli, 2004; Read & Bartkowski, 2000). Women's context-specific engagement with Islam to define gender empowerment is captured in ethnographic accounts of Muslim women's participation in diverse Islamic movements in Egypt and Indonesia (Mahmood, 2005; Rinaldo, 2013). In these contexts, Islam becomes a "dynamic tool kit" rather than a universal and fixed set of practices (Bartkowski & Read, 2003). In different Muslim societies, modernity and education are approached as Islamic, rather than Western, traditions (Adely, 2014; Khurshid, 2015; Rinaldo, 2013).

The feminist scholarship that highlights modernity and education as nurtured by Islamic values and cultures does not undermine or overlook the profound impact of certain patriarchal structures on the lived experiences of these women. Instead, it provides a critical insight into how these women creatively solicit support from Islamic teachings as well as from their families and communities to challenge and transform these structures. In other words, it challenges a simplistic reading of Islam, or of families and communities in Muslim societies, in contrast to the modern West.

It provides an in-depth understanding of how different colonial, postcolonial, and development projects have produced complex understandings of Islam, modernity, and the West. For example, the Muslim reformist movement in South Asia created a discourse that presented Islam, modern education, and science as complementary, rather than as incompatible, systems of knowledge (Metcalf, 1994; Minault, 1998)

This locally situated and dynamic approach to Islam, Muslim culture and gender helps us examine the multilayered nature of Malala's narrative. She challenged religious extremist ideologies and groups through asserting her identity as a Muslim girl who was empowered by her Pashtun culture and Islamic beliefs, rather than by the Western modernity. However, the mainstream narrative of Islam versus the West is unable to fully capture how Muslims who embrace Islam may pose the most effective challenge to groups like the Taliban. For example, Ayan Harsi Ali, another popular women's rights activist with a Muslim background, proposes Islam as the source of women's oppression and religious extremism. Ali uses her personal experiences as a "former" Muslim woman to reassert the binary of traditional Islam versus the modern West (Ali, 2008). This story better fits the narrative of oppressed Muslim women becoming agents through shedding their religion and culture and becoming immersed in the Western values. Malala's narrative, on the other hand, is a departure from Ayan Harsi Ali's story as Malala proposes Islam and her culture being central to her identity and struggle. Despite this fact, the media has told Malala's story in a manner that echoes Ali's story. This chapter examines how Malala's own narrative is transformed into a story in a manner that has reinforced, rather than challenged, mainstream perceptions of Islam and of Muslim women.

Methods

This chapter focuses on media coverage from two widely circulated United States newspapers, *The New York Times* and *The Wall Street Journal*. We selected these two newspapers because of their large printed and digital circulation as the United States Alliance for Audited Media (2013) reported both newspapers as being at the Top 25 United States Daily Newspapers in 2013. *The Wall Street Journal* was ranked first place, followed by *The New York Times* in the second place in the average circulation (print and digital) of United States daily newspapers. We recognize the existence of a large number of other national and local newspapers that impact public opinion. In addition, there is also a proliferation of Internet-based news sources and magazines. Our intention in this chapter is not to select a representation of different media sources but rather to critically investigate the mainstream media discourse on Malala. We believe that the selection of these two prominent and respectable newspapers effectively serves that purpose.

We used the ProQuest database to find articles in the two newspapers from the time of the incident, October 9, 2012 to May 2014. This timeline captures the international reaction to the attack on Malala to her becoming the Noble Laureate. For this search, we used the keywords "Malala Yousafzai," with the starting date of

October 2012. We originally identified 60 articles from *The New York Times* and 53 articles from *The Wall Street Journal*. Duplicates and irrelevant articles where Malala was not the main focus were excluded from the analysis. After this analysis, we focused on 45 articles from *The New York Times* and 31 articles from *The Wall Street Journal*.

We used conventional content analysis (Hsieh & Shannon, 2005) to conduct a systematic analysis of the text from two newspapers. Hsieh and Shannon define conventional content analysis as a method in which coding categories come directly from the text. Following this method, our first stage of analysis was directed by examining what kind of information was used to describe and explain Malala's story. Our analysis showed that *The Wall Street Journal* and *The New York Times* talked about education, the Taliban, Muslim women, Pakistani society, and Muslim societies. We used these themes as codes or categories to direct our second stage of analysis.

The first and second stages of coding were done manually by the second author and three other research assistants. This team of coders met with the first author before, during, and after the coding to discuss, compare, and clarify the emergent codes as well as to ensure consistency across coders. Berends and Johnston (2005) highlight how the presence of multiple coders can refine the coding system through inclusion of multiple perspectives. The findings revealed a complex media discourse that presented Malala not only as a brave and independent young girl who took on the Taliban but also as a victim oppressed by the patriarchal structures. Our analysis also shows how the media constructs agent/victim positionality by presenting Malala as a sole warrior, who challenged not only the Taliban but also the very principles that had shaped the institutions of family and community in her culture. In mobilizing the image of Malala as a victim/agent, this media discourse reinforces problematic stereotypes through conflating the Taliban with Islam and with the broader Pakistani society.

Malala as a Victim/Agent

A Taliban gunman singled out and shot the girl, Malala Yousafzai, on Tuesday, and a spokesman said it was in retaliation for her work in promoting girls' education and children's rights in the northwestern Swat Valley, near the Afghan border. (Walsh, 2012b)

The New York Times [*NYT*] described the tragic attack on Malala though connecting it to her activism. The Taliban's violent retaliation shows the powerful impact of her work. Interestingly, the same statement in NYT also presents Malala as a "girl." This is an obvious reference to her very young age. The story of her courage and bravery becomes even more striking because of her positionality as a girl as seen in the following quote:

On Tuesday, masked Taliban gunmen answered Ms. Yousafzai's courage with bullets, singling out the 14-year-old on a bus filled with terrified schoolchildren, then shooting her in the head and neck. (Walsh, 2012a)

This emphasis on Malala being a girl was a common theme in both *NYT* and *The Wall Street Journal* [*WSJ*] reporting on Malala. For example, *WSJ* reported: "The Pakistani school girl and activist who was shot by the Taliban last week is showing signs of recovery" (Bryan-Low, 2012). Malala's girlhood was used in two ways: to present her a particularly vulnerable and innocent victim, but also as a brave agent with the potential to make education available to all girls in her community. In other words, the media discourse presents Malala as a particularly vulnerable victim, as well as an assertive agent.

The agent/victim subjectivity becomes the lens through which media has approached and explained Malala's story to the audience. This "girl" subjectivity, however, is not neutral. It constructs girls as individual agents surrounded by ineffective and tradition-bound institutions. Despite being vulnerable and innocent, this "new girl" is expected to tap into her potential to serve social, political, and economic causes as the state and family fail to serve their purpose (Gonick, 2006). It is no surprise that girls in the so-called Third World are believed to be capable of ending poverty in their societies (Moeller, 2014).

Family, Community, and Islam in Malala's Story

In this media discourse, Malala's subjectivity as a "girl" was also a commentary on the failure of her family, community, and religion as portrayed in Western media. This failure was conveyed through the images of a limited role, absence, complacency, or hostility of these institutions as Malala became an activist and took on The Taliban. In the following discussion, we analyze how Malala was presented as vulnerable in this discourse not only because of her age, but also because her family, community, and society were depicted as not being able to protect her.

The media discourse presented Malala's family as either having a limited role or being largely absent as Malala asserted her role as an activist. For example, one article stated that no members of her family had come to the United Kingdom and there were not any plans for them to do so (Bryan-Low, 2012). The presentation of Malala's family as not opposing Malala, but also not being the driving force for her, was the most prevalent in this discourse. They were shown as tagging along as Malala took on her journey of becoming the global icon of girls' education and gender empowerment. The projected image of her family playing a marginal role, however, is in contrast to the way Malala describes her family and especially her father. Malala writes that her family had inspired her to raise her voice when others were silenced, and they continue to be her primary support structure (Yousafzai & Lamb, 2013). Moreover, it was her father who encouraged her to write the blog highlighting the atrocities carried out by The Taliban in Swat Valley. Nevertheless, the media has not underscored this supportive role of Malala's family. After the attack on Malala, her parents could not travel immediately to the United Kingdom to be present during her surgeries but were only able to arrive once their travel documents were arranged. However, this media-promoted image of an absent family during her stay at the United Kingdom hospital generated strong responses from the public.

Malala even received a marriage proposal, as well as an adoption offer (Yousafzai & Lamb, 2013).

Why would the media not tell the story of how Malala, as well as her family, have fought to support women's right to education? Why was their support not presented as being instrumental to Malala becoming a global activist? The media has projected a passive role of her family from the time she was attacked in 2012 to her receiving the Nobel Peace Prize in 2014 and onwards. We argue the active role of family cannot be integrated into the victim/agent discourse on Malala. It is not compatible with the framework that presents Muslim women's *agency* as an expression of individual rights against the oppressive structures of family, community, and Islam. Malala as an *empowered* Muslim girl has to be an individual agent who fought not only the Taliban, but also the institutions that supposedly embodied these ideologies. The media discourse, therefore, cannot present Malala's family and father as instrumental actors or even as complacent. Their unwavering and unconditional support for Malala and for girls' education, as well as their close relationship and presence in Malala's life, problematizes the image of Muslim families as oppressive structures. Thus, for the most part, the media rendered Malala's family as marginal or having an invisible role in her story.

On the other hand, the media presented Malala's community and Pakistani society as institutions that were complacent, indifferent, or even hostile towards Malala. *The Wall Street Journal* reports:

Last week, on the local Pakistani-language versions of the BBC website, in the national language Urdu and the Pashto spoken in her native Swat, the majority of comments were venomously against the schoolgirl. Some even described her as a "prostitute". (Shah, 2013)

Whereas the *WSJ* coverage of these baffling accusations against Malala was accurate, an editorial choice was made to focus on the incidence of negative comments while reporting on Malala. This *WSJ* report did not mention huge public rallies that were held in Pakistan to support Malala in the aftermath of the attack on her. The exclusion of these rallies is particularly glaring since other newspapers had reported, though in a very limited manner, on the support that Malala received in Pakistan. The *NYT* reported that the Pakistani President, Asif Ali Zardari stated that Malala, "… the schoolgirl had become a symbol of all that is good in us" (Kristof, 2012) and the Prime Minister Raja Pervez Ashraf said "… she is our daughter," (Walsh, 2012a). Walsh (2012a) follows up by stating:

That such figure of wide-eyed optimism and courage could be silenced by Taliban violence was a fresh blow for Pakistan's beleaguered progressives, who seethed with frustration and anger on Tuesday. 'Come on, brothers, be REAL MEN. Kill a school girl,' one media commentator, Nadeem F. Paracha, said in an acerbic Twitter post.

However, just like Malala's family, public support for Malala received nominal attention in media reports. More crucially, this support for Malala was not integrated in the reports about the incidents such as the comments made on the BBC website about Malala. In a global context where religious and racial stereotypes are the main lens to examine Muslim societies, the incidents such as the BBC event are viewed as a reflection of the Pakistanis society. The Western media has often used

Malala's story to solidify the stereotypical image of Pakistan. However, the Pakistani public unanimously condemned the attack on Malala, and the hostility of the audience during the BBC event is not commonly shared.

With the images of a complacent and hostile Pakistani society, the media presented Malala as a sole warrior who knew her voice was critical, "so she spoke up for the rights of children. Even adults didn't have a vision like hers" (Walsh, 2012a). Malala was projected as someone different from her community and society. She was seen as a "symbol of raw courage in the face of implacable evil" (Dhume, 2012). This difference is not merely a reference to Malala's courage and vision, but rather of an ideology that conflicted with the traditional values. An editorial in the *NYT* argued "This is not just Malala's war … It is a war between two ideologies, between the light of education and darkness" (Kristof, 2012). The media presented Malala as a choice that the Pakistani society has between the "darkness" of the religious extremism and the "light" of girls' education. Through using selective evidence, it also showed that the Pakistani society rejected Malala, which implies rejection of the "light" of Western, modern values of education and endorsement of the extremist ideologies. This framing of the issue, thus, blurs the boundaries between Malala's community and society and extremist groups like the Taliban. This discourse mobilizes the West–Islam binary by presenting the Pakistani society as *traditional* and *unmodern*, which opposes the Western enlightenment values of girls' education and gender empowerment.

Presenting girls' education and gender empowerment as Western institutions reinforces the belief that Malala became a target because she supported these Western values. For example, the *WSJ* and the *NYT* newspapers extensively reported on how the Taliban accused Malala of being "secular-minded," "pro-West," (Dhume, 2012), and "… pawn of the West or even as an agent of the Central Intelligence Agency" (Shah, 2013). Depicting the Taliban and the general Pakistani society as an inseparable entity, thus, make these assertions stand as a reflection of general sentiment in Pakistan. In other words, it is not just the Taliban, but also the Pakistani society that opposed the Western values of girls' education and gender empowerment. This perception completely overlooks the history of girls' education as an Islamic institution in Pakistan. It was the *ulema* [Muslim scholars] of nineteenth-century India who advocated the need to educate Muslim women. These *ulema* presented education as a right and responsibility for Muslim men and women, and conceptualized education as being central to Muslimhood through their reformist discourse (Minault, 1998). This historical discourse of Islamic modernity continues to shape the official and public imagination of girls' education in Pakistan (Khurshid, 2015). The Western media discourse has created a binary where Malala and girls' education are seen as being synonymous to Westernization whereas the Taliban, and by implication the Muslim society of Pakistan, are an antithesis of women's rights and modernization. As *The Wall Street Journal* states "Malala stands for education and the Taliban do not" (Shah, 2013). This simplistic presentation equates the Pakistani society as embodying the *traditional* vision of Islam, while completely overlooking the fact that majority of Muslims and Muslim scholars in Pakistan use Islamic teachings and script to oppose religious extremism.

The United States media's use of the Islam–West binary to describe and explain Malala's story is particularly startling given that Malala uses Islam to counter the claims made by the Taliban. In her autobiography (Yousafzai & Lamb, 2013), Malala argues that denying girls' education is un-Islamic:

> Today we all know education is our basic right. Not just in the West; Islam too has given us this right. Islam says every girl and every boy should go to school. In the Quran it is written, God wants us to have knowledge. He wants us to know why the sky is blue and about oceans and stars. (pp. 311–312)

Malala explicitly uses Islam as her framework to promote education and rights for Muslim. She argues that the Taliban, rather than the West, are an antithesis of Islam. She talks about her being a devout Muslim by mentioning how Islam is part of her daily life. For her, Islam is a modern and egalitarian religion that has informed the lives and beliefs of the majority of people in the Pakistani society. In summary, Malala talks about Islam, Pashtun culture, and her family, and not Western ideologies, as being the ideologies and institutions that have empowered her.

Malala's descriptions of Islam and Pashtun culture as her inspiration, however, disappeared from the mainstream media discourse about her. Instead, Islam is only referred to in the coverage of the Taliban justifying their attack. For example, *The New York Times* reported

> This week the militants published a seven-page justification for their violence against Ms. Yousafzai — 'Malala used to speak openly against Islamic system and give interviews in favor of Western education, while wearing a lot of makeup,' it read. (Walsh, 2012c)

This reporting explains how the Taliban use Islam to justify their attack on Malala. It also shows how the Taliban view Malala as an embodiment of Western values. The same media discourse does not explain that Malala not only challenges the Taliban, but also this version of Islam. On the contrary, this discourse argues that Malala became a *victim* because she challenged the traditions that define Islam as well as her community and society. Her *agency*, on the other hand, is presented as a reflection of Western institutions of education. In this context, the Taliban's narrative appears to represent Islam whereas Malala's story reinforces the binary of Islam–West.

Malala Yousafzai: A Counter-Narrative

In her autobiography, Malala discusses the triumph of individual will and the crucial role of education, as well as the dangers posed by religious extremism. She also affirms her family, culture, and Islam as being the sources of her empowerment and activism. In addition, Malala's visual image, as someone with a covered head and traditional Pakistani attire, is a physical embodiment of the mainstream Pakistani culture. Nevertheless, the media primarily employed the historical binary of *traditional* Islam versus the *modern* West to tell Malala's story. It is, thus, no surprise that many elements of her narrative became invisible in this media discourse.

In these media accounts, Malala appears as a *victim*; as a fighter; as an *agent*; and as a subject embodying Western values. When Malala was portrayed as a victim we see the emphasis of a "girl," "schoolgirl" and her young age and her innocence and this is compared to the Taliban's brutality and oppressive ways. Her aggressor, the Taliban, was portrayed as representing Islam. This presentation was not literal, but the distinctions were blurred in the narrative. Through this depiction, Malala becomes a victim of the Taliban and Islam and, thus, a representation of the plight of Muslim women.

Malala was also shown to have "raw courage." She is the opposite of a victim because she stood against the Taliban by advocating for girls' education. Malala and the Taliban represent opposing forces, two ideologies in one community. Malala represented the "light"—pro education and the Taliban the "dark"—against education. As the Taliban was represented as Islam, then Malala's image has become the opposite of Islam. Not only is she a fighter she is also an activist whose "weapons are books and pens." Depictions of the Taliban accusing Malala of being "secular-minded" and her community saying she might be a "CIA-agent," are used to reaffirm the construction of Malala's image as non-Muslim and non-traditional. These two newspapers neither mentioned that Malala is practicing Islam, nor that she wears a veil because these religious and cultural symbols are viewed as a threat to the West.

Conclusion

The media's presentation of Malala as an embodiment of *modern* Western values and in opposition to *traditional* Islam calls our attention to carefully engage with the global girls' education and gender empowerment discourses. These media discourses are the primary sources of education for the majority of the population in Western contexts (Macedo, 2007), and therefore impact public opinion as well as policy decisions. This discourse of *empowering* Muslim girls/women through education hinges on the binaries that associate women's victimhood with Islamic values. Family and community are viewed as institutions that manifest patriarchal religious values. On the other hand, education is mobilized as an embodiment of Western modernity that can help Muslim women assert their individual rights against these "unmodern" and "oppressive" institutions. The subjectivity of an educated empowered Muslim woman is of someone who has not only distanced herself from, but has also challenged Islam, family, and community.

The images of a homogenous Islam and oppressed Muslim women reinforce the problematic narrative of modernizing Muslim societies through educating and empowering Muslim women. However, instead of flatly rejecting these dominant discourses, we need to examine what images and understandings are mobilized to (re)produce certain subjectivities. This critical engagement can highlight the binaries embedded in these discourses without conflating the multilayered tensions, struggles, and complexities of the Muslim societies. Moreover, this engagement can also highlight the local understandings of modernity and girls' education that are shaped by the colonial and postcolonial histories of Muslim societies. This approach can problematize the static and homogenous notions of not only Islam but also of the West. We conclude our chapter by employing Malala's own words:

> I don't know why people have divided the whole world into two groups, west and east. Education is neither eastern nor western. Education is education and it's the right of every human being. (Yousafzai, n.d.)

References

Abu-Lughod, L. (1998). Introduction. In L. Abu-Lughod (Ed.), *Remaking women: Feminism and modernity in the Middle East* (pp. 3–32). Princeton, NJ: Princeton University Press.

Abu-Lughod, L. (2002). Do Muslim women really need saving? Anthropological reflections on cultural relativism and its others. *American Anthropologist, 104*(3), 783–790.

Abu-Lughod, L. (2009). Dialectics of women's empowerment: The International Circuitry of the Arab Human Development Report. *International Journal of Middle Eastern Studies, 41*, 83–103.

Adely, F. (2009). Educating women for development: The Arab Human Development Report 2005 and the problem with women's choices. *International Journal of Middle East Studies, 41*(1), 105–122.

Adely, F. (2014). Gendered paradoxes: Educating Jordanian women in nation, faith, and progress. *JMEWS: Journal of Middle East Women's Studies, 10*(3), 125.

Ahmed, L. (1992). *Women and gender in Islam.* New Haven, CT: Yale University Press.

Ali, A. H. (2008). *Infidel.* New York City, NY: Simon and Schuster.

Alliance for Audited Media. (2013). Top 25 U.S. newspapers for March 2013. Retrieved May 13, 2014, from http://auditedmedia.com/news/research-and-data/top-25-us-newspapers-for--march-2013.aspx.

Asad, T. (2003). *Formations of the secular: Christianity, Islam, modernity.* Stanford, CA: Stanford University Press.

Awan, K., Sheikh, M., Mithoowani, N., Ahmed, A., & Simard, D. (2010). Maclean's magazine: A case study of Media-propagated Islamophobia. Retrieved May 18, 2014, from http://www.safs.ca/issuescases/Report_on_Macleans_Journalism.pdf.

Bartkowski, J. P., & Read, J. G. (2003). Veiled submission: Gender, power, and identity among evangelical and Muslim women in the United States. *Qualitative Sociology, 26*(1), 71–92.

Berends, L., & Johnston, J. (2005). Using multiple coders to enhance qualitative analysis: The case of interviews with consumers of drug treatment. *Addiction Research & Theory, 13*(4), 373–381.

Bryan-Low, C. (2012, October 19). Pakistani schoolgirl shows signs of recovery. *The Wall Street Journal (Online).*

Chismaya, G., DeJaeghere, J., Kendall, N., & Khan, M. (2012). Gender and 'Education for All': Progress and problems in achieving gender equity. *International Journal of Educational Development, 32*, 743–755.

Dhume, S. (2012, October 12). A child soldier in the war for Pakistan: Fourteen-year-old Malala Yousafzai stood up for modernity. Few others do. *The Wall Street Journal (Online).*

Falah, G. (2005). The visual representation of Muslim/Arab women in daily newspapers in the United States. In G. Falah & C. R. Nagel (Eds.), *Geographies of Muslim women: Gender, religion, and space* (pp. 300–320). New York, NY: Guilford Press.

Gonick, M. (2006). Between "girl power" and "Reviving Ophelia": Constituting the neoliberal girl subject. *NWSA Journal, 18*(2), 1–23.

Guin'ee, N. (2014). Empowering women through education: Experiences from Dalit women in Nepal. *International Journal of Educational Development, 39*, 183–190.

Herz, B. K., & Sperling, G. B. (2004). What works in girls' education: Evidence and policies from the developing world. Council on Foreign Relations, Washington, DC. *International Journal of Educational Development, 25*(4), 395–407.

Hesford, W., & Kozol, W. (2005). *Just advocacy?: Women's human rights, transnational feminisms, and the politics of representation*. New Brunswick, NJ: Rutgers University Press.

Hirschkind, C., & Mahmood, S. (2002). Feminism, the Taliban, and politics of counter-insurgency. *Anthropological Quarterly, 75*(2), 339–354.

Hsie, H. F., & Shannon, S. E. (2005). Three approaches to qualitative content analysis. *Qualitative Health Research, 15*(9), 1277–1288.

Huisman, K., & Hondagneu-Sotelo, P. (2005). Dress matters: Change and continuity in the dress practices of Bosnian Muslim refugee women. *Gender & Society, 19*(1), 44–65.

Hutson, A. (2001). Women, men, and patriarchal bargaining in an Islamic Sufi order: The Tijaniyya in Kano, Nigeria, 1937 to the present. *Gender & Society, 15*(5), 734–753.

Jamal, A. (2009). Gendered Islam and modernity in the nation-space: Women's modernism in the Jamaat-e-Islami of Pakistan. *Feminist Review, 91*(1), 9–28.

Jhally, S., Earp, J., Shaheen, J. G., & Media Education Foundation. (2006). *Reel bad Arabs: How Hollywood vilifies a people*. Northampton, MA: Media Education Foundation.

Jiwani, Y. (2005). Orientalizing "war talk": Representations of the gendered Muslim body post-9/11 in the Montreal Gazette. In J. Lee & J. Lutz (Eds.), *Situating "race" and racism in the time, space, and theory: Critical essays for activists and scholars* (pp. 178–204). Montreal, BC, Canada: McGill-Queen's Press-MQUP.

Kandiyoti, D. (2005). *The politics of gender and reconstruction in Afghanistan: Occasional Paper 4*. Geneva, Switzerland: UNRISD.

Kandiyoti, D. (2007). Old dilemmas or new challenges? The politics of gender and reconstruction in Afghanistan. *Development and Change, 38*(2), 169–199.

Kapur, R. (2002). The tragedy of victimization rhetoric: Resurrecting the "native" subject in International/Post-colonial feminist legal politics. *The Harvard Human Rights Journal, 15*, 1–317.

Kassam, A. (2008). The weak, the powerless, the oppressed: Muslim women in Toronto media. *Canadian Journal of Media Studies, 4*(1), 71–88.

Khoja-Moolji, S. (2015). Suturing together girls and education: An investigation into the social (re)production of girls' education as a hegemonic ideology. *Diaspora, Indigenous, and Minority Education, 9*(2), 87–107.

Khurshid, A. (2012). A transnational community of Pakistani Muslim women: Narratives of rights, wisdom, and honor in a women's education project. *Anthropology and Education Quarterly, 43*(3), 235–252.

Khurshid, A. (2015). Islamic traditions of modernity: Gender, class and Islam in a transnational women's education project. *Gender & Society, 29*, 98–121.

Killian, C. (2003). The other side of the veil: North African women in France respond to the headscarf affair. *Gender & Society, 17*(4), 567–590.

Kristof, N. D. (2012, October 11). Her 'crime' was loving schools. *The New York Times*, p. A.31.

Lazreg, M. (1994). *The eloquence of silence: Algerian women in question*. New York, NY: Routledge.

Macedo, D. (2007). Introduction: Deconstructing the corporate media/government nexus. In D. Macedo & S. Steinberg (Eds.), *Media literacy: A reader* (pp. xxii–xxxii)., New York, NY: Peter Lang.

Mahmood, S. (2005). *Politics of piety: The Islamic revival and the feminist subject*. Princeton, NJ: Princeton University Press.

Marshall, G. A. (2005). Ideology, progress, and dialogue: A comparison of feminist and Islamist women's approaches to the issues of head covering and work in Turkey. *Gender & Society, 19*(1), 104–120.

Metcalf, B. (1994). Remaking ourselves. In M. E. Marty & S. Appleby (Eds.), *Accounting for fundamentalisms*. Chicago, IL: Chicago University Press.

Minault, G. (1998). *Secluded scholars: Girls' education and Muslim social reform in colonial India*. New Delhi, India: Oxford University Press.

Moeller, K. (2014). Searching for adolescent girls in Brazil: The transnational politics of poverty in "The girl effect". *Feminist Studies, 40*(3), 575–601.

Mohanty, C. T. (1988). Under western eyes: Feminist scholarship and colonial discourses. *Feminist Review, 30*, 61–88.

Najmabadi, A. (1998). Crafting an educated housewife in Iran. In L. Abu-Lughod (Ed.), *Remaking women: Feminism and modernity in the Middle East* (pp. 91–125). Princeton, NJ: Princeton University Press.

Predelli, L. N. (2004). Interpreting gender in Islam: A case study of immigrant Muslim women in Oslo, Norway. *Gender & Society, 18*(4), 473–493.

Read, J. G., & Bartkowski, J. P. (2000). To veil or not to veil? A case study of identity negotiation among Muslim women in Austin, Texas. *Gender & Society, 14*(3), 395–417.

Rinaldo, R. (2013). *Mobilizing piety: Islam and feminism in Indonesia*. Oxford, England: Oxford University Press.

Schultz, T. P. (2002). Why governments should invest more to educate girls. *World Development, 30*, 207–225.

Scott, J. W. (2007). *The politics of the veil*. Princeton, NJ: Princeton University Press.

Sensoy, Ö., & Marshall, E. (2010). Missionary girl power: Saving the 'third world' one girl at a time. *Gender & Education, 22*(3), 295–311.

Shah, S. (2013, July 18). World news: Pakistan teen is no longer hero at home. *The Wall Street Journal*, p. A.7.

Share, J., & Kellner, D. (2005). Toward critical media literacy: Core concepts, debates, organizations, and policy. *Discourse: Studies in the Cultural Politics of Education, 26*(3), 369–386.

Stambach, A. (2000). *Lessons from Mount Kilimanjaro: Schooling, community, and gender in East Africa*. New York: Routledge.

Stromquist, N. (2006). Gender, education and the possibility of transformative knowledge. *Compare: A Journal of Comparative and International Education, 36*(2), 145–161.

Tembon, M., & Fort, L. (2008). *Girls' education in the 21st century: Gender equality, empowerment, and economic growth*. Washington, DC: World Bank.

Walsh, D. (2012a, October 10). Taliban gun down a girl who spoke up for rights. *The New York Times*, p. A.1.

Walsh, D. (2012b, October 11). Pakistanis unite in outrage over girl's shooting by Taliban. *The New York Times*, p. A.6.

Walsh, D. (2012c, October 20). 'Malala moment' may have passed in Pakistan, as rage over a shooting ebbs. *The New York Times*, p. A.9.

Watt, D. (2008). Silent meaning: A cover photo of Muslim women. *J-Source: The Canadian Journalism Project*. Retrieved May 20, 2014, from http://www.j-source.ca/.

Watt, D. (2011). Juxtaposing *sonare* and *videre* midst curricular spaces: Negotiating Muslim, female identities in the discursive spaces of schooling and visual media cultures. Doctoral thesis. University of Ottawa, Ottawa, ON, Canada. Retrieved May 21, 2014, from http://www.ruor.uottawa.ca/handle/10393/19973.

Watt, D. (2012). The urgency of visual media literacy in our post-9/11 world: Reading images of Muslim women in the print news media. *The Journal of Media Literacy Education, 4*(1), 32–43.

Yousafzai, M., & Lamb, C. (2013). *I am Malala: The girl who stood up for education and was shot by the Taliban*. Cambridge, England: Hachette.

Yousafzai, M. (n.d.). BrainyQuote.com. Retrieved April 28, 2014, from http://www.brainyquote.com/quotes/quotes/m/malalayous569385.html.

Peers, Sexual Relationships, and Agency in Tanzania

Laura Wangsness Willemsen and Anna Ndesamburo Kwayu

Introduction

Recent efforts to reach the Millennium Development Goals, address the ongoing HIV/AIDS crisis, and confront uncertain youth livelihoods in sub-Saharan Africa have garnered increasing attention at the intersection of schooling, gender, and sexuality. Epidemiological perspectives that seek to promote safer sexual practices, educational perspectives that seek to improve schools' processes and outcomes, economic perspectives that seek to address youth unemployment, and feminist perspectives that seek to understand and critique systems of gender so as to promote female empowerment have all been brought to bear on young people's sexual relationships. We seek to add to these conversations by focusing on young people's voices and experiences with sexuality and agency, and by examining how young people in Tanzania simultaneously shape and are shaped by their peer and sexual relationships. More specifically, we seek to understand the ways in which students see their peer relationships as shaping their sexual relationships, as well as the choices they make around them. Our work, which is situated in critical and feminist perspectives, is premised on the assertion that foregrounding youths' own perspectives and experiences can lead to deeper, more illustrative understandings of complex social, cultural, material, and economic contexts and processes in which young people develop their agency with regard to sexual relationships.

L.W. Willemsen (✉)
Department of Organizational Leadership, Policy, and Development,
University of Minnesota, Minneapolis, MN, USA
e-mail: lauraw@umn.edu

A. Ndesamburo Kwayu
Policy Forum, Dar es Salaam, Tanzania
e-mail: anansian@yahoo.com

© Springer International Publishing Switzerland 2016
J.G. DeJaeghere et al. (eds.), *Education and Youth Agency*, Advancing
Responsible Adolescent Development, DOI 10.1007/978-3-319-33344-1_10

While many studies (Harper, Gannon, Watson, Catania, & Dolcini, 2004; Springer, Parcel, Baumler, & Ross, 2006) have examined how peers influence the identity formation, attitudes, behavior, and goals of young people worldwide, research that specifically examines how peer relationships shape youth sexuality in sub-Saharan Africa has been less prevalent (Muhanguzi, Bennett, & Muhanguzi, 2011). Much of the research has been aimed at understanding sexuality and peer relationships vis-à-vis the transmission and prevention of HIV infection in the context of the AIDS crisis (Mojola, 2014; Thorpe, 2005). While our work does in fact occur in contexts of relatively high prevalence of HIV, ours is not an epidemiologically focused study. Rather, this is an interpretive and critical study that draws on qualitative interview data to examine how students understand sexual relationships as they are intertwined with secondary schooling, peer relationships and notions of modernity in contexts of economic insecurity. We utilize Kabeer's (1999) empowerment framework of resources, agency and achievements alongside relevant literature to analyze how young people view sexual relationships and recognize their peers as influencing their decision-making in both desired and undesired ways. Our findings show how some youth use peers as resources to expand their abilities to act agentically in order to enter desired relationships or resist unwanted relationships, while other youth view their peer relationships as involving unwanted pressure to enter sexual relationships.

Our work here is a new analysis of qualitative interview data from two distinct studies of secondary schooling and sexual relationships in Tanzania. How young people view their peers as influencing their perceptions of and choices involving sexual relationships was not the initial foci of either of the two studies from which the data originates. However, the open-ended interviews with young people around sexuality and schooling repeatedly returned to this topic as interviewees described how their social contexts and perspectives of sexual relationships influenced each other. As such, we became increasingly attuned to young people's descriptions of their choices around their sexuality as being embedded in, and shaped by, their peer relationships and social structures. The question we began to ask, and the research question structuring this chapter, is: How do peers influence young people's choices around sexual relationships in rural Tanzanian secondary school contexts characterized by economic insecurity and a high prevalence of HIV?

Empowerment, Schooling and Sexuality: Theoretical Framework and Study Context

Framing Agency, Choice, and Empowerment

Emergent research paints pictures of both vulnerability and agency, at times simultaneously, of youth sexuality in sub-Saharan Africa. This recurring tension is most evident over differing viewpoints on the extent of female sexual agency such that a binary has begun to emerge; one view regards females as strategic and agentic around engaging in sexual relationships (Hawkins, Price, & Mussá, 2009; Leclerc-Madlala, 2003). The other view highlights vulnerability and situates female sexuality as constrained by prescriptive norms of male dominance or predation and female victimization, particularly within patriarchal and capitalist systems (Grant, 2012; Muhanguzi, 2011). Even as much research exists, and is explored more thoroughly in the subsequent section that questions, nuances, complicates or disrupts this binary, the extent to which these perspectives are contradictory or, perhaps, complementary continues to be debated around multiple issues including marriage norms, sexual desire, romance, sexual relationships between older and younger people, transactional sex, the use of contraception and other protective measures (Willemsen & DeJaeghere, 2015). So, too, does this tension exist around questions of the influence of peers on young people's sexuality in sub-Saharan Africa.

Our work, like the work of many others in this and related fields, is not premised neatly on either end of this agent–victim binary. Rather, we are interested in what has been succinctly termed "the dynamic interplay of agency and structure" (Monkman, Miles, & Easton, 2008, p. 108) for individuals and groups of young people in educational contexts. Further, we acknowledge the existence of multiple, concurrent experiences with sexualities among the young people in this study, from similar backgrounds in similar contexts. As Tamale states, "Researchers need to recognize that there is no uniform or monolithic way of experiencing sexualities within one culture or community, or even among individuals" (2011, p. 12). A nuanced examination of youth agency seeking to eschew binary thinking, therefore, requires lithe conceptual tools able to accommodate a range of experiences and perceptions.

Kabeer (1999) proposed a framework for conceptualizing and measuring empowerment, which she defined as "the process by which those who have been denied the ability to make choices acquire such an ability… the expansion in people's ability to make strategic life choices in a context where this ability was previously denied to them" (p. 437). Although we are not chiefly interested in measuring empowerment per se, and we examine the agency of both females and males, whereas her work has been concerned primarily with female empowerment, her conceptualization of the process of female empowerment offers several analytical tools that we find valuable for this work. Namely, her conceptualizations of resources, agency, and achievements can be fluidly applied to illuminate the ways in which peers influence youth sexuality. Furthermore, we hold that, given the precarious economic, material, and educational contexts of these young people, contexts which will be examined in subsequent sections, it is useful to apply Kabeer's framework as a means of analyzing their experiences and perceptions.

For the purposes of this chapter, we employ Kabeer's conceptualization of empowerment as a process due to its attention to agency and ease of applicability. This conceptualization has been used in analyzing agency and empowerment in educational settings in diverse contexts (e.g., DeJaeghere & Lee, 2011; Murphy-Graham, 2008). For example, Murphy-Graham (2008) drew on Kabeer to analyze the impacts and limitations of an empowerment-focused educational program for women in Honduras. She found that while the program cultivated advancements in women's inner-resources such self-confidence, knowledge and awareness of gender equity, there remained ways in which their agency was still constrained by social contexts. Unterhalter, Boler, and Aikman (2008) drew on Kabeer's concepts to analyze an ActionAid project in Tanzania devoted to girls' education and protection against HIV transmission. Quoting a 2007 Action Aid white paper, they describe Tanzanian girls as having both agency and constraints placed upon them:

> We understand girls as active agents, who think about their lives, articulate their views and act… We see the girls' lives as being constrained by a range of forces … but girls have some spaces and opportunities and act back in a range of ways, with different outcomes. (pp. 22–23, italics in the original)

Likewise, we find applying Kabeer's theoretical framework to analyze questions of youth agency in Tanzania proves simultaneously simple and comprehensive insofar as it allows us to consider young people's agency around sexual relationships while also attending to structures, and here we emphasize the social and educational contexts, which may influence the choices that young people make. As it has with programs aimed at women's empowerment, Kabeer's conceptualization, with its emphasis on decision making ability (agency) toward desired outcomes (achievements) with the use of resources (of several kinds), offers the appealing conceptual clarity for examining the interplay between peers and students' choices and values around sexual relationships. In the chapter that follows, we explore various meanings of Kabeer's dimensions alongside interview data while examining relevant literature. We find that peers serve as social resources to either enter or resist relationships. We find peers influence young people's desired outcomes insofar as peers may either valorize or eschew various types of relationships. And we find young people acknowledge ways in which peers both support and thwart the development of their own agency.

Context: Secondary Schooling in Tanzania

Young people's sexuality is but one of many areas in which the expansion of formal schooling in sub-Saharan Africa has ushered in social change. Where sexuality and marriage were once solidly within the domain of family control (Maticka-Tyndale et al., 2005), more extended transitions to adulthood occurring within educational spaces bring different balances of influences, including increased peer influence, to bear on young people's sexuality. "Today, prolonged education and economic changes has (sic) led to postponing marriage and the creation of adolescence. Schools place girls and boys in close proximity and … created a situation where non-marital, sexual liaisons are likely" (Maticka-Tyndale et al., 2005). Although two of the schools in this study are female-only boarding schools, interviewees described their adolescence as involving the negotiation of both peer and sexual relationships within and around schools, including within single-sex schooling sites. We therefore begin our analysis with a deeper examination of the educational, and, by extension, social contexts of the lives of the young people in this study.

Expanded access to secondary schooling is a recent development in Tanzania. In 1991, when many of the participants' parents were of an age to attend secondary school, the gross secondary enrollment rate was a mere 6 % for male students and 5 % for female students (UNESCO Institute for Statistics, 2014). More recently, the Tanzanian government has passed several educational reforms in an attempt to expand the provision and improve the quality of secondary schooling. Nevertheless, inequalities according to sex remain. In 2012, for example, only 33 % of young women were enrolled in secondary school, compared to 37 % of young men (World Bank, 2014). Beyond overall enrollment rates, which often mask other gender inequalities (see for example, Chisamya, DeJaeghere, Kendall, & Khan, 2012), there are other social, material and economic forces that likely differentially affect young women and men in Tanzania. For example, while corporal punishment is a routine form of discipline in Tanzanian schools (Feinstein & Mwahombela, 2010), sexual abuse of female students is also known to be prevalent such that one out of ten girls in recently reported having been sexually victimized by a teacher (United Republic of Tanzania, 2011).

Tamale notes that "sexuality is deeply embedded in the meanings and interpretations of gender systems" (2011, p. 11). Which normative notions of gender and sexuality are taught and reproduced in the classrooms of Tanzanian secondary schools, and how? Secondary schools, particularly in sub-Saharan Africa, are highly heteronormative contexts (Muhanguzi et al., 2011). Thomas and Rugambwa's (2011) multi-sited ethnographic study revealed how hierarchical, heteronormative conceptualizations of gender were at work in teaching and learning practices in northern Tanzania. Their findings suggest that even when some teachers felt they had a responsibility to promote gender equality in their classrooms, this responsibility was taken up in ways that were counter-productive. The authors argue that these conceptualizations reveal, and leave untouched, underlying beliefs that girls are less confident or less academically capable. In one example, a teacher's lesson portrays an "empowered Tanzanian woman" in conflict surrounding her vocational choice, the eventual resolution of which involves her securing her husband's permission to continue with her job (Thomas & Rugambwa, 2011). This example highlights the ways in which scripts of masculinity and femininity can be reinscribed in Tanzanian classrooms even when some teachers' lessons attempt to question them. With regard to what students may be directly taught about sexual relationships in Tanzanian secondary schools, Vavrus (2003) describes the tendency for teachers and students to replicate parent–child relationships that may involve moral instruction but often preclude as taboo the open discussion of sex. Sexual education is further complicated by other material and social constraints in Tanzanian schools, as Plummer et al. (2007) notes a severe shortage of educational materials, the use of didactic pedagogy, authoritarian teacher-student relationships, corporal punishment and sexual abuse of students.

In summary, though the provision of schooling may be expanding in Tanzania, the quality and relevance remains severely lacking, thus aggravating tensions between schooling and youth's economic and social needs during adolescence. Literature suggests that students are frequently taught in environments in which heteronormative, hierarchical, gender structures prevail, and in some cases are unsafe for female students. And while the state of sex education in Tanzanian secondary schools is less thoroughly researched, there are indications it is inadequate, particularly given the current AIDS epidemic. We conclude this section with a caveat in that we do not claim that all the educational conditions described above were being experienced by the interviewees in this study. We note, for example, that the schools in this study offer a life skills program, either embedded within the curriculum or as an extracurricular option. While we did not examine each of these programs, their presence suggests an institutional acknowledgement of young people's needs beyond learning the national secondary curriculum, if not some commitment toward providing some sexual, reproductive or social-emotional education. Further, at one of these schools, students described how their participation in the life skills program, which we did examine and found to be particularly robust, has enhanced their ability to make strategic choices in their sexual relationships and that at least some of the students are receiving relatively higher quality teaching in a more supportive atmosphere than is typical in many Tanzanian secondary schools (see Willemsen & DeJaeghere, 2015, for a more thorough description). Yet interview and observational data alike confirm that many of the pedagogical, curricular and social constraints described above have been experienced by the interviewees in this study, if not presently in these schools, then in their previous school experiences. In the following section, we look more closely at the educational and economic contexts of the young people in this study following an introduction to our own collaboration.

Methodology and Study Background

In order to situate this chapter and collaboration, we offer a brief introduction to our shared history of interest in issues of gender and schooling in Tanzania. We have been examining these and related issues since 1998, when Anna was one of Laura's English students at a secondary school in Tanzania. In the ensuing years—together with other colleagues, friends and students—we have had numerous conversations about education, development, globalization, sexuality, and female empowerment. Because we were both students at the same tertiary institution in Tanzania, albeit at different times, we compared experiences to examine the norms, structures and nuances of gender and relationships in this context. We observed the dissonances between the relationships around us and the notion of rational, dispassionate individuals armed with the knowledge, abilities and preferences to practice abstinence, monogamy and safe sex as promoted by ubiquitous anti-HIV transmission efforts. In time, both of us went on to study gender in graduate school, and each of us embarked on our own studies examining issues of gender in the context of Tanzanian secondary schools. Later we worked together with Joan DeJaeghere on one of the studies from which these data are drawn. During Laura's frequent trips to Tanzania while pursuing her doctoral work, we have spent weeks reading, critiquing, discussing, assisting with and shaping each other's work. It was during one such visit, when our discussions turned to how critical peers are in shaping young people's sexual relationships, that we envisaged bringing together data from different studies with a new framework.

What follows, then, is a secondary analysis of previously collected qualitative interview data from two different studies of schooling and relationships in Tanzania, collected at four secondary schools in 2013 and 2014. In one study, conducted in 2014, Anna Ndesamburo Kwayu investigated how school peer groups might be used to help adolescents avoid risky sexual behavior at three schools in northern Tanzania (Ndesamburo Kwayu, 2014). The other study, conducted in 2013, examined how life skills training impacted young women's relationships at an all-girls' school in central Tanzania.[1] Both studies relied extensively on qualitative interviews. The 2013 life skills study also made use of ethnographically informed participant-observation, and Anna made use of quantitative surveys in her study as well. The two studies allowed for interviews with 82 secondary students as well as nine parents and several teachers, and we examined any resulting data that was pertinent to our research question.

Each of the in-depth interviews we consider in this chapter was semi-structured and conducted in Kiswahili by Anna. The resulting dialogue was then translated and transcribed into English by Anna or, in the case of life skills study, with assistance from Laura. Laura and Anna then coded these interviews for themes related to their original studies (see Ndesamburo Kwayu, 2014; Willemsen & DeJaeghere, 2015), and then re-coded the interviews according to themes pertinent to this chapter's analysis. The intimate nature of our relationships with the sites and participants in the study makes the citation of participant interviews and dates problematic for ensuring participant confidentiality. Additionally, citing which specific study the data comes from has the potential to breach the anonymity for the participants. For these reasons, we have chosen not to attribute interview citations to individual participants at specific schools.

While we do include some adult interviewee data for additional perspectives, we focus primarily on relevant student interview data because our foremost aim is to examine youth experiences and perceptions with peers and sexual relationships. Student interviewees were in secondary school, from Forms One to Six (roughly equivalent to eighth through twelfth grade in a United States-based system), aged 15–22 years. Because two of the schools in these studies are all-girls' schools, there were 57 female and 25 male student interviewees. In most cases, teachers assisted in selecting students who they thought would be willing and informative participants, as well as those with whom it was convenient to talk. We found enlisting teachers' help in locating subjects (both youth and adult) was the least disruptive, most efficient and most courteous way of approaching this work at bustling school sites where national exams were looming. While this is a purposive and convenience sample from four schools and is not necessarily representative of their schools' student bodies, nor of Tanzanian young people in general, we contend that these young people's voices, contextualized as they are, provide valuable insights that contribute to the growing research and theoretical work on sexuality in educational spaces, peer relationships and youth agency in Tanzania.

---

[1] For this study, Anna Ndesamburo Kwayu served as the research assistant, Joan DeJaeghere was the principal investigator, and Laura Wangsness Willemsen was the coinvestigator (Willemsen & DeJaeghere, 2015).

As with schooling, youth's economic and material contexts shape their notions of sexual relationships. The young women and men who attended the four schools tend to be from less affluent families in rural or semi-rural areas of Tanzania. Two of these schools were, in fact, created to serve marginalized, underprivileged young women who would otherwise not attend secondary school. The other two offer relatively low cost secondary schooling for local families. Furthermore, the three schools in northern Tanzania draw significantly from the local population of nomadic and semi-nomadic families who historically had limited access to formal schooling. In each of these schools, the majority of students' parents attended little or no formal schooling themselves, usually limited to a few years of primary school, if any. Parents and guardians of students at all schools are primarily subsistence farmers or livestock keepers. Climate change, however, has caused weather patterns to be increasingly unreliable, making these livelihoods more and more tenuous. Accordingly, many families augment their agriculture-based incomes via engaging in small business ventures such as making charcoal, selling snacks or crushing rock to produce gravel. In summary, most youth interviewees at these schools come from economically disadvantaged backgrounds and, as part of Tanzania's recent expansion of secondary schooling, are among the first in their families to attend secondary school. With unemployment rampant, the likelihood of finding secure employment or self-employment post-graduation is low. Their broader economic and social challenges, therefore, are succinctly described by Honwana (2014), "African societies are struggling with economic decline, strained educational systems, high unemployment rates, and insecure livelihoods, all of which seriously weaken the social fabric" (p. 33). It is within such contexts that youth develop their notions of, and aspirations for, sexual, romantic, and peer relationships, as well as closely linked notions of modernity.

Social and Sexual Relationships in School: Resources, Risk, Resistance, and Agency

Relationships, Schooling and Modernity

We begin with an examination of these students' perceptions and experiences of sexual and peer relationships so as to better comprehend both individuals' choices and a variety of peer influences. Some of the young people we interviewed described an awareness of how their conceptualizations of sexual relationships were influenced from a variety of sources. At one site, young women described their life skills classes as having taught them about mutuality in relationships (Willemsen & DeJaeghere, 2015). Many interviewees made the overt distinction between what their families said or expected of them, and what they learned from other sources. For these interviewees, the concept of romantic sexual relationships was frequently attached to notions originating beyond the spheres of influence of their families and invoked the idea of more global youth cultures. This stands in contrast to the findings of a study nearly 10 years earlier on young people's sexuality in an adjacent area of rural northern Tanzania in which romantic love was not a primary consideration (Wight et al., 2006). The following is a quote from a Form Three student in which she described how information and notions of sexual relationships were shared in her school, "I am sure we (teens) know a lot about love, more than our parents can tell us. We learn through television, books and internet, and when we meet with our friends we share our experiences. It is very important." This quote highlights how conceptualizations gleaned from sources beyond the family are valorized and, in turn, disseminated by peers in educational spaces.

Although it is not the main focus of our analysis, we noted that parents similarly associated schooling with the introduction of notions of sexuality of which they disapproved. Here the mother of a Form Two student described her anger at her daughter's clothing choice, an area in which other researchers have noted sexuality is performed by secondary school students (Stambach, 2000; Muhanguzi et al., 2011). The mother stated:

> Many of our daughters today when they come back from school for holiday, we are expecting to see that they have changed in a constructive way, but … my daughter came back home dressed in very tight jeans. She had never done that in front of my eyes, it was quite shocking … I had to punish and warn her not to do it again because that is not our culture, it's very dangerous, she can be raped because of the way she is dressed.

This quote highlights two recurring tensions. The first tension involved families' expectations of what young people will learn in school and what young people actually experienced and learned around schooling. The second tension was between more "traditional" norms of sexuality and what may be considered more cosmopolitan notions and performances of sexuality. Stambach's (2000) ethnographic work in the context of secondary schools in the rapidly changing region of Kilimanjaro closely examines these and other tensions. She found a subset of adults in that community held a negative view of schooling. These adults made a distinction between young women's "traditional" transitions to marriage and motherhood, which they valorized, and "city sisters," whose schooling brings about a new set of aspirations, relationships, sexuality, and livelihoods.

Similarly, the young people in our study described schools as places in which aspirations for a consumptive modernity are cultivated among peers. They acknowledged that such aspirations, like more cosmopolitan notions of sexuality and romance, were in tension with families' economic abilities. In the following quote, a young male student suggested his generation was distinct in their awareness of, and desire for, global material goods that, in turn, fostered competition between peers for the status they bestowed on their owners:

> Teenagers of today know each and every thing. We want nice things such as expensive telephones, i-pods and laptops … We are competing with our friends in school without knowing their parents' status at home. For example, my mama sells *maandazi* (donuts) and through this business she gets money to send me to school expecting me to study so that I will come back and help her and my young sister later. She cannot afford those luxurious things. So I have to understand her situation.

Mojola's (2014) study in Kenyan secondary schools has similarly revealed this coupling of schooling and consumption. She described the dilemma of young secondary school women who needed goods, such as face creams, to enact notions of educated, modern, cultivated women: "The project of modernity, the implicit work of school, then, was arguably bound up with consumption—consumption that many could not afford" (p. 132). Likewise, the story of this secondary school student, the son of a *maandazi* seller who is charged with ensuring his family's well-being upon graduation yet who desires a laptop despite his family's financial constraints, well-represented our interviewees' struggles to cope with multiple tensions including between peers and families, and their desires and school's demands.

In short, interviewees described schooling as connected to romantic and globalized notions of sexual relationships, consumption, and recurring tensions between families and peers playing out in realms such as clothing choices and a desire for status associated with what young people term "luxurious" goods, which are indicative of modernity. Yet for the participants in this study, most goods associated with this modernity were still largely elusive and aspirational given their precarious economic status, relatively rural geography, student status and the fact that the majority of their parents were less-educated subsistence farmers engaged in small business ventures. It is within these consumptive educational contexts that both peer and sexual relationships became resources and risks, and that young people's agency was cultivated as well as thwarted.

Relationships as Resources

These young women and men described engaging in sexual and romantic relationships as a means of procuring a variety of resources of varying importance. Kabeer (1999) makes a distinction between first and second-order life choices, whereby first-order choices are "those strategic life choices which are critical for people to live the lives they want" and second-order choices are "less consequential choices, which may be important for the quality of one's life but do not constitute its defining parameters" (p. 437). Our analysis suggested that these young women and men held a range of viewpoints on sexual and romantic relationships. For some, the decision to enter a sexual relationship at times constituted a first-order life choice. For many others, such a decision may be considered more second-order insofar as an individual described being interested in prestige, romantic love, increased status or a measure of material or economic comfort. Nevertheless, neatly categorizing choices around sexual relationships was nearly impossible in part due to their inherent hazards, and young people described how they understood engaging in sexual relationships, for whatever reason, may involve incurring unwanted, harmful and potentially life-altering repercussions.

One young woman interviewee was a single mother who had reluctantly left secondary school shortly before we interviewed her. When her aunt who had been caring for her child became ill and could not work, her household descended into a state of severe need with insufficient food and clothing. Despite seeking help from multiple sources, sources of assistance were neither forthcoming nor sufficient to meet this family's needs. Eventually her boyfriend convinced her to leave school with the promise that he would then help support her family:

> [M]y boyfriend, I went to him and said that I had a problem .... He said, 'How can I help?' And I told him that for me it's very difficult to support my family because I don't have money, I was going to school and couldn't work and they don't have money. So what he said was, 'When you decide what you're going to do with your life, you can tell me. For me, I can't advise you anything, it's for you to decide. So when you decide to leave the school, you tell me.'

In this young woman's retelling, her boyfriend predicated the possibility of securing his further help for her family with the advancement of their relationship, which he positioned as incompatible with her schooling. Therefore, for this young woman, her relationship was the key resource that enabled her to care for her child, even though the pursuing this relationship entailed leaving school. This was a decision she made out of urgent necessity and with a measure of regret. While such a choice was likely a first-order choice, and may have constituted an act of what Kabeer (1999) terms "effective agency", it was not an act of "transformative agency" (pp. 452, 461) which would more fundamentally challenge the inequalities within which this young woman was forced to act.

She goes on to recount how, once she left school, her boyfriend arranged for her to work in a low-paying business venture with one of his relatives. While this was far from this young woman's vocational aspirations, it afforded her the opportunity to care for her family in a time of crisis. She expressed ambivalence about this relationship, yet she recognized that it provided some security. In the excerpt below, Anna had asked, "So, when you look at him, do you think there's a future between the two of you?"

> Hmmm ... I don't know ... he supports me a lot. For example, at the time when I was in school and when I was coming back home, he knew what to give me, he was buying me things to take back to school and he was supporting me. To be honest, he was supporting me to a great extent. So I don't know. Maybe he will change later, but for the time being he is the one ... I will be with him because he's a person who helps me.

In the quote above, the young woman stated a clear linkage between the continuation of a sexual relationship and its material, financial, and emotional support. There is extensive literature around aspects of exchange in sexual relationships in and beyond sub-Saharan Africa (Maticka-Tyndale et al., 2005; Nyanzi, Pool, & Kinsman, 2001; Wight et al., 2006), and the term "transactional" is commonly employed to signify this interchange. Leclerc-Madlala's (2003) work in South Africa reveals how, underlying these relationships is "the idea that sex was something valuable and therefore a man should not expect a woman to give it away for free. The exchange aspect of sex was implicit, whether it was an exchange of sexual favors for basic subsistence or for conspicuous consumption" (p. 220). The Tanzanian secondary students with whom we spoke also had conceptualizations of relationships in which gifting and love were intertwined.

While the previous story illustrated engaging in a sexual relationship out of necessity for purposes related to subsistence, young men and women frequently described pursuing relationships as a means of meeting desires. In terms of Kabeer's framework, these would be second order choices insofar as they are perceived to lead to romance as well as a desired augmentation of status or well-being, but do not, from the perspectives of young people, entail critical life choices. Many examinations of the "sugar-daddy" phenomenon, engaging in sexual relationships with older partners to access desired goods, have occurred via diverse lenses (Hawkins et al., 2009; Luke, 2005: Silberschmidt & Rasch, 2001) but this is not the main focus of this chapter. Some interviewees, however, specifically described relationships with older partners as more materially promising than entering into relationships with peers, as was the case for this young woman:

> I don't want to have an intimate relationship with my fellow student, because I know he doesn't have money to give me, he depends on his parents, and I want things which he cannot afford to give me—that's why I prefer going out with an old man, they know how to treat girls.

This quote echoes Silberschmidt and Rasch's (2001) research with sexually active young women in Dar es Salaam who chose partnerships with older men in what they described as "entrepreneurial and risk-taking" (p. 1822) behavior. Furthermore, this phenomenon was not confined to young woman, as in the case of this Form Five male student who described both the benefit and risk of taking on a "sugar-mommy":

> My friend has a very fancy phone and it was given to him by his girlfriend, an older woman. But this woman expects something in return, at the end of the day if we continue wishing for things we cannot afford will end up dying from HIV/AIDS.

Relationships as Risks

Echoing discourses of danger common in campaigns against the spread of HIV, many youth interviewees described sexual relationships in terms of the risks they posed. In this way, some youth were cognizant of the ways in which what Kabeer would term second order life choices, choices to enter sexual relationships that were unlikely to be long-term commitments, held the latent potential to bring with them life-altering misfortune and thus could become, retrospectively, first-order life choices. While contracting HIV was frequently mentioned as a possible risk, young women in particular described the immediate risk of an unwanted pregnancy as more pressing because it required dropping out of school. This Form One female student described her fear of entering a relationship:

> To me unplanned pregnancy is very risky, it cannot be compared to HIV/AIDS or VDs, if I get pregnant today and I don't have money to abort it, that means I will drop out of school and my family won't accept me because I will have brought shame in the family.

This viewpoint echoes previous research (see Wight et al., 2006; Willemsen & DeJaeghere, 2015; Grant, 2012) on the perceived incompatibility of schooling and pregnancy in Tanzania as well as reinforces research on youth sexuality in sub-Saharan Africa describing how females are expected to remain pure for the sake of their own and their families' honor (Nyanzi et al., 2001).

Male students also described relationships as jeopardizing their schooling. Here, a Form Three male offers his rationale for avoiding young women: "I haven't started yet to involve myself in love affairs because I know it will consume my time of studying." The sentiment in this quote was shared by young women as well, and was indicative of the widespread anxiety concerning academic achievement in a context where a form four certificate is required to secure most jobs that do not involve manual labor. In these contexts, students coupled their future livelihoods with their current academic effort, and many students—female and male—regarded sexual relationships as threatening to their future plans.

Peers Influencing Desired Outcomes

One area that has garnered widespread attention are the ways in which young people may exert influence on each other in ways that some adults consider to be negative, sometimes termed "peer pressure." This phenomenon was strongly evident in our data. Some parents blamed peers for their children's engagement in sexual relationships, as in this example of a secondary school girl's mother lamenting her daughter's relationship with an older man:

> Friends provide information of how sex is in stories. They go far on introducing their friends to partners. My daughter was having an affair with a military police man ... When I came to find out, I was very angry with her. When I inquired how she happened to know that man, she said a friend of hers in school had connected her to him. It is very painful.

This story aligns with other research showing peers serve as intermediaries between would-be sexual partners in educational spaces in sub-Saharan Africa (Maticka-Tyndale et al., 2005; Mojola, 2014; Nyanzi et al., 2001).

Some youth acknowledged that their peers could valorize sexual relationships to the extent that they may began to view such relationships as desired outcomes, overcoming their initial reluctance and enter them. For example, this young woman, a Form Two student, had not intended to have a boyfriend in school, yet she changed her mind:

> I didn't want to have any intimate relationship till I finish my O-level education. That was my plan. However, I found it changing after I met friends who hooked me up with a boy who is my school mate, I didn't want to disappoint my friends so I accepted him.

While it is unclear whether the friends she referred to were male or female, or the extent or type of pressure she received, her choice to enter a relationship with a classmate suggests she was not primarily motivated by obtaining "luxurious" material goods that are often associated with older men (Wight et al., 2006).

There is research suggesting peers differentially influence individuals' motivations to enter relationships (Maticka-Tyndale et al., 2005; Muhanguzi, 2011). We hypothesize that this young woman may have viewed her decision to enter a sexual relationship as potentially conferring her with higher social status in her school setting. The extent to which she viewed herself as agentic, however, in her eventual decision to enter this relationship, as well as her views on this relationship, are unclear.

Researchers also frequently describe negative motivation at the root of the decision to enter relationships, as in Muhanguzi's (2011) analysis of female sexuality in Ugandan secondary schools, where young women "risk harassment by boys for rejecting their sexual invitations and advances" (p. 717). We noted that while our interviews did not reveal any instances of rape or obviously coerced sexual relationships, we make no claims that that these have not occurred at these schools or to these same young people in other settings. In the case of the interviewee's decision above, there may likely have been an element of avoidance of stigmatization involved in her eventual decision to enter an intimate relationship with her classmate. Underscoring others' findings on the pressure that male students feel to perform a notion of masculinity that involves sexual conquest (Maticka-Tyndale et al., 2005; Nyanzi et al., 2001; Nzioka, 2001), some male interviewees described obscuring their actual sexual experiences in discussion with their peers, as in the case of this form three student who wanted to avoid sex while in school: "But when I am with my friends, I tell them that I have tried it so that they won't tease me."

In an attempt to understand how young people's peer contexts create circumstances in which sexual relationships become achievements they may not otherwise value, we return to Kabeer. She describes how it is "difficult to judge the validity of an 'achievement' measure unless we have evidence, or can make a reasonable guess, as to whose agency was involved and the extent to which the achievement in question transformed prevailing inequalities in resources and agency rather than reinforcing them or leaving them unchallenged" (1999, p. 452). By this definition, the agency exercised by students in this section is not transformative. Some interviewees reluctantly acted within the confines of social structures they would have preferred to eschew.

Peers as Social Resources and Fostering Agency

Having examined how sexual relationships can serve as resources and risks for young people in Tanzania, as well as the ways in which peers may shape each other's desires for relationships, we now examine how these secondary school students use their peer relationships as valued resources that may, in turn, foster the development of their agency. In Kabeer's (1999) conceptualization of the process of empowerment, she describes resources as needing to be defined "in ways which spell out the potential for human agency and valued achievements" (p. 444). Some interviewees described how they intentionally organized themselves in peer social groups according to shared values, or achievements to which they aspired, including organizing themselves according their experiences and aspirations with sexual relationships. One young woman detailed the existence of distinct social groups delineated along lines of those who had boyfriends or children and those who did not:

Anna:	What about the friends you have in school … do they have boyfriends?
Female Form Two interviewee:	Yes, they have boyfriends, the majority of them have boyfriends. For example, many of the girls who study here have babies … these girls talk about elder things … So when you hear these girls' stories and their stories of their boyfriends, their stories are different than mine, especially when they have babies … [T]hey just share experiences about their boyfriends and the relationships they have with them, and you can come across a group of girls who have boyfriends and who have babies sitting in a group by themselves.

Even as this young woman described this group of girls as her friends, she distinguished herself from them as having different stories, and sitting in a different space, separated from those with different life experiences around sexuality and reproduction. With our understanding of this school context, we suggest that the group of mothers sitting together may be offering each other companionship and encouragement toward sustaining their studies, particularly given the improbability and difficulty of their returning to school after bearing children.

Our data revealed instances in which young people purposively attended to their peer relationships in order to subtly resist inequalities or cultivate viable alternatives. In an interview excerpt that underscores both how young people are cognizant of how their peers shape which outcomes are considered desirable and how youth are accordingly agentic in how they engage with their peers, this student described her wariness at engaging in discussion of sexual relationships with young women from her home context:

Anna:	What do your friends discuss regarding relationships—do they have boyfriends?
Female Form Three student:	My school friends don't have boyfriends, but my friends at home do have boyfriends.
Anna:	How do these friends at home define relationships?
Female Form Three student:	Well, for me, when I'm sitting with her and she begins to talk about her boyfriend, I change the topic. Because, in short, nobody knows me that well, and I don't want to talk about relationships with boys. And if I tell them I don't want to hear about it, they may feel bad and so I just change the topic.

In the context of this particular school, which serves marginalized young women with high academic potential from backgrounds of extreme poverty, we understand this young woman's assertion that "nobody knows me that well" at home to mean that she recognizes how her relational aspirations are divergent from those of the young women in her home neighborhood. Her aspirations, the outcomes she has come to value for herself in the context of an all-girls' boarding school and among peers she has chosen who do not have boyfriends, and her subsequent sheltering of them, strongly suggested she has grasped what Kabeer termed "the possibility of alternatives" for herself (1999, p. 437). Furthermore, she viewed her home friend's potential influence on the topic of sexual relationships as possibly challenging her own well-being, and her response was to avoid the topic as a form of self-protection.

Occasionally young women and men described how their peers provided emotional support in the context of sexual relationships. Further, they distinguished this support from the support they may have received from adults, particularly parents: "I have a boyfriend, if he dumps me today I can't go to my mother and tell her that something like this has happened to me, she will be very mad at me, but if I go to my friends who are my peers, I will get help. They will be my crying shoulder and they won't judge me." In-depth examinations of the ways in which peers provided such emotional support were scant in the literature on youth sexuality in secondary schools in sub-Saharan Africa. We feel this is an area that deserves more attention, and were we to able to interview these young people again, we would probe for deeper understandings of this phenomenon.

We conclude this section with an examination of a final interview excerpt in which a young woman described how her group of friends provided each other with a different kind of pressure. While the previous section focused on how secondary school peers in Tanzania may exert pressure toward entering sexual relationships, here is a compelling opposite case:

Anna:	And how about these friends, do you talk about boyfriends?
Female Form Two student:	In my group we have made a promise not to have any boyfriends, so we have this agreement that until we finish school and we're ready we won't have boyfriends.
Anna:	Oh—what happens if one of this group decides to have a boyfriend?
Female Form Two student:	She will never be our friend again. We will call her and tell her the reason why we are taking her out of the group, because she will have made a fake promise. So we will leave her. But first before that, we should call and say that she has gone against the promise, but, however, I don't think any one of these girls will go against her promise. But if it happens, we will tell her and then we won't be her friend again.

When discussing how to consider agency, Kabeer (1999) writes, "We have to know about its consequential significance in terms of women's strategic life choices and the extent to which it had transformatory potential" (p. 452). For these young women, students at a school for marginalized girls, their understanding of the way in which sexual relationships may impact their lives (possibly thwarting their academic advancement) has caused them to intentionally structure their peer relationships in ways that makes it more likely for them to be able to withstand prevailing pressure to enter relationships. This is the strongest example in our data of young people's notions of sexual relationships influencing their choices and expression of peer relationships. We suggest it is an example of youth intentionally cultivating their agency through their peer relationships. Yet the extent to which this calculated structuring of peer relationships will ultimately foster desired life changes for these young women, whether this has or will result in effective or transformatory agency, remain unknown to us.

Conclusion

In reviewing literature in preparation for writing this chapter, we noted that much of the research on gender, sexuality, and schooling in sub-Saharan Africa does not explicitly focus on influences of peer relationships. It is not unusual for authors to employ the passive voice when describing youth sexuality and gender such that, for example, gendered identities "are constructed" but it's not completely clear by whom or how, or sexual roles "are learned," yet we're left uncertain who is actively teaching and in what ways. Thus peer influences, while alluded to, are not always clearly examined or defined. In contrast, the focus of this chapter has been to analyze previously collected interview data in an attempt to elucidate how youth see their peers as influencing their notions of and experiences with sexuality within the contexts of four secondary schools in Tanzania. Drawing on Kabeer's (1999) notions of resources, agency and achievements, we examined youth conceptualizations of sexual and peer relationships and revealed instances in which youth see their agency around such relationships as either supported or thwarted by their peers.

In her examination of sexuality in Kenyan secondary schools, Mojola (2014) references Pugh's work discussing "how young people's consumption desires are not just about wanting to possess material things; they are also about participating in their school culture and attaining social visibility among their peers" (p. 129). Our findings suggest that, for these Tanzanian secondary school students in precarious economic and educational contexts, schooling is similarly linked to notions of consumptive modernity, which are cultivated and valorized by peers and that, furthermore, youth frequently regard romantic, sexual relationships as a component of this modernity. Young women and men acknowledged that peers actively shape notions of and experiences with sexual relationships, which, like schooling, are viewed as potentially offering expanded access to social and material resources.

These young women and men described a diverse range in their experiences with the interplay between their peer and sexual relationships, and they recognized both welcome and unwelcome ways that peers influence their values and experiences with sexual and romantic relationships. Youth noted dissonance between their peers' and families understandings and values of sexual relationships. Young women and men alike described feeling pressure to enter sexual relationships for increased status and/or consumption. Finally, some youth used their peers as resources to cultivate their agency to eschew sexual relationships in the hopes of finishing school.

We conclude by considering Kabeer's (1999) distinction between effective and transformatory agency, which is agency that may be used to challenge inequalities. While some youth suggested their agency has been impeded by their peers' values and actions, others described instances in which their effective agency has been supported by peers, sexual relationships, or some combination of the two, particularly in order to procure resources, social status or well-being. Our analysis also reveals ways in which Tanzanian secondary school students from economically insecure families used peer relationships as resources in the pursuit of what may become transformatory agency toward their valued achievements. This is particularly true for young women from marginalized backgrounds who regarded schooling as essential for their current and future well-being. As these students navigated the tensions, contradictions, and possibilities with relationships, risks, and resources, they purposefully drew on their peers to cultivate and grow their agency.

References

Action Aid. (2007). *White paper: Transforming education for girls in Nigeria and Tanzania.* Nairobi, Kenya: Action Aid.

Chisamya, G., DeJaeghere, J., Kendall, N., & Khan, M. (2012). Gender and 'Education for All': Progress and problems in achieving gender equity. *International Journal of Educational Development, 32*, 743–755.

DeJaeghere, J., & Lee, S. K. (2011). What matters for marginalized girls and boys: A capabilities approach to exploring marginalization and empowerment in Bangladesh. *Research in Comparative and International Education, 6*(1), 27–42.

Feinstein, S., & Mwahombela, L. (2010). Corporal punishment in Tanzania's schools. *International Review of Education, 56*(4), 399. doi:10.1007/s11159-010-9169-5.

Grant, M. (2012). Girls' schooling and the perceived threat of adolescent sexual activity in rural Malawi. *Culture, Health & Sexuality, 14*(1), 73–86.

Harper, G. W., Gannon, C., Watson, S. E., Catania, J. A., & Dolcini, M. M. (2004). The role of close friends in African American adolescents' dating and sexual behavior. *Journal of Sex Research, 41*(4), 351–362.

Hawkins, K., Price, N., & Mussá, F. (2009). Milking the cow: Young women's construction of identity and risk in age-disparate transactional sexual relationships in Maputo, Mozambique. *Global Public Health, 4*(2), 169–182.

Honwana, A. (2014). Waithood: Youth transitions and social change. In D. Foeken, T. Dietz, L. de Haan, & L. Johnson (Eds.), *Development and equity: An interdisciplinary exploration by ten scholars from Africa, Asia, and Latin America.* Leiden, The Netherlands: Brill.

Kabeer, N. (1999). Resources, agency, achievements: Reflections on the measurement of women's empowerment. *Development and change, 30*(3), 435–464.

Leclerc-Madlala, S. (2003). Transactional sex and the pursuit of modernity. *Social Dynamics, 29*(2), 213–233.

Luke, N. (2005). Confronting the 'sugar daddy' stereotype: Age and economic asymmetries and risky sexual behavior in urban Kenya. *International Family Planning Perspectives, 31*(1), 6–14.

Maticka-Tyndale, E., Gallant, M., Brouillard-Coyle, C., Holland, D., Metcalfe, K., Wildish, J., et al. (2005). The sexual scripts of Kenyan young people and HIV prevention. *Culture, Health & Sexuality, 7*(1), 27–41.

Mojola, S. A. (2014). *Love, money, and HIV: Becoming a modern African woman in the age of AIDS.* Berkeley, CA: University of California Press.

Monkman, K., Miles, R., & Easton, P. (2008). The dance of agency and structure in an empower-ment educational program in Mali and the Sudan. In M. A. Maslak (Ed.), *The structure and agency of women's education* (pp. 107–126). Albany, NY: State University of New York Press.

Muhanguzi, F. K. (2011). Gender and sexual vulnerability of young women in Africa: Experiences of young girls in secondary schools in Uganda. *Culture, Health & Sexuality, 13*(06), 713–725.

Muhanguzi, F. K., Bennett, J., & Muhanguzi, H. (2011). The construction and mediation of sexual-ity and gender relations: Experiences of girls and boys in secondary schools in Uganda. *Feminist Formations, 23*(3), 135–152.

Murphy-Graham, E. (2008). Opening the black box: Women's empowerment and innovative sec-ondary education in Honduras. *Gender and Education, 20*(1), 31–50.

Ndesamburo Kwayu, A. (2014). *Prospects and challenges of using adolescent peer groups in dis-couraging risky sexual behaviours in Tanzania.* Unpublished master's thesis. University of Dar es Salaam, Tanzania.

Nyanzi, S., Pool, R., & Kinsman, J. (2001). The negotiation of sexual relationships among school pupils in south-western Uganda. *AIDS Care, 13*(1), 83–98.

Nzioka, C. (2001). Perspectives of adolescent boys on the risks of unwanted pregnancy and sexu-ally transmitted infections: Kenya. *Reproductive Health Matters, 9*(17), 108–117.

Plummer, M. L., Wight, D., Wamoyi, J., Nyalali, K., Ingall, T., Mshana, G., et al. (2007). Are schools a good setting for adolescent sexual health promotion in rural Africa? A qualitative assessment from Tanzania. *Health Education Research, 22*(4), 483–499.

Silberschmidt, M., & Rasch, V. (2001). Adolescent girls, illegal abortions and "sugar-daddies" in Dar es Salaam: Vulnerable victims and active social agents. *Social Science & Medicine, 52*(12), 1815–1826.

Springer, A., Parcel, G., Baumler, E., & Ross, M. (2006). Supportive social relationships and ado-lescent health risk behaviour among secondary school students in El Savador. *Social Science Medicine, 62,* 1628–1640.

Stambach, A. (2000). *Lessons from Mount Kilimanjaro: Schooling, community and gender in East Africa.* New York, NY: Routledge.

Tamale, S. (2011). Researching and theorising sexualities in Africa. *African Sexualities: A Reader,* pp. 11–36.

Thomas, M. A., & Rugambwa, A. (2011). Equity, power, and capabilities: Constructions of gender in a Tanzanian secondary school. *Feminist Formations, 23*(3), 153–175.

Thorpe, M. (2005). Learning about HIV/AIDS in schools: Does a gender-equality approach make a difference? In S. Aikman & E. Unterhalter (Eds.), *Beyond access: Transforming policy and practice for gender equality in education* (pp. 199–211). Herndon, VA: Stylus Publishing.

UNESCO Institute for Statistics. (2014). *Education profile: United Republic of Tanzania.* Retrieved December 13, 2015, from http://stats.uis.unesco.org/unesco/TableViewer/document.aspx?ReportId=121&IF_Language=eng&BR_Country=7620&BR_Region=40540.

United Republic of Tanzania. (2011). *Violence against children in Tanzania findings from a national survey 2009.* United Republic of Tanzania: UNICEF.

Unterhalter, E., Boler, T., & Aikman, S. (2008). Essentialism, equality, and empowerment: Concepts of gender and schooling in the HIV and AIDS epidemic. In S. Aikman, E. Unterhalter, & T. Boler (Eds.), *Gender equality, HIV, and AIDS* (pp. 11–32). Oxford, England: Oxfam Publishing.

Vavrus, F. (2003). *Desire and decline.* New York, NY: Peter Lang.

Wight, D., Plummer, M. L., Mshana, G., Wamoyi, J., Shigongo, Z. S., & Ross, D. A. (2006). Contradictory sexual norms and expectations for young people in rural Northern Tanzania. *Social Science & Medicine, 62*(4), 987–997.

Willemsen, L. W., & DeJaeghere, J. (2015). Learning to negotiate sexual relationships: A girls' school in Tanzania as a restrictive and agentic site. *Gender and Education, 27*(2), 183–197.

World Bank. (2014). *World Data Bank development indicators.* Retrieved November 7, 2015, from http://databank.worldbank.org/data/views/reports/tableview.aspx.

Part III
Youth Agency and Socio-Economic Contexts

Considering Children's Economic Agency: Work and School Decisions in Kanchipuram, India

Miriam S. Thangaraj

Introduction

What happens when children's situated logics for work and school encounter the child labor policy community in India that has repeatedly called for a "blanket ban" on child labor in the country? The answer is troubling, as I found: children's deliberate and deliberated decisions about work and/or schooling were typically dismissed as "misapprehension" or derided as "careless" and "rogue" behavior—paradoxically in the name of children's rights, and to education in particular. This chapter offers an ethnographic account of how constructions of "childhood," constituted in and by adultist discourses of child welfare (Sandin, 2009), international development arguments about educational returns (Psacharopoulos & Patrinos, 2004), and the global cultural politics of children's rights (Stephens, 1995), are experienced by children in contexts marked by increasingly neoliberal logics of production and consumption (Harvey, 2005). On the one hand, globally mandated policies to "combat child labor through education" (IPEC-ILO, 2009, p. 2) sought to restore working children to "childhood" (INDUS-ILO, 2006a); on the other hand, working children in Kanchipuram, in the light of their lived economic realities, responded to global mandates for schooling in "flexitarian" ways that belied straightforward conceptions of "childhood." By foregrounding the logics and aspirations of working children, the chapter seeks to acknowledge children's economic agency and frames their flexitarian strategies as a situated critique of global policy constructions of childhood and child labor.

This research was supported in part by the Social Science Research Council's International Dissertation Research Fellowship, with funds provided by the Andrew W. Mellon Foundation; and by the National Academy of Education/Spencer Dissertation Fellowship.

M.S. Thangaraj (✉)
Department of Educational Policy Studies, University of Wisconsin-Madison, Madison, WI, USA
e-mail: thangaraj@wisc.edu

© Springer International Publishing Switzerland 2016
J.G. DeJaeghere et al. (eds.), *Education and Youth Agency*, Advancing Responsible Adolescent Development, DOI 10.1007/978-3-319-33344-1_11

Origins, Part I: Out of the Mouths of Children

In the spirit of the argument I make in this chapter, it is important that I mark its origins in a conversation with 12-year-old Kanniappa.[1] "I want the 'minister' to know what I think—will you tell him what I said," he asked me urgently, one afternoon. It was several months into my fieldwork in Kanchipuram, a municipal corporation in the southern Indian state of Tamil Nadu—the primary site of my fieldwork in India, in 2009 and 2011–2013—and I was escorting Kanniappa back to his TEC (Transition Education Center) classroom. He had disappeared from the TEC earlier in the day, and I had finally run him to ground by the rubbish-dump that edged Pillayarapalayam, one of the key weaving "neighborhoods" (see Arterburn, 1982) in the area. He was scouring the area for "wire" he explained, referring to the increasingly lucrative trade in scrap metal—25 g of aluminum or 10 g of copper would fetch 10 rupees at the two scrap-metal shops he frequented. Ten rupees that, he grinned, would pay for the four eggs he planned to make a "grand egg-fry" with! I grinned back at his enthusiasm and promised not to tell his teachers.

K [loudly]:	But I want you to tell the "[education] minister" about it; I want him to know that people are nagging me about school. They are giving me *tholla* (trouble), and I want them to stop... It's a "waste", a "time-waste". I could be collecting "wire" instead.
MT [teasing]:	What if you don't find any wire?
K:	I'll work in a *kari-kadai* (butcher's-shop) instead. Do you know, they give you *kaas* (money) and *kozhi* (chicken). I can make a sizzling *biriyani*[2] with it.
MT:	And what if they don't hire you?
K:	I'll work in a *biriyani-kadai*[3] then.
MT:	But what ...
K [interjecting]:	And if they don't hire me, I'll work in the *mitai-kadai* (sweets-shop) then. And if they don't hire me, then the *pani-puri kadai* (*pani-puri* shop) near the main bus-stand. I have worked there before—last year—and they gave me fifty rupees as *naal-coolie* (daily-wage).[4]

[1] Pseudonyms have been used for minor-participants, as per IRB (Institutional Review Board) guidelines, though many of those quoted in this chapter were disappointed that their names would not be recognized and their opinions would not be attributed to them. In the case of interview-participants in the policy community in India, the large majority of whom requested that quotes not be attributed to them or their employers by name—child labor was a "sensitive issue"—I have elected not to name any of them.

[2] *Biriyani* is a popular and festive dish of rice, spices, and usually chicken or goat meat, and a staple at "special functions" like weddings, birthdays and other festive celebrations across India. Increasingly, they have also become a popular take-out food—the families I lived among in Pillayarapalayam, for instance, often ordered *biriyani*-packets to mark Sunday lunch.

[3] In the expanding "fast-food" markets of the post-liberalization era of India's economy, *biriyani-kadais* (*biryani*-shops) have mushroomed across Kanchipuram in the last few years—two new *biriyani*-shops sprung up in Pillayarapalayam during my field-work, attracting a constant crowd of boys and young men each evening.

[4] The quotes used in this chapter were excerpted from field-notes and transcriptions and, where required, translated from the vernacular (primarily Tamil). English words used by my participants

Kanniappa's impressive and intimate knowledge of the local economy had momentarily stumped me. "What about when you are older," I turned to ask him, "fifty rupees won't buy you and your family *biriyani*-packets, will it?" But Kanniappa was not to be moved in the slightest:

> *Thooh* [spitting on the ground], do you know where I'll be in two years' time? I'll be joining a road construction crew when I'm a little bigger—I don't need any more schooling for that! Do you know what the *naal coolie* is? Just the "starting [wage]" is more than two hundred rupees a day.

He would know—after all, his 16-year-old brother, a school drop-out himself, had been working for a few years now as part of a road-construction gang that included other relatives and family members. His *anna* (older brother) was making 450 rupees a day and had recently bought a second-hand motor-bike, Kanniappa crowed triumphantly. "A bike!" He repeated, dancing a little celebratory jig. "You are taping all this, aren't you," he stopped to ask again. "I want the minister to hear what I think, I want him to know what **Kanniappa** thinks."

A significant amount of my fieldwork in Kanchipuram, an "area of high child labor concentration" (INDUS-ILO, 2006b), was spent in the company of Kanniappa and others like him, who occupied a liminal space on the fringes of school as they engaged in the work-based pursuit of their diverse aspirations. While my larger research project considered older cohorts as well, in this chapter, I focus on a subset of participants, categorized as "children"—persons 14 years of age or below, as defined by the Indian Constitution—and identified as "child labor" by various state and non-state agencies. Fourteen boys and six girls, ranging in age from 11 to 14 or recently turned 15, they moved across—occasionally, circling through—the spaces of middle-schools (classes 6–8), state-run Transition Education Centers (TECs) and work. The targets of anti-child labor projects, they charged me—if not as eloquently and insistently as Kanniappa, then equally frustrated—with conveying their concerns to the *mel-adhikari* (top officials) whose efforts they experienced as unwelcome *thollai* (trouble).

Origins, Part II: Have We Asked the Children?

In 2013, about a year after my conversation with Kanniappa, I was invited to one of several "Civil Society Consultations" being held across the country to mobilize local non-governmental organizations (NGOs) and advocacy groups towards a

---

have been largely retained (in quotation marks), as have key phrases and terms in the vernacular (italicized) where useful.

"blanket ban" on child labor in the country—in particular, to ensure that all children enjoyed the right to elementary education. Organized in a southern Indian city and under the aegis of a transnational, child rights-based NGO, the Consultation brought together about 40 participants from a cross-section of regionally focused NGOs working on or researching child labor issues. I listened as participants shared advocacy, implementation and legal strategies for the prohibition of child labor in India; and when it was my turn, I voiced Kanniappa's frustration with similar anti-child labor efforts in Kanchipuram. Describing the manifold strategies that children like him had adopted in response, combining a variety of regular or casual work with varying amounts of schooling, I asked the participants if they had accounted for children's perspectives. When children often demonstrated extensive knowledge of the local economy and explained their school/work strategies in terms of present consumption needs like *biriyani* but also longer-term aspirations and opportunity costs, I asked those gathered: "Have we asked the children?"

I was only echoing Reddy's (1997) position paper "Have we asked the Children?" which recorded children's demands for rights and protections at work voiced during the first international meeting of working children and youth at Kundapur, India, in 1996 (see Miljeteig, 2000). Seventeen years later, and Consultation participants appeared to find the idea preposterous. "Would you take a child—a *child*—seriously?" one of them responded with exaggerated incredulity. Another suggested that I was being callous about working children: "Would you listen to your well-off children if they refused to go to school in order to work?" he snorted. An elderly researcher suggested that my research was, in effect, contributing to poor children's misapprehension; as his younger colleague added, "It is our work, our duty, to correct children like Kanniappa and educate them about the better future that is accrued from schooling." Still others muttered about my "western training," suggesting it inappropriately valorized children's opinions and aspirations. "Soon you will be asking the state to provide free cell-phones to keep them in school," laughed one of the invited speakers, or "free *biriyani*," added a voice from the audience. "What we need," concluded the speaker to loud applause, "is a blanket-ban [on child labor], not some handkerchief ban that rendered children's right to education ineffective."

Child Labor Policy and the Construction of "Childhood": The Erasure of Children's Economic Agency

This chapter is a consideration of children's economic agency: an ethnographic record of children exercising economic agency in making considered decisions for work and/or school in the light of global policy regimes that facilitate the ready erasure of children's economic agency and fuel the rights-based "blanket ban" discourse of the child labor policy community in India. I focus on the former to challenge the latter; and do so by drawing on two broad literatures, Anthropology of Policy and Childhood Studies.

If policy, as Shore and Wright (1997) observed, is a central regulating principle of modern society, that operates by constituting particular kinds of subjects, then— in the vein of the characteristic poststructural anthropological critique of international development (Escobar, 2011; Ferguson, 2006)—child labor policies represent "regimes of truth" about children and childhood that render particular children and childhoods as objects of and the grounds for protective state and, increasingly, global intervention. However, as Childhood Studies scholars have insisted and social and cultural anthropologists have demonstrated, children are not passive determinations of policy projects. On the other hand, they are social actors in their own right, effective in altering the conditions of their own childhoods (Bluebond-Langner & Korbin, 2007; Liebel, 2004; Mayall, 2000; Montgomery, 2008; Prout & James, 1997).

The Child Labor Policy Orthodoxy

Some of the earliest interventions on the grounds of children's rights—that is, on the grounds that the substance of children's "nature" was different from that of adults (Cunningham, 1995; Hendrick, 1997)—were in relation to the labor market. The first child labor laws in nineteenth century Britain reified a particular idea(l) of childhood as a distinct and inherently vulnerable condition, best served by the nurture of the family. Institutionalized in factory legislation, this middle-class, Victorian ideology of childhood rendered poor and working-class children as needy or deviant and the appropriate objects of protection and reform by state and society (Hendrick, 1997; Sandin, 2009). Child labor laws were an educational project[5] from the start, purposed to regulate factory-children by removing them into the expanding school-system. In effect, schooling working children out of their "precocity," "independence," and "self-reliance"—read as delinquency by the reformers of the day[6]—while schooling them into the dependence characterizing the "domestic ideal" of childhood and the discipline required of the "nation's children" for the success of British industry and empire (Davin, 1982; Hendrick, 1997; Johnson, 1970). In thus restoring the working child to childhood, reformers believed that an uncertain, rapidly industrializing society was also being restored to its stable "natural" (if adultist, patriarchal, classed, and imperial) order.

Child labor laws were not only one of the earliest labor standards, but one of the first to take on an international character (Engerman, 2003): Factory Acts targeting child labor, for instance, spread to the British colonies, including to India in 1881,

---

[5] The first child labor legislation, the Health and Morals of Apprentices Act (also known as the first Factory Act of 1802) not only required clean premises but basic education and religious instruction for factory apprentices.

[6] Mary Carpenter, for instance, leading Victorian educationist and advocate of "reform schools" (see Hendrick, 1997), or Dr. Kay, the chief administrator of the government grant for public education (see Johnson, 1970).

spearheaded by some of the same British reformers. Moreover, when the International Labor Organization (ILO), established in 1919, was tasked with the elimination of child labor as a foundational agenda, the British legislative approach was taken up as the proven model for state action; and with the influx of newly decolonized states into the ILO, post World War II, the British model was further internationalized and institutionalized (Cunningham & Stromquist, 2005; ILO, 2010). As child labor legislations spread across regions over the course of the twentieth century, in effect, the twinned languages of children's rights and socioeconomic progress, originating in nineteenth century Britain, became the predominant frame with respect to child labor everywhere.

The twinned logics of child labor laws were also readily amenable to the dominant two-pronged rationale of human capital and human rights that animated international development and education at the turn of the twentieth century. In the context of the Education For All (EFA) and Millennium Development Goals (MGDs) frameworks, child labor was not only a bad investment in human capital, whether at the household or national level, it was also, quite simply, bad for children. Thus, laws banning child labor were seen as both a marker and the means of modernization, intrinsic to the achievement of individual, national and even global development goals and intrinsic to the proper experience of childhood (Boyden & Levison, 2000; Grimsrud, 2003; Kendall, 2008; Psacharopoulos & Patrinos, 2004; Weiner, 1991; World Bank, 1995). This orthodoxy on child labor is currently represented by the IPEC, ILO's International Program on the Elimination of Child Labour[7] and the largest global effort against child labor. "[R]ecognizing the extent to which child labour elimination and implementing the right to education for all children are intertwined," IPEC issued a call for "Combating Child Labor through Education" (IPEC-ILO, 2009, p. 2); in effect, framing school and work as inherently oppositional spaces and reinscribing childhood as a period of appropriate dependence on adults and appropriate development and discipline in school.

The global orthodoxy on child labor has been increasingly taken up by the child labor policy community in India as the basis of their demand for a complete prohibition of child labor in the country. The state-appointed Study Group on Women Workers and Child Labour, for instance, signaled a departure from the extant "regulatory approach" of the Child Labor Prevention and Regulation Act (CLPRA) of 1986 and towards what Lieten (2002) has described as the "activist position" of banning all child labor. Where the CLPRA, India's primary child labor law, regulated child labor by employment-sector and working conditions, the Study Group declared that all forms of work, including home-based work, were "bad" for children and recommended new legislation that enforced compulsory education as a means of prohibiting child labor (Reports of the National Commission on Labour, 2003). With the Right to Education Act (RTE) signed into law in 2010, guaranteeing eight years of free elementary education to all children in the country, calls for abolishing child labor "in line with RTE" grew louder (Bring child labour prevention law, 2011),

---

[7] IPEC was established by ILO in 1992, in the wake of the United Nation Convention on the Rights of the Child (UN CRC), to promote a CRC-based approach to child labor.

with civil society consultations convened across the country to pressure for a rights-based, no-exceptions "blanket ban" on child labor.

Childhood and (the Erasure of) Children's Economic Agency

If classical economic thought has defined economic agency as the capacity of actors to make rational, autonomous decisions, then, as feminist scholarship has argued, it has also privileged men as the ideal, even sole, economic agents capable of reasoned and independent judgment (Bodkin, 1999; Pujol, 1995). The earliest labor laws in Britain were not directed towards men but children first and subsequently, women, because unlike men, children and women were not held to be agents capable of deciding or bargaining for themselves (Engerman, 2003). They warranted legislative protection therefore, including, for children, their removal altogether from the "hostile worlds" of rational and self-interested economic activity (Zelizer, 2005). The presumption of children's lack of agency has persisted in formal economic theory; as Nelson (1996) observed, children are either invisible in formal econometric models "due to the implausibility of treating [them] as the rational, autonomous agents who are the only residents allowed (so far) into the economists world" (p. 65) or because they are treated as private or public goods (Folbre, 1994; Zelizer, 1985). As a result, child labor was ignored by economists until recently,[8] or analyzed as a problem of market demand. Children, in this view, were merely instruments in the bargain between parents and employers (Gupta, 2000) — banning child labor, therefore, was the obvious, "natural" solution (Emerson, 2009).

The invisible or passive status of children in economic theory derives from the modern separation of the economic from the social and cultural that, in turn, drives the separation of children out of adult economic worlds and into the protective and pedagogic spaces of family and school. This "modern childhood" (Archard, 1993), reified in child labor laws such as those in Britain, emerged in the particular social and economic histories of western nations (Hendrick, 1997; Rahikainen, 2001). Globalized in the spread of child labor laws, modern childhood regulates children's lives everywhere (Boyden, 1997; Wells, 2009); in effect, privileging school over work and consumerism over productivity (Mayall, 2000), moralizing the economic uselessness of children (Zelizer, 1985) and rendering "other" working childhoods as stolen or lost (Bourdillon, 2006a; Nieuwenhuys, 1998). Childhood studies scholars, on the other hand, have critiqued modern childhood, first, on the grounds that any notion of universal childhood is ideological, and second, that the passivity of children is untenable. Indeed, a foundational claim of the field is that children are active in the construction and determination of their own lives and the lives of those around them, rather than merely the passive recipients of adult care or the passive victims of adult exploitation (Prout & James, 1997). As Liebel (2004) describes, working

---

[8] As Emerson (2009) notes in his review, there existed little formal economic theory of child labor until recently, when Basu and Van put forward their seminal work in 1998.

children have a "will of their own," used in service of their own visions of a better life; and as "change-makers," they contribute to the socioeconomic development of their communities (Karunan, 2005). Indeed, even when children work in extremely tenuous situations, they actively strategize to make the best of the material and sociopolitical conditions of their lives (Montgomery, 2001). As the accounts of Huberman (2012), Abebe (2013), Bissell (2003) or Nieuwenhuys (1994) amply demonstrate, children are active social (and economic) agents, working not only in response to familial and social obligations, but also to gain economic benefits and social recognition.

Few studies, however, have focused on children's economic agency per se. While the economic significance of children as consumers, in particular, is increasingly being acknowledged, children's behavior as economic agents in their own right is largely understudied; Iversen (2002) and Amigó (2010) offer exceptions. Iversen (2004, 2002), in his study of bonded migrant child labor in the Indian state of Karnataka, demonstrates that children autonomously negotiated work contracts without parental pressure or involvement, often as a means of rebelling against them, and that they were not necessarily worse off as a result. Similarly, Amigó (2010), in the context of work on Indonesian tobacco farms, insists on children's "own economic understanding," describing how children not only had a "remarkably clear knowledge of the local economy" but an equally "remarkable autonomy in making economic decisions" (p. 48). This chapter adds to their accounts of children's economic agency in the context of their decisions about work and school, as they negotiated the state's anti-child labor efforts in Kanchipuram. In particular, it considers children's economic understanding—their remarkable and ready knowledge of the local economy, but also their relatively sophisticated and longer-term calculations of economic outcomes and aspirations—as a challenge to the modern construction of childhood and as a critique of the school-versus-work frame of child labor policy orthodoxy.

Loom to School to Special Economic Zones: Changing Education and Economic Contexts

For centuries, children in Kanchipuram grew up on the world-famous handlooms, their lifeworlds materialized in relation to the silk and gold lace of the eponymous *kanjeevaram* sari.[9] Now old enough to reel the yarn, now adept enough to pick the *korvai* sari-borders, now tall enough to reach the pedal or harness, children's lives described the developmental arc from helper to apprentice to weaver. In the process, they progressively mastered weaving techniques and grew in economic worth and social status, en route to the "independent"/full-time weaver status that signaled

---

[9] In 2005, the *kanjeevaram* was awarded a "Geographical Indication" (GI) certificate, an intellectual property right of the United Nations Conference on Trade and Investment (Unctad), in recognition of its unique provenance.

adulthood and full membership in the occupational group. Children's work, as Arterburn (1982) detailed in her anthropological account of Kanchipuram's looms, was vital to the production and reproduction of the weaving household; and in producing the characteristic *korvai* border of the *kanjeevaram*, children were in turn (re)produced as the next generation of "Kanchipuram weavers." Earning and learning on the loom was thus inseparably interwoven in childhood and "more children work[ed] than attend[ed] school" (Arterburn, 1982, p. 36).

In 2004 however, Kanchipuram's looms became a site of global surveillance as the INDUS Child Labor Project commenced local operations. A transnational collaboration between the National Child Labor Project (NCLP) in India and the United States Department of Labor (USDoL), INDUS was implemented by the ILO with the support of local NGOs and the *Sarva Shiksha Abhiyan* (India's Education For All Program). Memorably described by an education official as the "no work, more school" mantra, INDUS represented the global orthodoxy on child labor and framed children's work on the loom as harmful because it "interfere[d] with children's schooling" (INDUS-ILO, 2006c, p. 8). Project officials, therefore, were tasked with "rehabilitating" working children in modern society by "rescuing" them from the looms, preparing them in Transition Education Centers (TECs) for formal education, and then mainstreaming them in state-run municipal schools. Between door-to-door enrollment drives, awareness campaigns, employer fines and child labor raids,[10] the no-work-more-school mantra was so effectively enforced that, by 2009, when I first arrived in Kanchipuram, the looms had been largely emptied of children.[11]

Even as INDUS-enforced loom to school trajectories were transforming Pillayarapalayam and other weaving neighborhoods in Kanchipuram into a "child labor-free area," other zoning policies were being effected 40 miles away: the state, in pursuit of export-led economic development, was carving out thousands of acres into Special Economic Zones (SEZs), seeking to attract foreign capital and technology into the country. The massive and multinational spaces of SEZs also attracted hordes of young contract workers from nearby areas, including those recently dislocated from Kanchipuram's looms. While the direct and opportunity costs of education after eight years of free elementary school put white-collar employment in the formal economy beyond the reach of most rescued child workers, the SEZs offered a ready alternative. SEZ factory-floors could be accessed with a "10th pass" or "10th fail" secondary-school certificate, or even with an "8th class TC" (transfer certificate) at the end of elementary school. As a result, "children were moving neat-*a* (neatly) from the loom into school onto class 10 and then into the SEZ—just like an

---

[10] Raids, conducted by district officials and Project staff, involved trawling weaving neighborhoods in Kanchipuram for children on the loom. Children were then "rounded up" and transported by a "raid-van" to the nearest school or TEC. While child workers have described such raids as being treated as if they were "stray dogs" (Bourdillon, 2006b), raids continued to be organized as a spectacular display of the state's care for child workers.

[11] After INDUS was wrapped up in Kanchipuram, the TECs continued to function in the area under the aegis of the National Child Labor Project (NCLP) and focused on non-loom-based child labor.

assembly-line!" described a municipal-school teacher approvingly. Indeed, teachers and INDUS Project-staff showcased SEZ-work as a "good opportunity" for girls in particular, as a means of retaining them in school. In effect, loom-to-school INDUS efforts were largely imagined and realized in Pillayarapalayam as a loom-to-school-to-SEZ trajectory. The promise of newly enforced formal schooling was embodied by SEZ-jobs, even though they were low-paid, low-skilled and contract-based.

School and/or Work "Flexitarianism"

It was in the context of SEZ-returns to schooling that children like Kanniappa were taking decisions for work, not only in the contract-labor spaces of SEZs but also in the booming informal sector work-spaces in Kanchipuram while still in middle-school (classes 6–8). Most middle-school children in Pillayarapalayam worked in the summer; and such economic activity was not perceived as problematic, as it was not in direct competition with school and indeed was often the means to buy new school supplies. Occasionally but increasingly, summer-jobs also translated into regular work through the year, slotted around school-hours in the evenings and weekends. More frustrating for teachers and Project-staff, however, and often, and without the knowledge of parents, a growing number of children, boys in particular, was also cutting classes or sneaking off during free-periods for an hour or so of work. An hour that could turn into a day or more during the various "seasons" in Kanchipuram when extra hands were needed in shops, rice-mills or temples. Yet newer modes of school/work combinations were being experimented with as well. Two of the municipal-school boys I spent time with, for instance, had shifted to "aided schools"[12] where well-intentioned, less-strict attendance policies meant that they could write their examinations despite having missed entire months of school for work. Still others, a significant number, had dropped out of school entirely for work, finding it quicker and more profitable to return to education when older, via night-schools or "corres-classes" (correspondence courses).

The "flexitarian"[13] ways in which boys and girls (to a lesser degree) sought and carried out a variety of paid work, negotiating no-work-more-school policies, was remarkable; though parents, teachers and Project-staff, of course, were less appreciative when they were made aware of such activity. "*Intha kaalathu pasanga* (children these days)," they chided, torn between resignation and outrage when they found children "simply roaming" outside the school with "cash in hand" to spend.

---

[12] "Aided schools" are run by a private management team and supported by the state through salary and non-salary grants. As a condition of state support, they offer free elementary schooling and maintain adequate enrollment of students warranting state funds.

[13] The striking description offered by a child rights lawyer and activist I interviewed in India, who shared similar examples of children in "difficult circumstances" dealing remarkably and ably with them, in unexpected ways.

With parents having made sacrifices, even borrowing money to keep their children in school, how could children be so "careless" (irresponsible) as to cut classes for *ur suththaradhu* (roaming around), they lamented. Project-staff chased after them, calling out threats of "hostel," referring to the NGO- and state-run residential schools that were increasingly seen as the "solution" for the rogue-*pasanga* (rogue kids) who were constantly "escaping" from their classrooms. "We can't 'control' these rogue-*pasanga* anymore," complained a teacher; "once they experienced cash-in-hand, then there was little one could do."

If the adults in their lives dismissed their activities as turning rogue or being careless, children pursued their "flexitarian" negotiation of school and work spaces, not only with facility, but a focus on the future. In the following sections, I describe four flexitarian trajectories I encountered in Pillayarapalayam, each organized by particular trade-offs between school and work, and each justified, not only in terms of immediate remuneration, but also longer-term life trajectories and economic aspirations. Thus, summer-work, with little direct trade-off between school-hours and work-time, was an opportunity to explore work-based fall-back options to school; short-term SEZ-work after dropping out of school was a means for girls, in particular, to pursue and prepare for good marriages (often with the expectation of returning to some form of education); "own business" work-trajectories rejected formal schooling entirely for long-term self-employment while resorting to night-schools for literacy and certifications; and opportunistic-work was pursued intermittently during school-hours and justified in terms of immediate needs but also in the expectation of unskilled, casual work futures.

Summer-Work and Fallback Options

Where casual work opportunities for some "cash-in-hand" were available year-round and taken on without much planning, summer-jobs were regular, full-time employment, assiduously planned by children, often with the support of their households. With children's time freed up over the summer, they and their parents hoped to recuperate some of the direct and opportunity costs of schooling. In the long row-house I lived in and shared with four other families (as was characteristic of weavers' neighborhoods), the talk among the children as early as March, even before final examinations had been completed, was about their summer-plans. As one of them put it, "I don't want to waste one second of summer," and he had already engaged his social networks to find suitable work opportunities. Thus, Selvi had arranged with her mother's master-weaver to assist on his looms while Chandra would keep accounts for the small cooperative enterprise where a distant aunt was employed. The boys, Mano and Yogi, less constrained by gendered notions of distance and safety, were headed to work in the bazaar-area: Yogi, to the hotel kitchen that had previously employed his father, and Mano to a "silk-house" that retailed the saris produced by his uncle and other weavers in the neighborhood.

While their earnings primarily paid for rising school-related expenses, additional tuition-classes in particular, or helped out with household *kashtam*s (hardships) such as outstanding debt, summer was also the time for exploring fallback options to academic trajectories. As Yogi explained, for all that he wanted to study for an engineering degree, his plans were contingent on the marks he scored in school. "Class 8 or 9 examinations are so difficult," he grimaced, adding, "learning to cook in a hotel is a handy skill if I don't do well in school." With a growing local economy in retailing, hotels, low-end services, transportation and construction, informal sector alternatives to higher-education mediated formal employment were increasingly available and increasingly lucrative. Fifteen-year old Mani, for instance, had spent his first summer working at a "mechanic-shop" in Class 6. The main push for work had been the difficult *soolnalai* (circumstances) the household faced at the time, as his father had been unable to work; but Mani had found working with (motor) bikes so appealing that he had since resolved to make it his future line of work. To that end, he had worked every summer, weekend and holiday at the mechanic-shop; not only had he never troubled his parents for a single rupee, Mani added proudly, he had progressed enough on the job to consider opening his own repair-*kadai* (shop) in the near future. He had been saving up his wages for some time now, and having assiduously followed the rising motorbike sales in Kanchipuram, expected his investment to pay off handsomely.

With the growth of such relatively long-term informal sector opportunities, summer-work was also increasingly a precursor to dropping out, as in Mani's case. As a Project field-worker grumbled in frustration, unless children were locked up during the annual school vacation, her work towards the elimination of child labor was impossible. For children like Mani or Yogi, however, summer-work was the means to identify, explore and build relationships and skills; in case formal schooling proved too difficult to complete or was irrelevant to their aspirations, summer-work generated the economic and social capital for alternative work-based trajectories in the local economy.

SEZ-Work and Planning for "Good Matches"

Shantha, barely 14, was the youngest SEZ-worker I met in Pillayarapalayam, employed at one of the SEZs an hour-long, company-van ride away. Having dropped out a few weeks into class 8, she had joined a "shoe company" as contract-labor, thanks to one of the *akkas* (elder sisters, as older females are respectfully referred to) in her neighborhood already contracted to the company. Determinedly pragmatic and forthright, marriage, Shantha admitted, was on the cards in a few years: "we are not like you Miss, and we don't want to grow old before we marry," she declared. Given her life goals therefore, schooling had not made sense to her; despite the effort it cost her, she had not made much headway in learning to read and write. "Why stay in school, when SEZ-work was available and it paid?" she had reasoned, and dropped out to work at the shoe-company. Getting around age restrictions on factory-floors by wearing "make-up" and a *salwar*-suit to look older, Shantha had found the work easy—"cutting" leather florets and "pasting" onto shoes—and learned quickly. "It is better than school," she insisted defiantly, describing the "jolly" atmosphere with the *akkas,* gossiping and teasing during lunch and tea-breaks. Crucially, she was saving up her "full salary"—in 5 years' time she expected to have put away enough for the dowry and wedding trousseau that would contract for her the marriage she sought. Yes, she acknowledged, she might come to regret her decision: she wouldn't be able to help her children with their school homework; then again, she reasoned breezily, she could always pay for their "tuition [classes]."

Shantha, at 14, had grasped the logics that drove thousands of older female teens onto the SEZ factory-floors near Kanchipuram: SEZ-work was the means to improve their marriage prospects, especially when educational qualifications beyond elementary/secondary school proved challenging, time-consuming or expensive. A "good match" in marriage depended on the number of "[gold] sovereigns"[14] you brought in dowry, as my neighbor often reminded her two daughters anxiously. Rather than depend on financially insecure parents, girls like Shantha secured their own futures by heading out to SEZs, the short-term nature of the work, aligning well with their planning horizons and translating into the requisite number of sovereigns. While the shift-work modalities of SEZs precluded formal education, many girls, keen to be the kind of good mothers who could "coach" their children for school, also planned to pursue their education after marriage. They hoped to join correspondence courses or complete secondary and higher-secondary school certifications as "private candidates" (typically, older candidates, were not required to enroll in regular school); in the meantime, however, they worked in SEZs to make good marriages that held out the best returns in terms of long-term desires and economic security.

Work-Based Trajectories to "Own Business"

For Daya, work modalities were more congenial and in line with his ambitions than school. An astute reader of the local economy if not of textbooks, he had spent the better part of the last 3 years evading school-teachers and Project-staff, working on the sand-moving *maatuvandis* (bullock-carts) instead and supplying local construction-sites. Starting out as loader, he had moved up to *maatuvandi*-driver, before renting a cart himself to run a sand-moving operation with a motley group of school-boys cutting classes. When Daya first set up as a sand-mover/supplier nearly two years ago, the price of sand had been 300 rupees for a full-load; once they had paid the 200 rupee hire-charge for cart and cattle and the 50 rupee *challan* (receipt)

---

[14] A sovereign is a standard measure/weight of gold, named for the British gold coin, that has entered the local vernacular.

cost to the police, there was enough left over for them, he explained, given they were supplying two to three loads a day. "These days, a load of sand costs 500 to 600 rupees, depending on the weather—do the math," he urged. If I was impressed with their fat profits, Daya's sights were set on bigger things: an "own business" in the logistics and transportation sector that he and his great friend Vijay hoped to start. Not only had they both dropped out of school to work in the construction industry supply-chain, thus learning the lay of the land, they were also saving up to buy a *chinna yanai* (a type of mini-truck) on installment to get their transport-company going.

While Daya steadfastly refused to talk about schooling, I was offered an insight into his logics one afternoon as we walked across the *thope* (tamarind orchard) in Pillayarapalayam. We had just been hailed by a student at the nearby municipal school: "What are you doing with this *porriki-payyan*,[15] Miss," he had called out, hooting with laughter as he cycled back to class after lunch. Offended on Daya's behalf, I asked him if he was concerned about being belittled for not finishing school. Time will be the judge, he shrugged.

> In another five years' time, I will have my "own business" and I'll be the one they call "boss." But he will be working in an SEZ, saying 'yes sir,' 'no sir' to his supervisor. I need to be able to read and write, yes? That I can manage; and if I need a "certificate", I can always join the night-school[16] for a couple of months and pass the exam. In five years' time, we'll see who the *porriki* is.

If Daya was comprehensive in his rejection of mainstream schooling, finding it largely irrelevant to his ambitions, then he was also conscious of institutional demands for educational-certifications and acknowledged the benefits of literacy. Drawing on his knowledge of local opportunity structures however, he reasoned that the SEZ-based returns to education did not justify the opportunity costs of schooling; particularly when those opportunity costs included the material, relational and informational resources that work-based trajectories offered towards an "own business" or becoming a "boss." Thus, Daya went about his sand-deliveries, biding his time until his "own business" was a reality and paying no heed to the naysayers or the haranguing project-staff in the meantime. While he himself was no longer on their list of "rogues," having recently turned 15, his ragged crew of three or four middle-school boys continued to be a target of their ire and rehabilitation efforts. Recently, two of them had enrolled in an 'aided school' nearby as a compromise, hoping to take advantage of the school's relatively relaxed attendance policies.

---

[15] Literally a rag-picker or those who once scavenged for a living; the term was typically used as an insult for young men who were wastrels, though young people often also used it in friendly name-calling.

[16] Night-schools, known as the *Nila Oli Palli* or Moonlight School in Kanchipuram, were popular thanks to strong support from the district administration in the late 1990s as part of The Literacy Mission efforts; however, their numbers have dwindled to two since INDUS.

Opportunistic-Work in the Informal Sector and Pocket-Money

The most irksome of children's flexitarian behavior, as far as school teachers and Project-staff were concerned, was the seemingly consumption-driven and unplanned casual work that students, more boys than girls, engaged in from time to time. Subbu, for instance, in Class 8 at the local municipal school, was (in)famous among his peers for slipping in and out of school unnoticed. Running into him one afternoon outside the school-gates, he admitted he had spent much of the afternoon, and many others as well, assisting his electrician brother-in-law on a job. "He gives me twenty rupees at least each time, Miss," Subbu added proudly. Parthi earned as much, each time the sand-cart made a delivery. Having disappeared from his TEC classroom one morning, I had found him in the *thope*, loading *bands* (baskets) of sand onto the waiting cart. He enjoyed it, he insisted; he was good at it, moreover—the cart-owner trusted him to get the number of *bands* in a load right. "Not like *padippu* (studies)," he added bitterly, "where you never *did* anything." Shankari was more sanguine about her lack of academic skills; and if teachers often upbraided her for taking an extra day off at the weekend from time to time, it was water off her back. Her weekends were usually spent weeding the paddy-fields where she lived, or cleaning out her neighbors' cattle-sheds—even half a day's work paid as much as 50 rupees. Taking a school day off now and again to compensate, she felt, was justified.

Such opportunistic work that brought in some "cash-in-hand" was available through the year, in the fringe economy of haberdashers and scrap-collectors, at food-stalls and marriage-halls, as domestic-help or helpers for house-painters, drivers, electricians, masons and bike-mechanics. At "season" time, it proliferated when crowds of shoppers or Hindu-devotees descended in Kanchipuram, presenting a captive market for groups of youthful sellers of water-packets, cheap toys, handkerchiefs or small eats. Parents and teachers, however, bemoaned their carelessness and irresponsibility in choosing cash over school, while Project staff roundly denounced them as "rogues." As one of the Class 8 teachers would often say, "the children are carelessly throwing their futures away for a bit of 'cash-in-hand'—it was bound to mire them in 'bad habits,'" she feared.

Such "cash-in-hand" moral panics among adults obscured children's view of their labor and consumption practices. "How can I ask my parents for pocket-money, Miss?" Subbu frowned. He knew the *kashtam* (hardships) at home and it was shameful to ask them for money when he could easily take care of his own needs. Undoubtedly, a spicy *biriyani*-packet or a cold-drink or, as in Shankari's case, a pair of earrings, fueled children's interest in paid work; but there was also honor in earning pocket-money instead of burdening parents with their demands. Moreover, while opportunistic work was relatively unplanned and contingent, children were not "careless" in their behavior—indeed, they were canny workers and consumers, with their ears close to the ground in the local economy. Their remarkable knowledge of wage-rates and "commissions" in a variety of sectors, or the best deals on second-hand mobile-phones or cheap *biriyani*, or a host of casual work opportunities, was acquired through the various kinds of work spaces and networks they participated in, even moving a veteran TEC instructor to reluctant admiration. "The children are very well-informed in these matters," she acknowledged; and already experienced in finding ways to make money in the growing, low-skilled services sector.

While opportunistic-work was an undeniable "escape" from the particular pedagogic modes of classrooms, children were also making considered judgments about their academic abilities and interests in the light of the work modalities and relationships they participated in. As Shankari candidly admitted, she was not academically inclined nor was she interested in SEZ-work with its grueling nightshifts. With little incentive for schoolwork, she was primarily waiting out the years of "automatic promotion" through elementary school (class 8) enshrined in recent education policy, till she could legitimately drop out and tend to home and (vegetable) garden. In the meantime, she felt her time was better spent on remunerative work at the weekends which was better suited to her present and future interests.

"Misapprehension" and "Carelessness" or Situated Logics, Aspirations and Agency?

Among the "constellation" of actors and activities (Wedel, Shore, Feldman, & Lathrop, 2005) that make up the child labor "policy community" in India, children's logics for work were persistently framed as "misapprehension" or "careless"/"rogue" behavior. Among those I interviewed in policy circles,[17] the very choice of work over or alongside school was proof of children's incapacity for rational and long-term returns calculations, prone, as children were assumed to be, to the present and perverse pleasures of "cash-in-hand." Their stance is perhaps best summed up by Burra (2003), an influential child labor researcher in India, who observed:

> Are children capable of being aware of [the] long-term consequences for their adult lives? I rather doubt it. Even if they were able to comprehend the impact of their perspectives, it is arguable as to whether their representations of their best interests should be taken literally. (p. 82)

These policy actors were, in effect, echoing the global orthodoxy on child labor: childhood was a period of dependency and discipline that—irrespective of the contexts and conditions of children's daily lives—precluded the exercise of economic agency on the grounds that it was unnatural or harmful to children. To "choose" to work, therefore, was easily dismissed as "misapprehension" or labeled as rogue behavior, "careless" of the future and driven by presentist desires for consumption.

On the other hand, I suggest that "misapprehension" and "careless" roguery are better understood as children's situated logics, responsive to the social and material

---

[17] These 20 interviews with state bureaucrats and policy-makers, multilateral agency specialists, staff at transnational and regional NGOs, and researchers/academics are analyzed elsewhere.

conditions of their daily lives; and, in a post-(neo)liberalization labor market of declining job security and shrinking formal employment, purposed towards informal sector futures rather than the formal sector employment trajectories assumed in education policies. For many children in Kanchipuram, work of varying duration, type and regularity was a mundane part of daily life, whether in addition to or instead of school. Given the longer-standing, local constructions of childhood as integral to the social and economic life of weaving communities, many children continued, in the present day, to identify and perform as economic actors in their own right. Not passively resigned to their relative poverty, nor readily reconciled to classroom modalities that they saw as irrelevant or uncongenial in the light of opportunities in the local economy, children made strategic calculations about work and school based on their abilities and aspirations—and they acted on their calculations.

Children's decisions for work, whether more or less opportunistic or purposive in kind, were framed and strategized in terms of a longer planning horizon. If summer-work compensated for educational costs or met household needs, then it also offered the means of exploring alternative careers in the informal sector; and SEZ-work, if short-term by nature, also offered longer-term utility in the socioeconomic security and status of "good matches." In the case of work-based trajectories—moving up from renting a *maatuvandi* to owning a transport-company, for instance—rejecting school was explicitly rationalized by children in terms of longer-term aspirations for ownership. Even the pursuit of opportunistic work was reasoned out and justified by children as a negative assessment of their academic futures. While the immediate satisfaction of buying a pair of earrings or eating *biriyani* was not a trivial consideration, present consumption in itself was rarely the end-game. Instead, children framed their participation in work as a strategic use of their time—a more efficient and enjoyable use of their time, when participation in classroom modalities did not support their interests or aspirations beyond narrowly conceived academic trajectories.

Children's school/work logics, therefore, were not only longer-term oriented, but also calculated in relation to alternative trajectories. Underlying their logics for work were probabilistic comparisons of school- and work-based outcomes that factored in their interests and abilities and were framed within larger structural/material constraints. In making decisions for work and/or school, children were, in effect, choosing between the school-based trajectories to formal employment assumed in policy orthodoxy, the school-mediated trajectory to contract-based SEZ-work as effected in Kanchipuram, and the opportunities available in the local informal economy via more or less organized work and apprenticing trajectories. Trajectories from school to formal employment presumed the absence of academic and economic constraints for post-elementary schooling and assumed the existence of capacious and local formal labor markets—conditions that did not apply to many children in Kanchipuram (or indeed, in many parts of India). On the other hand, school-to-SEZ trajectories were readily accessible to children in Kanchipuram; but while they offered girls, in particular, a route to achieving desirable marriages, the short-term, shift-based and closely supervised work modalities of assembly-lines did not appeal to all children. Consequently, children sneaked out or dropped out of school, or shrewdly exploited automatic progression policies and lax attendance policies in elementary school, to take up various combinations of work in pursuit of their informal sector aspirations.

Children's situated logics, in effect, embedded the opportunity costs of work and school in the immediate economic context. Whether "good matches," "own business," or a variety of skilled and unskilled work futures in the informal sector, children's aspirations were sensible to them in their everyday contexts in Kanchipuram; they were life-trajectories that were "real" and realize-able, given the sociocultural and material conditions of their life. And in rejecting post secondary education-mediated formal employment, children were responding to the incentives offered by opportunities in the local economy, whether for long-term employment, status or cash-in-hand. Their exercise of economic agency reflected both a sophisticated awareness of the local economy and the ability to act on such awareness in taking up work and school in various combinations. Transnational efforts like the INDUS Project that framed work and school as oppositional to "combat child labor with education" have, in the process, effectively erased children's demonstrable economic agency and foreclosed their own determinations of their futures.

The flexitarian strategies of children in Kanchipuram offer a critique of the orthodoxy on child labor policy and the underlying rights-based and utilitarian claims. Universalistic rights-talk, abstracted from the specificities of children's lived experience and context, has functioned in policy-contexts to preclude the need for engaging with "real" children and their lived situations. Consequently, law and policy in India have continued to veer towards the complete prohibition of child labor (Ramanathan, 2009) despite the tripling of "marginal" child workers[18] in the country since the 1990s (Registrar General & Census Commissioner, India, n.d.)—arguably, a sign of the growing incidence of flexitarianism among school-age children. Moreover, the human capital calculations underpinning formal schooling in international education discourses are weighted towards waged employment in the formal sector, a large proportion deriving from the public sector (Bennell, 1996a, 1996b). In the process, they overlook both the shrinking of public sector employment and the informal sector-driven growth in employment in India—mainly concentrated in the non-waged, self-employment category—since the (neo)liberalization reforms of the 1990s (Bosworth & Collins, 2007; Mazumdar & Sarkar, 2008; Sarkar & Mehta, 2010). With recent studies questioning the longstanding dogma on wage returns to primary education (Colclough, Kingdon, & Patrinos, 2010), the insistence that "If returns [to schooling] haven't been seen there [in Kanchipuram] yet, they have to come, they have to come" (as the child labor specialist at a multilateral agency in India said to me) is increasingly a statement of faith than a reflection of labor markets in many parts of India.

The faith in "no work more school" policies as the rightful—and rights-ful—response to child labor has undermined the search for alternative modes/models of

---

[18] "Marginal" child labor is defined by the decadal Census as children who are engaged in some economic activity but whose primary activity is not economic, i.e., they do not work full-time.

education that better accommodate, even support, children's aspirations and agency. For far too long, international development discourses have valorized formal schooling and formal sector employment, in the process, framing alternative trajectories such as the pursuit of "own businesses" and "good matches" as "a more brittle horizon of aspirations…and a thinner, weaker sense of career pathways" (Appadurai, 2004, p. 68). Given the informal sector in India accounted for 82 % of the country's non-agricultural labor force and given the growing power of informal sector workers as claim-makers, paradoxically, in a neoliberal environment that has disempowered traditional labor (Agarwala, 2008), the time has come to acknowledge that it is not the informal sector aspirations of children that are "brittle," but policy conceptions of formal schooling and school-based trajectories that are reductive.

Conclusion

Kanniappa decided that he did not want to return to the TEC with me—that was "final." "I have other options," he reassured me before taking off through the *thope* at a run. Extant child labor policies have little to offer Kanniappa or his friends, beyond pointing to their right to formal schooling; a few days later, project-staff would drag Kanniappa back to the TEC, quite literally. Given their mandate, there was no room to acknowledge his frustration with their efforts to school him; and given the constellation of actors and discourses that constitute the global orthodoxy on child labor there would be no "minister" to listen to Kanniappa or recognize his economic agency. On the other hand, the situated logics and informal sector aspirations underlying the flexitarianism of Kanniappa and other children in Kanchipuram are undeniable—and remarkably astute. Policy idealizations of childhood as a period of dependence and discipline effectively erased children's economic agency by reframing their flexitarian-ism as misapprehension or carelessness, thus dismissing their situated aspirations and logics, and are counterproductive therefore. In this context, it is worth reiterating the Kundapur Declaration at the first international meeting of working children: "We want respect and security for ourselves and the work that we do. We want an education system whose methodology and content are adapted to our reality" (Miljeteig, 2000, p. 20).

References

Abebe, T. (2013). Interdependent rights and agency: The role of children in collective livelihood strategies in rural Ethiopia. In K. Hanson & O. Nieuwenhuys (Eds.), *Reconceptualizing children's rights in international development: Living rights, social justice, translations* (pp. 71–92). Cambridge, England: Cambridge University Press.

Agarwala, R. (2008). Reshaping the social contract: Emerging relations between the state and informal labor in India. *Theory and Society, 37*(4), 375–408.

Amigó, M. F. (2010). Small bodies, large contribution: Children's work in the tobacco plantations of Lombok, Indonesia. *The Asia Pacific Journal of Anthropology, 11*(1), 34–51.

Appadurai, A. (2004). The capacity to aspire: Culture and the terms of recognition. In V. Rao & M. Walton (Eds.), *Culture and public action*. Stanford, CA: Stanford University Press.

Archard, D. (1993). *Children: Rights and childhood*. London, England: Routledge.

Arterburn, Y. J. (1982). *The looms of interdependence: Silk-weaving cooperatives in Kanchipuram*. Delhi, India: Hindustan Publishing Corporation.

Bennell, P. (1996a). Rates of return to education: Does the conventional pattern prevail in sub-Saharan Africa? *World Development, 24*(1), 183–199.

Bennell, P. (1996b). Using and abusing rates of return: A critique of the World Bank's 1995 Education Sector Review. *International Journal of Educational Development, 16*(3), 235–248.

Bissell, S. (2003). The social construction of childhood: A perspective from Bangladesh. In N. Kabeer, G. B. Nambissan, & R. Subrahmanian (Eds.), *Child labour and the right to education in South Asia. Needs versus rights* (pp. 47–72). New Delhi, India: Sage Publications.

Bluebond-Langner, M., & Korbin, J. E. (2007). Challenges and opportunities in the anthropology of childhoods: An introduction to "children, childhoods, and childhood studies". *American Anthropologist, 109*(2), 241–246.

Bodkin, R. G. (1999). Women's agency in classical economic thought: Adam Smith, Harriet Taylor Mill, and JS Mill. *Feminist Economics, 5*(1), 45–60.

Bosworth, B., & Collins, S. M. (2007). *Accounting for growth: Comparing China and India* (No. w12943). National Bureau of Economic Research.

Bourdillon, M. F. C. (2006a). Children and work: A review of current literature and debates. *Development and Change, 37*(6), 1201–1226.

Bourdillon, M. F. C. (2006b). *Violence against working children*. Stockholm, Sweden: Save the Children.

Boyden, J. (1997). Childhood and the policy makers: A comparative perspective on the globalization of childhood. In A. James & A. Prout (Eds.), *Constructing and reconstructing childhood* (pp. 63–84). London, England: Falmer.

Boyden, J., & Levison, D. (2000). *Children as economic and social actors in the development process* (Working Paper 2000:1). Stockholm, Sweden: Expert Group on Development Issues (EGDI).

Burra, N. (2003). Rights versus needs: Is it in the best interest of the child. In N. Kabeer, G. B. Nambissan, & R. Subrahmanian (Eds.), *Child labour and the right to education in South Asia. Needs versus rights* (pp. 73–94). New Delhi, India: Sage Publications.

Colclough, C., Kingdon, G., & Patrinos, H. (2010). The changing pattern of wage returns to education and its implications. *Development Policy Review, 28*(6), 733–747.

Cunningham, H. (1995). *Children and childhood in western society since 1500*. London: Longman.

Cunningham, H., & Stromquist, S. (2005). Child labor and the rights of children: Historical patterns of decline and persistence. In B. H. Weston (Ed.), *Child labor and human rights* (pp. 55–83). London, England: Lynne Rienner.

Davin, A. (1982). Child labour, the working-class family, and domestic ideology in 19th century Britain. *Development and Change, 13*(4), 633–652.

Emerson, P. (2009). The economic view of child labor. In H. D. Hindman (Ed.), *The world of child labor: An historical and regional survey* (pp. 3–9). New York, NY: M.E. Sharpe.

Engerman, S. L. (2003). The history and political economy of international labor standards. In K. Basu, H. Horn, L. Roman, & J. Shapiro (Eds.), *International labor standards: History, theory, and policy options* (pp. 9–83). Malden, MA: Blackwell.

Escobar, A. (2011). *Encountering development: The making and unmaking of the Third World*. Princeton, NJ: Princeton University Press.

Ferguson, J. (2006). *Global shadows: Africa in the neoliberal world order*. Durham, NC: Duke University Press.

Folbre, N. (1994). Children as public goods. *The American Economic Review, 84*(2), 86–90.

Grimsrud, B. (2003). *Millennium development goals and child labour.* Geneva, Switzerland: Understanding Children's Work (UCW) Project, UNICEF.

Gupta, M. R. (2000). Wage determination of a child worker: A theoretical analysis. *Review of Development Economics, 4*(2), 219–228.

Harvey, D. (2005). *A brief history of neoliberalism.* New York, NY: Oxford University Press.

Hendrick, H. (1997). Constructions and reconstructions of British childhood: an interpretive survey, 1800 to present. In A. James & A. Prout (Eds.), *Constructing and reconstructing childhood* (pp. 33–60). London, England: Falmer.

Huberman, J. (2012). *Ambivalent encounters: Childhood, tourism, and social change in Banaras.* India: Rutgers University Press.

ILO. (2010). *Accelerating action against child labor.* Geneva, Switzerland: ILO.

INDUS-ILO. (2006a). *Give then back their childhood: Sensitization module for school children and youth on child labour.* New Delhi: ILO Subregional Office for South Asia.

INDUS-ILO. (2006b). *INDO-USDOL child labor project.* New Delhi, India: ILO Subregional Office for South Asia.

INDUS-ILO. (2006c). *Communication in action: A handbook for social mobilization on child labor.* New Delhi, India: ILO Subregional Office for South Asia.

IPEC-ILO. (2009). *Combating child labor through education: A resource kit for policy-makers and practitioners.* Geneva, Switzerland: ILO.

Iversen, V. (2002). Autonomy in child labor migrants. *World Development, 30*(5), 817–834.

Iversen, V. (2004). On notions of agency, individual heterogeneity, and the existence, size and composition of a bonded child labor force. In S. Cullenberg & P. K. Pattanaik (Eds.), *Globalization, culture, and the limits of the market: Essays in economics and philosophy* (pp. 107–141). New Delhi, India: Oxford University Press.

Johnson, R. (1970). Educational policy and social control in early Victorian England. *Past and Present, 49*, 96–119.

Karunan, V. (2005). Working children as change makers: Perspectives from the South. In B. H. Weston (Ed.), *Child labor and human rights: Making children matter* (pp. 293–318). Boulder, CO: Lynne Rienner Publishers.

Kendall, N. (2008). "Vulnerability" in AIDS-affected states: Rethinking child rights, educational institutions, and development paradigms. *International Journal of Educational Development, 28*(4), 365–383.

Liebel, M. (2004). *A will of their own: Cross-cultural perspectives on working children.* London, England: Zed Books.

Lieten, G. K. (2002). Child labor in India: Disentangling essence and solutions. *Economic and Political Weekly, 37*(52), 5190–5195.

Mayall, B. (2000). The sociology of childhood in relation to children's rights. *The International Journal of Children's Rights, 8*(3), 243–259.

Mazumdar, D., & Sarkar, S. (2008). The employment problem in India and the phenomenon of the missing middle. Paper Presented in the Canadian Economics Association Meeting, Vancouver, Canada.

Miljeteig, P. (2000). *Creating partnerships with working children and youth.* Washington, DC: World Bank Global Child Labor Program.

Montgomery, H. (2008). *An introduction to childhood: Anthropological perspectives on children's lives.* Chichester, England: John Wiley & Sons.

Montgomery, H. (2001). *Modern Babylon? Prostituting children in Thailand.* Oxford, England: Berghahn

Nelson, J. A. (1996). *Feminism, objectivity and economics.* London, England: Routledge.

Nieuwenhuys, O. (1994). *Children's lifeworlds: Gender, welfare, and labour in the developing world.* London, England: Routledge.

Nieuwenhuys, O. (1998). Global childhood and the politics of contempt. *Alternatives, 23*(3), 267–290.

Prout, A., & James, A. (1997). A new paradigm for the sociology of childhood? Provenance, promise and problems. In A. James & A. Prout (Eds.), *Constructing and reconstructing childhood: Contemporary issues in the sociological study of childhood* (pp. 7–32). London, England: Falmer Press.

Psacharopoulos, G., & Patrinos, H. A. (2004). Returns to investment in education: A further update. *Education Economics, 12*(2), 111–134.

Pujol, M. (1995). Into the margin! In E. Kuiper, J. Sap, S. Feiner, N. Ott, & Z. Tzannatos (Eds.), *Out of the margin: Feminist perspectives on economics* (pp. 17–34). London, England: Routledge.

Rahikainen, M. (2001). Historical and present-day child labour: Is there a gap or a bridge between them? *Continuity and Change, 16*(1), 137–156.

Ramanathan, U. (2009). Evolution of the law on child labor in India. In H. D. Hindman (Ed.), *The world of child labor: An historical and regional survey* (pp. 783–787). New York, NY: M.E. Sharpe.

Reddy, N. (1997, June). Have we asked the children? Different approaches to the question of child work. Paper presented at The Urban Childhood Conference, Trondhiem, Norway.

Registrar General & Census Commissioner, India (n.d.). Census of India 2011: Series B Tables. Retrieved August 7, 2015, from http://www.censusindia.gov.in/2011census/B-series/B-Series-01.html.

Reports of the National Commission on Labour, 2002–1991–1967. (2003). New Delhi, India: Academic Foundation.

Bring. (2011). Bring child labour prevention law in line with RTE, says NGO. (2011, October 11). *The Hindu.*

Sandin, B. (2009). Coming to terms with child labor: History of child welfare. In H. D. Hindman (Ed.), *The world of child labor: An historical and regional survey* (pp. 53–56). New York, NY: M.E. Sharpe.

Sarkar, S., & Mehta, B. S. (2010). Income inequality in India: pre-and post-reform periods. *Economic and Political Weekly, 45*(37), 45–55.

Shore, C., & Wright, S. (1997). *Anthropology of policy: Critical perspectives on governance and power.* London, England: Routledge.

Stephens, S. (1995). Introduction. In S. Stephens (Ed.), *Children and the politics of culture* (pp. 3–48). Princeton, NJ: University of Princeton Press.

Wedel, J. R., Shore, C., Feldman, G., & Lathrop, S. (2005). Toward an anthropology of public policy. *The ANNALS of the American Academy of Political and Social Science, 600*(1), 30–51.

Weiner, M. (1991). *The child and the state in India: Child labor and education policy in comparative perspective.* Princeton, NJ: Princeton University Press.

Wells, K. (2009). *Childhood in global perspective.* Cambridge, England: Polity.

World Bank. (1995). *Priorities and strategies for education: A World Bank review.* Washington, DC: The World Bank.

Zelizer, V. (1985). *Pricing the priceless child: The changing social value of children.* Princeton, NJ: Princeton University Press.

Zelizer, V. (2005). The priceless child revisited. In I. Qvortrup (Ed.), *Studies in modern childhood: Society, agency and culture* (pp. 184–200). London, England: Palgrave.

Social Capital, Agency, and Creating Micro-enterprises: A Case of Entrepreneurship Education for Tanzanian Youth

Nancy Pellowski Wiger

Introduction

A high rate of youth[1] unemployment in Tanzania is a current and critical issue as in 2012 there were more unemployed youth aged 15–24 per capita than 109 other countries (Kushner, 2013). When youth employment prospects are poor, families have less incentive to send children to school and pay the associated costs (International Labour Office [ILO], 2015). Yet youth with less education are significantly less likely to have the skills needed for securing decent work (ILO, 2015). In Tanzania, youth confront a number of barriers to secondary education. Recent statistics show that only one in four secondary school-age youth was actually able to attend school, and youth from poorer households are disadvantaged in their educational outlook as they are less likely to attend, persist, and graduate secondary schooling (Economic and Social Research Foundation, 2014). It has also been predicted that around 55 % of young people in Tanzania will never secure stable employment (ILO, 2015). Given these education and labor market conditions, scholars have critically explored how youth can act agentically during life transitions, such as from schooling to employment (Jeffrey, 2012; Lloyd, 2005). One way to improve the school/employment linkage is through entrepreneurship education, efforts that aim for young people to create their own micro-enterprises and future livelihoods (ILO, 2009). Entrepreneurship education programming includes a mixture of academic, vocational, business, and life skills training (including mentorships) to help youth successfully participate in the labor market (Baxter, Chapman,

---

[1] I employ the UN definition of youth as those aged 15–24 (United Nations, 2013). In the 1996 National Youth Development Policy, the government of Tanzania also adopted this definition (United Republic of Tanzania, 1996).

N. Pellowski Wiger (✉)
Department of Organizational Leadership, Policy, and Development, University of Minnesota, Minneapolis, MN, USA
e-mail: pell0097@umn.edu

© Springer International Publishing Switzerland 2016
J.G. DeJaeghere et al. (eds.), *Education and Youth Agency*, Advancing Responsible Adolescent Development, DOI 10.1007/978-3-319-33344-1_12

DeJaeghere, Pekol, & Weiss, 2014). However, starting a micro-enterprise, particularly for youth, requires not only knowledge, but a combination of resources and networks. The question this chapter takes up is how youth from marginalized backgrounds strategically draw on their social capital—resources and relationships—built through education and at home to improve this education/employment linkage.

This chapter explores if and how youth from marginalized backgrounds are able to build relationships with peers at school and at home, and draw on such relationships to start or enhance their own micro-enterprises, thus improving their livelihoods. The chapter begins with an outline of the critical conceptualizations of social capital and youth agency that guide this work. Following that, I review the relevant literature and expand on the methodology central to this study. Lastly, I detail the ways in which youth use agency to draw on supportive peer relationships and actively detach from constraining peer relationships to expand or create new micro-enterprises.

Critical Conceptualizations of Youth Agency and Social Capital

Education scholars have postulated that youth may need to actively draw on social capital—defined here as the potential or actual resources gained from one's network of relationships utilized for purposive action—to transform the knowledge and skills learned through schooling into livelihood opportunities (Bourdieu, 1986). While there has been a wide array of social capital research to date, findings have been mixed as scholars have used varying definitions of social capital (Portes, 1998). For instance, some scholars have utilized a functionalist or normative perspective of social capital (Coleman, 1988; Putnam, 1993) and have found positive relationships between social capital and youth persistence in school (Coleman & Hoffer, 1987) and increased socioeconomic success in early adulthood (Furstenberg & Hughes, 1995). Yet these perspectives have also been critiqued as they do not often consider youth in such conceptualizations (Leonard, 2005), nor do they position youth as agentic (Morrow, 1999), and they discount issues of power and domination (Dika & Singh, 2002). Drawing on Bourdieu, my conceptualization of social capital assumes that agency is necessary to act on these relationships. Individuals with agency thus can actively draw on their social capital to find or create employment to improve their livelihoods.

In contrast to functionalist approaches, Bourdieu (1986) has critically linked the notions of habitus, structure, agency, and social capital as a way to describe how power and inequality are produced and potentially disrupted. I believe that a critical conceptualization is necessary when examining youth agency and social capital, as it considers how power and political, social, and economic structures in society contribute to inequalities for certain groups coming from disadvantaged backgrounds

According to Bourdieu (1990), the habitus is one's "durable, transposable dispositions," principles, or preferences formed by an individual's history and others she interacts with (p. 53). Bourdieu (1990) describes that the habitus "structures new experiences in accordance with the structures produced by past experiences, which are modified by the new experiences within the limits defined by their power of selection" (p. 60). Power relations among individuals and society can affect if and how one's habitus is changed or altered based on new experiences, as the habitus "is an infinite capacity for generating products – thoughts, perceptions, expressions and actions – whose limits are set by the historically and socially situated conditions of its production" (Bourdieu, 1990, p. 55). Related to the habitus, Bourdieu (1990) also described the concept of field as "a feel for the game" or the rules and relations that comprise daily life depending on one's status in the social world (p. 66). A field is a "global social space…within which agents confront each other, with differentiated means and ends according to their position in the structure of the field of forces, thus contributing to conserving or transforming its structure" (Bourdieu, 1998, p. 32). A chicken micro-enterprise is one example of a field, where youth may be treated with limited power and status (e.g., a female youth may be in charge of gathering eggs); yet as this youth learns new skills and gains new experiences through relationships with others, this same female youth may now be valued for her knowledge of treating diseases in chickens and preventing death.

Although Bourdieu stresses the strong, reproductive bias built into structures, scholars have critiqued Bourdieu's theorization as he gives less attention to the role of agency (Sewell, 1992). In this chapter, I draw on both Ahearn (2001) and Bajaj (2008) to define agency as action intended to improve individual social mobility, although such action is limited by one's network of social relations, or one's "individualized system of social capital" (Raffo & Reeves, 2000, p. 148), as these relations are affected by larger inequalities in society. Bourdieu (1998) argued that the value of social capital lies in an individual's ability to convert it into other forms of capital, and these forms of capital serve as important sources of power and are affected by wider structures in society such as economic and political relations.

Stanton-Salazar has complemented Bourdieu's social capital work while emphasizing youth agency to examine how youth are able to develop relationships with institutional agents, or "high-status, non-kin, agents who occupy relatively high positions" in society (Stanton-Salazar, 2011, p. 1066) who have the capacity to transmit, or negotiate transmission of, resources and opportunities. Relationships can provide institutional support or forms of social support to help youth effectively participate in mainstream institutions, such as school or the labor market, as youth can agentically draw on their social capital to reach certain goals (Stanton-Salazar, 1997). Yet relationships can be problematic because youth encounter barriers to participating in mainstream settings such as school and are expected to adapt to the cultural capital and standards of the dominant group; thus devaluing their own culture. While instrumental action occurs when youth convert their social capital into institutional support with the purpose of reaching certain goals, youth from marginalized backgrounds have limited agency and trouble accumulating social capital because these youth have differential value based on their class, ethnicity, or gender.

Scholars who conceptualize social capital from a critical perspective illustrate that the process for developing and utilizing relations with peers and adults is complex and nuanced in helping them make the transition from education to employment. For instance, research in Brazil and England explored schooling as a site for social capital development and found that youth from low-income families built strong relationships with both school peers and adults (Chattopadhay, 2014; Holland, Reynolds, & Weller, 2007; Morrow, 2002). While youth reported that these relationships were important in achieving their goals, results differed by gender, as some youth developed supportive relationships and others reported their relationships were discouraging. Similarly, other research found that youth from disadvantaged backgrounds navigated complex relationships when searching for employment. Non-university-going youth from minority immigrant families in Canada did not draw on relations with family members for help with their job search as their family members often lacked social connections, but instead drew on peers to act as references, share interview experiences, and provide motivational and emotional support (Yan, Lauer, & Chan, 2009). However, other youth in Ireland reported working in low-pay exploitative jobs, oftentimes for relatives, which they found boring, repetitive, and provided few opportunities to accumulate transferable skills (Leonard, 2005). While these studies highlight the importance of relationships to further youth livelihoods, it remains unclear if and how youth were able to act with agency to develop positive relationships, distance themselves from relationships that were stifling, and use agency to respond to challenges in schooling or once employed.

Linking youth agency to social capital, Morrow (1999) argued that research on youth lives must couple Bourdieu's conceptualization of social capital in relation to other forms of capital and as based in the practices of daily life while viewing children with agency, although constrained by power and structures, to "shape and influence their own environments" (p. 757). Similarly, Raffo and Reeves (2000) argued that an individual's social capital, or system of social relations, is directly related to agency, as different material and symbolic resources are available to different networks, thus supporting or constraining individual action. Youth's active decisions about their behavior or level of participation in school were "not completely open and free," but instead were mediated by structural factors such as class, race, gender, and ethnicity (Raffo & Reeves, 2000, p. 149). Thus, while youth could and did aspire for futures that might "transcend their objective reality," future success depended on youth's ability to develop a strong individualized system of social capital, albeit mediated by inequalities in society (Raffo & Reeves, 2000, p. 151).

There has been limited research linking social capital, agency, education, and employment using a critical lens to examine the lives of youth from marginalized backgrounds in Tanzania. Of the few studies conducted, scholars have found that the traditional familial relationships or ties were not always sufficient to help youth succeed, particularly when youth were forced to live on the streets due to maltreatment, abuse, neglect, or the death of one or both parents (Wagner, Lyimo, & Lwendo,

2012). While studies have shown that Tanzanian youth have been strategic and agentic in drawing on relationships with others outside the family to help improve their likelihood of success in school (Vavrus, 2013) and the labor market (DeJaeghere, Pellowski Wiger, & Willemsen, 2016), more longitudinal research is needed to further explore if and how youth agentically draw on their social capital to foster their future livelihoods.

This study seeks to understand how youth, who attend boarding schools in Tanzania, develop relationships and agentically draw on them to further their employment goals of starting or advancing their own micro-enterprises. As youth from marginalized backgrounds are often limited in their ability to develop relationships with institutional agents (Stanton-Salazar, 1997), and studies have found that agency can be developed in school (Bajaj, 2008), this study also explores if and how youth agentically draw on their social capital over time. In addition, this study adds to the literature by exploring the types of relationships that relate to youth micro-enterprise development and if/how youth from marginalized backgrounds act with agency to strategically draw on their relationships to further their livelihood goals given the structural inequalities they face.

Methodology

This study is grounded in the assumption that the youth face multiple inequalities in pursuing their educational and employment goals, and this study explored how youth from marginalized backgrounds were (or were not) agentic in developing and using their peer relationships at school to start or enhance their own micro-enterprises given discrimination in their lives. I utilized a concurrent mixed-methods design with quantitative methods to identify relationships between youth social capital and micro-enterprise creation, and qualitative methods to explore youth agency with their relationships to "get at the inner experience of participants [and] determine how meanings are formed through and in culture" (Corbin & Strauss, 2008, p. 16). This study attempted to "convey the trends and voices of marginalized groups of individuals" (Creswell, 2009, p. 121), in this case youth from disadvantaged backgrounds in Tanzania. These youth are disadvantaged for various reasons, including living in poverty, not being able to continue schooling (prior to enrolling in these schools, which offer scholarships); being orphaned (one or both parents); needing to work to support their families' basic needs; and becoming pregnant or ill.

This study focuses on youth that were attending two secondary boarding schools, Sasema Secondary School and Usawa School, located in two communities in Tanzania. And the names of all youth participants have been changed to ensure confidentiality. Sasema Secondary School is an all-girls school located in a central Tanzanian city, which is a center for agriculture with over 200,000 residents. In 2008 Sasema opened as a residential secondary school, including pre-form and Forms 1-4, and currently enrolls over 140 females. Usawa School is located in a rural area in the southern highlands that is currently expanding as a center for tea,

Table 1 Details of interview sample

Year	Total youth	Sasema females	Usawa females	Usawa males
2012	60	30	15	15
2013	55	30	12	13
2014	50	27	10	13
2015	43	26	8	9

forestry, and agricultural production. Usawa was created by a consortium of non-governmental organizations from Tanzania and other countries. Usawa operates within the formal Vocational Education and Training Authority (VETA) system and adopts and adapts the VETA curriculum. Usawa serves both female and male youth and enrolled its first group of students in 2012. Currently the Usawa school has 150 youths enrolled. Both schools have partnered with a non-governmental organization to implement a model of entrepreneurship education that integrates the officially recognized secondary school curriculum with educational-productive units to sell goods and services in the local market. The educational-productive units provide youth hands-on experiences developing vocational, financial literacy, and life skills while selling goods and services that generate income for the school and cover school operating costs (DeJaeghere, 2013).

For this specific chapter, I drew on survey and demographic data administered to all youth enrolled in the program from 2012–2014 (227 youth— 159 females and 68 males) asking about their financial literacy, entrepreneurship, employment, savings, and life skills (see USAID, 2013a, for an in-depth review of the tools used in this study). The survey questions asked if the youth had ever started their own micro-enterprise at two different time points, when we first started the study in 2012 and again in 2014. I combined these items at both time points to create a single variable to measure if youth had ever started their own micro-enterprise (and 54 of the 227 youth reported having ever started their own micro-enterprise). In addition, eight items about relationships with peers and adults at home and at school were asked and analyzed to measure change in social capital over time. To explore the relationship between social capital and micro-enterprise creation, I calculated the Pearson correlation between each item about relationships and if youth had reported ever starting up their own micro-enterprise.

In addition to the spoken survey, a team of researchers[2] conducted interviews each year with 60 youth from 2012–2015 to further understand how participation in the entrepreneurship education program affected youth livelihoods (see Table 1). At Usawa, all youth in the interview sample were enrolled in TVET 1 (Technical and Vocational Education and Training Year 1) in 2012. At Sasema, the interview sam-

[2]This study is a secondary data analysis of demographic, spoken survey, and interview data collected as part of a larger 6-year evaluation of three entrepreneurship education programs in Kenya, Tanzania, and Uganda, conducted by the University of Minnesota (UMN) and funded by The MasterCard Foundation. David Chapman and Joan DeJaeghere served as the principal investigators and UMN staff and graduate students and Tanzanian researchers conducted interviews, and collected spoken survey and demographic data between 2012 and 2015. The author served as the project director.

ple for 2012 was comprised of ten youth from each of the first three forms (the British O-level system of lower secondary school) for a total of 30 youths. For the final round of interviews in 2015, the Sasema youth were either enrolled in TVET 4, had dropped out of school, or had enrolled elsewhere, and the Usawa youth were either still in school in Form 4, graduated, or had dropped out/enrolled elsewhere. To delve deeper into understanding how youth agentically drew on their social capital to start or enhance their own micro-enterprises, I used a grounded theory approach to analyze the interview data (Corbin & Strauss, 2008). Much like DeJaeghere (2013) and McCleary (2013), I inductively analyzed the interviews in Nvivo to understand the themes in the data and develop codes. I "let the data speak for themselves" by exploring categories of data and connecting emergent codes to one another in my study (Andrade, 2009, p. 53). From the interview data, I investigated the extent that youth were able to utilize their schooling to agentically develop and mobilize their social capital to start or enhance their own micro-enterprises.

The Importance of Peer Relationships as Social Capital

Peer Relationships at Home

Contrary to Stanton-Salazar's (2011) definition of institutional agents as "high-status, non-kin" my results indicated that youth were agentic in drawing on their relationships with peers to start or enhance their own micro-enterprises, thus working toward their goals. The spoken survey data (from 227 youth) indicated that youth reported a significant increase over time from their peers at home helping them to achieve their employment goals ($z = -4.003$, $p < 0.001$). As previously mentioned, youth in this sample were from disadvantaged backgrounds, and many reported that their peers at home were not able to continue with their education and faced challenges with work, early pregnancies, and HIV. As one youth succinctly stated, "Life at home is quite hard." Despite that these youth lived in poor communities with limited resources, they learned how to identify peers who could help them and learned to strategically draw on these relationships to further their goals.

For instance, in our first interview with Anna in 2012, she described how she struggled with daily life as both of her parents had passed away and why she had re-joined school, "[To] develop my skills and to get education… [and have] a good life" (2012). When asked what a "good life" was, she replied, "I would depend on myself…[have] a good job, good house, eating well" (2012). To help her meet her basic needs, Anna worked during holiday breaks from school making and selling *kachori*, a porridge made from Irish potatoes mixed with wheat flour. To make her micro-enterprise successful, Anna described how she agentically drew on relationships with peers by specifically asking for a loan for her micro-enterprise. She explained, "It was 2100 (Tanzanian shillings, about $1 USD), that litre…I used that cooking oil, I used it to cook that *kachori*…just after 3 days I repaid the loan" (2013). While the amount may seem small, it was necessary to make any earnings, and Anna then used her earnings to pay back the loan and purchase "school materials, like shoes, socks, and clothes for home" (2013), thus making a small step toward her life goals of providing for herself.

Other youth described how they pooled together resources with peers at home to earn income to help support their goals. Maria had previously dropped out of school because she was pregnant with her first child. With the goals of either becoming a doctor or starting up her own micro-enterprise, Maria re-enrolled in school. In her final year of school when we interviewed her, determined to pass the Form 4 national exam, she shared, "I thank God I completed my form four studies. And the results are out and they're not bad, they're good" (2015). Her exam results gave her the opportunity to pursue further education and Maria decided to go onto college to study health sciences with a goal towards being employed as a nurse. While waiting for her application to be accepted, Maria started up a photography micro-enterprise with a friend in the community where she was living. Maria said, "I have a friend who has a camera and a small machine for picture cleaning. So I joined her and we are doing it together" (2015). While this was only a short-term micro-enterprise (as Maria was leaving to apply for an internship to prepare for college), Maria explained that this income was necessary to meet her school needs and future goals of employment and self-employment (raising chickens)[3] Drawing on her peer relationships, Maria created a plan that included working both for herself and others to achieve her long-term goal of having her own home.

Peer Relationships at School

In addition to agentically drawing on relationships with peers at home, spoken survey data showed that youth also were agentic with peers at school to start their own micro-enterprises. Over the course of their studies, youth reported a significant increase in their peers at school helping them achieve their employment goals ($z=-2.65$, $p=0.008$). In addition, it was found that this increased support from peers at school was positively and significantly correlated with youth starting their own micro-enterprise ($r=.147$, $p=0.027$). Interview data showed how the skills learned and relationships built at school were vital to success when youth strategically drew on those relationships to meet their needs. For instance, one male youth, Nelson, described how his life at home was hard. He started, "The economic situation of my parents is not that good" (2015) and he had re-enrolled in school to become "a livestock officer or keeper or agriculturist. If not this I want to become a poultry keeper" (2012). Nelson further refined his life goals after subsequent years of schooling and explained that he now wanted to be an agriculture professor. While at school, Nelson and his peers learned how to castrate pigs, give appropriate dosages of medicine, and treat pigs for diseases; Nelson then collaboratively worked with his school peers to start a new pig micro-enterprise to work toward his future

---

[3] Most Tanzanians have home or micro-enterprises in addition to employment, and Maria was planning for both.

long-term goals. Nelson described how he planned to use the profit from the group micro-enterprise to start raising chickens:

> Because one piglet is sold for about 70,000 tsh [about $33 USD] for now…After five years if things will be good, which means that I will have kept my chickens very well, I want to have a lot of money. Because that will help me to assist the orphans and the disabled people. And by that time I'll be studying if I get the opportunity, but also continuing keeping the chickens. (2015)

Like Nelson, a group of female youth at Nguvu drew on their peer relationships at school to start a small micro-enterprise. After graduating, a group of young women from the school participated in an entrepreneurship course offered through a collaboration by the school and a local entrepreneur. Upon completing the course, the seventeen graduates received a grant to start a micro-enterprise. One graduate who participated in the course, Joyce, then went on to explain how she agentically partnered with other peers to pool together their capital, while also drawing on their entrepreneurship knowledge, to start the Top Clothing Group. She said, "Everybody was given their own money to start the micro-enterprise. We decided to make the group, me and a couple of friends decided on charcoal and used clothes" (2014). Joyce

Described how the group micro-enterprise had benefitted her. She stated, "It helped me because I knew now to do a business in partnership, and how to do business with your fellows, how to divide responsibilities, like this one can do this and the other can do this" (2015). As Joyce's mother died when she was in Form 3, Joyce was intensely focused on her goals of furthering her education and becoming a businesswoman. In 2015, Joyce was in college in Dodoma studying biology, and she described the challenges of living in a new place and trying to start a new micro-enterprise, particularly when she did not have the relationships she had previously:

> You know, I'm new in Dodoma so when we arrived here we didn't know people. And we were not used to people here because you would find everyone is dealing with their own life, which is different when we were at Nguvu where we used to live together.
> I'm supposed to know the location of the business that I'm about to start so I need to find out where the location is for marketing and if my business will prosper. I can't just start without having a plan. (2015)

To learn about her knew environment, Joyce planned to strategically draw on her new peer relationships at school "by interacting with fellow friends and discuss[ing] about them" (2015), as Joyce clearly saw the value of her peer relationships at school.

Agentically Navigating Constraining Peer Relationships

Not all relationships with peers were reported as positive; thus some youth learned how to navigate their complex social fields and when to draw on relationships that help support their micro-enterprises and goals. For instance, Ester described the importance of selecting positive peer relationships and distancing herself from negative relationships. She said, "I have got good relationships with my fellow students, especially when we want to share good ideas with them. But you need to be selective. Things that are good, take them. The bad things should be left" (2013). In 2012, Ester described how she and her peers at school were learning "how we can develop a garden and how we can grow crops" (2012); yet she faced challenges to starting an agriculture micro-enterprise at home due to a lack of access to land because she was female. Ester's thoughts capture the challenges:

> There is no opportunity for females to get access and own land. Only males are allowed to own land. I have a good example from my family that my brothers own pieces of land and they are the only ones. The girls don't have access to land and so they kept complaining about access to land but they are not getting it. (2012)

When asked how she confronts such challenges, Ester responded, "When it happens that someone is discouraging me, I seek advice from my fellow friends. They advise me that I should not be discouraged" (2013). Using such advice, in addition to her knowledge of poultry rearing from school and more supportive relationships at home, Ester instead started a chicken micro-enterprise. Ester explained:

> My neighbor had a flock of sick chickens, so she brought one over. We brought the healthy one chicken home. After producing the chicks, the original mother chicken was returned to my neighbor. There are now seventeen. This will help me because I can sell then. In the future, in case I get stuck, I can sell the chickens and get money. (2013)

Yet Ester found it difficult to keep the micro-enterprise going while still in school, due, in part, to a lack of positive peer relationships at home. As both Ester's mother and father had passed away, she described the importance of peer relationships at home to keep her micro-enterprise going, "I find myself that I can't do it...I don't have someone to look after my chickens because I'm at school" (2015). As she stated that, "I could overcome them [my problems] if I can have someone to help look after those chickens" (2015). Ester understood the importance of drawing on relationships for her future success. Thus, Ester was learning how to agentically navigate her relationships, draw on her new skills such as life skills learned at school, and cope with structural barriers such as lack of access to land, to further her goals.

Female youth in this study also described negative pressure to engage in sexual relationships with boys. In particular, when these young women had started a micro-enterprise, they had to navigate young men's interests in them or their earnings. Grace re-enrolled in school after her father had passed away with the hopes of becoming a doctor and a businesswoman, and she earned money during holidays by cooking and selling *ubuyu* (baobab fruit) and *mandazi* (fried bread). Yet Grace faced challenges with male peers who came to her micro-enterprise:

> There are some boys, they see that you're doing a business and they may start as a friend, taking this or taking that...he takes it [your product for sale] as a friend – he just says he's taking it as a friend, he does not pay it back. That's a challenge...there are other things, first they want us to be in a relationship with them. You're having no plans to do so but they're forcing you to do so....it is only to women who are trying to do business. (2014)

Grace described how she dealt with this unwanted attention from an older boy in the past, "He wanted me to be his friend, I just told him that I don't have time to be with him" (2014). She succinctly described how she would achieve her goals, "I have confidence in myself…I've been able to get knowledge, skills, and I can do any kind of business" (2015). In her last interview, Grace described how she served as a positive peer mentor for others at home by sharing, "In the community, it's like when I was giving advice to girls on how to do business, those who did not go to school. When I was going from school I would meet them, and now they have their own businesses" (2015). Thus, Grace learned how to navigate negative relationships, such as unwanted romantic relationships with male peers, and she found ways to serve as a positive relationship for others in her community, which included working to promote micro-enterprises other than her own.

Susan's Story of Agency Through Her Relationships

Susan's story is one both of perseverance and constant struggle in the face of adversity. In 2012, Susan, then in Form 2, explained that she had previously dropped out of school when she was pregnant with her first son. While she had wanted to be a lawyer, she now had a new dream after re-enrolling at Sasema to become a businesswoman. Susan explained how she wanted to continue schooling and succeed in her goals: "I am not planning to go back again. I am planning to go forward and achieve more" (2012). In 2013, Susan described how she engaged in small micro-enterprises with peers when at home during school breaks to help with family expenses:

> For example, whenever I go home, I find my peers or siblings selling chips [french fries] and fried chicken…I say that well, I have this small amount of money and I can help you with capital, and we enter into a new small business agreement together. It's different than doing your own small business, so what I see most is it's like I'm joining them at the moment that I'm there and then we do a little bit of business together. (2013)

Susan also saw this experience as a step in fulfilling her longer-term goal of becoming self-employed. To enhance the chicken and chips micro-enterprise with her siblings and friends, Susan strategically pooled her capital and drew on her entrepreneurship skills:

> I added 10,000 shillings [about $5 USD], and what I discovered was that when it reaches 7 pm, they just felt like, oh the business was over – even if they didn't have a profit they said let it be done. But when we worked together, they discovered that if we work together, the customer needs like adding this, like maybe tomato sauce or chili sauce, and so when I joined them they saw some changes. (2013)

From this micro-enterprise, Susan was able to use the profits for both her school and home needs, such as buying soap, socks, clothes, and lotion.

When we interviewed her in 2014, difficult circumstances surrounding her mother's illness and caring for her child caused Susan to drop out of Sasema school. She shared:

> I wasn't able to go to school because of the responsibilities – the first responsibility was to help my mother, she was sick and was supposed to help me and my child depended on me – and you can't go to school with the fear of your family not being okay. So it wasn't easy for me to stay in school without knowing their needs are met. (2014)

Susan was now trying to make a profit as a food vendor, co-owning the micro-enterprise with her friend. Susan had limited start-up capital, only 50,000 Tanzanian shilling, about $23 USD, and her friend had 100,000 Tanzanian shilling, about $46, so they decided to start a micro-enterprise together. Susan explains the benefit of having your own micro-enterprise, partnering with a friend, and the pride she felt in earning her own money:

> Most of the time starting a business is hard, but as you continue things get a bit easier…the difference is when you're doing business on your own, if your capital decreases then you struggle on your own to find that capital. But also on the customer side you struggle on your own to find customers…when you have a partner you help each other. The difference is when you're employing someone, that employee is just waiting for a salary at the end of the day. But when you're two business owners, it's easier to find capital if your business decreases. It's easy because when you're together you find customers together compared to when you're alone.
> Now I can depend on myself…[and] I can help my family. They now know that there's someone else who can help so if any problems occur they can depend on me…on my side it's also that I feel like it's my responsibility to help her [my mother]. (2014)

Susan also described challenging peer relationships, especially with male peers:

> A boy might come and pursue you, but with the main goal of just eating the food for free. He doesn't have true love – he just wants to eat for free. This is mostly applied to girls whereby the boys want them as friends to eat for free.
> There was a boy that we used to be friends, he might come for the first day and he'll say that he doesn't have a single cent but he comes with his swagger. Give me food and I'll pay you back – he eats and you can't find him for 2 or 3 days. Then he comes back with his own stories he's saying that he loves you and so on, but this isn't true love….but me, I have my goals so I just say, please pay for the food but don't tell me anything else and he'll pay and not say again that he loves me. (2014)

When asked what happened with this boy, she explained, "He ate 1000 tsh of food [about $.50 USD]—that's it. He paid it back and he never came back" (2014). Susan was able to recoup the lost income, and she had strategically learned to avoid relationships that conflicted with her goals.

In her final interview, Susan described how she had another child and was struggling to make ends meet, as she was forced to close her restaurant because the location increased her rent significantly and she was unable to turn a profit. Yet, despite the constant challenges to her livelihood, she again reiterated her desire to partner with others as she recognized the need to draw on relationships to balance family with work:

> A child is a challenge because there is a time that he could get sick or he's not doing well and so you can't work at that time. And even if you do it will not be good. So that's why I'm saying I cannot work by myself because even if I open my own business I'll be closing it often. But if I have a business with my fellow that will be easy. (2015)

Thus, Susan understood the importance of strategically drawing on positive relationships and avoiding negative ones to succeed, although her ability to confront all challenges was often limited.

Discussion

In this study of youth from marginalized backgrounds in Tanzania, I found that they were agentic in drawing on their relationships with peers at home and at school to use their education and start or enhance their own micro-enterprises. Previous research has argued that schooling can be a problematic site for social capital development if bureaucratic processes at school are more important than the needs of youth (Stanton-Salazar, 1997). For example, the role of teachers may be inconsistent, contradictory, or ambiguous, and instructional methods are often rooted in the cultural capital of the dominant group such as the language of instruction (Stanton-Salazar, 1997). In this study, the school sites, along with the entrepreneurship education program, were seen as positive spaces for youth to build relationships and learn new technical and life skills, which youth then drew on to start their own micro-enterprises. While previous research has described schooling as a site for social capital development for youth from marginalized backgrounds (Chattopadhay, 2014), this study enhances previous work by exploring how school social capital can benefit youth to start or expand their own micro-enterprises, both while in school and upon graduation.

In addition, these data challenge Stanton-Salazar's (2011) definition of institutional agents, as the peers at home and at school in this study were not high-status nor well-positioned to provide key forms of support. Instead, peers were also from disadvantaged backgrounds and oftentimes had very limited resources. Yet youth in this study utilized their agency both in and through these peer relationships to improve their livelihoods. Youth acted agentically to draw on favorable relationships with peers to borrow money, pool capital to start micro-enterprises, share knowledge, offer encouragement, and learn new skills. In addition, youth were agentic in objecting to or navigating constraining relationships (for instance, exploitative relationships with boys) that limited their livelihoods or conflicted with their goals. Similar to Bajaj's (2008) work, youth in this study continued to describe challenging larger structural constraints. But in contrast to her findings, youth in this study reported that their schooling helped them to be agentic over time to confront or work around such challenges. For instance, the majority of females in this study described being pursued by males as some point in their lives to engage in relationships, either for money, basic needs, or school fees. These youth described how, before schooling, they did not always feel able to confront such challenges. Yet with new confidence, plans to achieve their goals, and encouraging relationships with peers developed over time, youth were able to agentically meet such challenges outside of school. While youth continued to face structural inequalities, such as gender discrimination, a lack of access to land for females, or economic marginalization in the larger community, youth were learning to actively draw on their skills and relationships in an attempt to mitigate such barriers.

Conclusion

While there has been considerable research done on how youth can succeed in school and find or create jobs to earn a decent wage, youth unemployment remains a significant challenge, especially in Tanzania. Entrepreneurship education has been suggested as an effective way to help youth from marginalized backgrounds gain the skills needed to get out of poverty (USAID, 2013b; World Bank, 2012). Other scholars have noted that youth livelihoods, particularly those from disadvantaged backgrounds, continue to be constrained by social, political, and economic factors outside of their control (Baxter et al., 2014). Researchers have suggested that the accumulation and utilization of social capital may help (Stanton-Salazar, 1997), but developing and utilizing social capital is especially problematic for youth from marginalized backgrounds because they are alienated and excluded from many structures in society. These data show these Tanzanian youth agentically developed and drew on their relationships with peers both at home and at school to create micro-enterprises amidst inequalities in their lives.

By exploring how relationships and related resources affect youth development and livelihoods, this study illuminates larger lessons. First, this study makes a theoretical contribution to illustrate how peer relationships are an important component, in addition to knowledge and skills, for fostering employment for youth from marginalized backgrounds. While these data are limited to two sites in Tanzania, they suggest that youth may be able to convert social capital, specifically relationships with peers, into economic capital by starting small micro-enterprises to help achieve their goals and earn an income.

Second, this study has important implications for practice. As new visions for education are developed and acted upon (see, for example, UNESCO, 2015), it is critical to consider schooling as an important and necessary site for youth to learn how to develop relationships with peers to foster learning and earning. Peer mentoring programs purposefully added into the school timetable could help deepen peer relationships. In addition, entrepreneurship education programming with a specific focus on building relationships with peers (both in and out of school) could help foster group enterprises.

Lastly, given inequalities in youth's lives, schools and entrepreneurship programs could provide counseling or support services to help youth learn to navigate constraints such as gender discrimination or sexual exploitation in the workplace. More research is needed to further understand if and how programs can build youth agency and help youth learn to actively utilize relationships to address structural barriers and succeed in education, secure employment, and enhance their livelihoods.[4]

[4]I would like to thank Joan DeJaeghere, Jasmina Josic, and Kate McCleary, editors of this book, for their collaboration and helpful comments. In addition, I am grateful to my colleagues at the University of Minnesota who assisted with this research, including David Chapman, Joan DeJaeghere, Chris Johnstone, Heidi Eschenbacher, and over 50 graduate students who have worked on the larger evaluation over the past 5 years. I am especially thankful for the kindness and collaboration from youth and staff at Sasema and Usawa, in addition to staff at Parka, as this work would not be possible without their support.

References

Ahearn, L. M. (2001). Language and agency. *Annual Review of Anthropology, 30*, 109–137.

Andrade, A. D. (2009). Interpretive research aiming at theory building: Adopting and adapting the case study design. *The Qualitative Report, 14*(1), 42–60.

Bajaj, M. (2008). 'I have big things planned for my future': The limits and possibilities of transformative agency in Zambian schools. *Compare, 39*(4), 551–568.

Baxter, A., Chapman, D. W., DeJaeghere, J., Pekol, A. R., & Weiss, T. (2014). Youth entrepreneurship education and training for poverty alleviation: A review of international literature and local experiences. In A. W. Weisman (Ed.), *International educational innovation and public sector entrepreneurship* (pp. 33–58). Bingley, England: Emerald Group Publishing Limited.

Bourdieu, P. (1986). The forms of capital. In J. G. Richardson (Ed.), *Handbook of theory and research for the sociology of education* (pp. 241–258). New York, NY: Greenwood.

Bourdieu, P. (1990). *The logic of practice*. Stanford, CA: Stanford University Press.

Bourdieu, P. (1998). *Practical reason: On the theory of action*. Stanford, CA: Stanford University Press.

Chattopadhay, T. (2014). School as a site of student social capital: An exploratory study from Brazil. *International Journal of Educational Development, 34*(1), 67–76.

Coleman, J. S. (1988). Social capital in the creation of human capital. *The American Journal of Sociology, 94*(Suppl), S95–S120.

Coleman, J. S., & Hoffer, T. B. (1987). *Public and private schools: The impact of communities*. New York, NY: Basic Books, Inc.

Corbin, J., & Strauss, A. (2008). *Basics of qualitative research: Techniques and procedures for developing grounded theory*. Thousand Oaks, CA: Sage Publications, Inc.

Creswell, J. W. (2009). *Research design: Qualitative, quantitative, and mixed method approaches*. Thousand Oaks, CA: Sage Publications, Inc.

DeJaeghere, J. (2013). Education, skills and citizenship: An emergent model for entrepreneurship in Tanzania. *Comparative Education, 49*(4), 503–519.

DeJaeghere, J., Pellowski Wiger, N., & Willemsen, L. (2016). Broadening educational outcomes: Social learning, skills development and employability for youth. *Comparative Education Review*.

Dika, S. L., & Singh, K. (2002). Applications of social capital in educational literature: A critical synthesis. *Review of Educational Research, 72*(1), 31–60.

Economic and Social Research Foundation. (2014). Tanzania human development report 2014: Economic transformation for human development. Retrieved October 21, 2015, from http://hdr.undp.org/sites/default/files/thdr2014-main.pdf.

Furstenberg, F. F., & Hughes, M. E. (1995). Social capital and successful development among at-risk youth. *Journal of Marriage and the Family, 57*(3), 580–592.

Holland, J., Reynolds, T., & Weller, S. (2007). Transitions, networks and communities: The significance of social capital in the lives of children and young people. *Journal of Youth Studies, 10*(1), 97–116.

International Labour Office (ILO). (2009). *Supporting entrepreneurship education*. Geneva, Switzerland: International Labour Organization.

International Labour Office (ILO). (2015). *World report on child labor: Paving the way to decent work for young people*. Geneva, Switzerland: International Labour Organization.

Jeffrey, C. (2012). Geographies of children and youth II: Global youth agency. *Progress in Human Geography, 36*(2), 245–253.

Kushner, J. (2013, October 29). Tanzania's perplexing youth unemployment crisis. Retrieved June 14, 2015, from http://www.globalpost.com/dispatches/globalpost-blogs/rights/tanzania-youth-unemployment-crisis.

Leonard, M. (2005). Children, childhood and social capital: Exploring the links. *Sociology, 39*(4), 605–622.

Lloyd, C. B. (Ed.). (2005). *Growing up global: The changing transitions to adulthood in developing countries*. Washington, DC: National Academies Press.

McCleary, K. (2013). 'Tomar decisions es el future de uno' [To make decision is one's future]: The gendering of youth agency within two Honduran communities. Doctoral dissertation. Retrieved from ProQuest, UMI Dissertations Publishing (3607817).

Morrow, V. (1999). Conceputalising social capital in relation to the well-being of children and young people: A critical review. *The Sociological Review, 47*(4), 745–765.

Morrow, V. (2002). Children's experiences of 'community': Implications of social capital discourses. In C. Swann & A. Morgan (Eds.), *Social capital for health: Insights from qualitative research* (pp. 9–28). London, England: Health Development Agency.

Portes, A. (1998). Social capital: Its origins and applications in modern sociology. *Annual Review of Sociology, 24*(1), 1–24.

Putnam, R. (1993). *Making democracy work: Civic traditions in modern Italy.* Princeton, NJ: Princeton University Press.

Raffo, C., & Reeves, M. (2000). Youth transitions and social exclusion: Developments in social capital theory. *Journal of Youth Studies, 3*(2), 147–166.

Sewell, W. H. (1992). A theory of structure: Duality, agency, and transformation. *American Journal of Sociology, 98*(1), 1–29.

Stanton-Salazar, R. D. (1997). A social capital framework for understanding the socialization of racial minority children and youth. *Harvard Educational Review, 67*(1), 1–40.

Stanton-Salazar, R. D. (2011). A social capital framework for the study of institutional agents and their role in the empowerment of low-status students and youth. *Youth Society, 43*(3), 1066–1109.

United Nations. (2013). *Definitions of youth.* Fact sheet. New York, NY: United Nations Department of Economics and Social Affairs. Retrieved May 14, 2015, from http://www.un.org/esa/socdev/documents/youth/fact-sheets/youth-definition.pdf.

United Nations Educational, Scientific and Cultural Organization (UNESCO). (2015). Education 2030: Incheon Declaration and framework for action. Incheon, Republic of Korea: UNESCO. Retrieved January 21, 2016, from http://unesdoc.unesco.org/images/0024/002432/243278e.pdf.

United Republic of Tanzania. (1996). National youth development policy. Retrieved June 21, 2015, from http://planipolis.iiep.unesco.org/upload/Youth/Tanzania%20UR/Tanzania_Nationalyouthdevelopmentpolicy.pdf.

United States Agency for International Development (USAID). (2013a). Scan and review of youth development measurement tools. Retrieved from https://www.usaid.gov/what-we-do/education/expanding-access-higher-education-and-workforce-development/Scan-Review-Youth-Development-Measurement-Tools.

United States Agency for International Development (USAID). (2013b). *State of the field report: Examining the evidence in youth workforce development.* Washington, DC: USAID.

Vavrus, F. (2013). More clever than the devil: Ujanja as schooling strategy in Tanzania. *International Journal of Qualitative Studies in Education, 28,* 50–71. doi:10.1080/09518398.2013.847508.

Wagner, C. M., Lyimo, E. D., & Lwendo, S. (2012). Matches but no fire: Street children in Dar es Salaam, Tanzania. In M. O. Ensor (Ed.), *African childhoods: Education, development, peacebuilding, and the youngest continent* (pp. 33–47). New York, NY: Palgrave Macmillan.

World Bank. (2012). *World development report 2013: Jobs.* Retrieved June 20, 2015, from https://openknowledge.worldbank.org/handle/10986/11843.

Yan, M. C., Lauer, S., & Chan, S. (2009). Social capital and the labour market process among new generation youth from visible minority immigrant families (Working paper No. 09-01). Vancouver, BC, Canada: Metropolis British Columbia. Retrieved May 9, 2015, from http://mbc.metropolis.net/assets/uploads/files/wp/2009/WP09-01.pdf.

Vocational Training and Agency Among Kenyan Youth

Acacia Nikoi

Education as a Site of Agency

Development discourse champions the completion of primary and secondary schooling as necessary for an individual's future and for their community's well-being. These arguments are backed by evidence that shows that by achieving schooling benchmarks, children and youth are more likely to have access to formal employment, earn higher incomes, and make contributions to more robust labor markets (Tembon & Fort, 2008; Warner, Malhotra, & McGonagle, 2012). There are also significant benefits to families as health and well-being improve and the time to first pregnancy is more likely to be delayed among girls (Ozier, 2011; Warner et al., 2012). Within this discourse, empowerment and agency have been frequently linked with schooling (which takes place in formal settings and within formal structures) and education (which can be formal, but also non-formal or informal and takes many different forms), especially in relation to gender inequalities (Murphy-Graham, 2012; Stromquist, 2015). Warner et al. (2012) argue that it is the process of empowerment in the transition to adulthood that connects schooling with the economic and social benefits identified above. Stromquist (2015) further states that schooling is a critical factor in increasing youths' knowledge—one of four dimensions of empowerment that she identifies—that can lead to increased youth agency. Despite this, research suggests that not all schooling experiences lead to agentic youth (Bajaj, 2011; Chismaya, DeJaeghere, Kendall, & Khan, 2012) and schooling alone does not guarantee success in the economic sector (Allison et al., 2014; King, 2007; Ohba, 2011). Furthermore, Stromquist argues that non-formal education programs have been more successful than formal schooling at engendering empowerment and agency.

A. Nikoi (✉)

Department of Organizational Leadership, Policy and Development, University of Minnesota, Minneapolis, MN, USA

e-mail: nikoi049@umn.edu

© Springer International Publishing Switzerland 2016

J.G. DeJaeghere et al. (eds.), *Education and Youth Agency*, Advancing Responsible Adolescent Development, DOI 10.1007/978-3-319-33344-1_13

With a global emphasis on providing schooling for all youth, the percentage of youth who are able to attain a basic or secondary education have increased in countries such as Kenya (Ministry of Education, 2012). Despite the fact that more youth are achieving benchmarks of schooling that are deemed necessary for them to engage in the workforce, many remain unable to do so (King & McGrath, 2012). To address this gap, vocational skills training and education through both governmental and non-governmental mechanisms have become increasingly popular. As these opportunities become more readily available and are presented as opportunities for youth empowerment, it is important to look at whether or not vocational training provides youth with the knowledge and skills they need to actively engage in different livelihood options, and in the process, if and how it contributes to developing youth agency.

In this chapter I explore how Kenyan youth who participated in a non-formal, vocational training program after completing their secondary education developed skills and knowledge and were able to utilize them in ways that demonstrated both individual and social agency. I begin this chapter by situating the study in the Kenyan education and employment sectors and introducing the site of study. I then examine the ways in which agency can be explored among urban Kenyan youth and in relation to their transition to adulthood. My discussion on methodology highlights how a longitudinal study helps us to understand the ways in which agency develops over time. Finally, I discuss the study findings that contribute to broader conceptualizations of agency and youth.

The Context of Education and Employment for Youth in Kenya

For the past 25 years there has been a significant emphasis around the globe on promoting formal education, most prominently with primary or basic schooling but also with secondary schooling. The introduction of the Education for All (EFA) initiative and the Millennium Development Goals (MDG) spurred these efforts to ensure that basic education would be available to all children and youth, regardless of gender or socio-economic class. In response, countries have used considerable resources to bolster the educational systems in their countries. In Kenya, free primary education was introduced in 2003 and resulted in an additional two million students entering into the primary education system over the next 5 years (Ministry of Education, 2012). This expansion of the education system was followed in 2008 with the introduction of the Free Day Secondary Education Program (FDSEP) (Ministry of Education, 2011). Even though attending secondary school remained difficult for many youth and their families due to associated costs of schooling (i.e., the cost of uniforms and the opportunity costs of not working in order to go to school) (Ohba, 2011), the rates of secondary school enrollment increased from 32.4 % to 45.3 % from 2008 to 2011 (Ministry of Education, 2012). This increased access to formal education provides youth with necessary credentials for finding employment or for continuing their education. However, youth and employers often view these schooling credentials as insufficient for providing the skills and knowledge that youth need to engage in the workforce.

Despite an increase in the number of youth who have been able to attain a formal education, concerns remain over the quality and relevancy of education, particularly in secondary schools. The rapid increase in enrollments has meant that schools are facing over-crowding, a shortage of teachers and a lack of resources, all of which have led to a decrease in the quality of education that youth receive (Oyaro, 2008). Coupled with declining quality, youth and parents have concerns over the relevancy of secondary schooling. Even after completing secondary school youth feel they do not have the skills and means to pursue desired employment opportunities (Ohba, 2011). Ohba's study on primary school leavers found relevancy of learning outcomes to be one of the factors that affected whether or not youth pursued secondary schooling. He states, "Although some [youth] valued the greater knowledge they might gain from secondary education, they were simultaneously concerned about what they would be able to do after they had finished school" (2011, p. 407). This gap in quality and relevancy of education results in questioning the value of education for youths' future livelihoods.

While the official, national unemployment rate is 10 %, youth unemployment ranges between 15 % and 35 % depending on age; additionally, 70–80 % of the unemployed population is below the age of 34 (Njonjo, 2010; UNDP, 2013). Youth unemployment rates are complicated by the fact that youth are not able to legally engage in formal employment until the age of 18 (Government of Kenya, 2010).[1] The majority of 15–16-year-old youth are still in school during this period and, therefore, they are not included in unemployment rates (UNDP, 2013). Within the broad range of youth, 18–20-year-olds have the highest unemployment rate at 35 %. Rates of employment trend downward with age and 25 % of 25 year olds are unemployed, while 15 % of 30-year-olds face unemployment (UNDP, 2013).

In response to the employment challenges and the lack of quality and relevant education in preparing youth for the workforce, urban youth in sub-Saharan Africa seek to identify targeted non-formal education that will allow them to gain specific skills within a limited time period and in turn to start their own businesses (Sommers, 2007). Although the number of organizations that provide targeted non-formal education has increased over the past decade, the impact of non-formal educational programs that provide vocational training remains an under-studied area and little research has been done on the role of this type of education in fostering agency for youths' future livelihoods.

---

[1] The Kenyan constitution defines the stage of being a youth as being between the ages of 15 and 35 (Government of Kenya, 2010), but the life experiences and needs of youth within this broad category vary significantly.

Njia as a Site of Study

The *Njia* Youth Empowerment Program (*Njia* YEP, referred to throughout as "*Njia*")[2] is one organization that aims to address the gap between what youth learn in school and what they need to secure their livelihoods and achieve their career goals. Established in Kenya in 2010, *Njia* is a 4-month program that provides older youth (18–25) with basic employability skills in select vocational areas, introductory knowledge of entrepreneurship, work readiness skills and life skills. In addition to classroom teaching, the program uses hands-on learning experiences in entrepreneurship and technical areas, facilitates mentorship opportunities between business community members and youth, and places youth in attachments where they work with businesses in selected vocational fields for 1 month or more to learn about the field and further develop their skills. The attachment is frequently unpaid, though employers who choose to offer attachments longer than 1 month are required to provide a stipend or salary. Youth in this study participated in one of five vocational/technical fields that were regarded as meeting employer demands in the urban area of Nairobi: hospitality, customer relations and sales, automotive, electrical, and industrial garment manufacturing.

In keeping with the mission of Njia, youth who participate in the program are considered economically marginalized. Youth typically come from informal settlements or other low income areas and the majority of youth spend at least 1 year "idle" in which they were unable to engage in employment opportunities or to continue their education. At the same time, many youth defy other descriptors of marginalization. Most youth are not orphaned and have support, either financial or emotional, from family members. Furthermore, the majority of youth have completed secondary school, which requires access to financial resources or scholarships. In many ways these youths occupy an "in-between" space—they are neither the most marginalized in their communities nor are they the ones who are identified as leaders for the next generation. They are youth who have hopes and dreams for their future and anticipated that completion of secondary school would have provided them with the opportunities they needed to achieve those dreams. However, after spending at least 1 year after Form 4 (completion of secondary school in Kenya), being unemployed and unable to pursue further education, they entered the program expecting to gain the necessary skills to pursue their livelihoods. This chapter explores how after participating in the program, acquiring technical skills and developing new ways of thinking and perceiving themselves, youth demonstrated agency as they navigated economic opportunities and made decisions about their livelihoods and futures. In this process, I place youth agency within the social and economic environment in which the youth live and work, and discuss how these environments shape youth's agency.

---

[2] Pseudonyms are used throughout for the organization and all individuals.

Conceptualizing Agency and Empowerment

"Youth empowerment" has increasingly become part of the development lexicon. Throughout Africa, and in Kenya specifically, there have been strategic efforts to empower economically and socially marginalized youth through a variety of initiatives sponsored by governments, international organizations, international non-governmental organizations (NGO), and local NGOs. Frequently these initiatives emphasize the role of economic empowerment on youths' lives and equate vocational training or job placement with empowerment (Betcherman, Godfrey, Puerto, Rother, & Stavreska, 2007; McGrath, 2012). However, the different ways in which empowerment might be experienced, how youth agentically enact their empowerment, and the multiple dimensions of youths' lives that extend beyond their economic needs are frequently under-emphasized. It is against this backdrop of youth empowerment programming that this study on youth agency took place. This chapter positions agency within the process of empowerment (Kabeer, 1999; Murphy-Graham, 2012) and examines how youth who participated in non-formal, vocational training experienced agency. This study conceptualizes agency in three ways: (1) as a component of the process of empowerment, (2) as action that both impacts and is impacted by the individual and the social, and (3) as an act that is a part of everyday youth encounters and not just an extraordinary response to crisis conditions.

First, in this chapter I situate agency as a phenomenon that happens within the process of empowerment (Kabeer, 1999; Murphy-Graham, 2012). Kabeer (1999) identified agency as one of three inter-related dimensions of empowerment, including resources and achievements, and defined it as "the ability to define one's goals and act upon them" (p. 438). Murphy-Graham's (2012) framework extrapolated on this by demonstrating that the ability to act is influenced by changes in the ways one thinks and the development of new skills and knowledge. In her work with women's educational initiatives in Honduras, Murphy-Graham identified three inter-related yet distinct dimensions of empowerment–recognition, capacity development and action. The recognition dimension encompassed new ways of thinking about oneself and others and was evidenced through increased self-confidence, self-awareness, and an open mind. Capacity development referred to critical thinking and a more technical or cognitive type of knowledge, while the action dimension spoke to the ways in which those skills and knowledge are put into practice. In this study, all three dimensions are present, beginning with the new ways youth think of themselves upon developing new skills through vocational training to relating the obtained skills and knowledge in their daily lives and goals for their future. Similar to Murphy-Grahams' study, this study demonstrates youth agency through the enactment of various types of knowledge, skills, and ways of thinking. The three dimensions presented by Murphy-Graham therefore provide one framework to understand how non-formal, vocational education can act as a catalyst in youth's agency through the process of empowerment.

The second way in which this chapter conceptualizes agency is as socially embedded. While vocational skills training is primarily interested in giving youth the tools necessary to secure certain types of employment, pursue additional schooling, and set new livelihoods goods, youth are not isolated as they engage in these actions. Rather, the goals they set and actions they take are informed by social norms, societal expectations, and family (and other's) needs (DeJaeghere, McCleary, & Josić, 2016). In a study of low-income youth in Botswana, Joseph (2012) identified "familial-belonging" as intricately linked to the agency and livelihood trajectories of the young women in his study. His findings suggest that the decisions youth made regarding their livelihoods were impacted by both the needs of those around them and the aspirations youth had for themselves and for others.

The final way in which agency is explored among these youths in Nairobi is through recognition of "everyday agency" (Payne, 2012). Payne introduced the notion of everyday agency in the context of child-headed households to counter discourses that describe children's and youth's agency as a response to a crisis or a situation that is inherently abnormal. Instead, she chose to view agency in these situations through the lenses of the children who saw their decisions and actions as a part of the normal, everyday life that they were living. Similarly, within a discourse where youth are often seen as either the "makers" or "breakers" (Honwana & De Boeck, 2005) or the "vandals" or "vanguards" (Abbink & van Kessel, 2005) of society, the notion of everyday agency removes the stigma of a crisis situation and the pressure of becoming the heroes through broader social change. The concept of everyday agency recognizes that agency is not always a conscious action that youth take in response to a perceived injustice, nor does it necessarily take the form of active social change. Rather, everyday agency acknowledges that youth "view their actions as a part of their everyday life rather than as being constrained or viewing them through a 'coping lens'" (Payne, 2012, p. 403). While there were instances in which youth did act agentically in crisis situations such as a family member's illness or sudden death, the vast majority of decisions and actions that youth took happened in the everyday.

Methodology

This chapter draws on qualitative findings from longitudinal interview data that were gathered over a period of 4 years (2012–2015) with youth who participated in the *Njia* program.[3] The first interviews in 2012 were conducted with 64 youth from two cohorts of 162 youth as they completed the program and were engaged in or had just ended their attachment. Thirty of the youth participated in the Taharuki site,

---

[3] This study is a secondary analysis of interview data that was collected as part of a larger, 6-year evaluation of three entrepreneurship programs in Kenya, Tanzania, and Uganda, conducted by the University of Minnesota (UMN) and funded by the MasterCard Foundation. David Chapman and Joan DeJaeghere served as principal investigators and a team of 28 UMN faculty, staff, and graduate students and Kenyan researchers conducted interviews, and collected spoken survey and demographic data between 2012 and 2015. The author served as the lead project fellow for qualitative data collection in Kenya during that time period.

located in the center of Nairobi serving lower-income communities and 34 had participated in the Sukumiza site, in a peri-urban industrial area that serves a transit community. There were 33 males and 31 females. Follow-up interviews with these same youth were then conducted each subsequent year for the next 3 years. Although the sample size fluctuated between 64 and 46 youth each year, 34 youth were interviewed all 4 years. As a longitudinal study, sample attrition was anticipated and most attrition was due to youth movement away from the project site, unavailability of youth due to their long working hours or inflexible schedules or, in some instances, personal or family illnesses at the time the interviews were conducted.

Interviews were conducted by teams of researchers, including the author, from the United States and Kenya and were conducted in English, Swahili, or Sheng—a mix of Swahili, English, and other Kenyan languages. The ability of the team to use English, Swahili, and Sheng often put youth at ease and encouraged them to tell us their successes and challenges. Interviews with NGO staff and stakeholders provided additional information about the context in which youth live, work, and enact the skills and knowledge they have learned.

As a lead project fellow over the 4 years, I worked closely with the research team, facilitating and conducting interviews, training interview teams, and conducting analyses. The analysis of the interviews was a multi-step process that began in the field within the two to three person interview teams and amongst the broader data collection team. Analysis continued once field-work was complete through coding with NVivo software to identify themes. Although our understanding of youth's lives may have been constrained because the interviews were conducted on an annual basis and thus what youth related to the researchers reflected their reality at a specific point in time each year, a number of factors in the research design helped to mitigate this. As a longitudinal study we had an opportunity to further explore themes that emerged in the first years of the study through follow-up interviews that were designed to further probe salient themes, seek clarification of unclear or surprising findings and follow changes in youths' lives from one year to the next. In addition, the diverse research team, which included Kenyan researchers and United States university researchers who were from the region or had extensive experience in the region, allowed us to contextualize youth responses.

I came to the study with 15 years of prior experience in East and West Africa and as such was able to contextualize those stories within a Kenya and Nairobi specific context. Furthermore, my ability to speak and understand Swahili not only provided a space whereby youth felt comfortable using language fluidly, it also was a mechanism through which to understand the nuances with which the youth spoke and that sometimes could be lost in the translation process. As a researcher with the project during the 4 years of the study, I became intimately familiar with the stories youth shared of the changes that were taking place in their lives and livelihoods. I began to explore how empowerment and subsequently agency were being demonstrated in youth's lives. Drawing on empowerment frameworks and concepts of agency developed by Kabeer (1999), and Murphy-Graham (2012), I reanalyzed interview data from 2012–2014 to identify ways in which the process of empowerment was evident in youth's lives. Using that analysis, I incorporated a set of questions into the fourth year of interviews to illicit a discussion of youth's conceptualizations of empowerment and whether or not they saw this evident in their own lives. I then analyzed the ways in which youth conceptualized empowerment, together with their life experiences over 4 years, to examine how youth enact empowerment and agency in their own lives.

Developing Youth Agency Through Njia

Upon completion of the 4-month *Njia* program, almost all interviewed youth sought stable employment in the fields they studied or in a related field. For many youth, employment was a means to achieve a variety of goals, including supporting their families by providing school fees for siblings or buying basic needs, saving money to return to school or saving enough capital to pursue entrepreneurial opportunities. The majority of youth engaged in multiple earning and learning activities at any given time and most, though not all, saw shifts within their earning mechanisms from year to year. The trajectories that youth lives took in the 4 years after their participation in the *Njia* program demonstrated multiple ways in which youth experienced the process of empowerment and acted in agentic ways. More than being empowered by their employment, the stories of these youth over 4 years shows how they developed self-awareness and confidence, among other skills, and put these skills into action. It is through this process in which the youth became agentic by navigating livelihood opportunities, developing new goals and aspirations, and making life decision. In addition, their stories showed ways in which those trajectories were impacted by social and economic conditions that influenced their agency, at times constraining it.

Personal Development and Critical Skills and Knowledge

Over the 4-year period of the study, youth identified a number of ways in which they felt that participation in the *Njia* program had impacted their personal development and their acquisition of skills and knowledge. Youth frequently demonstrated a better understanding of themselves and those around them, increased self-confidence and self-awareness, improved communication abilities and an ability to relate with a wide range of people, all of which are identified by Murphy-Graham as aspects of recognition. These skills are frequently inter-related, as self-confidence leads to a greater willingness and ability to talk to people or openness to taking on other people's perspectives. Nathan[4] discussed these changes a year after completing the program:

> Something that has changed a lot – I'm able to interact with people in a good way. In a makeable way. I'm able to solve issues in a way that I can say is good. I don't find myself getting angry at people. I know how to express myself. When I go for a job interview, I will

---

[4] Pseudonyms are used throughout this text for all study participants in order to protect anonymity. The year of the interview is included next to the quotes from participant interviews to provide insight into changes in participants' perspectives over the course of the four year study.

be able to express what I feel and what I have ... So I would say that my personal skills have improved big time. (Nathan, personal communication, 2013)

In addition to demonstrating new ways to interact with people, Nathan also highlighted that one year after participation in the program he was able to recognize his emotions, engage in conflict resolution and put his newfound skills in relating to people into action in the workplace and in his community. He did not view these situations as unduly difficult or traumatic, rather his ability to navigate encounters in the workplace and with people in his community demonstrated his ability to be agentic in everyday activities.

In the first year following their participation in the program, youth emphasized the ways they had experienced and used increased self-confidence and improved communication skills. Over time, as youth became more engaged in their communities and in employment or self-employment, their perspectives on how these skills impacted them shifted. In the third year of interviews, youth continued to highlight their ability to communicate and have self-confidence, but they also indicated that as their self-knowledge increased, their mindset had changed and they had increased motivation in their lives. Describing how he viewed himself, Thomas said that increased self-confidence and self-awareness contributed to increased motivation in his life. He explained that "[increased skills and self-confidence] gave me that desire to grow. I always say that. It gave me the inner passion and the self-drive to keep on moving." After describing a classroom interaction where Thomas felt motivated, he further explained, "From there, [that situation] I said let me believe in myself. I always believe in myself. From [that point] I have never looked back. I have to keep moving" (Thomas, personal communication, 2014). While Thomas referred to this changed perspective as an inner passion and self-drive, other youth described this change as a new hope for their future or an opening of their minds.

Youth also demonstrated and valued increases in vocational skills, work readiness skills and improved financial literacy, all of which can be categorized as capacity development in Murphy-Graham's (2012) dimensions of empowerment. Whether the vocational skills were the basic knowledge of how to wire a house, use an industrial sewing machine or how to fix a car, obtaining this knowledge also served to boost youth's confidence as they completed the *Njia* program, in part because of the potential they saw in using these work readiness skills and knowledge in their employment. Andrew studied electrical wiring at *Njia* and his confidence in the second year of interviews remained strong. He indicated that having new skills improved his chances at securing employment:

For now what I can say is *Njia YEP* has opened my hopes. Like for me I did electricals and electronics, and before [participation in the program], in terms of fighting for a job, I could not go and find any job. I did not have any skills. But for now, I have the skills in electrical and electronics. I am able to do that. (Andrew, personal communication, 2012)

In year four Andrew was still gainfully employed by a contractor to do electrical wiring and frequently traveled to different parts of Kenya for contract jobs.

Even when technical skills did not lead directly to employment in the specific vocational field, youth often expressed pride in having knowledge that could be used in different ways. James shared how learning automotive skills served as a mechanism for contributing to his family despite the fact that soon after the first year he left the automotive field to first set-up a food stall in a local market and later go to work at a supermarket. He said:

> I got skills in automotive engineering. Those skills have helped me a lot. If the car breaks down, some parts I can fix instead of calling a mechanic. Then at least I am able to do services with the vehicles – minor services. (James, personal communication, 2013)

When asked if he charged a fee for working on vehicles, he replied, "When I am called by someone I charge you. But when I am travelling with my uncle, because he has his own car, if there is a problem with the car I can just fix it." For James, the skills were useful for making small amounts of money on the side, but were more useful as a service that could be given to family members.

While the specific vocational skills that youth learned appeared to be less impactful over time, youth credited these skills with setting them on their current path and contributing to their initial employment experiences. Nathan, whose perspectives on confidence were shared above, described how learning electrical skills was a catalyst for the three jobs he held in 2014 that were not directly related to his vocational field. He explained it in this way:

> I became a real estate manager with the training I received at *Njia*. I was able to study electricals. I was so good at it, the boss [of the NGO he now works at and who owns multiple properties] needed someone he could trust and I was that person. We had interacted before. He had seen me and had called me for quite sometime to look at his electricity. One day he called me and told me, 'I need someone to work on my estate. I don't think you would be a bad idea' … If it wasn't for the electrical part that I did, I'm pretty sure that I wouldn't have gotten where I am today. I would not be able to repair electronics and electrical anywhere. Therefore I wouldn't have met [my boss]. I met him through knowing to repair electricity, then that means that repairing electricity has made me a better person in this life. (Nathan, personal communication, 2014)

Whether or not youth were employed in the field in which they received training, youth perceived these tangible skills and knowledge as providing them with opportunities and increasing their self-confidence.

Putting Skills and Knowledge into Action

Youth demonstrated agency through using these tangible skills and knowledge as well as personal development as they actively navigated new opportunities, expanded their aspirations and made decisions that affected their livelihoods and personal trajectories. As youth completed the program they entered into vocational settings that were unfamiliar and into situations that were uncertain. Youth put into practice their reported increased self-confidence, newly acquired ability to relate to people along with new technical skills to navigate these difficult situations. One young man talked about his ability to handle difficult customers without feeling belittled during the conversation. Another youth, Abigail, used those skills to negotiate a difficult situation with her boss:

> I've gained confidence. I've gained confidence. And then when I saw that money was not enough, I approached my boss, I told her this and this – this money is not enough, I'll appreciate if you could add me some (i.e. give me a raise) ... because she saw my work was good so she just [increased my pay]. (Abigail, personal communication, 2014)

In this situation, Abigail used the financial literacy skills she gained through the program to plan a budget and see how much money she would need to make, not only for her current needs but also what would be needed to reach her future goals. Having identified these goals, she used her increased self-confidence and ability to communicate with her boss to seek out a raise. Her efforts were rewarded and she was given a raise and later received a promotion.

Not all youth were able to work directly with their managers or bosses to effect change within their work environment. Youth, particularly females, who had gone through vocational training in hospitality frequently noted that there were many challenges that they faced in the hospitality industry (Nikoi, Krause, Gebru, & Eschenbacher, 2013). These ranged from feeling unsafe in work settings, facing discrimination and sexual harassment, and working late into the night which made their commutes back home unsafe. Some youth found ways to navigate the challenges within the workplace by discussing problems with their supervisors, like Lucy who has worked at the same hotel for four years in different capacities:

> Sometimes people want a room, others just want to have a relationship and if I refuse they tell the manager some lies and *I have had to learn how to defend myself*[5] because at the office the motto is customers are always right, so it becomes hard. (Lucy, personal communication, 2015)

Lucy's ability to stand up to difficult customers and communicate with her supervisors is in contrast to the how she describes herself prior to the program. In 2012, she indicated that before gaining communication skills and self-confidence she "was *so* shy actually. I could not speak." Furthermore, the ability to confidently relate with her supervisors has meant that rather than having accusations from customers hinder her employment options, she has been able to defend herself and, over the four years, move into more desirable employment types within the company (i.e., from room attendant, to front desk receptionist).

Navigating employment conditions or changing the types of employment was not only observed with youth who worked in the hospitality industry. Youth in other sectors also found it necessary to make changes to their employment situations, often because the working schedules, the sense of job security or working conditions made it difficult for them to make progress toward other goals. Since many youth saw their current employment not as an end goal but rather a means to an end, they often sought new employment opportunities that would give them more flexibility. For instance, a young man who worked in a security firm requested the night shift so that he would be able to go to school during the day. Other youth requested that their employers give them consistent day hours so that they could enroll in night courses. While not everyone was successful in getting supervisors to agree to these

---

[5] Emphasis added by author.

changes, those who were unable to change their schedules were looking for other job opportunities that would be more flexible or they had established a savings plan in the hopes that they would be able to quit their jobs in the future to pursue their education.

Leaving employment was not always a youth's choice but also came about because of changes in management, the closing down of companies or because certain employers preferred to hire people on a short-term basis to avoid paying higher wages. Edward had lost a job due to a personal illness and found that once he was well his employer was not willing to take him back. Although able to find other employment in the hospitality industry he decided that until he found a stable, well-paying job he would only look for casual[6] employment opportunities:

> For now I am doing casuals. Permanent jobs, they did not pay good money which can cater you for other things like [transportation] fares and rent. Casual jobs give you a chance to go forward and apply for other jobs, even as you are already employed. If you are employed [in contract or permanent positions] in which they pay you low money, you will not have a chance to apply to another job that is good. That is why I do casuals for the time being and I will get a better [job] as time goes on. (Edward, personal communication, 2014)

Like many youth, Edward found himself in an undesirable situation due to unforeseen circumstances. However, he credits the recognition skills, including self-knowledge and an ability to think about and plan for his future, for his ability to navigate the situation in a way that would satisfy his immediate needs, benefit his long-term goals and assist his family (by paying his brother's school fees). Although offered more secure but low-paying employment, he felt that those positions limited his ability to pursue better work placements or the opportunity to further his education.

In the process of pursuing their goals, youth enacted their financial literacy and planning skills by developing business plans, identifying potential education centers to attend, ascertaining how much money they would need to save to take the next step and engaging in multiple ways of saving and planning to get there. In order to pursue business ideas or continue their education, youth were aware that their first step needed to be accruing capital or identifying funds for school fees. In the same way that youth navigated their employment and self-employment opportunities, youth navigated the financial systems to find the best fit for their needs. The decision to save was not made without sacrifice by youth. Despite the fact that by the fourth year of the study many youth were in positions where they could meet their needs and assist family members, saving for yet unknown future needs was not always an easy decision to make, as demonstrated by Dorothy:

> First, I'm saving for my school. Because I want to do my degree. And in case anything happens, I just want to have something that will be able to help me ... When I decide to save I must deny myself some things. I have to sacrifice so that I save because if I decide I have to use all my money, I won't be able to save. (Dorothy, personal communication, 2014)

---

[6] Casual employment are work opportunities that are not stable or guaranteed. Casual employment takes several forms, including waiting outside of companies or factories each morning as workers for the day are selected.

Identifying her goals, planning for her future and taking the necessary steps and decisions to achieve those goals highlights one way in which Dorothy agentically advanced her personal aspirations. However, youths' actions to pursue their desired livelihoods were not solely based on their own desires and goals, but by the needs of those around them as well.

Agency as Socially Enacted

The needs of family and community also impacted the decisions youth made as they sought to achieve their goals and they received either financial or emotional support from them. For example, as the youth's opportunities and financial well-being increased they were expected to contribute to their families as well. At times this meant that youth had to delay their own goals in order to meet others' needs. David described the way his family impacted his decision-making in this way:

> I was planning to go back to school to continue with my diploma, but I didn't have that chance to save due to unavoidable circumstances. I was not able to raise that amount. But this year I am planning to go back to school …. [Last year] instead of saving I used that money to pay for my brother's fees because he is in Form 4 right now. At that time the principal needed the whole amount for the school fees, so I chipped in the amount I had already saved. I paid for his school fees. That way, I was unable to go and enroll. (David, personal communication, 2014)

While family obligations may appear as a constraint to youths' abilities to achieve their livelihood goals, youth were aware that their willingness to step in and assist in family matters shaped their role within the community and in the family. Financial contributions for family well-being were an avenue to engage with the community in new ways, as youth were more likely to be invited into community discussions or family-decision making or serve as role models to other youth. This change in stature and in the ways in which they were perceived within their family or community provided youth with a sense of pride.

The youth supported their families and communities not only through their financial contributions, but also by sharing their knowledge and ways of knowing that they learned in the program. Their changing status within the community as someone who had accomplished their goals afforded them with an opportunity to encourage others to think similarly about the future by setting long-term goals and making plans for achieving those goals. Edward, the youth who decided to work in casual employment rather than in long-term jobs that did not pay well, described how the changes he experienced in his life and the agentic actions he took affected his friends. He explained:

> [My friends] do look at me as I was and they look at me as I am now, and they see change. They have a hope of asking 'How? What do you do?' I give them stories about *Njia* and I show them some things. I have realized that as we talk, as we share, as we do our music, they are really changing. Some used to drink, some used to just be there with nothing – but they have a knowledge on how to look for their survival so that they can be better people in the future. (Edward, personal communication, 2014)

Edward's accomplishments, which he has attributed to a new self-confidence, a renewed way of thinking about his future and the ability to use the technical work-related skills he had received, were evident to other youth around him and afforded him the opportunity to share these skills and new ways of thinking on to others. His ability to act toward his goals also influenced how he engaged with his family and friends to affect their ways of thinking.

Discussion

The urban Kenyan youth in this study demonstrated everyday agency as they set goals and took the necessary steps to achieve them. They also demonstrated that their ability to agentically engage in achieving their livelihood and personal goals were facilitated by both personal development, identified by Murphy-Graham (2012) as recognition, and technical and financial skills and knowledge, which is similar to her conceptualization of capacity development. Youth's ability to apply skills and knowledge to new and ever-changing settings spoke to both their willingness and ability to adapt their goals as needed as well as to some of the challenges youth faced in their lives. Goal-setting and decision-making highlighted how youth used individual agency to navigate their own lives. In putting skills and knowledge into practice to further their economic opportunities and pursue their chosen livelihoods, youth demonstrated the importance of individual agency in changing their life situation. In essence these new skills and knowledge were a platform from which to imagine and actively pursue new possibilities.

Despite their ability to use their personal development, skills and knowledge as they navigated their livelihood opportunities, youth faced difficulties that influenced their opportunities, decisions and the goals they set for themselves. The economic sector where youth worked and engaged in earnings opportunities was competitive and while some youth were able to put their recognition skills into practice and negotiated for raises or more suitable work hours, many other youths were still searching for positions that would give them more opportunities. Other youth attempted to overcome these challenges by starting their own small businesses, which was often constraining as youth rarely had access to the capital needed to start a business or to sustain it in difficult business environments. These constraints presented obstacles that frequently shaped the decisions youth made and the trajectories—both economic and social—that their lives took. Youth who had difficulty overcoming constraints in the workplace often expressed frustration and less confidence in their ability to change their immediate situations. On the other hand, youth who had successfully navigated difficult situations felt that the ability to enact skills and knowledge in turn increased the confidence they had in themselves and their capacity to impact their current situations.

Moreover, youth agency was socially embedded and was demonstrated through the everyday changes in their families and communities. Similar to Joseph's (2012) study, family support systems greatly impacted the decisions youth in this study made and the ways in which they enacted new skills and knowledge. While youth may not have enacted large-scale social change, they consciously applied their skills and knowledge in ways that impacted their larger family structures and, at times, the communities where they lived. For example, they were able to help siblings continue schooling or they encouraged other youth to change their goals or approach to life. While social factors at times impacted youths' ability to pursue personal goals, I would argue that their actions are part of the social fabric where youth lived. While the need to pay for a sibling's school fees may have meant that a youth had to delay opening their own business, their family was the same social fabric that supported youth when they participated in the *Njia* program and they needed transportation money each day, or from whom they received the necessary encouragement to go ahead and try a small-business venture. Youths' livelihood decisions were not made independently and these factors, while perhaps unusual or unexpected outside of this context, were part of the "normal lens" through which youth viewed their lives.

Payne's (2012) concept of everyday agency was evident in these youths' actions. Youth did not discuss their decision-making process or livelihoods within a context of extraordinary situations, or as steps that would promote extraordinary results. Instead they saw their everyday needs and relationships and pursued ways to improve their immediate and long-term situations. In addition to their own situation, they desired to help those with whom they had the most contact—their families, peers, and local community—to effect change in their daily lives.

Conclusion

This chapter examined the role non-formal, vocational training can play among urban Kenyan youth in fostering agency. For economically marginalized youth, skills and knowledge that provided entrée to employment or entrepreneurship opportunities were important elements that enabled youth to agentically engage in livelihood opportunities and pursue both personal and socially informed goals. However, this chapter also demonstrates that beyond gaining technical skills associated with vocational training and putting them into practice, youth agency hinged on an increase in personal development skills as well. Like Murphy-Graham's (2012) description of recognition and capacity development, the combination of new ways of thinking, technical skill development and self-knowledge were important elements in youth agency. Furthermore, youth agency was constructed within a social setting that both supported youth and placed expectations on them, influencing their decisions and livelihood trajectories. Although youth used their personal development and technical skills to advance their personal goals, they did so in a social setting in which they also accounted for the needs of those closest to them. Additionally, youth did not envision the decisions they made, or the actions they took, as countering or contributing to discourses of youth writ large as either trouble-makers or as the hope for the future. Rather their agentic actions were understood as logical next steps to achieving their goals and meeting the needs of those around them.

The integration of Murphy-Graham's (2012) framework for empowerment and agency with socially embedded, everyday agency provides a refined avenue through which to understand youth agency and the role of education in fostering agency amongst urban youth. This study has implications for development organizations and policy makers as they strive to address high youth un- and under-employment rates through vocational skills training or by providing employment and entrepreneurial opportunities to youth. The study demonstrates that the value of technical and vocational skills is enhanced when youth also develop a greater self-awareness and confidence in their ability to effect change in their lives. In addition, the value that youth place on increased skills and knowledge is only in part related to their desire to achieve personal livelihood goals. This type of educational programing is most compelling for the opportunity it affords to engage with youth as they navigate opportunities and reposition themselves as agents of change in their larger family settings, communities where they live and in their own lives.

References

Abbink, J., & van Kessel, I. (Eds.). (2005). *Vanguard or vandals: Youth, politics and conflict in Africa*. Leiden, The Netherlands: Koninklijke Brill NV.

Allison, C., Krause, B., Jaafar, A., Liuzzi, A., DeJaeghere, J., & Chapman, D. (2014). Youth prospects in East Africa: Current evidence and knowledge gaps in youth employment and livelihood programming. Unpublished manuscript. Minneapolis, MN: University of Minnesota.

Bajaj, M. (2011). *Schooling for social change: The rise and impact of human rights education*. New York, NY: Continuum International Publishing Group.

Betcherman, G., Godfrey, M., Puerto, S., Rother, F., & Stavreska, A. (2007). A review of interventions to support young workers: Findings of the youth employment inventory. *Social Protection Discussion Paper No. 0715*. World Bank. Retrieved December 24, 2015, from http://siteresources.worldbank.org/SPLP/Resources/461653-1253133947335/6440424-1271427186123/6976445-1271432453795/YEI_2007_full_report.pdf.

Chismaya, G., DeJaeghere, J., Kendall, N., & Khan, M. (2012). Gender and 'Education for All': Progress and problems in achieving gender equity. *International Journal of Educational Development, 32*(6), 743–755.

DeJaeghere, J., McCleary, K., & Josić, J. (2016). Conceptualizing youth agency. In J. DeJaeghere, J. Josić, & K. McCleary (Eds.), *Education and youth agency: Qualitative case studies in global context*. Cham, Switzerland: Springer.

Government of Kenya. (2010). *The constitution of Kenya*. Nairobi, Kenya: Government of Kenya. Retrieved December 17, 2014, from https://www.kenyaembassy.com/pdfs/The%20Constitution%20of%20Kenya.pdf.

Honwana, A., & De Boeck, F. (Eds.). (2005). *Makers & breakers: Children and youth in postcolonial Africa*. Trenton, NJ: Africa World Press, Inc.

Joseph, M. C. (2012). Social agency of low-income 'young' women in Gabarone City, Botswana. *Studies of Changing Societies: Youth Under Global Perspective, 1*(5), 37–62.

Kabeer, N. (1999). Resources, agency, achievements: Reflections on the measurement of women's empowerment. *Development and Change, 30*(3), 435–464.

King, K. (2007). Balancing basic and post-basic education in Kenya: National vs. international policy agendas. *International Journal of Educational Development, 27*(4), 358–370.

King, K., & McGrath, S. (2012). Education and development in Africa: Lessons of the past 50 years for beyond 2015. In *Conference Proceedings: CAS @50*, 6–8 June 2012. Edinburgh, UK (Unpublished). Retrieved April 2, 2013, from http://eprints.nottingham.ac.uk/1640/.

McGrath, S. (2012). Vocational education and training for development: A policy in need of a theory? *International Journal of Educational Development, 32*(5), 623–631.

Ministry of Education. (2011). *Free day secondary education Programme*. Nairobi, Kenya. Retrieved November 1, 2012, from http://www.education.go.ke/Documents.aspx?docID=2019.

Ministry of Education. (2012). Education statistics: Facts and figures [data file]. Retrieved April 5, 2012, from http://www.education.go.ke/Documents.aspx?department=52&id=868.

Murphy-Graham, E. (2012). *Opening minds, improving lives: Education and women's empowerment in Honduras*. Nashville, TN: Vanderbilt University Press.

Nikoi, A., Krause, B., Gebru, E., & Eschenbacher, H., with Chapman, D., DeJaeghere, J., & Pellowski-Wiger, N. (2013). *The MasterCard Foundation learn, earn, and save initiative: Synthesis report for Njia Youth Empowerment Program*. Minneapolis, MN: University of Minnesota, Department of Organizational Leadership, Policy, and Development.

Njonjo, K. S. (2010). *Youth fact book: Infinite possibility or definite disaster?* Nairobi, Kenya: Institute of Economic Affairs.

Ohba, A. (2011). The abolition of secondary school fees in Kenya: Responses by the poor. *International Journal of Educational Development, 31*(4), 402–408.

Oyaro, K. (2008, March 26). Kenya: Free secondary schooling policy faces testing times. *Inter Press Service News Agency*.

Ozier, O. (2011). The impact of secondary schooling in Kenya: A regression discontinuity analysis. Unpublished manuscript. University of California at Berkeley.

Payne, R. (2012). 'Extraordinary survivors' or 'ordinary lives'? Embracing 'everyday agency' in social interventions with child-headed households in Zambia. *Children's Geographies, 10*(4), 399–411.

Sommers, M. (2007). Creating programs for Africa's urban youth: The challenge of marginalization. *Journal of International Cooperation in Education, 10*(1), 19–31.

Stromquist, N. (2015). Women's empowerment and education: Linking knowledge to transformative action. *European Journal of Education, 50*(3), 307–324.

Tembon, M., & Fort, L. (Eds.). (2008). *Girls' education in the 21st century: Gender equality, empowerment and economic growth*. Washington, DC: World Bank.

United Nations Development Programme. (2013). Kenya's youth employment challenge. Discussion paper. New York, NY: UNDP.

Warner, A., Malhotra, A., & McGonagle, A. (2012). *Girls' education, empowerment and transitions to adulthood: The case for a shared agenda*. Report for International Center for Research on Women (ICRW). Retrieved December 1, 2015, from http://www.icrw.org/publications/girls-education-empowerment-and-transitions-adulthood.

Youth Agency and Education: Reflections and Future Directions

Roozbeh Shirazi

Introduction

The chapters in this book represent an important and timely contribution to the study of youth agency and its relation to processes of and participation in education. They are important because the development of "agency" is a strategic aim for educational policymakers and practitioners globally, and timely because they present their readers with a broad range of how the notion can be conceptualized. In spite of the plasticity of the term, cultivating youth agency is increasingly seen as necessary to addressing the pressing challenges of our times. Herrera and Bayat's (2010) observe that "youth coming of age in the postcolonial South, already in difficult circumstances brought about by poverty, fragile economies, conflict, authoritarian and corrupt governments … are highly critical, frustrated, and sometimes overcome by powerlessness" (p. 361). Contemporary states are unwilling or unable to provide social and economic guarantees to their citizens, so the task of securing the future is increasingly depicted as an individual odyssey. Amid the diminished capacity for states to harness and direct the energies and bodies of youth—or rein in the host of external forces that affect their lives (Comaroff & Comaroff, 2005)—the "agentic youth" has become a highly desired subjectivity of the twenty-first century, as marginalized youth are being told that education is their surest path towards a viable life and secure livelihood in an uncertain and precarious future.

R. Shirazi (✉)
Department of Organizational Leadership, Policy, and Development,
University of Minnesota, Minneapolis, MN, USA
e-mail: shir0035@umn.edu

© Springer International Publishing Switzerland 2016   251
J.G. DeJaeghere et al. (eds.), *Education and Youth Agency*, Advancing
Responsible Adolescent Development, DOI 10.1007/978-3-319-33344-1_14

In this volume, there is a clear commitment to situating the key ideas of youth and agency in relation to how they resonate and acquire meaning across distinct social, material, and discursive contexts. Drawing upon anthropological approaches, feminist studies, and critical policy studies, DeJaeghere, McCleary, and Josić's comprehensive theoretical overview illustrates how various scholars have grappled with ideas of what young people can and should be able to do on their own behalf. In this spirit, the volume does not set out to answer the question, "What does it mean for a young person to have agency?" because such a question suggests modularity to the ideas of "youth" and "agency" and a frictionless transposability of these concepts' meanings across distinct social and educational settings.

Instead, these scholars put education (conceived broadly) into a dialectical relationship with youth agency, where expressions of agency are mediated by several interrelated factors, including social, economic, and cultural dynamics that affect educational systems and their youth participants. Their studies consistently argue that agency may be cultivated by different means for different ends, whether that is the ability to act and make decisions on an individual behalf, on behalf of others, or towards the transformation of contemporary structural conditions. Organized thematically, these essays refine and enhance questions of agency in relation to youth citizenship in society; the interplay of agency with gender, class, and religion; and the intersections of economic agency of youth with social and economic policies. The result is a nuanced treatment of youth agency, in which the local material conditions, educational experiences, cultural politics, and social relationships of youth lives take on clear prominence across these studies. This framing allows readers to see the broad extent to which youth agency is contingent and mediated by context and spatially situated factors.

Methodologically, the ethnographically informed approaches that drive the majority of these essays effectively work, to paraphrase Tsing (2005), to interrupt stories of a unified and successful regime of developing youth agency through education. As a collection, they succeed in showing how the promises of education are often fraught with hope, contradiction and ambivalence. The immersive aspect of ethnography allows for the potential to connect the everyday conditions, social relations, and structures that provide the contours for youth action in distinctive contexts. The longitudinal designs of many of these qualitative studies provide an oft missing temporal dimension to how youth make decisions and take action on their own behalf, and how their decisions may reverberate into their futures. The authors' engagement with the nuance of localized conditions, and the situated logics that frame youth decision-making and future aspirations across different contexts, empirically build upon the editors' larger claims that agency cannot be understood outside of the social and material conditions in which it emerges. For these reasons, this volume makes several unique contributions to the study of youth agency and education. Many of these warrant deeper examination, but here I highlight three such contributions that are particularly compelling and well developed across the chapters, namely, the imaginative work of youth agency, connecting representation to youth agency, and relational aspects of agency.

The Imaginative Work of Youth Agency

A recurring thread among these chapters can be seen in how educational experiences of youth—and their experiences of specific educational spaces—may serve as a potential site of re-visioning the present, to reframe and reimagine their possibilities, and thus what they see as possible for themselves. As the editors note, there is a long history of scholarship that explores the relationship between critical awareness, education, and agency. Experiences of education have the potential to facilitate youth's "seeing" of the possibilities differently/critically, which is integral to the development of youth agency, but they do not ensure it, or may contribute to it in unanticipated ways. Across many of these case studies, youth exercise agency by acting upon and imagining their futures in spite of their formal educational experiences, through their participation and membership in alternate publics, collectivities, and educational programming.

To the extent that educational processes provide the opportunity and space for youth to see differently and to connect these alternative visions to practice, then we may understand the cultivation of agency through education work of the imagination (Appadurai, 1996). Appadurai's (1996) conception of imagination is integral to his larger arguments about "modernity" in an era of globalization, and how it is heterogeneously constituted and experienced unevenly by different individuals and communities. The term imagination is not only used to describe an individual's sense of the (increasingly globalized) world, but also broader collective or shared experiences of it. In this milieu, imagination is vital not only for the creation of new forms of subjectivity and community across locales and states, but as "a staging ground for action" (Appadurai, 1996, p. 7). The global movement of ideas, media, and people critically contribute to new self-imaginings and new subjectivities, which may serve as a prelude to collective action.

Appadurai's (1996) model of transnational flows through various "scapes" has been employed to theorize the global movement of educational policies, norms, and management systems (Carney, 2009). Combining this structural analysis with the study of youth's imagination, or self-imaginings, may also be productive for understanding how notions of youth agency are produced in relation to evolving spatial, material, and social factors through education. Several of the contributors to this volume suggest educational programs are a critical site to understand and gain insight into the lived experiences of youth within such scapes. Context matters a great deal in how these scholars have conceptualized their analyses of youth agency, but it is important to note that context itself is mutable—localities are dynamic, in process, and being made and remade as conflicts, people, information, infrastructure, and environmental changes alter our landscapes.

Acknowledgement of the contingency of agency on the one hand, and the contingency of structures on the other, complements the editors' argument that agency is socially embedded and conditioned by the differentiated operation of structural factors across localities. The dialectical relationship between education and agency described by the editors is seen in several chapters in how educational conditions discipline or create opportunities in how youth see themselves and their possibilities in relation to others and to their social and material environments. As a result, we can trace how the re-visioning that youth in these chapters undertake in their lives and for their future possibilities is mediated by different cultural, economic, and political conditions/structures that characterize their localities in the present historical moment.

The imaginative work of agency through schooling is performed in divergent fashion by youth, as evidenced (but not limited to) in the studies from the United States, Jamaica, India, Honduras, and Senegal. McCleary draws our attention to how the educational program of an NGO provides a reflective space and directive force for Honduran youth as they interrogate the norms and social practices that contribute to gender inequity in their communities. Drawing our attention to different enactments of agency—resistance, transgression, and *desalambrar* or "undoing fences"—undertaken by youth affiliated with the NGO's program, McCleary argues that these forms of agency contribute to meaningful micro-transformations of gender norms in the communities of these youths.

In the United States, Josić and Dierker highlight examples of non-formal educational programs that contribute to youth's ability to imagine themselves as citizens and to center their historically marginalized experiences of citizenship and belonging. Josić's chapter employs a comparative analysis of youth in differently resourced schools and communities to explore how these differences contribute to varied practices of youth citizen agency. Is it possible, she asks, for citizen agency to be produced equally amid varying conditions of communities? Though she does not definitively answer this question, her consideration of youth's ability to imagine themselves and equally be citizens despite different social, material, and surveillance conditions is vital in light of broader shifts in governance and emphasis on self-making that are discussed in the introductory chapter of this volume.

Josić draws our attention to how youth understand their neighborhoods and schools as sites of community. Despite the students' participation in extracurricular programs to cultivate civic engagement, their attachments to their schools and neighborhoods vary, and are bound up in the material and social conditions of these sites. In this respect, Josić's chapter illustrates the dialectical relationship between education and the development of youth agency, and how youths' experiences are mediated by structural factors that constrain and enable their practice as citizens.

Beth Dierker's chapter similarly considers the relationship between youth attachments and practices of agency. She presents a longitudinal examination of six African American youth who participate in a church-based youth development program. Integrating the ideas of praxis and coalitional agency, she analyzes how agency is cultivated by the youth in terms of their relationships and commitments to each other and to the African American community. The Youth Space in her study is a site of intergenerational praxis, where program "elders" encourage youth engagement in different social initiatives, and provide support and opportunities for their critical reflection as well. The "counterspace" of the Youth Space is productive of counter-narratives that allow participants to critically interrogate the history of African Americans in the United States and to re-center their African American identity in a white-dominant society. In doing so, her study highlights the importance of critical self-imagining to the agentization of youth and, like McCleary's chapter, prompts an interesting set of questions about the possibilities to cultivate and sustain transformative agency.

Is transformational agency, when interwoven with coalitions, narratives, and relationships, more resilient? Does transformative agency, when supported by a sense of belonging and embeddedness, sustain agency across contexts and/or over time? These questions direct us away from schools, and into new spaces of inquiry, where coalitional agency may gestate when individual relationships develop alongside of larger social aims and shared commitments. Such questions prompt educational researchers to take seriously the pedagogical work of coalitions, collective action, and social movements as under-examined terrains in the scholarship on youth agency and education. Dierker's work is all the more relevant, given the growth and impact of recent African American social movements such as #BlackLivesMatter, and how contemporary coalition-building and Black counter-narratives are being rethought along intersectional and diasporic lines (Meyers, Jeffers, & Ragland, 2016).

The articulation and enactment of counter-narrative constitutes a form of political agency in which notions of community are created around collective aims that are connected to historical experiences that are shared by members. The ability of these youth to affect change is contingent on these youths imaginative labor, on seeing themselves and their shared experiences of racial struggle as bound up with one another. These aspects of Dierker's chapter resonate with Stafford's examination of Senegalese student activism and improvisation in the face of shorter-term challenges of faculty strikes, and larger structural constraints related to the attrition of the higher education budget.

As discussed by the editors, the discourse of generating youth agency through education, and the concomitant aim of "empowering youth," often rest upon uncritical and unspecified assumptions about what schooling does. Through schooling, it would seem, youth should acquire skills and dispositions that imbue them with the ability and intention to act in particular ways, namely, as productive, self-reliant, and democratic members of society. In Stafford's study, the experience of higher education contributes to Senegalese youth agency, but not in the ways typically prognosticated by policymakers. The crisis in Senegalese higher education—lack of resources, overcrowding, and ineffectiveness of administration—reflects the situatedness of educational institutions and processes, and their inability to produce agency in universal ways. Rather, Stafford's portrayal of students acting *in loco cura* captures how youth organize and attempt to stand in for defunct or ineffectual state institutions. His participants refer to this as "filling gaps" to avoid the "rule of failure" that threaten their educational experiences.

Certainly, the inventiveness and practices of improvisation of these youth to move forward with their studies in light of structural constraints highlights their agency to act on behalf of their interests and to imagine and organize themselves as a political constituency. At the same time, Stafford draws attention to how the practice "filling in the gaps" has transformed the experience of pursuing higher education and strains the aspiration of becoming an "educated person" in Senegal.

The activism and collective action of these youth represents a creative mitigation of external constraints imposed upon them, but one that does not transform these limitations. Although Stafford focuses more on the experiences of students, discussing their activism along with the faculty strikes mentioned in the chapter would provide expanded perspective, as those strikes seemingly allude to a larger set of economic and political struggles in a postcolonial state negotiating the difficulties of structural adjustment competing in what Harvey (1991) terms a global economy of "flexible accumulation."

While Stafford's university-level participants are invested in becoming "educated persons," the high school boys in Shawanda Stockfelt's chapter are ambivalent about the promises of higher education. Her work examines family, diaspora, donor-driven educational policies, and school-based screening practices as the structural means by which to understand how educational aspiration of Jamaican boys is generated. Stockfelt's focus is on how aspirations for higher education are influenced by distributions of social and economic capital; drawing on Bourdieu's theory of practice, she argues that boys who have limited access to resources see little to be gained by the pursuit of higher education. Despite rhetoric that links their educations to Jamaica's economic well-being and national security, the actual educational experiences of boys in Jamaican educational context are mediated by a confluence of structural factors. For boys who do not succeed in the current regime of high stakes testing and academic sorting, schooling does not reduce disparities in capital; Stockfelt argues it contributes to their reproduction insofar as boys who are unable to connect their educations to their wider aspirations "are unlikely to aspire accordingly." This is particularly true for boys who see their lives continuing on in Jamaica. However, the possibility of migration and connections to members of the Jamaican diaspora in wealthier countries also has a positive effect on the educational aspirations of Jamaican boys. As a result, her work pushes us to consider how "context" must accommodate transnational social forms and relationships generated by migration. Diasporic communities and connections have an intriguing, though somewhat briefly discussed, role in shaping the ways in which Jamaican boys imagine themselves and the degree to which they decide to fashion their future possibilities through education. Thangaraj's chapter, similar to Stockfelt's, documents how youth assess the returns of schooling versus participating in paid work. The decision-making of youth happens with an eye to what is around them, and the success of others who have come before.

The youth depicted in these studies are making strategic decisions about their futures in ways that trouble popular discourses around schooling, their own subjectivities, and what kind of mobility schooling can provide to "vulnerable" or "threatening" subjects. In doing so, the contributors to this volume push past simply cataloguing and evaluating the efficacy of skills, knowledge, and attitudes that youth are encountering in schools; the studies presented here offer tantalizing glimpses into how youth around the world imagine and locate themselves in relation to structural forces and social institutions that give shape to their everyday conditions. This imaginative work is the prelude to their actions and decision-making. While youth in these different localities make sense of their conditions in distinct ways—through embrace of and ambivalence towards educational programs and schooling—they are in aggregate interrogating modernist and universalizing promises of education, and strategically engaging with institutions of schooling in ways that push educators, policymakers, and researchers to rethink their own assumptions.

Connecting Representation to Youth Agency

Another unique contribution of this volume lays in its attention to processes of representation, and how they produce knowledge about youth through media, policy language, and other signifying practices. In doing so, these contributors illustrate that social meanings about a community or population are not just produced and confined to the spaces they inhabit, but that social meanings and their representations are mobile and produced in different ways in different sites. The ability to represent is a form of power, as representations ascribe meanings to that which they depict (Hall, 1997). Accordingly, media and policy depictions of youth as victims, empowered, threatened or threatening all serve political purposes, and may orient popular and policy understandings of youth. As Stafford's, Sallam's, Stockfelt's, Khurshid and Guerrero's, and Thangaraj's contributions indicate, dominant representations of youth lives and the promise of education are often at odds with lived experiences and decision-making practices of youth, and advantages that schooling actually delivers. Educational policies, media coverage, and international development efforts targeting youth reinforce particular "regimes of truth" about youth that occlude and devalue the situated logics of their decision-making and long term strategizing. Said's (1978) conception of Orientalism as a system of representation, discussed in this volume by Sallam, provides an excellent example of how practices of representation delimit what counts as acceptable agency. In the case of the Middle East and North Africa, agency is often framed as resistance to localized hegemonic patriarchal structures, in accordance with "Western" norms and values. Modes of thinking and action that do not conform to these dominant norms then, are not readily recognized as agentic in an Orientalist framework. Khurshid and Guerrero's chapter, similarly, takes up representations of Malala in media in the United States as individually agentic in line with modernist assumptions in contrast to representations of an unmodern Islam, silencing other possible explanations of her agency as embedded within family, community, and Islam. Therefore, critical engagement with how youth are imagined and represented by their powerful external interlocutors, and the system of meanings that such representations map onto, is needed to better recognize their agentive possibilities and constraints in light of the social, material, and discursive conditions that frame them.

These contributors draw our attention to how the lives, choices, and activism of youth are appropriated to reinforce ideological agendas that may contrast with their own aspirations. In each instance, youth are ascribed social positions that suggest modal ways of working with them or defining their interests. In the existing representations of youth in Senegal, Jamaica, Egypt, India, and Pakistan, we see paternalistic and deficit/danger discourses that tells us that young people, when left to their own devices, are unequipped to make "correct" decisions about their futures.

Consequently, they embody conditions and anxieties that are not only detrimental to their well-being but to that of their societies. Youth may become productive members of society, but only by heeding the guidance and authority of the state and/or its external proxies. Thus, in these chapters, education—and its ancillary benefit of empowerment—can also be understood as a regulatory practice to produce particular youth subjects and may ironically constrain self-determination of their own future trajectories. This takes on additional salience in Stockfelt's and Thangaraj's chapters in which youth decisions with respect to schooling were not only longer-term oriented, but also calculated in relation to the possible returns of pursuing alternative possibilities and outcomes.

On this last point, there is room for debate. Certainly, as Thangaraj shows, there are those who continue to question whether youth, particularly pre-adolescent children, are mentally equipped to make decisions about their futures. Theoretical and disciplinary approaches explored in this collection, such as anthropology of childhood, as well as postcolonial and poststructuralist critiques of universalist truth claims, work to unsettle knowledge and policies about youth that are rooted in the convergence of human rights, human capital, and psychosocial development discourses.

As these authors convincingly illustrate, young people do not live and make their decisions in a vacuum; the social, discursive, and material conditions of their lives vary greatly and do much to delimit their subjectivities and the scope of their decisions and actions. As a result, there are clear limitations to employing a universalist understanding of what youth need and staged models to capture their development. Moreover, the authors' foregrounding of youth voices across these studies allow for how young people articulate and negotiate their agency in relation to complex and situated processes that are remaking their environments, often with different access to resources and forms of capital. Such depictions complicate representations of youth in media, policy documents, and educational sector reports that often collapse their lives and subject positions into monoliths or oppositional binaries, such as the "agent–victim" or "order–chaos" critiqued by Khurshid and Guerrero and Sallam. These studies suggest that more attention is needed to the politics of youth representation: notably, how, why, and in response to what conditions, youth are represented in hortative calls to become empowered and entrepreneurial citizens. Through their diverse conceptual and methodological approaches, these contributions not only highlight the importance of attending to what youth do and say in order to understand how they enact agency, but also critically juxtaposing such practices against those of external interlocutors seek to speak on their behalf.

Relational Aspects of Agency

In their efforts to move past binary and holistic perspectives on agency, DeJaeghere, McCleary, and Josić propose a dialectical model of agency, in "which the individual is always socially embedded in different structures and norms." Such a model moves to position "youth agency in relation to others; young people do not necessarily learn and act alone, but rather with and through others." The emphasis on relational forms of agency constitutes a notable contribution of this volume to the study of youth agency and education. In particular, the chapters by Nikoi, Pellowski Wiger, Shah and Wangsness Willemsen, and Ndesambaro Kwayu richly delve into the work that relationships do to shape how young people learn to think and act with and through others, and in doing so, present more hopeful conceptualizations of youth agency. Furthermore, these studies push back upon binary constructions of marginalized youth as victims/agents to highlight the creative and relational enactments of their agency without losing sight of the inequalities that frame their choices and access to opportunities.

Wangsness Willemsen and Ndesambaro Kwayu's exploration of how Tanzanian youth make decisions to enter into sexual relationships provides valuable insight into how students recognize their peers as influencing their decision-making in both desired and undesired ways. The chapters by Nikoi and Pellowski Wiger draw upon longitudinal data, which facilitates a deeper understanding of how youths' agency has developed not only in response to their engagement with their educational training, but also to deepening conditions of economic uncertainty. Pellowski Wiger's study draws attention to the importance of peer relationships over time, by highlighting how Tanzanian youth in boarding schools turned to each other to finance and support each other's microenterprises. For Nikoi, Kenyan youths' participation in vocational training represents a strategy of safeguarding their socioeconomic well-being and basic rights in an evermore-flexible economy. Flexibility as a mode of participation in the labor market celebrates a certain kind of youth subjectivity, that of the entrepreneurial youth subject who has skills, ability, and desire to navigate the competitive uncertainty of the labor market. That youth have the possibilities to acquire the knowledge and skills needed to survive in precarious conditions is vital, given the diminishing abilities of states to control their economies and labor markets. But in examining the agentic possibilities of youth through education in conditions of precariousness, researchers must also be willing to consider, as DeJaeghere, McCleary, and Josić state in their introduction, whether programs training youth to survive "seemingly intractable material and social inequalities" can be considered to be productive of transformative agency (Bajaj, 2009), or further normalizing the uncertainty of their social lives and material conditions.

Shah's portrayal of two young women in Western Gujarat skillfully explores this tension. In her study, she holds up the importance of education, as well as familial and other relationships in contributing to a continuum of agency, but also with explicit recognition of how the norms of a patriarchal social order inform those relationships. For Shah, the triumph of education over this order is the exception rather than the rule, but her chapter astutely considers how social norms and cultural practices imbricate with material conditions. As a consequence, Shah is able to critique the social order of her participants without falling back on a "culture as problem" argument, which is instructive for future educational researchers and practitioners who seek to cultivate and understand contextually driven constructions of youth agency across the global South.

The emphasis on relational agency across these studies is important because it allows for more than individualized portraits of agency, which are by definition, snapshots of structural conditions, and how they impose constraints. Additionally, situating the inquiry longitudinally is useful because this approach gives a compelling sense about how action-taking and decision-making of youth is a dynamic ongoing process, which is situated in social relationships and larger processes of transformation and tenuousness.

Future Directions

These rich qualitative studies from across diverse contexts provide insightful findings on the complex relationship between education and different forms of youth agency. Together, these cases highlight new connections that need further exploration and theorizing. A central contention of this volume is that education is in dialectical relationship with youth agency. This is a promising framework, and the studies here signal that there is room to develop new research questions to discover the different permutations of this dialectic, and relatedly, need for new methodological and ethical approaches to answer these questions.

If producing agentic youth has become a fixture in global discourses of educational policymaking and reform, as these and other scholars suggest, then greater engagement with the *movement* of this discourse across educational contexts is needed. Highlighting contextual differences and the social embeddedness of agency allows for scholars and practitioners to understand how "global" norms and policies are appropriated and localized differently as they travel. Yet not enough is still known about what larger debates or processes connect these cases, and the studies presented here are uneven in theorizing the local, national, and global structures that frame youth possibilities for agency. If policymakers and practitioners in different contexts are calling for schooling (non-formal, formal, vocational, etc.) to cultivate youth agency, why are certain scripts of agency, such as entrepreneurialism and civic engagement, so prevalent across programs of educational reform and development? What recurring forms of political labor, such as Stafford's students acting *in loco cura*, are educators and youth being asked to assume in place of the state? What forms of agency "count," and how do youth actions and decision-making get interpreted and ordered in value? What "imagined communities" or collectivities materialize in conjunction with the transnational spread of discourses of youth crisis and educational failure? Finally, how might such exhortations provide us with new perspectives on the changing nature of governance and relations of production that agentic youth must navigate?

The flows of globalization described by Appadurai (1996) and Carney (2009), and evidenced by the global spread of "youth agency talk" push us to think beyond the state and its economic, social and educational policies. The majority of these studies, while spatially grounded in particular localities and social relations of families and communities, could further complicate the nation-state as the level of analysis or locus of economic, social, and political change. For example, several contributors in this volume examine education and youth's agency as "citizens." It is worth asking whether state-based citizenship can provide a framework for us to understand and value the rights and needs of all, when the "right to have rights" (Arendt, 1958) is mediated by the bodies of those who seek such rights. Critical race scholars and anthropologists of youth citizenship argue that youth's ability to think, act, and be recognized as citizens is inflected not only by class and gender, but also by their race, religion, sexuality, and national origins. In other words, practices of citizenship are contingent upon the bodies that practice them, and the embodiment of difference confers partial and contingent access to seemingly universal rights. Rather than to persist in questioning if we can all be citizens despite these differences—a question which may mute the importance of intersectional and situated analyses of rights and struggles for justice—it might be worth asking instead what spaces and communities are marginalized young people finding room for their political expressions in the wake of increasingly hierarchical access to rights of citizenship and recognition as citizens. How does a regime of tiered membership inform the political subjectivities and agency of youth that cannot exercise citizenship as it is popularly imagined? Josić's questions have the potential to contribute to that line of inquiry, and Dierker's study pushes us to consider how embodied differences contribute to conceptions of political membership beyond state-based citizenship.

In developing their notions of the "youthscape" from Appadurai's (1996) movement of global forms and processes, Maira and Soep (2005) acknowledge the possibility of researcher fatigue with using concepts of "resistance" and "transgression" to frame and theorize youth political practices. Resistance, in particular has a history of being paired alongside cooptation, creating binaries that "lose touch with the actual, complex meanings and consequences" (p. xxxi) of youth actions and agency. Still, Maira and Soep (2005) argue that "young people are very much seeking vernaculars of dissent, and we [researchers] may be missing the depth and subtlety of their critiques … out of the fears of pinning our politics and hopes for a new theory of resistance onto young people" (p. xxxi).

For youth agency to be linked to sustained social change, we have to ask another question: how, and to what extent, do micro-transformations of youth accumulate and acquire larger transformative force? In her analysis of Judith Butler's work on performativity and its linkages to agency, McNay (1999) likens agency to an iterative process, meaning that its effects materialize over time, even if they are not immediately visible. Following McNay (1999), agency is not limited to an individual's actions in distinct moments or venues, but should be seen as "a process of materialization in which the constraints of social structures are reproduced and partially transcended in the practices of agents … the identifactory processes through which norms are materialized enable the formation of a subject who is capable of resisting those norms" (p. 177).

Considering, as many contributors argue here, that agency is contingent, and structures are mutable, how might we investigate the relationship between contextually distinct repertoires of youth agency and sustainable social change as an ongoing and iterative process? If agency towards the transformation of social structures is a question of interest, then this points us towards an even greater need for engagement with the temporal dimensions of context, and looking for agency not just within relations among social actors, but with respect to broader structural constraints over time. While several these studies present valuable longitudinal perspectives on how the actions and decision of youth resonate over time in their own lives, there is also a need for further analysis of how these decisions, in concert with their educational experiences, contribute and possibly transform social relations and conditions of their communities through the building of new collectivities and movements. As formal schooling becomes increasingly regimented and assessed through global norms of performance and accountability, such investigations will entail fore-grounding not only the non-formal realm of educational programs provided by civil society, but also informal spaces of youth re-visioning. There is still ample terrain for educational researchers to investigate and mainstream the pedagogical work of youth-based collective actions and counterpublics, particularly those that may materialize translocally in response to recurring global structural pressures.

In such a move, there are methodological and ethical implications to consider as well. The strength of this volume lies in its contextually driven challenge to total-izing stories about how education contributes to youth agency. While the ethno-graphically informed studies of this volume are valuable in foregrounding global youth perspectives in social and policy debates where they have often been absent, at times the authorial voice of the contributors predominate youths' accounts of their practices of agency. This tension reflects ongoing contests over the politics of voice and representation in ethnography. Within critical qualitative research debates, there is growing acknowledgement of the need to move from researching marginal-ized youth to researching with marginalized youth—to mitigate the epistemic vio-lence of the research encounter, and in doing so, "to name, unlearn, and interrogate our privileged analytical frameworks (Nagar, 2014, p. 3)." Particularly for research-ers invested in ethnographically examining practices of youth agency across the Global South, there is a need to incorporate a clear practice of reflexivity in research, to account for how power inflects their practices of research, their access to and relationships with their participants, as well as their interpretive practices. The abil-ity to travel and study others, who are located in unequal relationships with those who seek to research them, represents a form of power, the power to represent, to deem aspects of their lives as important or inconsequential, which must be accounted for and visible in producing the ethnographic account.

Certainly, no single research design, no one theoretical framework, or method will ensure this process; nonetheless it is incumbent upon researchers to seek out a greater engagement with methodologies, modes of collaboration, and writing practices that allow youth an equitable role in producing critical knowledge of themselves and of their relationships and communities while connecting their strug-gles to larger structural factors and processes. These studies represent an energetic and significant step in that direction, and together they push future researchers to articulate modes of inquiry and collaboration that allow the further decolonization of knowledge production on the lives of youth, and the conditions, events, and relationships that frame how they make decisions and take action in their lives.

References

Appadurai, A. (1996). *Modernity at large: Cultural dimensions of globalization*. Minneapolis, MN: University of Minnesota Press.
Arendt, H. (1958). *The origins of totalitarianism*. Orlando, FL: Harcourt Brace.
Bajaj, M. (2009). 'I have big things planned for my future': the limits and possibilities of transformative agency in Zambian schools. *Compare 39*(4). 551–568.
Carney, S. (2009). Negotiating policy in an age of globalization: Exploring educational "policyscapes" in Denmark, Nepal, and China. *Comparative Education Review, 53*(1), 63–88.
Comaroff, J., & Comaroff, J. (2005). Reflections on youth: From the past to the postcolony in Africa. In A. Honwana & F. De Boeck (Eds.), *Makers and breakers: Children & youth in postcolonial Africa* (pp. 19–30). Trenton, NJ: Africa World Press.
Hall, S. (1997). *Representation: Cultural representations and signifying practices*. London, England: Sage Publications.
Harvey, D. (1991). *The condition of postmodernity: An enquiry into the origins of cultural change*. Malden, MA: Blackwell Publishers.
Herrera, L., & Bayat, A. (2010). Knowing Muslim youth. In L. Herrera & A. Bayat (Eds.), *Being young and Muslim: New cultural politics in the Global South and North* (pp. 355–365). Oxford, England: Oxford University Press.
Maira, S. & Soep, E. (2005). "Introduction." In Sunaina Maira & Elizabeth Soep (Eds.) *Youthscapes: The Popular, the National, the Global*. Philadelphia, PA: University of Pennsylvania Press.
McNay, L. (1999). Subject, psyche, and agency: The work of Judith Butler. *Theory, Culture, and Society, 16*(2), 175–193.
Meyers, M., Jeffers, N., & Ragland, D. (2016, January 18). Refusing to choose between Martin and Malcolm: Ferguson, Black Lives Matter, and a new nonviolent revolution. Retrieved January 18, 2016, from http://www.counterpunch.org/2016/01/18/refusing-to-choose-between-martin-and-malcolm-ferguson-black-lives-matter-and-a-new-nonviolent-revolution/.
Nagar, R. (2014). *Muddying the waters: Coauthoring feminisms across scholarship and activism (dissident feminisms)*. Champaign, IL: University of Illinois Press.
Said, E. W. (1978). *Orientalism*. New York, NY: Vintage Books.
Tsing, A. (2005). *Friction: An ethnography of global connection*. Princeton, NJ: Princeton University Press.

Index

© Springer International Publishing Switzerland 2016
J.G. DeJaeghere et al. (eds.), *Education and Youth Agency*, Advancing
Responsible Adolescent Development, DOI 10.1007/978-3-319-33344-1

CPSIA information can be obtained at www.ICGtesting.com
Printed in the USA
BVOW05*1112050916

461160BV00009B/24/P